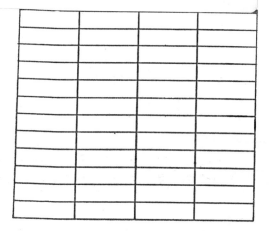

DEMCO

Modern International Economics

To Our Siblings

Helen, Joe, Marco,
Mark, Mary-Clare,
Teresa, Tracy, Virginia

Modern International Economics

Shelagh Heffernan
Peter Sinclair

Basil Blackwell

First published 1990

Basil Blackwell Ltd
108 Cowley Road, Oxford, OX4 1JF, UK

Basil Blackwell, Inc.
3 Cambridge Center
Cambridge, Massachusetts 02142, USA

British Library Cataloguing in Publication Data

A CIP catalogue record for this book is available from the British Library.

Library of Congress Cataloging in Publication Data

Heffernan. Shelagh A., 1956–
    Modern international economics/S. A. Heffernan, P. J. N. Sinclair.
    p.   cm.
    ISBN 0-631-16603-3—ISBN 0-631-16604-1 (pbk.)
    1. International economic relations.   2. International trade.
3. International finance.   4. Economic policy.   I. Sinclair, P. J. N.   II. Title.
HF 1359.H44 1990
382—dc20   89–18199
                                       CIP

Typeset in 10 on 12pt Times
by Colset Private Limited, Singapore
Printed in Great Britain by TJ Press Ltd, Padstow

Contents

Acknowledgements

A number of colleagues read and commented on different parts of the book. We should like to thank them, and particularly Roy Batchelor, Alec Chrystal, Alfred Kenyon, Maurice Scott, Tony Venables, and Alan Winters. We have also had valuable discussions on international economics with, among others, Michael Beenstock, David Begg, Christopher Bliss, Max Corden, and Peter Neary, and we thank them warmly. Our numerous graduate and undergraduate pupils at City University Business School and Oxford deserve our thanks too. We thank Xander Alpherts, Doug Fraley and Steve Potter for help with reading proofs, and Charles Stewart for the index. Finally, we are especially grateful to John Black, who read the entire manuscript and gave us helpful and detailed comments. Any errors in the book are entirely the responsibility of the authors.

1

Introduction and Overview

1.1 Why Study International Economics?

'No man is an island, entire of itself', wrote John Donne. Nor is a national economy. Microeconomics and macroeconomics are too often studied in a closed economy framework. This is not just an unhelpful oversimplification. With every day that passes, it becomes more anachronistic. Domestic firms are increasingly checked by competition from imports and export a rising proportion of their output. The ownership, production, and sales operations of large companies straddle international boundaries more and more. Today's world of high capital mobility integrates national asset markets, and transforms longer-run supply relationships in factor and product markets. Exchange rates play a central role in determining output, prices, and interest rates within national economies. Sudden changes in international commodity and capital markets send shock-waves into every country.

   Yet the international economy is composed of its parts. It cannot be studied independently of them. Further, the movement of goods and factors across frontiers is impeded by numerous obstacles, many of them imposed by governments. The overall picture is one of increasing but still definitely incomplete integration. Heated debate continues to rage, as it has done for centuries, on whether governments should accelerate or obstruct the process of economic international integration. New twists to the old controversies are provided by growing recent attention to imperfect competition and questions about international coordination of economic policies. These new developments and others, ranging from the nature of expectations formation in foreign exchange markets to applications of uncertainty and duality techniques, have a major impact on international economics. They make what has always been an important subject a lively and exciting one.

1.2 Outline of the Book

The book is divided into two parts, 'The Microeconomics of the Open Economy' and 'The Macroeconomics of the Open Economy'. Chapters 2–4 cover a number of topics related to trade between nation states: the pattern of international trade and its effects on output and factor incomes (chapter 2), tariffs and trade policy (chapter 3), and the implications of market imperfections, in particular, imperfect competition (chapter 4). Chapter 2 focuses on why trade occurs, why it takes the form it does, who gains from it and who might not and why. Chapter 3 is devoted to exploring the complex effects of trade restrictions, why governments might apply them, and when, if ever, they could be justified. The central questions that chapter 4 seeks to answer are: what role do market imperfections, those rising in oligopoly and monopolistic competition, play in trade and how do they affect the case for trade?

In chapter 5 we turn to the issue of trade integration, and the welfare effects of one form that trade integration can take, customs unions. We also examine the performance of the European Community, a prominent contemporary experiment in trade integration. Chapter 6 explores the long-run questions about the effects of changes in factor endowments, international factor movements, and changes in technology on trade.

The last chapter (7) of this part investigates the multinational enterprise (MNE), the reasons for its existence, and its implications. In one section econometric tests of the determinants of the MNE are reviewed.

The second part of the book covers the macroeconomics of the open economy. In chapter 8 we review the key concepts of the open economy. We explore the interrelations between a country's money supply, its trade balance, and the allocation of resources in a system of fixed but adjustable exchange rates. We proceed to set up a simple model to identify some of the main issues in open economy macroeconomics. In chapter 9, we turn to models of exchange rate determination. We review four: Keynesian, Dornbusch, monetarist, and portfolio balance. These models all differ in their explanations of exchange rate changes. In chapter 10, the empirical evidence on exchange rate determination is reviewed in an attempt to identify the key factors influencing the movements of exchange rates between countries.

Chapter 11 explores three related contemporary issues, all concerned with some aspect of international macroeconomic interdependence. In the first section, the problem of developing country external debt is explored. We discuss the causes of the problem, the current situation, and future prospects. The second section considers the debate on exchange rates: is there a need for currency reform, such as a formal agreement to manage or fix exchange rates? We review the key arguments on both sides and examine the European Monetary System as a case study in managed exchange rates. In the final section, issues related to international policy coordination are explored. A game-theoretic approach is used to identify the key problems related to the coordination of macroeconomic and trade policies. Is international coordination desirable, unnecessary, or even counter-productive? What effects does it have? These are among the questions asked and answered.

1.3 Whom this Book is For

This book is a textbook, designed for students taking courses in international economics. It has been written primarily for students in universities that follow British or American models of tertiary education. The book is appropriate for undergraduates in their last two years, and requires only an introductory course on microeconomics and macroeconomics as a background. It should also appeal to graduates, such as MBA students, taking economics for the first time. The emphasis of the book is on explaining the key ideas intuitively and geometrically. It is sparing in its use of algebra, and only elementary mathematics are employed. But we have strived to present a reasonably thorough account of many recent contributions to international economics, and to provide some examples to bring out the concepts and highlight their practical significance. The book embraces both micro (trade) and macro (payments, exchange rates) subjects. So, for example, the MBA for business student who is taking the course as part of an international finance requirement can concentrate on certain chapters or sections of the book. On the other hand, advanced undergraduates seeking a comprehensive self-contained text in international economics should find the book well suited to their needs. Also, postgraduate students planning to specialize in international economics as part of their graduate degree should find this volume a valuable introduction to modern international economics.

Part I

The Microeconomics of the Open Economy

The Theory of International Trade

This chapter is concerned with the fundamental questions of trade. Why does international trade occur? Why do countries export the goods they do? Whom does trade favour? Who gains from it? And who could lose and why?

Section 2.1 looks at trade and arbitrage between countries. In section 2.2. we analyse two-way trade in two goods, production possibility frontiers, and community indifference maps. The Ricardo model of trade, where production possibility frontiers are linear, is considered. In section 2.3, attention moves to the Heckscher–Ohlin model, where frontiers are typically concave, and its results. The question of who gains from trade in this two-good, two-factor framework is considered in section 2.4 and the discussion is broadened to a many-good many-factor setting in section 2.5. Finally, section 2.6 examines major evidence on international trade issues. The focus of this chapter is on positive trade theory rather than trade policy, on perfect as opposed to imperfect competition, and on static not dynamic analysis. Chapters 3, 4, and 6 extend the model to cover protection, imperfect competition, and growth.

2.1 Trade and Arbitrage between Countries

Trade means an exchange of goods between two parties. If parties reside in different countries, the trade is international. Often one of the goods involved is 'monetary', such as units of one of the parties' national currencies, or a currency of a third country, or gold. When neither of the goods exchanged is monetary, the trade is barter. Barter is a direct swap of one physical commodity or service for another.

Parties that engage in international trade may be state agencies, private companies, or individuals. Neither party will presumably undertake a trade unless it sees some advantage in doing so. Consider the case of international trade by private merchants. The advantage here will be profit gained by buying cheap and selling dear. Buying a good cheaply in one country and selling it for a higher price in another is an example of international arbitrage. Arbitrage is defined as the profitable exploitation of price discrepancies.

Suppose a trader can buy a good a in one country A at x per unit and sell it in country B at y per unit. Assume the cost of transport is negligible. If $y > x$, there is an incentive to purchase in A and sell in B. The profit from doing so is $(y - x)$ per unit, if transactions costs are also negligible, so that the trader can buy or sell y in B and x A. Profitable arbitrage requires buying in B and selling in A if $x > y$.

If trade is conducted on a modest scale by just a handful of traders, the gains from trade will accrue to the merchants. Trade will not be substantial enough to influence the prices x and y. But if there is free entry into international arbitrage, profits will act as a magnet and induce others to conduct trade. In the absence of transactions and trading costs and entry barriers, arbitrage will continue increasing until the prices of good a in countries A and B converge. If the pre-trade prices of x and y in A and B are such that $x > y$, the price in A will be bid down and that in B raised until they are equal. At this point, profitable arbitrage will have been exhausted. But the arbitrage will continue; if it did not, price discrepancies would reemerge.

These findings are illustrated in figures 2.1–2.3. Figures 2.1(a) and 2.1(b) depict the forces of local demand and supply in the two countries, establishing distinct equilibrium prices in the absence of trade. In 2.1(a) this is x in the absence of trade, and y is the pre-trade equilibrium price in country B, shown in 2.1(b). The curves D_A, D_B, S_A, S_B represent demand and supply in the two countries. p_A and p_B stand for the dollar prices in A and B and q_A and q_B denote quantities demanded and produced in the two countries. A single merchant, trading in small

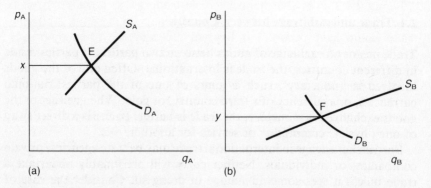

Figure 2.1   Pre-trade (autarkic) equilibria in countries A and B: (a) pre-trade equilibrium at E, where $p_A = \$x$; (b) pre-trade equilibrium at F, where $p_B = \$y$.

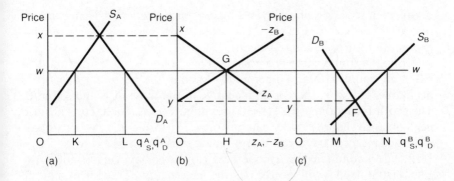

Figure 2.2   Complete arbitrage, with no trade barriers: (a) country A; (b) trade volume; (c) country B.

amounts, will barely disturb the two prices. In the absence of trade barriers, he will earn $\$(x - y)$ per unit of trade.

Large scale arbitrage, unfettered by trade barriers, is depicted in figure 2.2. Figure 2.2(b) shows country A's excess demand z_A, which is the amount by which domestic demand q_{DA} outstrips domestic supply q_{SA} for any price below x. In country B, when price exceeds y, there is excess supply, or negative excess demand, labelled $-z_B$. If the world consists of these two countries, the international equilibrium price is established at G where z_A and $-z_B$ intersect. World excess demand is zero because B's excess supply (MN) just matches A's excess demand (KL).

The common international price is $\$w$. The volume of trade between the two countries is OH, which equals both A's imports KL and B's exports MN. The new world price w must lie between x and y. If the z_A and $-z_B$ curves are linear and have the same gradient (in absolute value), w will equal $(x + y)/2$.

Figure 2.3 shows what happens when traders face a trade barrier of given height per unit, shown by the vertical gap RS in future 2.3(b). No trade would have occurred if RS had exceeded $x - y$. In figure 2.3, RS $< x - y$ and so there is trade but on a smaller scale than in figure 2.2. The price falls from x to x' in A and rises from y to y' in B. Trade is OH', which equals A's imports (K'L') and B's exports (M'N'). The trade barrier RS might be due to international transport and trading costs. Alternatively it could result from the imposition of an import tariff by country A's government or an export tax levied by B's.

Our major conclusions thus far are as follows. First, if there are no trade barriers, international arbitrage will establish a common international price. Second, the direction of trade follows that of profitable arbitrage: countries will export goods which in the absence of trade would have been relatively cheap and import goods which would have

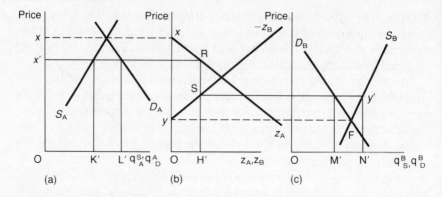

Figure 2.3 Incomplete arbitrage: (a) country A; (b) trade volume; (c) country B.

been relatively expensive. If trade barriers are allowed for, trade will still occur provided that the barrier is less than the price discrepancy on an autarkic (pre-trade) basis. In these circumstances, the second conclusion remains valid but the first does not because the process of arbitrage stops short of price equalization.

Country A imports the good in question but country B exports it because the price in A (x) exceeded that in B (y). But this is only a superficial answer because it does not explain the reasons behind the price discrepancy. If we restrict attention to the case of perfect competition there are two possible explanations. Either demand in A is high relative to B or supply in A is more inhibited than in B. The first possibility can arise as long as the supply curves are upward sloping (and, in particular, not horizontal); and the second, as long as demand curves are downward sloping and not horizontal. Had supply curves been horizontal, differences between x and y (the pre-trade equilibrium prices) would have been an entirely supply side matter, since the level of demand would have no influence on price. With horizontal demand curves, supply is irrelevant to price determination.

A may be importing the good because of a demand bias in favour of it in comparison with B (with supply curves sloping up). Alternatively, B may have exported it because of a supply bias in favour of the good compared with A. In this second case, B's producers may have lower costs of production because of a technological advantage; or because a factor of production employed intensively in this industry (for example land in agriculture) may have been relatively abundant in B and hence, probably, less expensive; or because a factor of production specific to this industry (such as specialized labour or machinery) may be more plentiful in B than in A. The notion that trade occurs because of international differences in technology is associated with the name of David

Ricardo. The hypothesis that countries differ in factor endowments, and goods in factor intensities, and that these differences explain trade patterns is due to Eli **Heckscher** and Bertil **Ohlin**. These ideas will be explored in a more general setting in sections 2.2 and 2.3.

We saw that a lone merchant trading internationally in small amounts could make large profits. But the very process of arbitrage in which he is participating will erode these profits if trade is unrestricted. What happens to the profits or gains from trade in that event?

The demand curve for a good shows the highest price that consumers are willing to pay for each unit. The total area under a demand curve up to the quantity $\bar{q}$ currently purchased (figure 2.4) represents the willingness of consumers to pay. It gives a measure, in money, of how much they gain from the quantity $0\bar{q}$. If consumers face a price $\bar{p}$, quantity $\bar{q}$ will be purchased. So the vertically striped area represents what they actually pay. The diagonally striped area captures the net gain that buyers obtain from the good. This is the excess of the total willingness to pay over the sum actually paid. It is known as consumers' surplus.

For sellers, there is the analogous concept of producers' surplus. The supply curve shows the minimum price which must be paid to ensure the production and sale of each unit. The total area under the supply curve must be paid to the producers. It represents the bare minimum of receipts which have to be earned in order to obtain a given total output. This is the diagonally striped area in figure 2.5, for a given output $\bar{q}$, If all producers obtain a market price of $\bar{p}$ for all their production, then given an upward-sloping supply curve, their actual earnings ($\bar{p}\bar{q}$) exceed the minimum

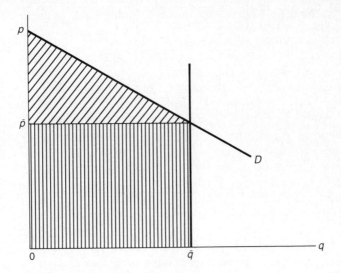

Figure 2.4   Willingness to pay, amount paid, and consumer's surplus.

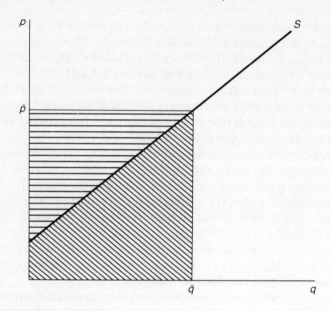

Figure 2.5 Producer's surplus.

necessary. This difference, producers' surplus, is the horizontally shaded area.

Returning to figure 2.2, examine what happens to consumers' and producers' surpluses. In country A consumers' surplus increases as the price declines from $x to $w but producers' surplus is squeezed. However, the consumers' gain outweighs the producers' loss because the demand curve lies to the right of the supply curve. International trade makes A's consumers who buy this good better off. It also reduces the real incomes of individuals who own factors of production specific to or intensively employed in this industry in country A. However, in an aggregate monetary sense, the gainers' gains outweigh the losers' losses.

In country B, it is producers' surplus which increases and consumers' surplus that is squeezed. But because the supply curve lies to the right of the demand curve, as price is bid up from $y towards $w the producers' gain exceeds the loss in consumer surplus in monetary terms. The gain in producers' surplus takes the form of increased rewards and income to those lucky enough to own factors specific to or intensively employed in the expanding industry. For example, if the industry were agriculture, the extra producer surplus would take the form of increased rent on land to landowners and improved prospects of pay for specialized agricultural labour. Since the gainers' gains exceed the losers' losses, it would be possible in principle to devise a set of lump sum transfers from the gainers to the losers that made everyone in country B better off. Whether such a scheme could be practical is a different matter.

The next question to be addressed is what happens to profits from trade under complete arbitrage? The merchants do not get them. Instead they accrue in the form of higher consumer surplus (net of producer surplus) in A and higher producer surplus (net of consumer surplus) in B. These net gains from trade, and who receives them, are the subject of section 2.4, later. It is not possible to say that the societies in A and B both gain unless strong assumptions are imposed, such as that the marginal value of money is identical for all members of society and that social welfare is the sum of everyone's utilities. However, the potential levels of domestic welfare rise in both countries since there is in principle an opportunity to redistribute income between individuals in such a way that everyone could be better off.

2.2 Two-way Trade and Ricardo's Model

Up to now we have examined international trade in a single good, which is exported from A to B. Although this has highlighted most of the central issues, such as why the direction and volume of trade are as they are, and who gains and loses from trade, the story is far from complete. Earlier, it was observed that trade can take the form of a direct swap of one good for another. At the micro level, merchants can trade on a barter basis. At the macro level, country A will not be able to continue importing for long if it does not export something in return.

The analysis may be expanded by introducing a second good b. As before, the key factor giving rise to trade is autarkic price discrepancies. But in a two-good context price discrepancies mean differences in the ratios of the two prices, for example, the price of good B in terms of good A. Let P be the ratio p_b/p_a, so that P represents the number of units of a that can be exchanged for one unit of good b. For trade to occur between the two countries A and B, the pre-trade price ratios P_A and P_B must be unequal. If they are equal, there is no incentive for international arbitrage.

Assuming the absence of trade barriers, any discrepancy between the two price ratios will lead to trade and the process of arbitrage expands until P_A and P_B have converged. If $P_A < P_B$, it is country A that exports good b and country B that imports it. In equilibrium, the two prices ratios converge on a common price ratio P^* lying between P_A and P_B. Also, B's excess demand for b (z_{bB}) will have to equal A's excess supply for it ($-z_{bA}$) and similarly for good a. If trade is to be balanced, the value of B's imports of b will equal its exports of a. Hence

$$z_{bB} + z_{bA} = 0$$

$$z_{aB} + z_{aA} = 0 \tag{2.1}$$

and

$$p^* z_{bB} + z_{aB} = 0$$

$$p^* z_{bA} + z_{aA} = 0 \tag{2.2}$$

That is, world excess demand for both goods is eliminated (2.1) and values of imports and exports are equalized (2.2).

The phenomenon of two-way trade may be explored geometrically. Consider a closed economy A. The concepts of domestic demand and supply presented in 'partial equilibrium' terms for good a alone are depicted in figure 2.1(a). However, if two goods are involved the function of depicting demand is taken over by an indifference map. It is simplest to assume that there exists a unique set of indifference curves that describe how the community of A's residents will arrange their aggregate purchases of goods a and b, with given incomes and prices. For a community indifference map to be uniquely defined, it is sufficient that every individual in the community has a unique set of indifference curves and that at least two of the following conditions hold.

1   Everyone in the community has identical preferences, that is, the same indifference map.
2   Everyone in the community has homothetic preferences, that is, their demands for each good always increase in direct proportion to their incomes.
3   The distribution of incomes between individuals is fixed.

Under these conditions we can always predict what society as a whole will buy with given aggregate income and prices. But the conditions do not necessarily imply that a society's welfare rises if a higher indifference curve is attained. For example, if (3) fails, we may encounter a situation where some people's incomes fall and others rise but the community as a whole spends more. However, we may not deem the new position to be an improvement in social welfare. We return to this point later (section 3.1). Figure 2.6 illustrates a typical community indifference map, if it is uniquely defined.

In a two- or many-commodity context, the role of the supply curves is performed by the production possibility frontier (PPF). It shows the maximum combinations of outputs that an economy can produce with

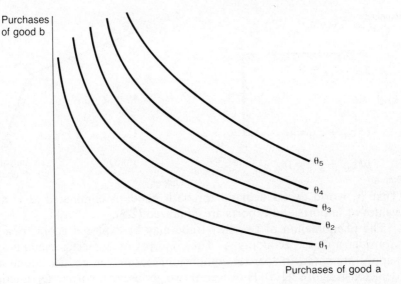

Figure 2.6   A community indifference map.

given resources. The PPF can have many shapes. These are illustrated in the different frames of figure 2.7. A PPF separates feasible from non-feasible sets of commodity outputs. Points on or to the left and below the PPF are feasible. Points above and to the right are unattainable with present resources.

Figure 2.7(a) applies when all factors of production are specific to particular industries to which they are assigned and cannot move between industries, and also when the two goods are produced jointly, in fixed proportions. The maximum outputs of goods b and a are uniquely defined at C. The rectangular PPF corresponds to vertical supply curves for the goods in question. One can think of 2.7(a) as depicting a very short-run position where the output levels of the different industries have been predetermined.

Figure 2.7(b) applies when the two industries enjoy constant returns to scale, operate independently, and employ two factors of production (for example, capital and labour) in different but fixed proportions, and when the factors can be moved between industries. If good b is relatively labour intensive and a relatively capital intensive, the only point where both factors of production are fully employed is at the kink, C. To the left of C, along BC, the economy is using all its labour but some of its capital stock is unemployed. This must be true because b is more labour intensive than a: as the output of a is reduced the capital and labour employed in a are both reduced but industry b, which is more

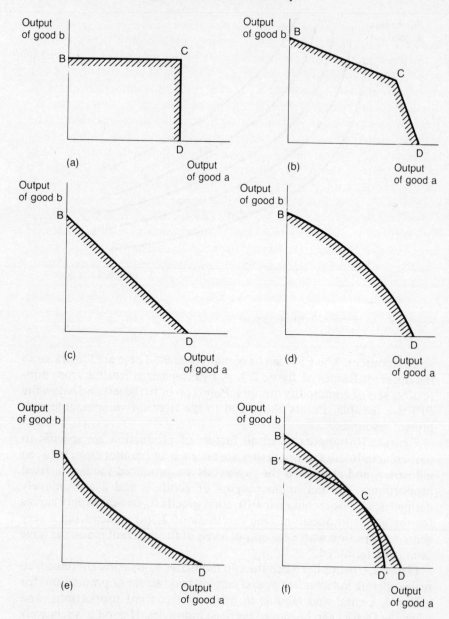

Figure 2.7 Various production possibility frontiers: (a) rectangular; (b) piecewise linear; (c) linear; (d) smooth concave; (e) smooth convex; (f) short-run (B'CD') and long-run (BCD) smooth convex.

labour intensive than a, has no use for some of the capital, which is released. Along the steep facet CD, some of the economy's labour force is unemployed. The reason for this can be seen in figure 2.8, which depicts an 'Edgeworth factor box'. The height of the box is the economy's endowment capital K. The length is its labour endowment N. The bottom left corner is the origin from the standpoint of industry a, 0_a. Here, a employs none of the two factors and produces nothing. The analogous point for b is 0_b in the upper right corner. The steep arrowed line R_a from 0_a depicts the fixed capital–labour ratio in industry a. If a is to increase its output, it must move outwards along R_a. The flatter broken line R_b from 0_b shows the expansion path for industry b. R_a is steeper than R_b because a is more capital intensive.

The L-shaped curves a_1, a_2, a_3, and a_4 depict isoquants for industry a. An isoquant is defined as the locus of combinations of the factors of production along which the level of output is constant. They are L shaped because the industry employs capital and labour in fixed proportions. Since constant returns to scale are assumed, the output level on isoquant a_1 at F is only one-third of that along a_3 at C if $0_aF/0_aC$ equals one-third. The dotted L-shaped curves b_1, b_2, and b_3 are isoquants for industry b,

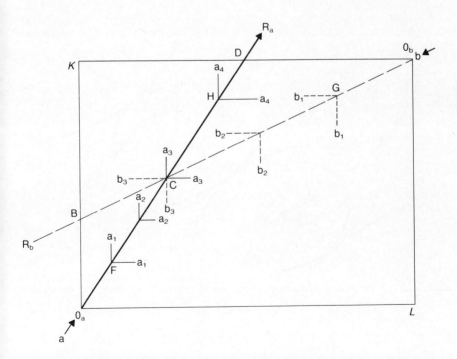

Figure 2.8   Edgeworth factor box with fixed but differing factor proportions and constant returns to scale in the two industries.

again L shaped to reflect the fixed proportions. If $0_bG/0_bC = 1/3$, b's output at C is three times higher than at G.

The only point in figure 2.8 where the economy employs all its capital and labour endowments is at C. This corresponds to point C in figure 2.7(b). It is the only point where the two expansion paths cut. If a were to expand its output, say to a_4 at H, industry b would have to cut back output to G in order to release the additional capital needed in sector a. But this would imply labour unemployment equal to the horizontal distance from G to H. The maximum possible output of a is given by point D in figure 2.7(b) and figure 2.8. Here, industry b produces nothing and labour unemployment is 0_bD. Similarly, the highest possible output of b is given by point B, where 0_aB units of capital are unemployed.

In figure 2.7(c), the PPF is linear. This state of affairs will hold if the two industries have constant returns to scale, operate independently, and employ capital and labour in common (not necessarily fixed) proportions in a context where both factors are mobile between the two industries. Figure 2.9 depicts this set of conditions and smooth convex-to-the-origin isoquants are introduced.

Suppose that both countries A and B have linear PPFs. Before trade is introduced the relative prices of the two goods are given by the slopes of

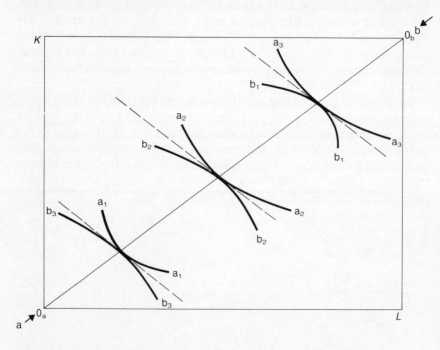

Figure 2.9 Edgeworth factor box with variable but common factor proportions.

the PPFs. If the PPFs have the same slopes, the pre-trade price ratios will be the same. In this case, merchants will gain nothing from international arbitrage. There is no incentive to conduct international trade and there will be no trade.

If the autarkic price ratios differ, however, trade is profitable. This can only happen if the PPFs differ in gradient. The country where the PPF is flatter, country A say, will display a lower pre-trade price of the horizontal axis good a than country B. The flatter PPF tells us that A enjoys a comparative technological advantage in the production of good a. B, where the PPF is steeper, exhibits a lower pre-trade relative price of the vertical axis good b, and so B has a comparative technological advantage in the production of b. Since merchants will buy cheap to sell dear, the pattern of trade will involve B exporting b to A and importing a from A. Trade patterns depend on pre-trade price ratio divergences, and in this case, where the PPFs are linear, such divergences can only be caused by international differences in technology.

This technological basis for international trade was first promulgated by Ricardo. Ricardo asked why England exported cloth to Portugal and imported wine from Portugal. His answer: resources (reduced for simplicity to labour) had a comparative advantage in wine production in Portugal and a comparative advantage in cloth production in England. An English worker might produce more wine and more cloth in a day than his or her counterpart in Portugal but, if the ratio of labour productivity in cloth to wine were higher in England than in Portugal, Portugal's comparative advantage lay with wine and England's with cloth.

To formalize this idea, suppose labour is the only factor of production. Labour productivity h, is the ratio of output Q to labour N. With constant returns to scale, h is independent of the level of outout in the industry in question; with independent production (that is, no joint production), one industry's Q is independent of the other's. For the two industries a and b in the two economies A and B, we have four independent constant returns production functions:

$$Q_{Aa} = h_{Aa}N_{Aa} \tag{2.3}$$

$$Q_{Ab} = h_{Ab}N_{Ab}$$

$$Q_{Ba} = h_{Ba}N_{Ba} \tag{2.4}$$

$$Q_{Bb} = h_{Bb}N_{Bb}$$

If there is full employment in the two countries, N_a and N_b must add to the total labour supply N in each:

$$N_{Aa} + N_{Ab} = N_A \qquad (2.5)$$
$$N_{Ba} + N_{Bb} = N_B \qquad (2.6)$$

Inserting (2.3) into (2.5) and (2.4) into (2.6) establishes that

$$N_A = \frac{Q_{Aa}}{h_{Aa}} + \frac{Q_{Ab}}{h_{Ab}} \qquad (2.7)$$

$$N_B = \frac{Q_{Ba}}{h_{Ba}} + \frac{Q_{Bb}}{h_{Bb}} \qquad (2.8)$$

Equation (2.7) is country A's PPF, and (2.8) is B's. Both PPFs are linear. A has a comparative advantage in a and B in b if p_b/p_a before trade in A which is equal to $h_{Aa}/h_{Ab} > h_{Ba}/h_{Bb}$ (equal to p_b/p_a before trade in B).

This corresponds to a steeper PPF in B than in A, as depicted in figure 2.10. If the world consists of only these two countries and a and b are the only two goods, A will export a and B will export b. The post-trade price ratio will lie somewhere between the autarkic price ratios.

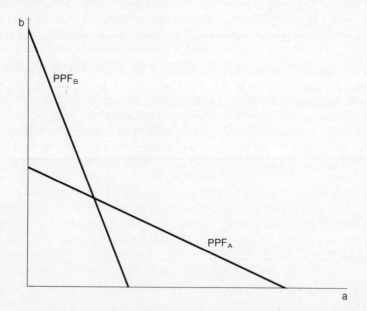

Figure 2.10   The Ricardian basis for trade, with linear production possibility frontiers.

2.3 The Concave Production Possibility Frontier and the Heckscher–Ohlin Theory

This section is devoted to exploring the idea of concave PPFs and the theory of international trade, constructed originally by Heckscher (1949) and Ohlin (1933), which is based upon them. In section 2.2 we examined various possible PPF shapes. In the case of a single factor of production or when both industries employ factors in the same proportion, we saw that the PPF is linear if both industries display constant returns to scale, factors are mobile between the industries and production is independent. Retaining the other assumptions but introducing increasing returns makes the PPF convex to the origin, as in figure 2.7(e). The PPF is concave to the origin if returns to scale are decreasing.

A concave-to-the-origin PPF also arises in other circumstances. Suppose the two industries employ factors of production in different proportions but enjoy constant returns to scale, produce independently, and operate in an economy where all factors of production are fully mobile. If capital and labour are the two factors of production, let good a be relatively labour intensive and good b be relatively intensive in capital. If industry a expands and b contracts, the economy's overall demand for labour increases, while that for capital falls. If both factors of production are supplies inelastically, so that the economy's total endowments of labour and capital are given, the aggregate changes in factor demands will raise the price of labour and lower that of capital. The ratio of average costs in industry a to average costs in industry b rises. Given long-run perfect competition, the price of each good will equal its average cost and so the price ratio p_a/p_b will rise.

Under perfect competition, the gradient of the PPF will equal (minus) the price of good a in terms of good b. So the gradient of the PPF will be steeper in the new equilibrium than in the old equilibrium. A rise in the output of b, however, has to be accompanied by a fall in that of a when the economy is operating on its PPF, and so the frontier becomes flatter as one moves northwestward. The frontier of production possibilities is necessarily concave to the origin. This is depicted in figure 2.11.

The degree of concavity of the PPF depends on the differences between the industries' factor intensities and the ease with which they substitute between the factors. If capital and labour are easily substituted for each other in both sectors and their factor intensities are not very different, the PPF will be close to linear. Quite large changes in the pattern of production will occur in response to small changes in the price ratio for the two goods. Each of the industries will display an elastic (but not infinitely elastic) upward-sloping supply curve. However, if opportunities to substitute between the factors are limited, isoquants will

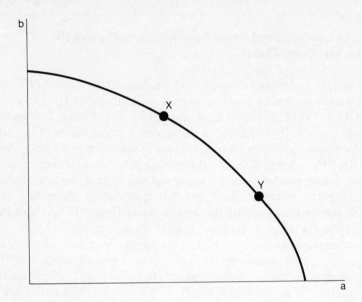

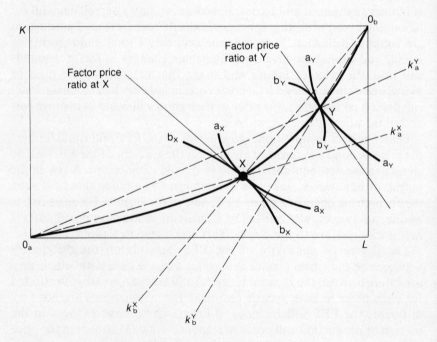

Figure 2.11   The concave production possibility frontier.

display considerable inflexibility and appear nearly L shaped. If their factor intensities differ, this will lead to greater concavity along the PPF, and the more their factor intensities differ, the more pronounced the concavity will be. Only a small rise in the output of a (and a fall in b) will require a large jump in p_a in terms of p_b and a large rise in the price of labour relative to capital.

Let us explore the link between factor demands, factor prices, and average costs (and hence prices) of the two goods in greater detail. Consider first the relation between a firm's capital–labour ratio k and the ratio w/r of the wage rate paid to labour to the rental on capital. A competitive profit-maximizing firm will seek to minimize its costs and this will require employing capital and labour in proportions where the slope of an isoquant (the ratio of the marginal product of labour to that of capital) equals w/r. Its cost-minimizing k will increase with w/r: the higher the relative price of labour, the greater the incentive to substitute capital for labour. If the firm's production function is Cobb–Douglas, the cost-minimizing k is proportional to w/r. When returns to scale are constant, the Cobb–Douglas production function makes output a weighted geometric average of the quantities of the factors of production employed. Put another way, the logarithm of output is linear in the logarithm of factors. For example, $Q = TK^c N^{1-c}$ or $ln Q = ln T + c\, lnK + (1 - c)\, ln N$, where Q, T, K, and N respectively denote output, a technology index, capital, and labour. If industry a is composed of identical competitive firms, industry a's capital–labour ratio will also be directly proportional to w/r, as shown in figure 2.12.

The Cobb–Douglas production function generates a set of isoquants along which substitution between factors is unit elastic. That is, production is neither flexible nor inflexible. If substitution is more elastic than in the Cobb–Douglas case, the industry is flexible in its inputs and the cost-minimizing value of k responds more than proportionately to a higher value of w/r. As in figure 2.13, w/r can be portrayed as a concave function of k. If the industry is inflexible, k responds very little to w/r and w/r is a convex function of k, as in figure 2.14.

If the two industries have the same degree of flexibility along their isoquants (that is, the same elasticities of substitution), one industry will always employ a higher capital–labour ratio than the other, whatever the common wage–rent ratio they face. But if the industries differ in their substitution elasticities so that one (say a) is more flexible than the other, as in figure 2.15, we cannot say that one of them is unambiguously more capital intensive than the other. It all depends on the wage–rent ratio. If this is low, so that labour is cheap, the flexible industry is likely to be relatively labour intensive, since it is in a much better position to take advantage of the low price of labour. At very high values of w/r, the flexible industry is likely to be the more capital intensive of the two. In

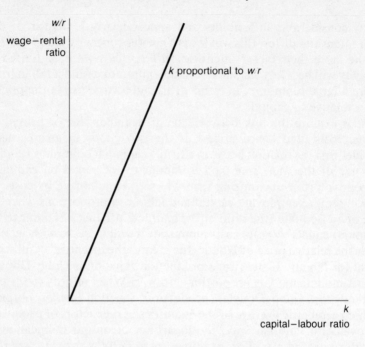

Figure 2.12   The Cobb–Douglas relation between the capital–labour ratio and the wage–rent ratio.

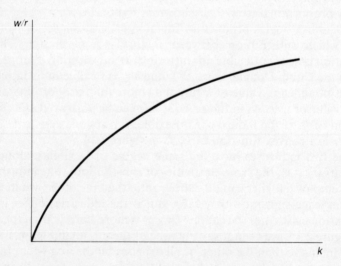

Figure 2.13   The relation between *k* and *w/r* when production is flexible.

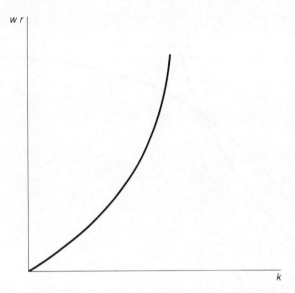

Figure 2.14 The relation between *k* and *w/r* when production is inflexible.

figure 2.15, the two industries' (capital–labour ratio)/(wage–rent ratio) functions intersect at point F. When the wage–rent ratio is at $(w/r)^*$, the two industries have the same capital–labour ratios. With w/r above $(w/r)^*$, the flexible industry is the more capital intensive. With w/r below $(w/r)^*$, it is the more labour intensive. Point F is known as a factor intensity reversal (FIR) point, where the ranking of the industries by factor intensities reverses itself. There is never a factor intensity reversal if the two industries are equally flexible, but if they differ in flexibility, the less flexible sector is the more capital intensive of the two at sufficiently low wage–rent ratios and the less capital intensive of the two when the wage–rent ratio is sufficiently high.

In the the absence of a factor intensity reversal (that is, if industries are equally flexible), one industry is always more capital intensive than the other. In that case, a rise in the wage–rent ratio will always lower relative average cost and hence relative price for the capital-intensive industry. If industry a is always capital intensive the price ratio p_a/p_b always falls as w/r rises. This is depicted in figure 2.16(a). The curve is 'monotonic', upward sloping in 2.16(a) and downward sloping in 2.16(b) where it is industry b that is relatively capital intensive. This curve is known as the commodity price–factor price correspondence (CFC). However, if there is a factor intensity reversal such as in figure 2.17, the CFC is no longer monotonic. It is downward sloping when w/r lies below $(w/r)^*$ and upward sloping above it. In this case there are two possible values of w/r

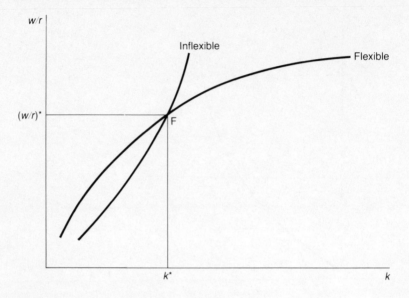

Figure 2.15   Factor intensity reversal at F: industries differ in flexibility.

associated with a single commodity price ratio in figure 2.17. In figure 2.16, however, where the CFC is monotonic, there is only one possible value of w/r for a single commodity price ratio. A final feature of the CFC worth noting is that it is inelastic, whether it is monotonic or non-monotonic. A given proportionate change in w/r is associated with less a than a proportionate change in the commodity price ratio because

$$(\dot{p}_a - \dot{p}_b) = (s_b - s_a)(\dot{w} - \dot{r}) \tag{2.9}$$

where $\dot{p}_i$ is the proportionate change in p_i ($i \equiv$ a, b), s_i is capital's share in i and a dot denotes a proportionate change in the variable beneath it. Capital's share in a sector is the ratio of capital costs to the value of that sector's output, so that $s_a > s_b$ if and only if a is more capital intensive than b.

We are now in a position to examine the **Heckscher–Ohlin** (HO) theory of international trade. The HO theory begins with two assumptions.

1   Countries differ in their relative factor endowments.
2   Industries differ in their relative factor intensities.

In its simplest and strictest form, the HO theory restricts attention to a world with just two countries (A and B), two factors of production (K and L), and two goods (a and b). There is perfect competition and each

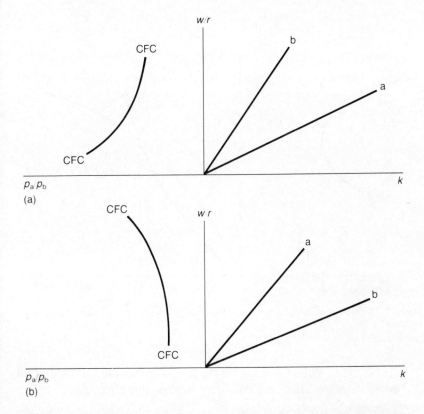

Figure 2.16 Monotonic commodity price correspondences with different relative factor intensities and no reversals: (a) industry a is always more capital intensive; (b) industry b is always more capital intensive.

industry employs the same constant returns to scale technology. The assumption of identical technology may be defended as a long-run state of affairs, where state of the art technology has had time to travel within and across national frontiers. This simple '2 × 2 × 2' model is further assumed to apply in a world where each country has uniquely defined and similar community preferences. Finally, the factors of production are freely mobile within countries but not between them, the supplies of factors to each country are uniquely given, and each country's isoquant map displays continuous limited substitutability between the factors (smooth convex-to-the-origin isoquants). There is no joint production of goods.

Under these strict conditions, the HO theory claims that

1   the country will export that commodity which is relatively intensive in its relatively plentiful factor of production and

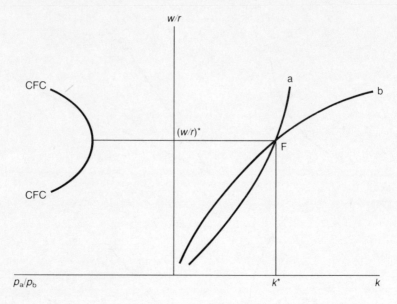

Figure 2.17   Non-monotonic commodity price correspondence with a factor intensity reversal.

2   free trade in goods is a substitute for international factor mobility because factor prices are equalized across countries.

Neither of these claims is fully valid even under the highly restrictive assumptions given. But they may be true. Let us see how the argument runs.

A country relatively well endowed with capital would, in the absence of trade, find that its capital-intensive good was plentiful and cheap. That particular commodity would be relatively more expensive in the other country where labour is plentiful. So as soon as international trade is allowed, this good should be exported from the first country to the second and the other relatively labour-intensive good would be bartered in return. The process of trade would cause the first economy to move along its PPF, raising the output of its exportable at the expense of its importable. Since the first good is relatively capital intensive, there would be a rise in the rental on capital, and downward pressure on wages. The opposite would happen in the second economy. There, international trade would compensate for its low endowment of capital since it would concentrate on producing the more labour-intensive good.

Under the conditions stipulated above, claim (1) is valid if the same good is relatively capital intensive in both countries, so that any factor intensity reversal, if it occurs, happens outside the range of the wage–rent

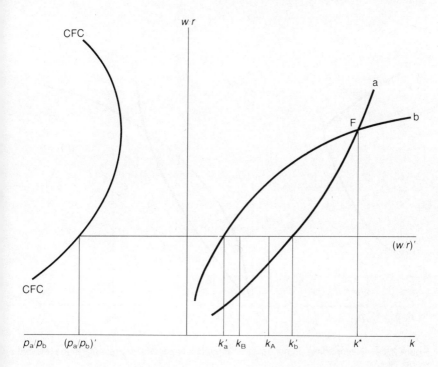

Figure 2.18 Factor prices equalize: there is no factor intensity reversal in the relevant range.

ratios in which we are interested. Claim (2) is valid given this proviso and the further qualification that both countries continue to produce both goods in the new free trade equilibrium. Figure 2.18 illustrates this case. The absence of a factor intensity reversal within the relevant range is evident here since the two countries' capital–labour endowment ratios lie on the same side of the particular value k^* at which the industries' capital–labour ratios are equal. Here country A exports the relatively capital intensive good a and imports b; in the absence of trade, the price ratio $P(=p_a/p_b)$ is lower in A than in B. Furthermore, the ratio of factor prices equalizes in A and B (the w/r ratio falls in capital-rich A where labour was expensive before trade and rises in labour-rich B) and both goods continue to be produced in both countries. The two endowment ratios k_A and k_B, both lie between the capital–labour ratios k_a', k_b' for the a and b industries that they will exhibit in free trade.

Figure 2.19 shows what happens in the presence of a factor intensity reversal in the relevant range. Now it is impossible for both countries to export the good which is intensive in their locally plentiful factor of production. Good a is capital intensive in A but in B it is good b that is

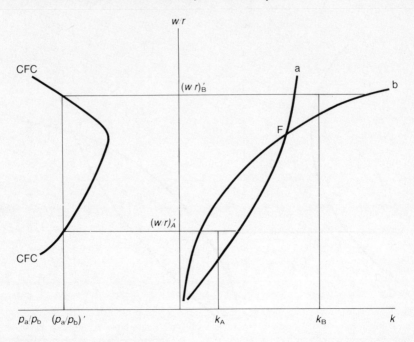

Figure 2.19   Factor prices do not equalize: there is a factor intensity reversal in the relevant range.

capital intensive! So either both countries export their capital-intensive good and country B violates claim (1) or they both export their labour-intensive good and country A violates claim (1). What is more, a common commodity price ratio P' now corresponds to two very different wage–rent ratios. Country A will tend to the low w/r, $(w/r)'_A$, and B the high one, $(w/r)'_B$. Hence claim (2) fails because factor prices will not equalize across countries. International factor mobility is needed to achieve that.

In figure 2.20 there is complete specialization in the production of good b in country B because its capital endowment ratio k_B is too low to permit any of good a to be produced. There is an incomplete tendency towards factor price equalization, too: the wage–rent ratio in B can rise no further than $(w/r)_B$. So claim (2) is invalid. Country B has to attract more capital before factor prices can equate with those in country A.

If the HO model is widened to include a less restrictive set of assumptions, it is clear that the two claims may fail for other reasons. If demand patterns are allowed to differ between the two countries but the community indifference curves of each are still uniquely defined, we encounter the possibility of a 'demand reversal'. This happens if country A, for example, has such a strong domestic preference for good a that its

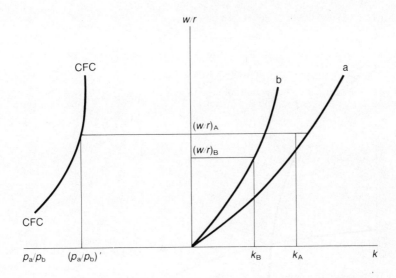

Figure 2.20   Complete specialization in country B: factor prices do not equalize.

relative price is higher before trade than in B, despite the relative physical abundance of capital, the factor in the production of which good a is relatively intensive. This demand reversal case is illustrated in figure 2.21. Here, claim (1) will be falsified but claim (2) can still go through; this time, free trade will have the effect of reducing the price of capital in terms of labour in A.

If the assumption that the community indifference map is uniquely defined is repealed, it is possible that an economy will display more than one pre-trade equilibrium (figure 2.22). This could happen if the economy's capitalists, who own the factor used intensively in industry a, have a strong demand bias in favour of good a while its labourers prefer good b, the product of the industry where their factor is intensively employed. In such a case, we would not know where the price ratio P at the moment when international trade was permitted actually lay; it might lie above or below the rest of the world's P, implying that with international arbitrage the good will be imported or exported. Again, claim (1) would fail, although claim (2) would not be violated.

Much more potential damage to the two HO claims is created if we introduce a phenomenon which the theory's authors, Heckscher and Ohlin, dispute – international differences in technology. Suppose country A has a relative technological lead in the production of good B. Geometrically, this would imply a stretching of A's PPF along the good b dimension. It is now quite possible that the autarkic price of a in terms of b in A would be higher, not lower, than in B, and if this were the case A

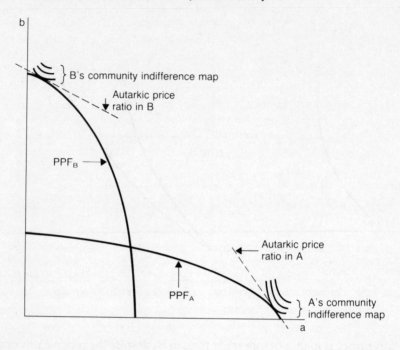

Figure 2.21   A demand reversal.

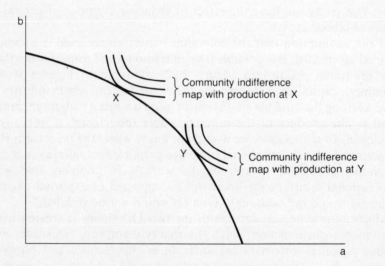

Figure 2.22   Multiple equilibria under autarky.

would export good b, not a. So claim (1) fails. The hypothesis of factor price equalization also collapses. The reason here is that the CFC would very probably no longer be common to both countries since it is constructed from isoquant maps which differ between them for one of the goods. If the CFCs differed, a common price ratio for goods would now typically entail two different price ratios for the factors.

Imperfect competition also wreaks havoc. Good a might be relatively expensive in A before trade because it was produced by a profit-maximizing monopolist who set price above marginal cost. In this event, good a might be imported into country A rather than exported from it. Imperfect competition would upset claim (2) by breaking the link between the reward paid to a factor and the value of its marginal product in each of the sectors. One of the many possibilities that emerges with the introduction of imperfect competition is a discrepancy in factor prices between the industries of a single country. A union might monopolize the labour employed in industry a but not in b, thereby driving up the market clearing wage in a and reducing it in b. Chapter 4 explores imperfect competition in greater detail.

To sum up, the HO claim that a country exports a good intensive in a locally plentiful factor may fail in several cases

1   factor intensity reversal;
2   demand reversal;
3   international technological differences;
4   non-unique community preferences;
5   imperfect competition.

Of these, (1), (3), and (5) could also violate the factor price equalization result as could

6   complete specialization and
7   trade impediments such as tariffs and international transport costs that prevent goods price equalization.

2.4 Who Gains from Trade?

In the initial stages of trade it is the merchants who garner the gains from trade. They earn arbitrage profits, but if arbitrage is pushed to the limit this source of profit is eliminated. So who gains?

In the $2 \times 2 \times 2$ model of perfect competition where factors are perfectly mobile within national boundaries, gains accrue to the owners of the factors of production employed intensively in the country's expanding exportables industry. If this factor is labour, the wage rate increases in terms of both exportable and importable goods. But the price of the other factor (for example, capital) falls, the rental rate declining in terms of both goods.

These results are seen most simply through the medium of isoprice curves. An isoprice curve for a particular perfectly competitive industry links the combination of prices for factors of production consistent with a particular value of the price of its product. The lower the rental on capital is, the higher is the wage rate that the firm can afford to pay. It embeds two assumptions: that the industry produces under conditions of constant returns to scale, and that all the firms in the industry select their inputs to minimize costs, with a common technology. If the isoquant map for an industry displays no substitution between factors, so that isoquants are L shaped, the corresponding isoprice curve is linear. If the factors are perfect substitutes, so that the isoquants are linear, the corresponding isoprice is L shaped.

The isoprice curve is generally convex to the origin, and the greater the degree of substitutability between factors is, the more pronounced is its curvature. The essential reasons for these properties can be seen by considering the gradient of the tangent to an isoprice. This is (minus) the capital–labour ratio if the wage rate is placed on the vertical axis and the cost of capital on the horizontal axis (as in figure 2.23). By contrast,

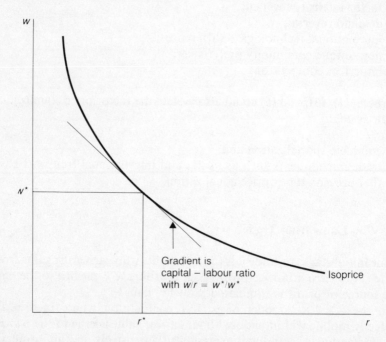

Figure 2.23 A typical isoprice curve. An isoprice curve links values of the wage rate w and the capital rental r at which the unit cost or price of the product is constant.

the slope of the tangent to an isoquant, given perfect competition, is (minus) the ratio of the prices of the factors of production. When there is no substitution, so that isoquants are L shaped, the capital–labour ratio is unique, and so the isoprice is linear. At the other extreme, where the factors are perfect substitutes and the isoquants are linear, the same wage–rent ratio is compatible with any capital–labour ratio, and so the isoprice is L shaped.

Figures 2.24–2.26 display isoprice and isoquant curves for an industry under different assumptions about substitution ranging from complementarity (figure 2.24) to perfect substitution (figure 2.26). In

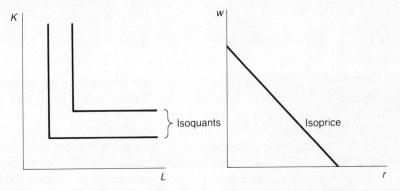

Figure 2.24   Isoquant map and isoprice when the factors are perfect complements.

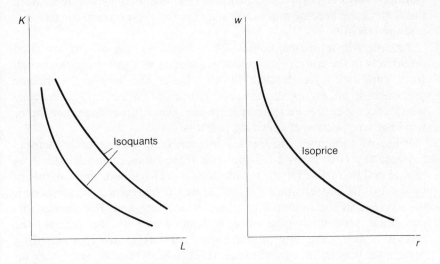

Figure 2.25   Isoquant map and isoprice when there is limited substitutability between factors.

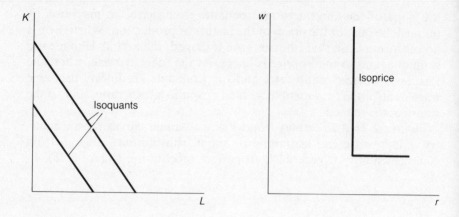

Figure 2.26   Isoquant map and isoprice when the factors are perfect substitutes.

figure 2.27 we superimpose isoprice curves for two industries, exportables (good a) and importables (good b). The a industry isoprice is defined for a price of good a scaled to unity. The two curves for good b represent before and after trade prices for that product. Opening the country up to trade means reducing the price of good b, from p_b^0 to p_b^1 in this case. Since good a is relatively labour intensive, the effect of trade is to lower the value of r, the rental on capital, in terms of both good a and good b; r falls more than p_b. The old capital–labour ratios in the two industries can be seen as the tangent slopes of the a and b industry isoprice curves at point C, while those at D give their new values. Both industries have become more capital intensive in response to the rise in w and the fall in r.

Anyone whose income comes solely from the sale of a factor used intensively in the country's exportable industry will gain from the switch from autarky to free trade. However he or she spends the income generated, it will go up, since w rises in terms of both p_a and p_b. Anyone whose income comes exclusively from the ownership of the other factor will lose, irrespective of spending patterns.

What of someone who derives income from selling both factors? Suppose the country is endowed with three times as much labour as capital and that these are the proportions in which labour and capital are owned by our 'representative agent'. If he has preferences identical with the average in the community, there is a clear gain. The keener this individual is on buying importables (compared with the average) the greater is this gain. But if the individual has a sufficiently strong preference bias in favour of exportables, whose relative price goes up when the country starts trading abroad, he or she stands to lose. We have therefore identified two sources of possible losses from free trade: those

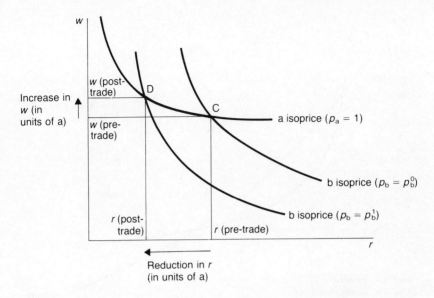

Figure 2.27   Isoprice curves for two industries a and b.

whose income comes from the ownership of the factors used intensively in the importables industries and those individuals with mixed incomes whose preferences are strongly biased towards exportables.

To this list we must add a third category of persons – those who own a factor specifically employed in the country's importables industry. This is considered below. Before examining this case, we return briefly to the isoprice diagrams to illustrate the various cases where the factor price equalization proposition of the HO theory fails.

The case of a factor intensity reversal is easily depicted (figure 2.28). Here, two isoprice curves corresponding to the free trade prices of goods a and b intersect twice, at E and F. This occurs because industry a is less flexible (has a lower substitution elasticity between capital and labour) than industry b. If the home country's capital–labour endowment ratio lies between the gradients of the isoprice curves at E, under free trade it will move to point E and wage rates and capital rentals of w_1 and r_1 will be established in the two industries. If the capital–labour endowment ratio is much lower than this and lies between the gradients of the isoprice curves at F, it will be to point F that the economy moves and w_2, r_2 will be established. If one country's endowment ratio corresponds to E and the other to F, so that a factor intensity reversal does occur within the relevant range, factor price equalization is violated. The point at which the factor intensity reversal arises is given by G, where the two industries' capital–labour ratios are equal.

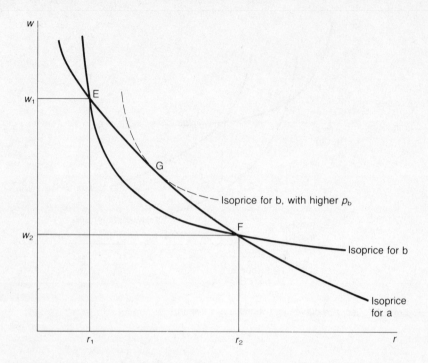

Figure 2.28 Factor intensity reversal: isoprice curves intersect more than once.

The case of technology differences is straightforward. The isoprice curves for at least one of the goods will now differ between countries, even under free trade (figure 2.29). Two countries A and B have common technology for good a and hence a common isoprice for good a under free trade. But A has an absolute technical lead over B in the production of good b, so that B's isoprice is closer to the origin when the price p_b' of b is common. A can afford to pay higher prices for capital and/or labour than can B, as shown by an isoprice further from the origin, which represents superior technology. Given this state of affairs, factor prices in A will be w_A and r_A and in B will be w_B and r_B.

We now revert to consider what happens when it is no longer assumed that both factors are perfectly mobile and free to move between sectors inside the economy. If both factors are sector specific, each industry will have fixed allocations of capital and labour and the PPF will be rectangular. There is no substitution in production. However, if one factor, labour say, is free to move but the other, capital, is sector specific, some substitution in production can occur. The PPF is more concave than it would have been had both factors been mobile. Except at one point, where the allocation of capital between industries is just what it would have been had capital been mobile, the former PPF lies wholly

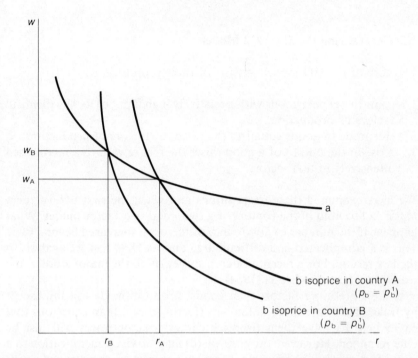

Figure 2.29 Isoprice curves for A and B when A has a technical lead over B in the production of good b.

inside the latter. The major income distribution of the change from autarky to free trade when one factor is sector specific is that the reward to the factor specific to the expanding exportables sector goes up in real terms but the price of the factor specific to the contracting sector falls. Those who own capital specific to the importables industry will experience a fall in their real incomes, even in terms of the importable good. For a more detailed discussion of the significance of specific factors, the reader is referred to chapter 6.

Those likeliest to gain from trade, therefore, are individuals who own factors of production specific to, or (if mobile) employed intensively in, the economy's expanding exportables industry. But we should emphasize three qualifications. If a country specializes completely in the production of a single good, increased trade (in response to a rise in the world price of that commodity) will raise the reward to both (mobile) factors. Second, as we shall see in chapter 4, increasing returns could provide gains from trade for everyone. Last, under conditions of uncertainty, and in the absence of futures markets, trade could be deleterious to the welfare of all. This point, due to Newbery and Stiglitz (1984), is also examined in chapter 4.

2.5 Generalizing the $2 \times 2 \times 2$ Model

The core of the HO model consists of three propositions:

1   countries export goods with a relatively high input of locally plentiful factors of production,
2   free trade in goods equalizes the prices of factors of production;
3   a rise in the output of a good raises the real reward to a factor used intensively in that sector.

We have examined these propositions and when the first two of them might fail to hold in the context of a two-good two-factor model. What happens if the number of goods and/or factors is increased beyond two? This is a complicated and difficult area and we shall restrict analysis to the key results. For a recent in-depth survey of all the major studies, the reader is referred to Ethier (1984).

If there are more factors than goods, proposition (1) will fail except by fluke. There are more unknowns (factor prices) than equations that could help to solve them (isoprice curves): factor prices will just be undetermined. However, proposition (2) may survive generalization to a many-factor many-good world if there are at least as many traded goods as factors. What is needed in addition to common technology available to each country and perfect competition is sufficient similarity in the country's factor endowments. Endowments do not need to be identical except at a point of factor intensity reversal. Figure 2.30 presents the concept of an 'endowments cone' for the three-factor case. Panels 2.30(a)–2.30(c) portray different capital–labour–land 'boxes' corresponding to different possible endowment patterns. In 2.30(a), two units of capital K are available and only one unit each of land L and labour N. In 2.30(b) there is one unit each of K and L but two of N; and in 2.30(c), two of L and only one of K and N. Figure 2.30(a) might correspond to Switzerland, 2.30(b) to Portugal, and 2.30(c) to New Zealand.

The endowment proportions in the three cases are given by the rays R_a, R_b, and R_c. These three parts are combined in 2.30(d). What factor price equalization needs in this three-factor and three-or-more-good world is that each country's factor endowment lies within the cone formed by the three rays R_a, R_b, and R_c. The precise cone depends on the prices of the goods. Any country with an endowment of the factors outside the cone will have factor prices that depart from world levels, essentially because its production will be too specialized to conform to the other countries' values of wage, capital rental, and rent on land.

Proposition (1) is problematical as soon as the number of factors or goods is increased beyond two. If there are three or more goods and two

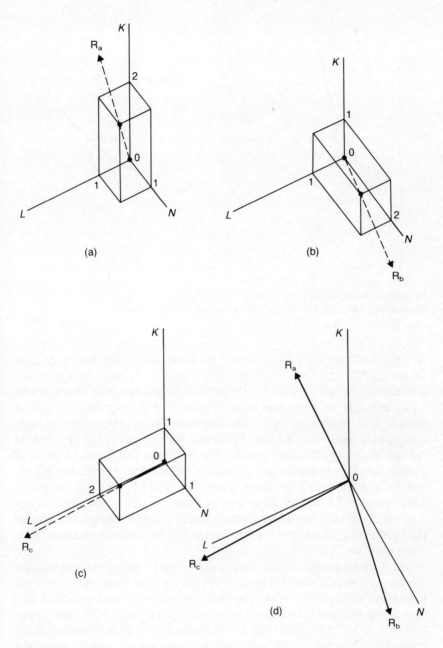

Figure 2.30   The endowment cone for factor price equalization: (a) endowment box with large K; (b) endowment box with large N; (c) endowment box with large L; (d) endowment cone R_a, R_b, R_c, and points within.

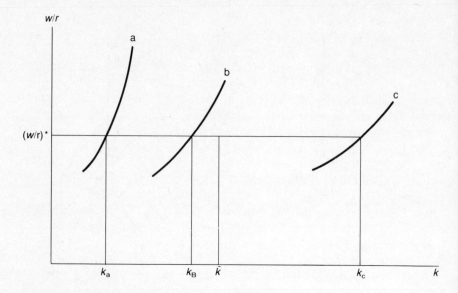

Figure 2.31   Output indeterminacy with two factors and three goods.

factors, for example, the pattern of production and hence exports becomes arbitrary. To see this, examine figure 2.31. Here there are three industries, labelled a, b, and c, the capital–labour ratios in which will be k_a, k_b, and k_c if the wage–rent ratio is $(w/r)*$. The problem is that, with an overall endowment of k', full employment of these factors and competitive factor pricing are compatible with a wide range of different output levels for the three goods. The economy can produce more of good b, and less of good a and c, while still employing capital and labour and fully adhering to the same wage–rent ratio. Essentially the three-dimensional PPF has straight line or 'flat' sections in it. If it is the number of factors, not goods, that is increased, the concept of 'relative factor intensity' ceases to have a precise meaning, and proposition (1) has to be reworded.

The third proposition, often called the Stolper–Samuelson results after Stolper and Samuelson (1941), survives in modified form. As long as the expanding sector starts with a positive output level, and provided that each factor it employs continues to be employed in some other industry as well, there will be some factor of production which becomes more expensive in terms of all other goods, possibly all goods, when the expanding sector's product price is increased. With the same provisos, there must be at least one other factor which suffers a price decline in terms of all goods.

2.6 International Trade: The Evidence

In 1988, the total value of world trade in goods and services was close to $US3 trillion. This vast figure was not much below US national income (some US$4.2 trillion) in that year. It represents about one-sixth of the world's aggregate income. So, on average, one dollar in six or so is earned from the sale of goods and services to foreigners.

Since 1945, international trade has grown faster than world income in most years. World trade in manufactures grew at some 7 per cent per annum from 1950 to 1986, as against annual income growth of about 4 per cent and manufacturing growth of 5 per cent. Much of the impetus towards trade expansion came from progressive cuts in tariff barriers by most developed countries. By contrast, the years between the world wars had witnessed a contraction in world trade: in the 1930s, in particular, individual countries sought to insulate themselves from world depression by restricting their imports. Countries which have expanded their exports fastest since 1950 include Italy, Japan, and West Germany (all shattered by defeat in world war), and other countries with high rates of national income growth are Hong Kong, Singapore, South Korea, Taiwan, Brazil, and Spain.

The geographical composition of trade has also changed in a further respect: trade between neighbours has grown with exceptional rapidity. Bilateral trade flows across the Canadian–US trade border, between France, the Netherlands, the UK and West Germany, and between Japan and the countries once known as her 'co-prosperity' sphere have risen a great deal more quickly than intercontinental trade.

The commodity composition of international trade has also been changing. Primary products (foodstuffs, fuel, metals) account for a declining proportion of the value of international trade. This downward trend is especially noticeable if the period begins in years such as 1951 or 1974 when primary product prices were high, but it is still visible, in the main, for other sets of years. Several factors help to explain it: policies to promote agricultural self-sufficiency, for example in the European Community and Japan; a long-term process of miniaturizing machinery, as mechanical engineering has yielded to electrical and electrical to electronic; and adverse long-term trends for some of the commodities involved. Iron and steel, textiles, and ships, which for so long dominated the exports of Britain and other early industrializing countries, also account for the falling shares in world trade. Steel exports are frustrated by protection, especially in Japan, the USA, and Western Europe; textiles are frustrated by the Multi Fibre Arrangement by which 36 countries restrain their imports to shield domestic producers; and ships are frustrated by the switch towards air and overland transportation of people and freight. The expanding sectors include aerospace, armaments, banking and other financial services, chemicals, computers, other electrical and electronic products, pharmaceuticals, tourism, vehicles, and vehicle parts. This range of products has benefited from a combination of freer trade and favourable world demand trends.

The above is a thumbnail sketch of a few statistical features of international trade. To what extent do such cross-border flows of goods and services corroborate the theory? We are faced with one immediate problem. International trade is arbitrage, a response to price discrepancies. But these prices discrepancies are *hypothetical*. In the limit, international trade eliminates them. Pre-trade or autarkic price differences cannot be observed. So our counter-factual explanation for international trade (if it did not occur, there would be a tempting plum of price differences) is singularly hard to test.

Allied to this is another difficulty. In the arbitrage theory of trade, autarkic price discrepancies are only an intermediate explanation. Something has to underlie them, be it differences in technology, factor endowments, or tastes. The frailty of the human mind encourages us to hope that a phenomenon has a single cause. The French Revolution occurred because of bad harvests, or people read *L'Encyclopédie*, or the middle class wanted political power to match its wealth. Many a third-rate historian falls for what one might call the fallacy of unicausality. Strict versions of Ricardo's model of international trade, and likewise the HO model, are unicausal. Everything is attributed to a single respect in which countries differ. It is easy to see such models as rivalrous. The student is excited by the thought of a battle royal between their protagonists, where one veridical victor ultimately triumphs in the tournament and the impostors limp off in ignominy. Such an all or nothing adversarial view is not helpful. Technology, factor endowments, and tastes can each play a role; no doubt they all do.

In the past four decades or so, most applied writing on international trade has been of three types. First, there have been tests, indirect and incomplete tests in the main, of the Ricardo and HO models. Then there has been statistical work linking countries' bilateral trade to their national incomes and the geographical distance between them. Finally there have been a number of different informal accounts, most of them yet to be modelled or tested rigorously.

The first type began with studies by MacDougall (1951, 1952) and Leontief (1954, 1956). MacDougall asked whether different countries' shares of exports of particular products to third markets were correlated in pairwise comparisons, as Ricardo's theory would presumably imply they should be, with relative labour productivities. It turned out they were, positively and significantly, in a UK–US comparison for 1939 data. Later work corroborated these findings (MacDougall et al., 1962, Stern, 1962; Balassa, 1963).

There are two difficulties, however: first, in its simple form Ricardo's model predicts that either the USA or the UK, say, would export a good to third markets (rarely, if ever, would both do so) and, second, relaxed versions of the HO model could give rise to the same finding. Leontief (1954, 1956) compared the capital–labour ratios in US export and import substitute production in 1947 and found that the ratio was about one-third higher in the latter. This is a paradox if one holds that the USA is relatively well endowed with capital (Leontief argued that America's education and training were so lavish that she could be relatively plentiful in labour in 'quality adjusted' or human capital augmented terms).

The paradox, if such it be, can be resolved in several ways: by invoking demand or factor intensity reversals, as noted in section 2.3; by introducing international technology differences, against the spirit of the strict HO model, which gave America's labour-intensive industries a cost advantage that offset any handicap due to factor endowments; or by showing that, in the disturbed economic conditions that prevailed in the immediate aftermath of the Second World war, the USA had a large trade surplus which could distort normal trading conditions (Leamer, 1980). Although confirmed by some later studies, Leontief's findings may apply no longer. Stern and Maskus (1981) find that, by 1972, US exports shared a 5 per cent higher capital–labour ratio than her import substitutes. Be that as it may, the HO predictions of trade direction involve cross-country comparisons of factor endowments and trade flows and cross-industry comparisons of factor intensities, but have yet to be tested in full. Maskus (1985) takes a major step forward by investigating all three of these variables for the USA. He concludes that the data do not lend support to the HO predictions.

The statistical inquiries in the second category were initiated by Linnemann (1966). In a major study of all bilateral trade flows between more than 40 countries, he regressed one country's total trade with another (exports and imports) against the former's national income, the latter's national income, and a term reflecting the geographical distance between them. Unlike the MacDougall and Leontief studies, he attempted to answer questions concerning the volumes of bilateral trade and the relative sizes of trade with different trading partners – the geographical composition of trade rather than its commodity composition. It turns out that countries trade much more with their close neighbours than with more distant countries: international transport costs matter. The size of trade also increases with the size of the exporter's national income (reflecting its productive potential) and the importer's national income (testifying to the size of its potential market). All these three variables prove significant. There are some exceptions to the 'gravitational hypothesis' that geographical propinquity encourages trade: Cuba's trade with the Soviet Union after 1960, Albania's with China, and the traditionally large trade between certain West European powers with their far flung current and former dependencies, could be attributed to tariff distortion or political links. Yet plausible as proximity and national income may be as influences on trade patterns, and however much they may matter in practice, they have yet to acquire a firm and intellectually appealing basis in received theory. This may reflect the fact that rigorous trade theory has yet to develop a properly articulated spatial dimension. Once it does, the studies pioneered by Linnemann will be enriched and extended.

The third strand to the recent applied literature on trade has taken the form of informal arguments and reflections on particular observations. Some of this has been stimulated by reactions to the unsatisfactorily extreme views implicit in the Ricardo and HO models, in their simplest forms, on the issue of technology. Ricardo has technology uniform within one country for a particular good, yet unaccountably at a different level in another, presumably in perpetuity. Heckscher and Ohlin insisted that the laws of physics held everywhere and that technology is therefore common to all. In practice technology does travel across international boundaries. Patents expire. There is imitation, legal or otherwise. Patentees licence production by foreign firms. Multinational companies apply ideas developed in a plant in one country to others abroad.

Yet stacked against these numerous routes of technological diffusion, which all support the HO view of uniform international technology at least as a central long-run tendency, is the important concept of 'learning by doing', due first to Arrow (1962). Learning by doing associates productivity with experience. Today's state of the art technology employed in a company in Yokahama or La Jolla may filter through to Lagos or Sofia in a few decades. But by that time the leading Japanese or American company will be several strides further forward. Diffusion undermines technological differences. Learning by doing may recreate them. Sometimes the fruits of experience can be transferred in full from one plant to another, if needs be across international boundaries; if this is so, international companies might be expected to determine an international pattern of production which minimizes costs, including those of transport, and the HO view will be vindicated. But if full transfer takes time and involves costly training, international productivity gaps, and the trade patterns they will give rise to, could persist. There could also be 'forgetting by doing'. Old-established plants or companies may become arthritic, inflexible, reluctant to sustain the momentum of change. Today's initiator may be tomorrow's sluggard. It has often been argued that Belgium, Sweden, and the major English speaking countries, which were relatively unharmed by the Second World War and grew relatively slowly in the three or four decades after it, lacked the benefits of a fresh start and new capital stock which destruction and defeat provided for some others, such as Japan and West Germany.

Some of these ideas are discussed by Posner (1961), and developed further by Hirsch (1967) and Krugman (1979). The application of learning by doing to international trade owes much to Clemhout and Wan (1970). Vernon argued that product innovation is mothered by perceptions of unsatisfied potential demand in a rich country. That is where it will first be produced for domestic and later foreign sale. Overseas production follows if conditions favour it. Hirsch suggested that products go through three phases, a 'product life cycle'. First, they are new, then growing, and finally they mature. New products need specialized skilled labour to produce them (Boston?, San Francisco?, Munich?). The second, rapid expansion, stage requires plentiful capital (Tokyo?). Stage three, maturity, requires large supplies of cheap, unskilled, and semi-skilled labour, such as exists in Seoul, São Paulo, or, in the next century, perhaps Calcutta and Shanghai.

There is clear evidence of a link between exports and technology. Stern and Maskus (1981) find a highly significant position association between net exports and research and development spending in 74 US industries. However, it is unclear which way causation runs. At the sectoral level, high profits from healthy net exports could stimulate research and development spending, and import penetration squeeze it.

Trade between countries is essentially the same as trade between regions. The goods an area exports are goods it produces. The exact location of production owes something to chance. Why are aircraft made in Seattle and Toulouse, not St Louis and Tours? Why ballbearings in Sweden and not the Saar? Why cars in Coventry, Detroit, Oshawa, Stuttgart, and Turin and not Leicester, Pittsburgh, Hamilton, Frankfurt, and Bologna? Increasing returns tell us why these products are not manufactured everywhere, but not why they are made where they are made. Often what mattered was the accident of where the successful entrepreneur happened to reside and work. Once production got going, he would incur the heavy costs of relocation only if these were outweighed by the discounted value of the stream of savings in expected transport and other costs. In the early stages of industrialization, proximity to power and ports was crucial. Electricity and the internal combustion engine liberated location decisions considerably, and propinquity to customers, labour, and component suppliers came to dominate. The peripheries of large conurbations, often centrally planned for cheap distribution, were favoured: hence the industrial expansions of the Los Angeles, Paris, and Toronto regions, and the valleys of the Po and Rhine. The high technology industries of the late twentieth century flourish near leading centres of learning, west of Boston and south of San Fancisco in the USA, and close to Cambridge in England. In Europe, some governments have intervened to bribe firms into regions of high unemployment and underemployment, such as Clydeside, Merseyside,

Naples, and the south of France, not always with happy results.

For raw and processed primary products, climate and geology are decisive. Cyprus has exported wine and, until 1988, Cornwall tin for over three millenia. Much trade between western European and the richer countries of the southern hemisphere conforms to the HO model: Argentina and New Zealand, for example, are land rich and relatively unpopulated and export land-intensive agricultural products in return for labour-intensive manufactures. Exporters of oil in the Middle East and elsewhere are not just exporting products intensive in a locally plentiful resource – they are exporting the resource itself. The same is true for metals, and for Australia, Bolivia, Chile, South Africa, Zaire, and Zambia. Differences in climate also help to explain why Canada exports grain; Southern California, Israel, and Spain citrus fruit; Scotland oatcakes and whisky; and Caribbean and Mediterranean countries tourist services.

The rapid and fast growing level of trade in manufactures between advanced countries in the western hemisphere is harder to explain. Japan, the rich countries of northwest Europe, and even Canada and the USA differ relatively little in factor endowments, climate, or geology. It is curious how much of this trade is two way, even at the level of individual industries and products. Many of these countries both export and import cars with each other, for example. The same is true for chemicals, steel and a wide range of machinery. How are we to explain this intra-industry trade?

We could explain cross hauling in building materials, for example, between France and Germany, or Canada and the USA, because at some points the most plentiful source lies on one side of the border and at others on the other side. Britain and France may come to engage in substantial two-way trade in electricity if they continue to apply different time zones. But for manufacturers the most appealing answer lies with imperfect competition and increasing returns. As will be seen in chapter 4, international oligopolists producing in different countries are likely to sell each other's home bases if transport costs allow. Increasing returns for the producers of differentiated products will mean that each country confines itself to producing just a few types of the good for the worldwide market, leaving imports to cater for domestic customers who prefer a different combination of characteristics.

2.7 Conclusions

The major reason for trade between countries is that it is a natural and profitable response to the price discrepancies that would exist without it. Such discrepancies are largely attributable to international differences in technology and factor endowments. This chapter has concentrated in the main on a framework of idealized perfect competition. Market imperfections such as oligopoly and monopoly, and problems concerned with uncertainty, will be expanded in an international context in chapter 4. We have seen, in a perfectly competitive setting, that international trade can bring big gains to certain groups, such as those who consume cheaper importable products or derive their incomes from ownership of factors associated with their country's exportables. We have also identified potential groups of losers.

International trade brings large gains to many individuals. It is a universal phenomenon, hallowed by antiquity. But just as deeply rooted in history are attempts by governments to regulate and restrict it. Why do governments so often do this? What do they gain and lose by doing so? These are the central questions addressed in chapter 3.

3

Tariffs and Other Forms of Protection

This chapter begins, in section 3.1, with a review of the welfare economic concepts that underlie the 'political economy' of international trade. It includes an analysis of why protection is typically inefficient, because it distorts the international allocation of resources. Section 3.2 investigates the effects of a tariff imposed by a small country in a simple partial equilibrium context and 3.3 looks at estimates of the cost of imposing tariffs and effective protection. In section 3.4 we look at four particular arguments in favour of protection. Section 3.5 widens the discussion to a simple general equilibrium model of the small economy. In section 3.6, the 'small country' assumption is repealed and the optimum tariff argument is examined. Section 3.7 contrasts tariffs with other instruments of protection.

3.1 The Inefficiency of Protection

3.1.1 Concepts in Economic Welfare

When does a change in the allocation of an economy's resources bring a gain to society? Pareto (1909) argued that social welfare improves only when all members of society are better off as a result of the change. This is called a 'strict Pareto improvement'. If someone gains and no one loses, that is a 'weak Pareto improvement'. Similarly, a strict Pareto deterioration in social welfare occurs if everyone is made worse off, and a weak Pareto deterioration occurs if at least one person loses and no one gains. If a certain change brings gain to some members of society and losses to others, the new and old states of affairs cannot be Pareto ranked as far as social welfare is concerned. Hence the ranking of different resource allocations or different 'states of the world' is seriously incomplete if Pareto's definitions are used.

Other social theorists have proposed definitions of social welfare that differ from Pareto's. Bentham (1789) equated social welfare with the sum of the welfare levels, or utilities, of all members of society. Bentham's criterion does not suffer from incompleteness but it is controversial. How are we to compare one person's utility with another's? How is utility to be measured? Even if we can deal with these problems, are we really to call a change a social improvement if it brings a larger utility gain to someone who is already well off than the utility loss suffered, for example, by someone with lower utility? In contrast, Rawls (1971) suggested that we should identify social welfare with the welfare level enjoyed by the least advantaged person, arguing that if we were unaware of our position in society we should all be so frightened of being the least advantaged individual that we would assent to any policy that increased that person's welfare. While Rawls's and Bentham's criteria may get us further than Pareto's, both the average utility test and the minimum utility test seem to occupy opposite extremes on a spectrum of possibilities. Roberts (1980) offered a weighted average of minimum and average utilities, with the relative emphasis one of us might place on these two depending on his or her subjective degree of aversion to inequalities in utility.

Although Pareto's ranking of social states is incomplete, there is another Paretian concept which is far more robust. This is the notion of Pareto efficiency. A state of the world is said to be Pareto efficient if it is impossible to make everyone better off by changing it. If it is possible to increase everyone's utility by enacting a change, the initial situation is Pareto inefficient. A Pareto-inefficient state is Pareto improvable; a Pareto-efficient (PE) state is not. A change from a Pareto-inefficient state to a PE state is neither a necessary nor a sufficient condition for a social improvement, however, as figure 3.1 illustrates.

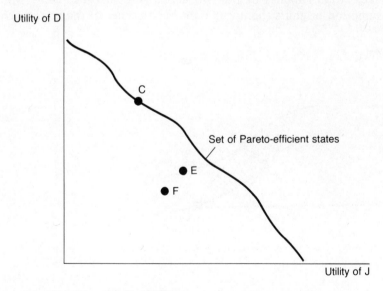

Figure 3.1   The utility possibility frontier.

Suppose society consists of two individuals, Jane (J) and Dick (D). The set of PE states shows the maximum possible utilities that can be enjoyed by one of them for different given levels of utility for the other. Points northeast of this set are unattainable. Pareto-inefficient states lie inside this frontier. Both F and E are Pareto inefficient, but a move from F to E is a Pareto improvement. C is PE but a move from F (or E) to C is not a social improvement because, while Dick clearly gains, Jane loses.

3.1.2 The Welfare Effects of Tariffs

A tariff on imports, the classic instance of protection, is almost certain to create Pareto inefficiency. It does this in two ways: by infringing conditions for efficiency in consumption or exchange between individuals who reside in different countries; and by violating conditions for efficiency in production across national boundaries. Why is this? Pareto efficiency in consumption is fulfilled when it is impossible to make all individuals (two people in a simple case) better off by reallocating fixed supplies of goods between them. That requires a *common* marginal rate of substitution (MRS). If individuals' indifference curves have different gradients (differing MRSs) at a particular point, such as Z in figure 3.2, both could gain by exchanging goods between them, that is, by moving to a point such as Y.

Point Z in figure 3.2 is an example of an allocation where two people's indifference curves intersect. Jane gets $0_J b_J$ units of good b and $0_J a_J$ units of good a, enabling her to reach indifference curve I_{J0}. The remainder of the fixed total supplies of the two goods goes to Dick. Dick, whose consumption origin is the upper right-hand corner of the box, reaches

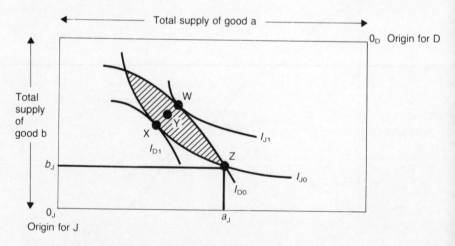

Figure 3.2   The condition for Pareto efficiency in exchange.

indifference curve I_{D0}. Because I_{J0} and I_{D0} intersect at Z, there is a set of allocations Pareto superior to it. This is given by the shaded area. All points inside this region will be preferred by the two individuals to point Z.

Where do tariffs fit into the picture? Point Z can only be an equilibrium for the two individuals if they face different relative prices of the two goods. I_{J0} is flatter at Z than I_{D0}. So Jane must face a lower relative price of good a (in terms of b) than Dick. Individuals optimize by finding a point of tangency between a convex portion of their indifference curve and the budget line facing them if they opt for positive amounts of both goods. The gradient of the budget line will be (minus) the ratio of the price of horizontal good to the price of the vertical. If D and J are residents of different countries and the government of one of them imposes a tariff on imports, the relative prices of the goods facing them will differ. A tariff is a tax on imports. A good on which it is levied will be more expensive at home than abroad. The good imported by country A will be more expensive in A than in country B, relative to a good exported from A to B. With free trade and no transport costs, the relative price of the two goods will be the same.

Given that consumers optimize so that the price ratio will equal their MRSs, free trade will achieve Pareto efficiency. PE allocations will display indifference curve tangency, not intersection, and free trade will give rise to this. Interrupt free trade by a tariff, so that relative prices differ, and a wedge is driven between the indifference curve tangents, creating a Pareto-inefficient allocation such as Z. The two individuals could be made better off, with no extra call on resources, by allowing them to exchange goods between them on equal terms. Tariffs are Pareto inefficient because they violate conditions for efficient exchange or consumption across international boundaries.

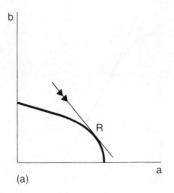
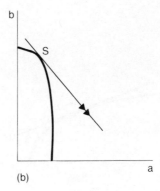

Figure 3.3 Efficient production within and across two countries: (a) production in A; (b) production in B.

Tariffs also infringe efficiency in production. Suppose there is perfect competition, full employment, and efficient allocation of resources within two countries A and B. Each country will produce a combination of goods on, rather than inside, its production possibility frontier (PPF). The slope of the tangent to the PPF, the marginal rate of transformation (MRT) will equal (minus) the ratio of prices of the goods facing producers inside the economies. Under free trade and in the absence of transport costs, these price ratios are the same in both countries. So the MRTs will be the same too, as shown in figure 3.3. Country A produces at R, country B at S. What happens if a tariff is introduced? Suppose country A exports good a and imports good b but levies a tariff on its imports. The price of b in terms of a must be higher in country A than in B. Producers inside the two economies now face different relative prices. The result of this is shown in figure 3.4. The higher relative price of b inside country A encourages producers to switch the pattern of production from R to R', where the value of total production at local prices, given by the slope of MM, will be maximized. More b is produced and less a. Country A now exports less a and imports less b. So inside country B good a becomes scarcer and hence more expensive. The relative price of good a in country B rises and the pattern of production responds to this by moving from S to S'. The new relative prices inside country B are given by the slope of NN.

The new pattern of production is internationally inefficient because world production of both good a and good b could be increased. Consider a marginal one unit cut in b output in country A and a rise in b output in B. The addition to the output of a in A will be greater, starting at R', than the fall in the output of a in B, starting at S'. This must be so because the MRTs differ. So countries A and B, taken together, could

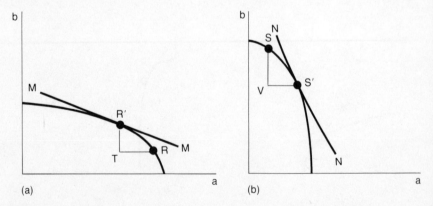

(a)   (b)

Figure 3.4   Inefficient world production after a tariff is introduced: (a) production in A; (b) production in B.

produce more b with no overall loss in output of a by marginal moves along the PPFs: from R' to R for A, and from S' to S for B. Compare R' and S' with R and S. Moving from the R'S' combination to RS will entail higher total output of good a (since RT > S'V) *and* good b (since SV > R'T).

To summarize, producing maximum combinations of goods in the world as a whole requires a common MRT for all countries as in figure 3.3. If MRTs differ between countries (which will happen if one country imposes a tariff levy on imports), the world will be producing less of both goods than it could. If goods were perfectly divisible, and circumstances were ideal, getting rid of tariffs could in principle allow us to give more of every good to every person in the world!

We have shown that import tariffs violate conditions for efficient production and consumption (or exchange) at the world level. It is not just tariffs that do this: so will quotas that restrict the volume of imports, any other non-tariff barrier (NTB) that achieves that result, and taxes or subsidies on exports. Any form of protection or government intervention in the pattern of international trade will threaten to infringe Pareto efficiency at the world level.

Are there any exceptions to these propositions? For example, could import tariffs ever be Pareto efficient at the world level? There are certain exceptions which merit mention, although they may be of limited practical significance. First, it is just possible that import tariffs do no damage. Suppose the PPFs of the two countries are rectangular and that the same is true of the indifference curves of their residents. As we saw in chapter 2, PPFs will be rectangular under conditions of complete joint production or total sector specificity of all factors; indifference curves are rectangular if consumers always want goods in fixed proportions. A rectangular PPF will have no defined MRT at its upper right-hand corner. The patterns of production will be frozen inside the countries independently of the relative prices facing the two sets of producers. If indifference curves are rectangular, the MRS will be similarly undefined and consumption patterns are independent of the prices facing consumers. In this extreme limiting case, phenomena such as import tariffs do not infringe efficiency in production or exchange because they have no effect on production and consumption patterns. From a welfare standpoint, tariffs are irrelevant.

Second, it is possible that there are international externalities in consumption, production, or both. Suppose that country B is very poor, with many of its citizens threatened by starvation in a drought, and run by a government which values armaments (good a) quite highly in relation to bread (good b). Suppose that neither the residents nor the government of country B are concerned by the pattern of consumption within the rest of the world (country A). But A's residents derive utility not just from their own consumption of armaments and bread but also from bread consumption by B's residents. Efficiency in the presence of this asymmetric commodity-specific consumption externality now requires that the residents of B face a lower relative price of bread in terms of armaments than those in A. Some departure from free trade, such as a negative import tariff or export subsidy, could achieve this, although the best instrument for correcting this externality will probably be a consumption subsidy on bread in B (otherwise production efficiency is violated).

There could also be international production externalities. Take the example of electricity generation. Electricity generated in the USA could adversely affect forestry production in Canada. The same could be true of the UK, France, and Germany on the one side and Scandinavia on the other. Acid rain falling on country B could distort B's PPF as a result of particular production patterns inside A. In such a case, worldwide efficiency calls for different relative prices facing producers in the two countries; and again, a tariff could achieve this, but a tariff is typically an inferior solution to the problem because it induces a consumption distortion.

Lastly, economic agents may fail to act in their own true interests, perhaps because they are imperfectly informed. If we rank different consumption bundles from the standpoint of person J's *preference* and

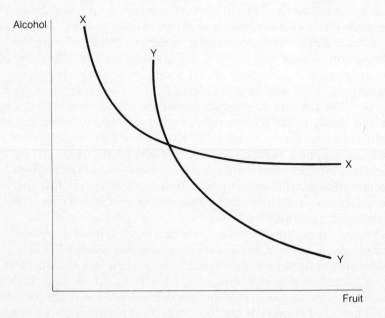

Figure 3.5   Preference and welfare rankings of consumption bundles differ.

compare the ranking from the standpoint of J's *welfare*, the results might not be the same. Figure 3.5 illustrates this possibility in the case of two goods, alcohol and fruit. The curve XX represents one of J's preference indifference curves while YY links combinations of alcohol and fruit consumption that yield a common level of true welfare. This argument appeals to liberals much less than to paternalists; many will question its applicability and argue that government intervention should be limited to ensuring that citizens are fully informed about the characteristics of the goods they buy. But, controversial as it may be, the idea can be made the basis of an argument for saying that relative prices confronting consumers in different parts of the world should differ. For example, if consumers are fully informed in A but not in B and welfare and preference maps for B's residents differ, the relative price of the 'demerit' good (alcohol) should be higher in B than in A for true Pareto efficiency in consumption. Once again, tariffs could achieve this, although at a cost in distorted production. Heroin provides a particularly powerful instance of this: many governments try to enforce an infinitely high tariff on heroin imports by an outright ban on them.

However, in the absence of international externalities or preference–welfare divergences, free trade is Pareto efficient under otherwise ideal conditions; and any restriction on trade (import tariffs, export subsidies) generates Pareto inefficiencies at the world level if there is any flexibility in production and consumption patterns.

3.2 The Partial Equilibrium Effects of a Tariff in a Small Country

In this section the domestic effects of an import tariff are explored in detail. We investigate the import tariff in partial equilibrium; attention is directed only to the domestic market for the good on which the tariff is levied, and not to the economy as a whole (see section 3.5). The size of the country levying the tariff is, for the present, assumed to be small. The significance of this assumption is that the country will be a perfect competitor in international markets, unable to affect world prices of the goods it buys or sells in them. This assumption is relaxed in section 3.6.

Referring to figure 3.6, begin with the case of free trade. The world price p^* is given. In the absence of a tariff or international transport costs, the home price p will equal p^*. In figure 3.6, SS depicts the supply curve of domestic producers of the importable good that we are considering, while DD is the demand curve of domestic consumers. Faced with a domestic price p^*, home firms produce at F, supplying S_0, and consumers will consume at J, demanding D_0. The excess demand FJ (or $D_0 - S_0$) for importables will be met by imports. The area FJD_0S_0 represents the economy's total value of imports of this product.

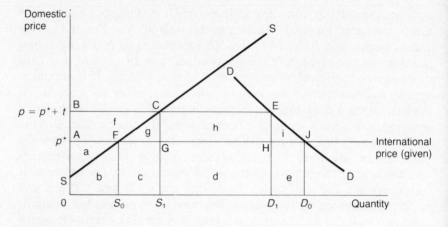

Figure 3.6   The partial equilibrium effects of an import tariff.

Domestic *producers' surplus* is given by area *a*, the amount by which total receipts $p*S_0$ exceed the bare minimum required to ensure production at S_0, the area under SS between the origin and S_0. *Consumers' surplus* is the area under the demand curve DD between 0 and D_0, above $p*$.

Suppose the government imposes a tariff at rate *t*. A specific tariff like this is imposed at a specific rate per unit, such as £1,000 per car or £1 per bottle of wine. An *ad valorem* tariff is levied on the value of the imported good at a particular proportionate rate. Since the country is small, nothing happens to the world price $p*$, and the home price rises to $p* + t$, point B on the vertical axis. Domestic production rises to C, from S_0 to S_1; domestic consumption drops back to E, from D_0 to D_1. The new import bill falls to area *d* ($= GHD_1S_1$) by virtue of this double-edged squeeze on imports.

Look first at the good news. The domestic government captures revenue from the tariff equal to area *h*. This rectangle (CEHG) is the product of the surviving import volume $D_1 - S_1$ and the tariff rate *t*. Domestic producers' surplus rises by area *f*. Area *f* will accrue, given perfect competition, to those individuals who own factors *used intensively* or *employed specifically* in this importables industry. If we are considering New Zealand, for example, which imports labour-intensive manufactures and exports land-intensive agricultural products, area *f* may be taken to represent the gain to labour in the form of higher wages. In the case of Japan or Western Europe on the other hand, which, by the logic of international trade, should import foodstuffs, area *f* will be increased rent on land, or perhaps the increased wage for agricultural workers if those elements in the labour force are specifically employed there and not free to move between sectors. So f and h represent gains for particular institutions or groups within the home economy. The bad news is the loss in welfare for consumers. Consumers' surplus falls by the total area ABEJ, that is, by $f + g + h + i$: this is the reduction in the amount by which consumers' total willingness to pay exceeds what consumers actually pay.

What can be said about the net effect on social welfare? If we employ Bentham's criterion of total or average utility in the community, and further assume that the marginal utility of money is constant and common for all, we can infer that total welfare must fall, in aggregate, by the sum of the two areas g and i. This is the amount by which the fall in consumers' surplus exceeds the sum of gains to producer surplus and government revenue. Put another way, areas f and h might in principle be returned to consumers but this would fail to compensate them for their total loss. Areas g and i are the deadweight loss from the tariff. If the domestic demand and supply curves are linear, the deadweight loss will equal $t\mathrm{d}M/2$, where $\mathrm{d}M$ is the tariff-induced fall in the volume of imports. Triangles CFG and EHJ have a total area equal to $t/2\mathrm{d}M$. Since $\mathrm{d}M$ is proportional to t, the damage done by tariffs will be related to the square of their size. Large tariffs will be disproportionately more injurious than small ones. The deadweight loss area depends on the elasticities of domestic demand and supply. If the two curves were completely inelastic (vertical), the loss would be zero. In general, the larger the elasticities of demand and supply are, the greater is the damage done.

If we adhere to Pareto's definition of social welfare, we have to be very careful. Society is worse off if everyone suffers, or at least if someone suffers and no one gains. We have seen that certain groups are likely to gain from the tariff: those who derive all or part of their incomes from ownership of factors specific to, or intensively employed in, the expanding domestic importables industry. We can add to this individuals with mixed incomes (derived, say, from the ownership of factors used intensively in both the importables and contracting exportables industries) but a pronounced taste bias, compared with the community average, towards exportable goods. Of course there are losers but Pareto's social welfare definition is unable to handle contrasts between positions where some people gain and others lose. From a Paretian standpoint, the social welfare levels in the two states, free trade and protection, are not comparable, and this statement is quite compatible with the fact that free trade is Pareto efficient while protection is not.

Could the tariff shown in figure 3.6 be Pareto efficient after all? Certainly not, if the domestic economy is immune from any other type of distortion save the tariff under consideration. In the absence of any other distortions, the domestic demand curve DD will represent the social marginal utility (SMU) of domestic consumption and SS the social marginal cost (SMC) of domestic production. In a partial equilibrium setting, Pareto efficiency calls for

$$SMU = SMC = SMCM$$

where SMCM is the social marginal cost of imports. Assuming the absence of international trade externalities, and given that the home country has no monopsony power that could enable it to influence the world price p^*, we know that SMCM $= p^*$. Therefore free trade is Pareto efficient.

Figure 3.7 illustrates the case, really an extreme special case, where it just happens that the tariff t' levied equates both SMU and SMC with p^*. Suppose that the domestic consumption of tobacco imposes a negative consumption externality. SMU for tobacco consumption lies below 'private' marginal utility, as reflected by the demand curve. At the same time, domestic tobacco production has a favourable production externality (tobacco farmers clean up rivers, train labour employed elsewhere, or perform some other meritorious service to the community that is not rewarded by the price system). So the SMC of home production lies below the private marginal cost borne by the farmers, given by the supply curve SS. If, by happy accident, the values of the two externalities are equal, a tariff of t' will be optimal. There is no deadweight loss from a tariff of t' but a policy of free trade with no intervention generates social deadweight losses equal to areas j and k. In this very special case the import tariff is the 'first best' solution. It is the ideal method of correcting the distortion. In every other case, a small

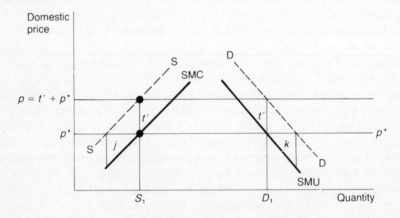

Figure 3.7   The freak case of a Pareto-efficient tariff on imports imposed by a small country.

country would do better to correct distortions by other means. 'Whatever a tariff can do, something else can do better' is a good general maxim. This argument owes much to Bhagwati (1971) and is developed further by Corden (1974, 1984b).

Figure 3.7 demonstrates the point that a tariff is equivalent to an equal subsidy on domestic production and tax on domestic consumption of the protected good. In an otherwise perfect economy as in figure 3.5, these tax-cum-subsidy effects are not just unwanted, they are deleterious in the sense of generating Pareto inefficiency and, applying Bentham's criterion, an unambiguous loss in social welfare. In the admittedly freakish circumstances of figure 3.7, the tariff is Pareto efficient if applied at the rate t'. A production subsidy and consumption tax are exactly what is needed to correct the externality.

If those who benefit and suffer from the externalities are limited in number, there are likely to be better ways of internalizing them, such as assigning property rights to one set of the agents affected in each case, encouraging cooperation and negotiation (through mergers, for example), or creating a market for the externality, such as pollution or training. Nationwide subsidies and taxes are too aggregative and create new distortions, and the same must be said for tariffs. Furthermore, it is always true that direct correction of a distortion at source, if this is the only distortion that is relevant, will be at least as good as imposing a tariff on imports.

Suppose there is one externality involved, say, consumption. If figure 3.7 is modified to banish the production externality, the optimum policy will be a consumption tax. This is preferred to a tariff because the latter involves a production subsidy which is damaging. If the ideal response,

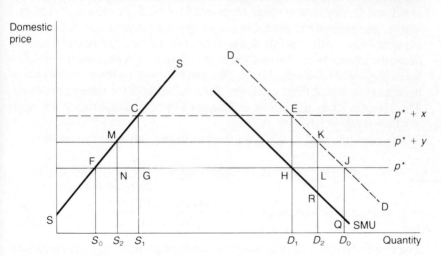

Figure 3.8 Responses to a consumption externality.

the consumption tax, is for some reason unavailable, the import tariff will be better than nothing ('second best') but the rate at which it should be applied is approximately $t'/2$ (exactly this if the gradients of the demand and supply curves are of equal magnitude in absolute value). In figure 3.8 the optimum rule for the small country (SMU = SMC = p^*) calls for a consumption tax at the rate x. This will lower domestic demand to D_1 and leave domestic production at its optimum level S_0. A policy of no intervention generates a deadweight loss of area HJQ. A tariff at the rate x means not just a consumption tax but a production subsidy at that rate, generating deadweight loss of area CFG. If the ideal policy, the pure consumption tax at x, is for some reason ruled out and the import tariff is the only device the authorities can employ, it should be set at rate y. Here the deadweight loss will be HLR + FMN.

3.3 Measuring the Effects of a Tariff

3.3.1 Studies on the Cost of Protection

This section reviews a selection of recent studies which have attempted to measure the welfare effects of imposing a tariff. The reader is referred to the excellent survey by Baldwin (1984) on empirical studies before that date. Morgan (1984) estimated the effects of doubling 1981 European Community (EC) tariff rates on manufactures from an average of approximately 5 per cent.

To compute the effect of the increase in tariff rates on the *value* of imports, we need an estimate of the import elasticity of demand, that is, the proportionate response of import demand to a proportionate change in price. Most estimates range from -0.5 to -2.5. For the EC taken as a whole, the estimate is probably closer to -2.5 because non-Community suppliers have only a small share of the market and are competing with domestic products and intra-Community imports. A particular manufactured good will have substitutes. This estimate will be lower in the case of products for which there are fewer close substitutes for foreign products. The Morgan study used three estimates of import elasticities of demand: -1.0, -0.69, -1.83.

The formula used to estimate the fall in the value of imports was

% change = % change in import price × the price elasticity of
demand for imports

$$\% \text{ change in import price} = \frac{\text{change in tariff rate}}{\text{original tariff} + 1}$$

The computation assumed there was no change in foreign supply prices. Morgan found that a doubling of tariff rates would cut imports of manufactures by between 4 and 10 per cent depending on the import elasticity of demand.

To compare welfare loss, Morgan employed the formula

$$\% \text{ change in import value} \times \tfrac{1}{2} (\text{new tariff rate} - \text{old tariff rate})$$

This is the simple partial equilibrium 'Benthamite' formula discussed in section 3.2. The reduction in welfare was found to be a very small percentage of gross domestic product. However, the formula does not take into account market imperfections or feedback effects on other sectors. For example, it does not consider the impact of tariff increases on a country's exchange rates. *Ceteris paribus*, increased protection may cause the value of a country's currency to appreciate as its balance of payments improves. Appreciation would worsen the competitive position of the country on world markets, with adverse effects on the economy's other traded goods industries. Market imperfections, such as imperfect competition or rent-seeking activity, could modify the welfare loss measure substantially. We return to this point in chapter 4.

Morgan also computed the effect of a doubling of EC tariff rates on tariff revenues:

$$\begin{aligned} \text{change in tariff revenue} = {} & (\text{new tariff rate} \times \text{reduced new} \\ & \qquad\qquad\qquad\qquad \text{volume of trade}) \\ & -(\text{old tariff rate} \times \text{old trade volume}) \end{aligned}$$

The increase in tariff revenue was about US\$5 billion, as against a 1981 EC budget of approximately US\$20 billion. Morgan found that, if the tariff rate was increased to an average of 50 per cent, there was a very large fall in imports and, for the smaller elasticities, an increase in tariff revenue. But for an import elasticity of -1.83, the rise in tariff revenue was similar to that for a doubling of the present tariff rate.

Deardorff and Stern (1981) examined the welfare effects of the Tokyo Round of tariff reductions, negotiated under the auspices of the General Agreement on Tariffs and Trade (GATT), 1974–9. Imposing estimates of the price elasticities of demand and supply, they computed welfare changes from the Tokyo Round based on what happened to the size of producer and consumer surplus. They also allowed for terms of trade effects, exchange rate adjustment, changes in consumption and production, and substitution between factors of production.

Deardorff and Stern showed that the Tokyo Round brought developing countries either negligible gains or losses. A reduction in tariffs reduced the revenue gains made by tariff impositions in developing countries and these countries continued to confront other forms of protectionism not considered in the Tokyo Round. For industrial countries, the gains were quite small – 0.3–0.5 per cent as a percentage of national income. The gains were not evenly distributed among countries, a large country such as the USA showing virtually no improvement.

Hufbauer et al. (1986) looked at 31 cases of protected industries in the USA. Each had trade volumes in excess of US$100 million and was protected by trade restrictions. Their calculations showed an annual consumer loss that exceeded US$100 million in all but six cases. The worst losses were in textiles and apparel, carbon steel, automobiles, and dairy products. The consumer losses per job saved were over US$100,000 per year in 18 of the 31 cases. Domestic producers were the main beneficiaries of the consumer loss, although in the car industry foreign producers gained 38 per cent of what consumers lost because foreign exporters to the USA had agreed to restrain exports. The authors found the production efficiency loss to be small in comparison with the consumption loss.

A World Bank (1987) study examined 41 developing countries. It compared two types of developing country: those that adopted an outward-oriented policy where trade and industrial policy did not discriminate between foreign and domestic production or consumption; and those that adopted an inward-oriented strategy in which trade and domestic policies were biased towards production for the domestic market relative to the export market. The study found a large difference (of the order of 5 per cent) in the growth rates of real income per head when the two groups were compared, over two different periods. The outward-oriented group grew faster.

Lastly, Cox and Harris (1985) (see also Whalley, 1984) examined the likely effects of Canada's removing tariffs against imports from the USA in a detailed multisector setting. They found that the changes in the allocation of resources would be large, with many industries contracting or expanding output substantially. The net welfare gain to Canada was equivalent to over 8 per cent of its gross national product, while a slightly smaller gain would result from her trading freely with all countries. Scale economies play a major part in these welfare effects. In another study by Wigle (1988), where scale economies are much less important, Canada seems to gain from a multilateral free trade agreement with all countries and lose slightly from one confined to the USA.

3.3.2 The Effective Rate of Protection

Up to this point we have looked at the effects of nominal tariff protection: a tariff applied to the finished product. But many intermediate commodities are traded internationally, and if tariffs are imposed on these then the profits of the industry using the protected factor inputs are likely to fall and the industry is 'disprotected'. In these cases the full impact of the tariff will not be captured by measuring the effects of the nominal tariff. However, if a tariff is levied on a final product and not on importable inputs used to produce it, the true level of protection is understated by the nominal tariff. The concept of effective protection receives its fullest treatment in Corden (1969).

The effective rate of protection is defined as the percentage by which a tariff raises an industry's value added per unit of output. It is expressed as

$$g = \frac{V_i' - V_i}{V_i}$$
$$= \frac{t_i - \sum_j a_{ij} t_j}{1 - \sum_j a_{ij}}$$

(3.1)

where V_i' is the value added in sector i in the presence of tariffs, V_i is the value added under free trade, t_i, t_j are the tariffs levied on the final product i and the intermediate product j, and a_{ij} is the input of j into the production of one unit of i. The **value added** of a firm is its sales income during a given period less the total value of bought-in materials, services, and intermediate inputs. For example, suppose that a car costs £5,000 to import but the inputs used to make it (steel, transmission system, etc.) cost £4,000 to import. Then the value added in car manufacture, in world prices, is £1,000.

If the nominal rate of protection on cars was 100 per cent, the car would be sold for £10,000. If the nominal rate of protection on inputs was 50 per cent, they would cost £6,000 instead of £4,000. Therefore the value added when both the cars and the factor inputs are protected is £4,000. The effective rate of protection is 300 per cent, the difference between the value added in world and domestic prices (£4,000 − £1,000) divided by the value added in world prices (£1,000) multiplied by 100 per cent. Of the £4,000 earned by domestic factors of production, £3,000 is the tax on consumers.

In our example, the nominal rate of protection of 100 per cent is much lower than the effective rate of protection of 300 per cent. Therefore it is possible that the protected industry will attract more resources than that indicated by the nominal rate. However, if tariffs on intermediate goods are high but the final good is protected by a lower duty, the effective rate of protection may be negative. In the above case, if cars were protected by a nominal rate of 50 per cent and inputs by a rate of 100 per cent, then the effective rate of protection is −150 per cent. The car industry is effectively disprotected because of the high rate of protection on intermediate goods. The effective rate is greater than (less than) the nominal rate of protection if the output of an industry is protected by a higher (lower) duty than its factor inputs.

Most studies have found, like Balassa (1965), that the effective rate of protection usually exceeds the nominal rate because nominal rates tend to be higher for industries producing finished products than for those producing intermediate products. In one celebrated study of some developing countries, Little et al. (1970) found that effective protection rates varied widely, with the highest, on light bulbs in Pakistan, exceeding 10,000 per cent!

3.4 Four Arguments for Protection

Figure 3.8 and extensions to it can be made the basis for various other arguments for protection. These include

1   the infant industry argument,
2   the public finance argument,
3   the unemployment argument, and
4   the income distribution argument.

We investigate each of these in turn.

The **infant industry argument** runs thus. Suppose an importable can be produced at home by recently formed firms or by firms which could be brought into existence. These 'infant' firms incur high initial costs and cannot compete in their first few years with long established overseas rivals. Eventually they will mature and make profits. A free trade policy will stifle them at birth. A temporary tariff against imports will allow them to grow to maturity, protected from the chill wind of overseas competition.

The first point to be made about the infants is that they may be able to borrow to finance their early losses. If there are future profits to be earned, why do they not invest in the industry and repay the initial set up or learning costs out of the profits they will earn later? If the domestic firms are unwilling to do this, perhaps they should be stifled at birth. The retort to that could be threefold: the new domestic firms are not prepared to take the risk, or they cannot borrow at appropriate interest rates, or they will bring external benefits to society for which they are inadequately remunerated. The first retort is unpersuasive, since it may be better to nationalize or to invite foreign firms to take them over, to remedy the defect in domestic private sector entrepreneurship. The second turns out to be a call for repairing the deficiencies in the domestic capital market, and the third for a production subsidy or other arrangements to internalize the externality. In this third case, there may be a good reason for setting up the industry but not for making consumers pay for this in the form of temporarily higher prices.

Arguments for production subsidies for both infant and mature firms acquire more force under conditions of imperfect international competition. This forms much of the subject matter of chapter 4. Under perfect competition, the case for production subsidies turns on the existence of externalities which cannot be internalized successfully by more direct means. The case for import tariffs, as opposed to production subsidies, is distinctly weak, since the former lead inevitably to a distortion in consumption. The only major qualification here relates to the fact that a government may have to deploy distortionary taxes anyway to defray the costs of production subsidies. By contrast, import tariffs, for all the damage they do to domestic consumption, actually contribute revenue to the state and allow for other forms of distortionary taxation to be reduced. These observations lead us directly to (2), the public finance argument for protection.

The **public finance argument** for tariffs on imports is built on the principle that governments either cannot or should not levy lump sum taxes. Lump sum taxes have the great merit of not distorting economic agents' marginal decisions. But they are widely perceived as unfair. The simplest form of lump sum tax, a poll tax, is imposed on everyone at the same level and is therefore highly regressive because it fails to take account of differences in income, wealth, or earning power. Governments need revenue to meet the costs of public goods provision, debt servicing charges, and transfer payments. If lump sum taxes are ruled out as infeasible or unfair, the government has the task of collecting its taxes in the least distortionary fashion it can. Sales taxes on goods and income taxes levied on individuals are distortionary. The mere fact that tariffs are also distortionary should not exempt international trade from taxation if other activities are also being subject to distorting taxes. For example, in geometrical terms, one could argue that area h in figure 3.6, the government rectangle, may be more valuable in the hands of the government than the consumers' surplus it displaces. That is because, up to a point, area h may allow the government to reduce other distortionary taxes which create no less serious deadweight losses elsewhere. The 'shadow value' of government revenue may be very high.

The problem with this line of thinking is that the government could go further. Why not get rid of the production subsidy element implicit in the import tariff and impose a straight consumption tax? The government's revenue from this, in figure 3.6, would not be limited to area h: it would gain areas f and g also. Furthermore, it would avoid the deadweight loss area g by a consumption tax at the rate t: there would be no incentive for domestic producers to expand their output of importables and, by implication in a fully employed economy, to expand their output of importables at the expense of more valuable output of other goods forgone. By itself, the public finance argument for import tariffs is less appealing than the more general case for consumption taxes. Ramsey

(1927) showed that, if the government is to raise a given revenue target by taxes on consumption in the least distortionary fashion, it should so arrange them that the quantities of each good bought should be lowered equiproportionately. In the simplest case, this means making the rate of tax on each good inversely proportional to the price elasticity of demand for it.

There are two points that can be stated in defence of import tariffs in this context. The first is that they are cheap to collect, much cheaper in many cases than consumption taxes where the number of collection points is usually vastly higher. The Roman Empire relied heavily on tariffs levied on maritime trade, partly because this was funnelled through relatively few ports, evasion was difficult, and many other types of taxation (for example, on incomes) were infeasible. The second is that the production subsidy implicit in tariffs may be desirable in its own right, particularly when the economy is suffering from unemployed resources. This leads us to (3), the unemployment argument.

The **unemployment argument** for tariffs rests on the claim that the true opportunity cost of domestic production may be very low, certainly less than the marginal costs faced by firms which are reflected in the supply curve in figure 3.6. Area g exaggerates the deadweight loss in such circumstances. Firms may have to pay wage rates to labour far in excess of what the workers could earn elsewhere. The additional production and employment of import substitutes which the tariff induces may be very welcome.

The difficulty with this argument is not that the tariff may be better than nothing: it could be. The issue is whether it is the appropriate means for combating unemployment. Suppose the country is suffering from nationwide unemployment. Wage rates exceed the opportunity cost of labour throughout the economy. The most direct and appropriate response to this distortion is a subsidy for employment, applied at least on the marginal worker in every industry where labour is hired. This policy, if feasible, amounts to a direct attack on the source of the distortion.

In a sense, a tariff on imports is an employment subsidy. But it is also much more and much less than that. It is less because it subsidizes employment in the domestic importables industry only and not elsewhere in the economy. It is sector confined, in an unhelpful way. It is also more: it subsidizes not just labour employment but the hiring of other factors too, such as land, capital, and raw materials, which may be unnecessary or worse. A production subsidy is equivalent to an equiproportionate subsidy on the hiring of all factors, not just labour. Worse still, it is also a consumption tax on importable goods, creating a distortion there (the deadweight loss area i) where there was presumably none before. Added to this, there is the risk that other countries will retaliate, squeezing exports and the jobs associated with them; and even if they do not, the reduction in imports which a tariff will bring about could lead to an appreciation of the exchange rate which may undermine exports through a different route.

Unemployment, therefore, does not justify the imposition of tariffs. In principle, at least, other instruments are better directed to combating it. All that can be said by way of qualification is that tariffs bring revenue to the government while employment subsidies will probably cause funds to flow in the opposite direction. Thus, if the government is in acute need of additional revenues as well as beset with nationwide unemployment, a combination of the public finance and unemployment arguments may call for some modest departures from the principles of free trade.

The fourth argument for protection is the **income redistribution** to which it leads. We have already seen who will gain the extra producers' surplus area f in figure 3.6. It could be argued that social welfare places a higher weighting on the incomes of certain groups than others. This would be a modification of Bentham's average utility test, perhaps on Rawls's lines (for instance, if the favoured groups were poorest). It is not an argument which Pareto's approach to social welfare could accept.

In geometrical terms, the social welfare effect of a transfer of f from, let us say, richer consumers towards the favoured group would be so beneficial as to swamp the deadweight loss areas g and i. If so, the tariff is socially beneficial. But there is a problem. Suppose we could find some other way of redistributing income towards these individuals whom society wishes to favour. A straight transfer of income to them would have all the alleged advantages with none of the defects, because the deadweight areas would not be lost. If consumers could simply be persuaded to transfer area f to the relevant individuals, society would surely gain even more than with the tariff. The levies on imports of agricultural goods imposed by Japan and the EC are an interesting example. If they are defended on the grounds that poor domestic farmers need higher incomes, there are surely better ways of achieving this objective. Cash transfers and free trade are preferable to tariffs. Incidentally, many farmers are far from poor and many consumers of agricultural products are far from rich, so that it is most doubtful whether policies to restrict agricultural imports even reduce the inequalities in the distribution of income.

3.5 The General Equilibrium Effects of a Tariff in a Small Country

In this section we employ a simple general equilibrium framework to investigate the consequences of imposing a tariff in a small country. We shall assume that the economy produces and consumes two goods a and b,

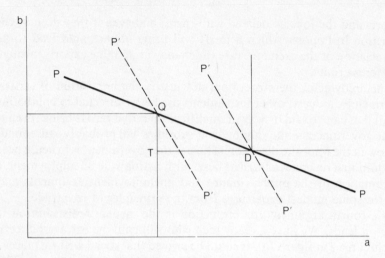

Figure 3.9   Production, consumption, and the irrelevance of tariffs when these display no substitution.

that its two factors of production K and N are given in total supply, fully employed and perfectly mobile between the two industries, which employ them in different proportions. It is also assumed that the community indifference map is uniquely given and, as elsewhere in this chapter, that there is perfect competition and constant returns to scale in the production of each good.

Figure 3.9 illustrates the case where production and consumption are completely inflexible. To have this under the above assumptions, one industry must employ K only and the other N only. It is therefore a limiting special case of little intrinsic interest, but it is useful as a comparitor. The pattern of production is frozen at Q. The world terms of trade are given by the slope of the line PP. The country exports b and imports a. The value of its total output at international prices allows it to consume at point D. It will have a 'trade triangle' QTD, exporting QT units of b and importing DT units of a in return.

This equilibrium is, interestingly, completely unaffected by tariffs. The domestic government taxes imports of a and the tariff changes the relative price to the gradient of the broken lines P'P'. It also hands back the import tariff revenue to domestic consumers. With no substitution in production or consumption, nothing changes as far as quantities are concerned. In terms of figure 3.6, it is as if the domestic demand and supply curves are vertical. In that case, we saw that the deadweight losses would vanish. Tariffs would do no damage.

Figure 3.10 modifies figure 3.9 by allowing substitution in consumption only, and figure 3.11 modifies figure 3.9 by allowing substitution in

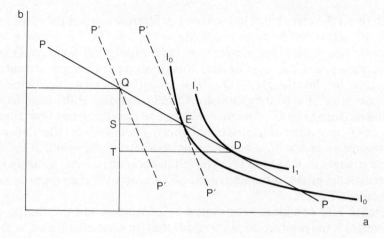

Figure 3.10   The effects of a tariff when consumption is flexible.

production only. Under free trade, consumers face the world price ratio *P* and spend their aggregate incomes at D. The trade triangle is QDT. But with a tariff that raises the relative price of good a to the gradient P′P′, consumers switch to E on the community indifference curve I_0. Trade shrinks to the new triangle QES. The fall from indifference curve I_1 to I_0 registers the consumption efficiency loss from the tariff. This is the analogue of area *i* in figure 3.6.

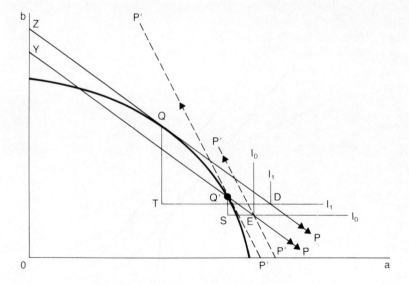

Figure 3.11   The effects of a tariff when production is flexible.

In figure 3.11 we return to L-shaped indifference curves for consumption but allow flexibility in production. The new PPF is concave and smooth, not rectangular. Under free trade, production occurs at Q and consumers spend the value of their total incomes at D. Suppose trade is captured by the triangle QDT. With a tariff that raises the domestic relative price of a to the gradient of the broken line P'P', production switches from Q to Q'. The new budget line for consumers now comes out of Q', measured at international prices. The complete inflexibility of consumption means no substitution by consumers, who spend at E. The trade triangle shrinks to Q'ES. The fall in national income, measured at international prices, is the equivalent of YZ units of b; the proportionate fall equals YZ/0Z.

Figure 3.12 combines substitution by consumers and producers. As before, Q is the production point and D that for consumption under free trade, where the relative price confronting households and firms is the slope of line P. QTD is the trade triangle. A tariff raises the domestic relative price of good a, the importable, to the gradient of the bold line P' and production shifts to Q'. Consumption occurs at F, the point on the budget line from Q', parallel to the P line, where consumers' MRS equals the new domestic price ratio P'. The trade triangle shrinks to Q'FS, and consumption falls to community indifference curve IC_0 from IC_2. The shift from D to E represents the consumption effect of the fall in real income (at international prices) due to substitution in production; the further decline from E to F is due to substitution in consumption.

This section concludes with a short discussion on the factor price effect

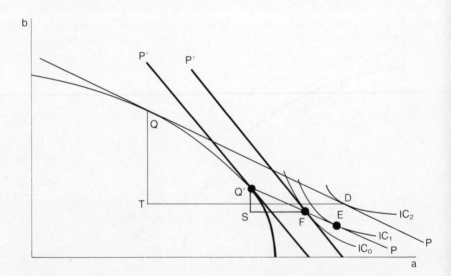

Figure 3.12   The effects of a tariff when both consumption and production are flexible.

in the context of this two-good, two-factor model. We have explicitly assumed that the production of goods a and b requires the employment of two factors, K and N, in different proportions. Perfect competition, full internal factor mobility, and constant returns to scale together imply that

1   each factor will be paid the value of its marginal product in each industry,
2   the unit costs of producing a and b will equal their prices, and
3   the wage rate w paid to labour and the capital rental r will each be uniform in the two sectors.

The use of isoprice curves is legitimated by these conditions. They are illustrated in figure 3.13. If good a is relatively capital intensive, the unit isoprice for good a will be steeper than that for b where they intersect. The slope of the tangent to the isoprice is the capital labour ratio. This intersection point is C under free trade where the prices of labour and capital are w_0 and r_0 measured in units of good b. The government introduces a tariff on the imported good a, raising its domestic price. The new a isoprice is the broken curve, which crosses the unchanged b industry isoprice at D. In units of b, the wage rate falls and the capital rental rate rises. The wage rate also falls (even more) in terms of good a; and the rental on capital actually rises in units of a. This can be seen from figure 3.13: the proportionate price increase for a is equal to $ED/0E$, while the rise in the capital rental $(r_1 - r_0)/r_0$ is relatively larger than this.

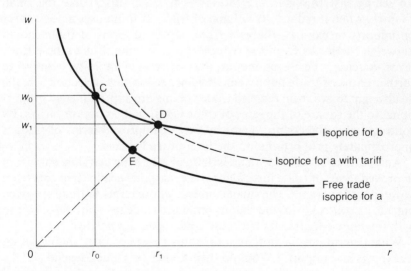

Figure 3.13   Factor price changes induced by the tariff.

So those who own capital, and derive their income from this, will be better off after the tariff increase. This is true however they allocate their incomes between the goods: even in units of dearer importables they are better off. The owners of labour are absolutely worse off.

3.6 Tariffs and the Large Country Case

In this section we repeal an assumption that has underlain the analysis throughout the chapter so far: the assumption that the home country is small. A small country is a perfect competitor in international markets for its exports and imports. It is a price taker for these goods. Its terms of trade, the ratio of the price for its exports to the price of its imports, are given. The terms of trade may change but never as a result of its own actions.

A large country, by contrast, can influence its terms of trade. If it imports more, it will drive up the world prices of the goods it imports. It has 'monopsony power', the power that accrues to a sole buyer or major buyer. Similarly it will drive down the world prices of its exports if it tries to export more. In export markets, it enjoys monopoly power. If the large country seeks to increase its volume of trade, it will suffer a deterioration in its terms of trade. Its export prices will fall relative to its import prices.

A large country can gain by restricting its trade in a way that a small country cannot: such action leads to an improvement in its terms of trade. The buying power of its exports, measured in imports, will widen. To set against this gain are the losses it must suffer, like the small country, when it reduces its volume of trade. If it imposes modest taxes on imports or exports, the gain from improved terms of trade should outweigh the losses from the reduced trade volume. But as these trade taxes increase, the losses mount with increasing rapidity, relative to further terms of trade improvement gains. As we saw in section 3.2, the deadweight losses from reduced trade volume are approximately proportional to the square of the rates of trade taxes, such as import tariffs. By contrast, what the country gains by way of improved terms of trade is approximately proportional to the level of trade taxes.

An optimum set of trade taxes is defined where the marginal gain from improved terms of trade just balances the marginal deadweight cost from lowered trade volume. The small country, whose terms of trade are given outside its control, will find that its optimum trade taxes are zero. Not so with the large country. Its optimum trade taxes are positive.

What determines the optimum tax rates a large country should set on its exports and imports? What do their numerical values depend on? To answer these questions and explain the reasoning behind them, we shall look first at partial equilibrium analysis. Then we shall generalize the story, first using duality to illustrate a country's trading pattern and how, if it is large, it can gain from taxing its trade. Then, by introducing the concept of offer curves, it is possible to show what an optimum tariff on imports, or an optimum export tax, looks like, and what effects it will have.

3.6.1 Partial Equilibrium Analysis of the Large Country Case

We begin by making a number of assumptions.

1   All residents of the country have identical homothetic preferences, so that a community indifference map is uniquely defined.
2   The government redistributes income between gainers and losers so that no one is allowed to lose from potentially socially advantageous changes. This ensures the Pareto comparability of different positions from a social welfare standpoint.
3   The rest of the world continues to trade freely, so that retaliation possibilities are ignored.
4   There are no distortions or market failures within the economy.
5   Domestic firms engaged in international trade enjoy no monopoly or monopsony power of their own.
6   The home country cannot discriminate in overseas markets, and so there is a single price for each of its imports that rules throughout the rest of the world.

With these assumptions it is possible to embark on illustrating the partial equilibrium story of how a large country can gain by taxing its imports. Figure 3.14 presents demand and supply for the home country's exportable, both at home (3.14(a)) and in the rest of the world (3.14(c)). Figure 3.14(b) depicts the home country's excess supply ES and the rest of the world's excess demand ED*. Under free trade a common world price p_0 is established in equilibrium. The quantity of exports is x_0. Under autarky the prices of the good would have been p_4 at home and p_3 abroad.

Had the home country been a perfect competitor in this world market, ED* would have been horizontal. But ED* slopes down because the country is large. It is this that gives the home country its monopoly power. The monopoly power is exploited to the full when the home country maximizes its profit from exports. This occurs where the marginal revenue from exports, MR*, intersects the domestic excess supply curve ES. The absence of domestic distortions ensures that the domestic price corresponding to this excess supply curve measures both the social marginal utility of consuming exportables at home (captured by D) and the social marginal cost of producing exportables, given by S. ES is the marginal cost of exports.

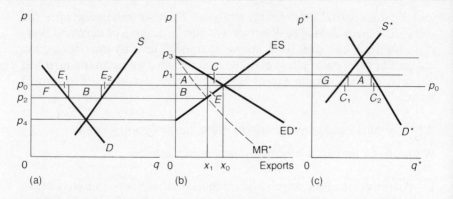

Figure 3.14   The home country's optimum export tax: (a) home demand and supply; (b) home country exports equal to rest of world imports; (c) rest of world demand and supply.

The optimum export tax is the vertical distance between p_1 and p_2. p_1 is the high price that will rule in world markets when the optimal tax is applied and exports are cut back to their optimal value x_1. The corresponding domestic price will be p_2, where the vertical line at x_1 intersects the domestic excess supply curve ES. Thus the application of the optimum export tax raises the world price and lowers the domestic price.

The government earns tax revenue equal to areas A and B. At home, domestic producer surplus falls by areas $F + E_1 + B + E_2$ in 3.14(a). Areas E_1 and E_2 sum to the area of triangle E in 3.14(b) and this reflects the deadweight loss from tax suffered at home. Domestic consumer surplus rises by area F. So, in crude partial equilibrium terms, social welfare rises by $A - E$. Indeed, since the export tax is levied at an optimal rate, we know that $A - E$ is not merely positive. It is maximized.

Abroad, the only good news is area G, which represents a gain to foreign producer surplus. To set against this, foreign consumer surplus falls by $G + C_1 + A + C_2$. $C_1 + C_2$, which represents area C in 3.14(b), is the overseas deadweight loss burden. But foreign social welfare falls by more than area C: the area A is part of the tax revenue accruing to the home country's government. Thus foreign welfare falls by $A + C$. If we value money at the margin equally between the two countries, as well as between their residents, the *world's* welfare has fallen by the sum of the two deadweight loss areas $E + C$. But the transfer of A from the rest of the world to the home country makes the latter a net gainer.

It is possible to be more precise about the size of the optimum export tax. Since there is a single world price that will be charged to all foreign buyers, the rest of the world's demand curve ED* represents the home country's average revenue from exports (AR). We also know that

$$MR = AR(1 - 1/e) \tag{3.2}$$

where e, defined as a positive number, is the elasticity of ED*. Profit maximization implies that $MR = MC$, and MC will equal the domestic price, while AR is the foreign price p^*. Let t be the export tax rate defined by

$$p = p^*/(1 + t) \tag{3.3}$$

Hence $MC = MR = p = p^*/(1 + t) = p^*(1 - 1/e)$, and so

$$t = 1/(e - 1) \tag{3.4}$$

In words, the optimum tax rate on exports is the reciprocal of the elasticity of foreign demand minus 1. If $e = 5$, the optimum tax rate is 25 per cent; if $e = 3$, 50 per cent. Formula (3.4) seems to break down if e is unity or less. This is not really so, but it reminds us of the result that a non-discriminatory profit maximizing monopolist only sells at the point where the demand for his product is elastic ($e > 1$). For if e were less than 1, marginal revenue would be negative, and a cutback in sales would have to increase profits not just by reducing total costs but by raising total receipts as well.

At this point it is worth noting how important it was to specify the assumptions given above. The significance of the first of these assumptions will be apparent later, but the others can be seen to play an important role in the argument behind figure 3.14. Assumption (2) enabled us to sweep aside the social implications of factor price changes. The factor used intensively in the exportable industry will suffer a decline in real reward in the two-good, two-mobile factor case as the domestic industry contracts. This effect is visible in the fall in producer surplus $F + E_1 + B + E_2$ in 3.14(a). Also, had the industry employed a factor specific to it, its owners would have suffered a fall in their real income. Assumption (3) ruled out foreign retaliation. Retaliation by the rest of the world would complicate and possibly negate the net gain to the home country since import tariffs could be erected to squeeze the trade volume still further. If they were imposed, the home country's terms of trade would deteriorate.

Had assumption (4) failed, the domestic excess supply curve ES would no longer be safely identified with the social marginal cost of exports. Relaxing assumption (5) would lead us to the observation that, had the home country's exporting been in the hands of a single firm or single group of colluding firms, they would already have recognized the logic of figure 3.14 and squeezed exports on their own. Lastly, if instead of assumption (6) we had assumed that the home country could discriminate

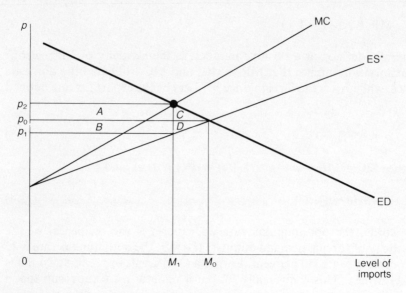

Figure 3.15   The home country's optimum import tariff.

perfectly in its export markets, the rest of the world's excess demand curve ED* would actually be the home country's marginal revenue for exports. The optimum export level would be as in free trade, x_0, but all but the marginal unit of exports would be sold at prices above p_0.

An analogous story can be presented for import tariffs. The large country enjoys monopsony power for its imports. It recognizes that the rest of the world's excess supply of importables (the supply curve for imports) is upward sloping and not horizontal as it would have been for a small country. In the absence of price discrimination, the marginal cost of imports lies above the supply curve. It is the former, not the latter, to which the domestic price of imports should be equated (p_2 in figure 3.15). The level of imports is M_1 rather than M_0, the free trade volume. The rest of the world price is cut from p_0 to p_1, and the domestic price rises to p_2.

The optimum tariff is $(p_2 - p_1)/p_1$. Areas A and B measure the tariff revenue accruing to the government. A is a transfer from domestic consumer surplus and B from foreign producer surplus. The home country's welfare rises by $B - C$, and welfare abroad falls by $B + D$. The deadweight losses are D abroad and C at home.

3.6.2 General Equilibrium Analysis of the Large Country Case

We turn now to exploring the optimum tariff argument in a more general setting. It is helpful to begin by introducing two new concepts. These are the national income function $Y(p, F)$ and the expenditure function

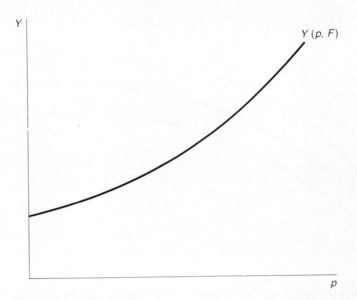

Figure 3.16   The national income function.

$E(p, U)$. Here p denotes a list or vector of prices of goods, F is a vector of factor endowments, and U is the utility of the representative individual residing in the country. For simplicity, assume there are just two goods, one imported (with the price of 1 throughout) and one exported with a price of p. The function $Y(p, F)$ shows how national income will vary with the price p of exports and also with factor endowments, which we take to be given. National income is the sum of the values of outputs of exportables and importables, in units of the latter. As p increases, production will shift towards exportables, and y will rise. The function $Y(p, F)$ is based on the premise of optimization by competitive firms. It is illustrated in figure 3.16 as a convex upward-sloping curve. The slope of the tangent to the curve at a point will equal the level of output of exportables, Q_X.[1] Since the curve is drawn convex, it increases steadily as p rises.

The expenditure function shows the smallest amount that the representative individual must spend to attain a given utility level. It is depicted in figure 3.17. He is assumed to want, and buy, some exportables as well as importables, and so his expenditure rises with their price. The curve is concave because of the non-perversity of the substitution effect. An increase in p for a given utility level cannot increase purchases of exportables. The slope of a tangent to the expenditure function gives the quantity of consumption of exportables. If higher utility is to be

---

1 National income is equal to $pQ_X + Q_M$, where Q_M is the output of importables. So $d(pQ_X + Q_M)/dp = Q_X$.

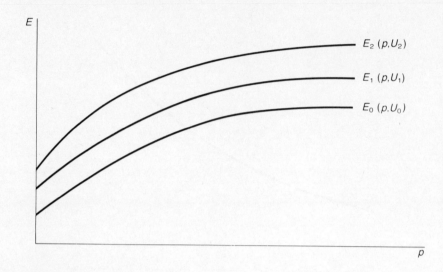

Figure 3.17   Various expenditure functions corresponding to different utility levels.

attained, the consumer must spend more at each price, so a higher E function is reached.

Figure 3.18 contrasts the autarkic and free trade equilibria. Under autarky, output and demand for exportables must be equal, and so the Y and E_0 functions are tangent at point A. In free trade, the price of exportables rises from p_A to p_H and so national income rises along the Y curve to H. The representative individual can now attain a higher utility level U_1 and reaches a higher expenditure function E_1. The free trade output and demand levels for exportables are given by the gradient tangents at H to the Y and E curves respectively.

Figure 3.19 shows the large country gaining from an export tax. The domestic price is reduced to p_j but the overseas price rises to p_k. The gap between these prices is the export tax wedge. The value of national income is augmented, beyond point B on the Y curve, by the level of export tax revenues. These are found by multiplying $p_k - p_j$ by the excess of exportables output (gradient of BD) over exportables domestic consumption (gradient of LD), which is the tangent to the expenditure function E_2 at L. Export tax revenues equal CG, therefore, and BL:DG/CD is the proportion of exportables output consumed at home. As it happens, in this case utility is increased by the export tax from U_1 to U_2. This could not have happened had the country been small, since the world price of exportables would have been stuck at p_H and expenditure would have been reached at a point below M.

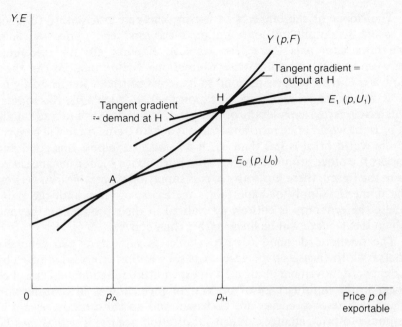

Figure 3.18 Autarky and free trade compared in the large country case.

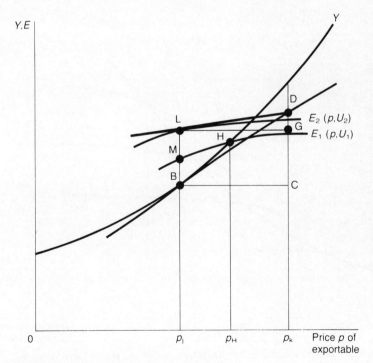

Figure 3.19 A large country gains from an export tax.

The slopes of the tangents to the income and expenditure function measure the output and consumption of the good whose price is given at the horizontal axis (here, exportables). Exports are the difference between output and domestic consumption. These functions can show how a country's exports respond to its terms of trade. Return to figure 3.18. When the relative price of exportables, p, equals p_A, the country will have a zero excess supply of this good. It will not wish to trade at all. If p_A is the world price ratio at which it is able to trade, trade will be zero. If the world price is less than p_A, it will wish to import this good and export the other product. But with the price above p_A, for instance at p_H as in the figure, there is positive excess supply of exportables. As p rises, the domestic supply of exportables increases, at least until the point where the economy is entirely specialized in their production, beyond which the Y curve will be linear rather than convex.

The domestic demand for exportables is subject to two generally contrary influences as p increases. The substitution effect is indicated by a rightward movement along a given expenditure function, which will be linear in the limiting case of perfect complementarity in consumption where indifference curves are L shaped and no substitution occurs in response to price changes. When substitution occurs, it will always be away from the good the relative price of which has risen, that is, as p

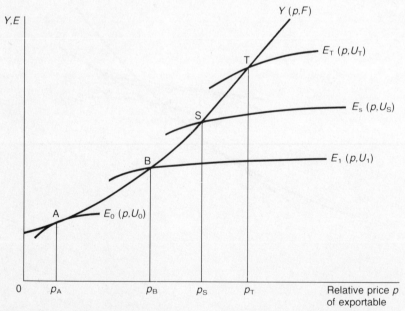

Figure 3.20   Income and expenditure functions and domestic demand and supply of exportables for different terms of trade.

rises, away from exportables towards importables, so that the expenditure function is always concave when the indifference curve is other than L shaped. But a rise in the relative price of exportables (with p above p_A) must imply a utility gain from improved terms of trade, so that there is also a shift to a higher expenditure function. If the exportable is a normal good, this effect on its own will raise the demand for it.

The typical response of exports to a rise in p (beyond p_A) will be positive at first and then eventually negative (figures 3.20 and 3.21). p_A is the autarky price: if the world price is at this value, Y is tangent to the autarky expenditure function $E_0(p_1, U_0)$ at A. Excess demand for exportables (z_X) is zero, because domestic demand and supply are in balance. When p is below p_A, there is excess demand ($z_X > 0$). The Y curve will be flatter than the expenditure functions intersecting it to the left of point A. When p exceeds p_A, the Y curve will be steeper than the expenditure functions intersecting it (at B, S, and T). In this region, there is excess supply of the exportable. S is the point of specialization: at and above p_S, the economy is producing the exportable goods only and so Y is linear to the right of S. The expenditure functions drawn in figure 3.20 display at first flatter gradients at their intersection with the Y curve, but somewhere before S has been reached their gradients at intersection have started to steepen. At a point between p_B and p_S the excess supply of the

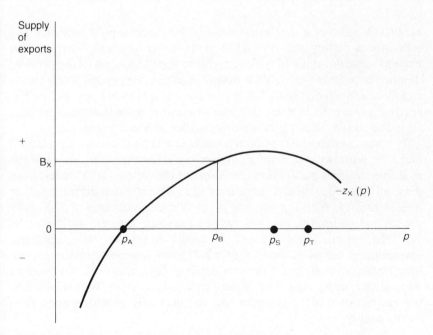

Figure 3.21   Excess demand and supply for the exportable in terms of its relative price.

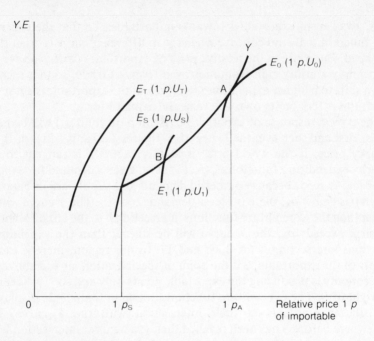

Figure 3.22   Income and expenditure functions and domestic demand and supply for the importable, for different terms of trade.

exportable reaches a maximum; beyond it, excess supply tails off. The economy is getting steadily richer as its terms of trade improve, and beyond some point it will typically wish to spend more on its exportable, despite the price increase. Since output does not rise beyond S, the excess supply of exportables must fall in that region. It even happens before S is reached, where the increase in home demand exceeds the rise in output, since the rise in output gets steadily smaller as S is approached.

The way the demand for imports reacts to p is illustrated in figures 3.22 and 3.23. Autarky is at A and p_A. When $1/p$ is less than $1/p_A$, for example at B, importables production (the slope of the tangent to Y) is less than demand (the slope of the tangent of the relevant expenditure function intersecting Y). With $1/p$ below $1/p_S$, the Y curve is horizontal. Domestic production of importables has vanished because they are so cheap. As $1/p$ falls, production drops and eventually disappears, while domestic consumption increases. So in figure 3.23 there is excess demand for the importable ($z_M > 0$) and a positive demand for imports of this product when p exceeds p_A. As p rises, import demand increases. With p below p_A the pattern of trade is reversed and the normally imported good is in excess supply.

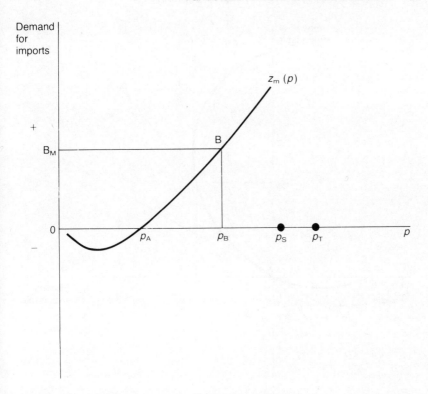

Figure 3.23 Excess supply and demand for the importable in terms of its relative price.

3.6.3 The Offer Curve

The excess demand for the importable, z_M, and the excess supply of the exportable, $-z_X$, are linked by the condition

$$pz_X + z_M = 0 \qquad (3.5)$$

if trade is to be balanced. This means that the $z_X(p)$ and $z_M(p)$ curves in figures 3.21 and 3.23 are interdependent. They are combined in figure 3.24 which presents the home country's offer curve. The offer curve for a country depicts its equilibrium trades (export supply and import demand) for all possible relative prices between the two goods. When world prices are the same as in autarky so that $p = p_A$, the country will not trade. At this point the offer curve passes through the origin. With the exportable more expensive than this, that good is exported and the other good imported. Consider point B. The gradient of the ray 0B in figure 3.24

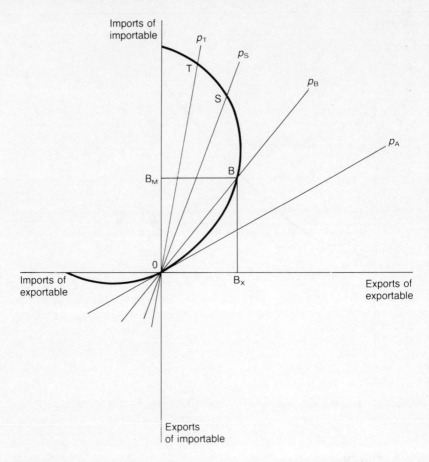

Figure 3.24   The offer curve.

gives the relative price of the exportable in terms of that of the importable (p_B). Imports are at B_M (corresponding to B_M in figure 3.23). Trade is balanced in conformity with (3.5). If the terms of trade improve further to p_S (or p_T), the country's equilibrium trade moves to S (T). Imports of the vertical good go up, while the volume of exports at first rises and then falls. Had p been less than p_A, the pattern of trade would have been reversed: the vertical axis good is exported and the other good, now so much cheaper is imported.

An equilibrium without tariffs between two large countries occurs at point C in figure 3.25. The foreign country's offer curve OC* intersects the home country's at C. The gradient p_C of OC gives the equilibrium terms of trade. The home country imports (and the foreign country exports) 0D of the vertical good, while 0E measures the former's exports

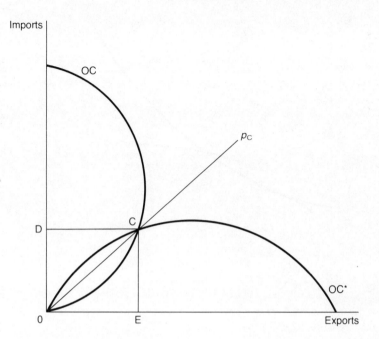

Figure 3.25   Free trade equilibrium at C.

and the latter's imports. The two countries' domestic demands and supplies of the home country's exportable are given by the tangents to E, E^*, Y, and Y^* in figure 3.26 when their terms of trade are p_C.

The key difference between a large and a small country may be stated as follows. The small country faces an offer curve from the rest of the world which is linear. OC* would be a ray from the origin and not, as in figure 3.25, a concave curve. A linear offer curve from the rest of the world means that the home country is a terms of trade taker. The price line p_C would in fact represent the rest of the world's offer curve. Any policy of trade restriction by the home country merely reduces the volume of trade; it cannot make imports cheaper in terms of exports. But a large country faces a curved OC*, and so a trade cut back which it initiates must result in a terms of trade improvement. All else equal, a terms of trade improvement must be beneficial for the society as a whole: it can buy the same volume of exports at less cost in exports forgone, or alternatively it can export the same and enjoy a higher volume of imports. However, a trade restriction at an unchanged terms of trade is damaging for potential welfare.

A country applies its optimum tariff when the gain from the improved terms of trade, net of losses from the reduced trade volume, is as high as possible. For the small country facing a linear OC*, the optimum tariff is

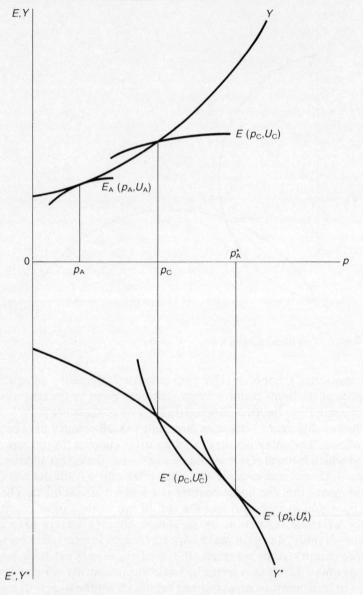

Figure 3.26   Expenditure and income functions for the two countries with free trade equilibrium.

zero. But for a large country, it is positive. Geometrically, the optimum trading position for the home country occurs where the foreign country's offer curve is tangent to the highest domestic country trade indifference curve that it can attain. The tangency condition is illustrated in figure 3.27 at point G. A trade indifference curve is defined as the locus of all trades of exports for imports between which the country can be said to be indifferent. It is the locus of all trades where potential domestic welfare is unchanged. A set of trade indifference curves is a trade indifference map (TIM). TIM is related to a country's offer curve in the following way: the OC in figure 3.24 is the locus of tangencies between successive price lines and successive trade indifference curves. When the terms of trade are given by the slope of the ray p_B, for example, B is the optimum trading point, on the offer curve, because B is a point of tangency between the ray p_B and a trade indifference curve, and likewise S and T for the rays p_S and p_T. Domestic welfare increases northwestwards since the move in that direction, if available, will involve additional imports and reduced exports.

In figure 3.27 the home country is applying its optimum tariff. C is the free trade point, and G is the optimum trade point from the home country's standpoint. The terms of trade swing around from p_C to p_G, illustrating a fall in the relative price of importables in world markets. The domestic price ratio of importables to exportables goes up, however. It will be equal to the slope of the tangent to OC* at G, that is, equal to

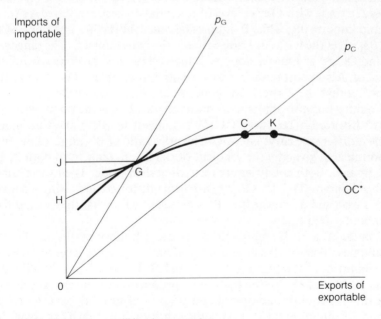

Figure 3.27 The optimum tariff in a large country.

the gradient of HG. The difference between the slopes of $0p_G$ and HG is the wedge that the tariff drives between the domestic and foreign relative prices of importables. The elasticity of the foreign offer curve OC* at a point such as G is defined by the ratio 0J/0H. In figure 3.27, it is approximately equal to 4/3. At K, where OC* is horizontal, the elasticity of OC* is unity; to the right of K, where OC* is downward sloping, it is below unity. In fact the optimum tariff at G is defined by the formula

$$t^* = 1/(e - 1) \tag{3.6}$$

where e is the elasticity of the rest of the world's offer curve OC*. This is exactly the same formula that we obtained earlier for a country's optimum export tax in conditions of partial equilibrium (equation (3.4)) where e was the elasticity of the rest of the world's demand for our exports. The formula also shows that a small country's optimum tariff is zero because e is infinite.

What one large country can do to improve its terms of trade by tariffs (or export taxes) can also be done by its trading partner. In figure 3.28 we illustrate the case of a two-large-country two-good world where each country is applying an optimum tariff against imports from the other. Country A is levying an optimum tariff by trading at L because L is the most attractive feasible trading point, given country B's tariff-distorted offer curve OC_B**. Point L is the point where OC_B** is tangent to A's highest attainable trade indifference curve θ_A. Everywhere else on OC_B** gives A a trade with a lower level of potential domestic welfare. A exports 0S and imports 0R, while B imports 0S and exports 0R. The slope of the ray $0p_0$ gives the terms of trade between the two countries. The tangent to θ_A and OC_B** at L has a slope p_1, which represents the domestic relative price of A's exportables in terms of its importables. This line is flat, implying that the vertical axis good is very expensive inside A.

Country B is *also* applying its optimum tariff. L is the point where A's tariff-distorted offer curve OC_A** is tangent to B's highest attainable trade indifference curve curve θ_B. The price ratio of B's importables to its exportables is given by the gradient of the line p_2 tangent to both θ_B and OC_A** at L. Both countries are restricting their trade. Their offer curves in this diagram (OC_A**, OC_B**) are tariff distorted and swing leftwards in A's case and downwards in B's compared with what they would have been under free trade.

Points M and N represent domestic equilibrium inside the two economies. Treating 0 as the origin, M and N give the level of domestic consumption of the two goods in A and B. If the origin is redefined to point L, M and N give the pattern of production of the two goods in A and B. This equilibrium describes a state of affairs where each country applies its optimum tariff, taking the other country's tariff as given. It is

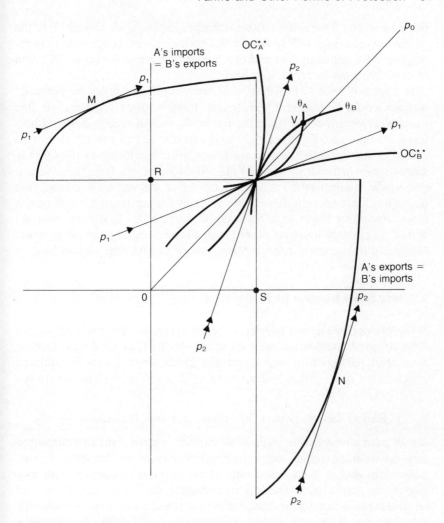

Figure 3.28 The Nash solution to the optimum tariff game.

an example of a Nash non-cooperative equilibrium, where each agent acts to maximize his own payoff, taking the other player's actions as given.

The Nash double optimum tariff equilibrium is not efficient. Examine the two trade indifference curves θ_A and θ_B which intersect at L. Every trading point to the left of θ_A offers a higher domestic welfare to country A. Every trading point below θ_B offers greater domestic welfare to country B. Thus points northeast of L but southwest of V (V and L give each country the same welfare levels) offer greater welfare to both A *and* B. Both countries would gain by trading more with each other at the given price ratio p_O. To return to the concepts explored in section 3.1, the trading equilibrium at L is simply Pareto inefficient. It generates distortions in both consumption and production: everyone in the world could in principle gain by removing them.

It does not follow, however, that both countries' levels of potential welfare would be higher if they traded freely with each other. The free trade equilibrium could lie to the left of θ_B, in which case B would be a loser. It could also lie to the right of θ_A, so that A was a loser. If the two countries are similar, the free trade equilibrium will lie on the $0p_O$ ray somewhere northeast of L, and both would gain from free trade. So it is essentially dissimilarity in countries' offer curves that creates the possibility that one country could be a net winner from a tariff war, a move from free trade to a Nash equilibrium at L. If it is to be a net winner, a country must be either larger than its trading partner or more flexible in its domestic consumption and/or production patterns.

3.7 Non-tariff Barriers to Trade

NTBs are defined as any barrier, other than tariffs, that distorts the free flow of goods across national frontiers. NTBs may be direct, that is, specifically designed to protect certain goods, or they may be indirect, imposed for other policy purposes but with a spillover effect on trade.

3.7.1 Export Taxes, Export Subsidies, and Import Quotas

As we have already seen, a tariff on imports is equivalent to a consumption tax on importables and a production subsidy for domestic importables, imposed at a common rate. If the economy produces only two goods, an exportable and an importable, an import tariff is also equivalent to a tax on exports. An export tax drives down the domestic relative price of the exportable relative to its world price. The domestic output of exportables will be squeezed and production will switch in favour of the importable, which is now relatively more expensive in the home economy. The real reward to the factor used intensively in importables increases, while the real reward to the other factor falls, just as would happen with an import tariff. Consumers substitute away from the now dearer importable in favour of the exportable.

Thus both an import tariff and an export tax will reduce the excess demand for the importable and the domestic excess supply for the exportable. If the economy produces three or more goods, a non-traded good, for instance, as well as an exportable and importable, import tariffs and export taxes cease to be equivalent, since they have different effects on the non-traded-goods industry.

Some countries tax their exports. Zambia has taxed its copper exports at varying rates, for example. The big rises in oil prices in 1974 and 1979 imposed by the Organization of Petroleum Exporting Countries (OPEC) can be thought of as increases in export taxes. But in the developed world export taxes are very rare. It is more common to see export subsidies, although the form they take is typically indirect. Production for exports is sometimes favoured by lower taxes on inputs, such as labour or electricity. More generally, countries with a value added tax (VAT, as in EC countries and Scandinavia) rebate the tax on exports. However the exports are subsidized, an export subsidy is equivalent to a negative export tax. VAT is generally levied on imports and so it resembles an import tariff on the goods on which it is applied, minus the element of subsidy on domestic production of importables.

In the developed world, major steps have been taken to reduce tariffs on imported manufactures. These were approximately halved in the 1968-9 Kennedy Round of the General Agreement on Tariffs and Trade. The Tokyo (1974-9) and Uruguay (from 1986) Rounds have led to further reductions. However, progress on eliminating import tariffs has been accompanied by a growing tendency to place quotas on certain categories of imports.

The relationship between an import tariff and import quota is as follows. The effect of a tariff or quota on the volume of imports will be the same under three conditions:

1   licences to imports are auctioned by the government;
2   domestic and foreign demand and supply conditions are known with certainty;
3   there are numerous independent domestic producers of the importable good.

The best way of seeing the significance of these conditions is to explore what happens when each of them fails to be met. If the licences to import are not auctioned, the government loses all the revenues it would have received with an otherwise equivalent tariff. The tariff revenue rectangle in figure 3.6 accrues instead to the lucky firms who get the import licences. Some of these firms may of course be foreign. If quotas are levied on imports, the government which applies them is well advised to auction the quotas. At various times Brazil and Israel have done just this. But there are exceptions: the quotas currently imposed by many European governments on imports of textiles (in accordance with the Multi Fibre Agreement) from southeast Asia, for example, are not accompanied by import licence auctions.

If condition (2) fails, there can be a difference between an import tariff and a quota. The import quota has a completely predictable effect on the volume of imports, assuming the quota 'binds', that is, is not set above the volume of imports that would have occurred in any case. With a tariff, the volume of imports is unpredictable, since it will vary with the world price and the positions of the domestic demand and supply curves. Quotas are an example of a quantity intervention instrument while tariffs are a price intervention instrument. Weitzman (1974) shows that it is sometimes better to intervene by quantity controls, and sometimes by price controls, under conditions of uncertainty. The two are equivalent under conditions of certainty, but not under uncertainty.

If condition (3) fails, there are only a few, perhaps just one, domestic producer of the importable. This takes us into the realm of imperfect competition, which forms the subject of chapter 4. As will be shown in section 4.2, a quota on imports confers some degree of monopoly power on the domestic producer(s) while a tariff will not, if the world price is given. The quota should trigger a larger domestic price increase than would have occurred with a tariff which restricted imports to the same degree, with consequently greater damage to consumer surplus.

3.7.2 Other Non-tariff Barriers

There are a host of NTBs apart from the three discussed above. The variable import levy (VIL) and the voluntary export restraint (VER) are types of import quota and tariff. The VIL has been imposed by the EC on agricultural produce. A reference price is fixed for each good. Foreign suppliers pay a tariff that brings their net price up to this reference price. This effectively fixes the domestic price of the good. Unlike an exogenous tariff, foreign suppliers confronting a VIL have no incentive to reduce their costs, reducing the pressure of competition on domestic and foreign suppliers.

A VER is a voluntary agreement between foreign suppliers and a domestic government to restrain the quantity of exports of a certain good to the country. Thus it is a type of voluntary import quota, although in the absence of licences the government earns no revenue. It is the exporting firms that gain from the higher price. VERs have been reached between Japanese car exporters and the US and EC governments during the 1980s. Using 1985 data, Digby et al. (1988) showed that for the UK the annual cost of VERs per job saved in the car industry was between £50,000 and £70,000. If VERs were removed and UK Japanese car sales increased by 55 per cent, the authors estimated that the UK would gain between £95 million and £130 million per year.

Indirect taxes may also act as a barrier to trade across countries. In the EC, variations in VAT and excise taxes across member countries mean that some types of production are protected. The way car taxes vary with engine capacity in Italy, for example, is widely thought to give an advantage to domestic firms, and similarly for excise taxes. Luxembourg attracts nationals from neighbouring countries, where taxes are higher, to take advantage of its negligible taxes on alcohol and petrol products.

As noted earlier, state aid may also act as an NTB by protecting imports and/or promoting exports. Subsidies may be granted to industries or regions, or may take the form of subsidized loans made to firms by the government. Purchases of domestic goods by national governments is another form of indirect NTB if foreign goods are cheaper.

Official and technical standards are often imposed by a government. But if one country imposes different standards from its neighbours, it may effectively block out imports. Foreign firms may find it too expensive to produce a variant of their product especially for one market. For example, in Italy a law requires that pasta be made from durum wheat, thereby preventing other types of pasta from reaching the Italian market. Time-consuming customs procedures at ports of entry act as an indirect NTB.

3.8 Conclusions

If a country puts a tariff on its imports, a number of things happen. Imports fall, squeezed between higher domestic production of importables and lower home demand. The government gains revenue. Factors employed intensively or specifically in the home importables sector get paid more. But consumers suffer from the price increase. In simple cases, what consumers lose exceeds the other types of gain. A small country is all too likely to lose on balance by taxing its trade. Even if it does not because of externalities, unemployment, or some other distortion, it will do best to dispose of the distortion directly rather than attacking it by the clumsy instrument of a tariff. Many of these results also hold for other forms of trade restriction.

A large country can gain or lose on balance by taxing its exports or imports in order to improve its terms of trade; if its trading partners do nothing in response, its optimum trade taxes will be positive. But retaliation is likely, and the end result is a tariff war in which all parties may well be worse off and one will certainly be worse off than it could be.

4

Market Imperfections in the Open Economy

In previous chapters it has been assumed that individual firms are small enough to be price takers. In this environment, price equals marginal cost and factors of production are paid the value of their marginal products. This chapter is concerned with the consequences of relaxing this assumption. New arguments for expecting international trade appear. These can go some way to explaining the phenomenon of 'intra-industry' trade, that is, countries exporting and importing similar products. New reasons emerge for thinking that trade is gainful. However, there are also cases when it can be harmful, and novel arguments for protection, peculiar to imperfect competition.

The chapter is organized as follows. Sections 4.1–4.3 are concerned with oligopoly. We start with Cournot's classic model and extend it to international trade (section 4.1), and then turn to trade policy (section 4.2) and to generalizations (section 4.3). In section 4.4 attention switches to the other major form of imperfect competition, monopolistic competition. In section 4.5 we examine increasing returns, the crucial phenomenon that goes furthest to explaining imperfect competition of all types, first in the context of external economies (section 4.5.1) and then in the context of internal economies of scale (section 4.5.2). In section 4.6 we look at other types of market imperfection in an international context: the striking result of Newbery and Stiglitz that autarky may be better for everyone than free trade if markets are incomplete; the significance of import quotas under imperfect competition; and the phenomenon of rent seeking.

4.1 Oligopoly and Trade

An oligopoly is a market with a few sellers. Oligopoly occupies the vast ground that separates the monopolist, a single seller, from perfect competition where the number of sellers is so large that none can influence price. Oligopolists are not price takers: they will recognize that their own output decisions affect the market price. But they are not monopolists: the effect on price of changing their own output will depend critically on how the other firms respond. Oligopolists are interdependent.

4.1.1 Assumptions

There are a number of choices about assumptions that we have to face in exploring the concept of oligopoly. We begin by stipulating the following assumptions:

1 The products of the firms are homogeneous, not differentiated.
2 Firms' objectives are to maximize profits.
3 Each firm is an output setter.
4 Each firm thinks that its rivals will not respond to its own decisions.
5 Firms' marginal cost curves are common and horizontal.
6 The number of firms is exogenous, fixed at n.
7 The model is static.
8 There is no intervention in the market.

These assumptions follow those made in the classic model of oligopoly, due to Cournot (1838).

Assumption (1) rules out product differentiation, an extra complication, which is discussed below in section 4.4. Profit maximization and output setting seem natural for assumptions (2) and (3), although there could be others. Assumption (4), that firms will assume their rivals' output rates to be given independently of their own actions, is the central feature of Cournot's model. The assumption of common costs ensures symmetry: all the firms behave alike, and horizontal marginal costs are the simplest to handle. The given number of firms, n, plays an important role, as we shall see. Assumptions (7) and (8) are for convenience rather than realism. After exploring the implications of these assumptions, we shall consider briefly what can happen if they are relaxed.

We begin by looking at Cournot's oligopoly model, first in a closed economy (which could be the world as a whole) and then in a multi-country framework. Assumptions (2) and (3) imply that each firm will set output where its perception of its marginal revenue (EMR) equals marginal cost (MC). By assumption (5), MC will be common at a given value, say c. What of EMR? This is equal to $p(1 - 1/en)$, where p is price, e is the price elasticity of product demand, and n is the number of firms. When $n = 1$ we have the familiar monopoly result that

MR $= p(1 - 1/e)$; when n is infinite we have the perfect competition condition that MR $= p$. In oligopoly, EMR will be less than p because the firm will reckon that an increase in its own output will depress the market price a little, and the gain in receipts from an additional volume of output has to be qualified by the loss from a lower price for the intramarginal output that it would have sold anyway. The larger the number of firms is, the smaller is the market share of each, and the weaker is the downward pressure on market price that results from one firm's raising its output. So the more numerous the firms are, the closer to p the expected marginal revenue will be.

So far we have established that $p(1 - 1/en) = c$, so that

$$p = \frac{c}{1 - 1/en} \tag{4.1}$$

Price exceeds marginal cost. The markup $(p - c)/p$ of price above marginal cost is equal to $1/en$, and is therefore inversely proportional to the number of firms. Oligopoly therefore fails to meet the Pareto conditions for efficiency in an idealized perfect economy, where price would have to equal marginal cost. Oligopoly therefore involves waste, a deadweight loss. The size of this welfare loss increases if the number of firms goes down. So the Cournot model suggests that entry of new firms is socially beneficial. But a fall in n, due to merger, takeover, or bankruptcy, has adverse effects. Price rises, profits go up, industry output shrinks, and the oligopoly slides further from the competitive ideal in the direction of monopoly.

Exact expressions for the oligopolistic industry's output and price can be obtained if we go further and assume that the market demand curve for the product is linear. In that case,

$$\text{industry output} = \frac{In}{n + 1} \tag{4.2}$$

$$\text{price} = \frac{z + cn}{n + 1} \tag{4.3}$$

where I is industry output in perfect competition (when $p = c$) and z represents the vertical intercept on the market demand curve, the price at which demand vanishes. Each firm's profits will be $(1/b)[(z - c)/(n + 1)]^2$ where $-b$ is the slope of the demand curve, so that $I = (z - c)/b$.

4.1.2   Cournot's Model in an International Context

We can now illustrate the Cournot oligopoly in international trade. Let there be two countries A and B. We focus on trade in one product between them. If A and B are of equal size with similar demand patterns and an equal number of firms enjoying common horizontal marginal costs, both production and consumption in A and B will be equal. There will be no net trade for this product between the countries, that is, if there is any trade in this good at all, quantities of the product will move across national frontiers in equal amounts. There is likely to be two-way trade in the good, however, even in the presence of transport costs, as long as they are modest enough. The reason for this is that, if there were not, the number of firms selling inside each country would be half the world number, prices would be correspondingly high, and firms in each country would be attracted to sell some of their product abroad, where marginal revenue would look higher than at home. This must follow, at least, if the two countries' markets are treated as distinct. Different national markets are 'integrated' if buyers can switch at will from purchases in one country to purchases in another, paying only any tariffs if they are applied; if they cannot, markets are 'distinct'. As Brander and Krugman (1983) first showed, international oligopoly is likely to lead to 'cross hauling' or intra-industry trade: the same good is exported and imported.

There is likely to be net trade, unbalanced trade (the quantities of the product that move between the two countries differ), between the countries in two sets of circumstances: (a) different demand conditions and (b) an unequal number of firms. Trade is balanced if and only if the ratio of home to foreign demand equals the ratio of the number of domestic to foreign firms. Cases of unbalanced trade are illustrated in figures 4.1 and 4.2. The first of these depicits conditions where demand differs between the two countries. In the second, the number of firms differs: there is a triopoly, consisting of one domestic firm and two foreign firms.

Consider figure 4.1. There is a duopoly here. One firm produces at home and one produces abroad. Figures 4.1(a) and 4.1(b) depict demand and production in countries A and B, while figure 4.1(c) presents equilibrium for the world as a whole. Demand is higher in A than in B, although both curves, for convenience, have the same vertical intercept z. The world demand curve D is the horizontal sum of D_A and D_B. All demand curves are linear. The horizontal line c shows the value of marginal cost, common to both firms. The ideal perfectly competitive output for the world is labelled U': this arises naturally if the number of firms is infinite. But with n restricted to just two, given that demand is linear and marginal costs are common and horizontal, world output at U is only two-thirds of its optimal value U', in accordance with (4.2). This gives rise to an equilibrium world price of R. From (4.3), we know that price will be one-third of the distance from marginal cost c to z. At the world level, the triangle RR'Z represents consumers' surplus, and the rectangle 0L'LU total variable costs of the two firms. The area of the rectangle R'RLL' is profits, net of any fixed costs. Triangle RLM is the

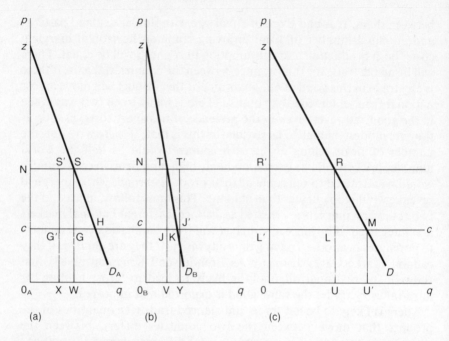

Figure 4.1   Two-country Cournot duopoly with different demands: (a) country A; (b) country B; (c) world.

deadweight loss: this is the increase in the money value of potential world welfare which would come about if the industry could be induced to behave as under perfect competition and produce at U' rather than at U.

Turning to the two countries, S and T depict the levels of equilibrium demand in A and B. Since the two firms enjoy the same costs and behave identically, they each produce half the world's output. Country A's firm produces $0_A X$ ($= \frac{1}{2} 0U$), and B's firm produces the same ($0_B Y$). But because demand is stronger in A than in B, country A has net imports equal to XW and B has net exports equal to VY. In country A, consumers' surplus and producer's surplus are NSz and NS'G'c respectively, and the comparable figures in B are NTz and NT'J'c. Compared with autarky, where $p = (z + c)/2$ in both countries, consumers are better off since trade reduces the price. But it also cuts the firms' profits. It is just possible that A is better off in autarky: if welfare is defined as consumers' plus producer's surplus, trade could lower the profits of A's firm more than it raises its consumers' surplus. This could happen if demand is much higher in A than in B, as shown by Smith and Venables (1986). A's consumers would gain from the price cut as B's firm exported into A, but their rise in consumer surplus could be more than offset by the reduction

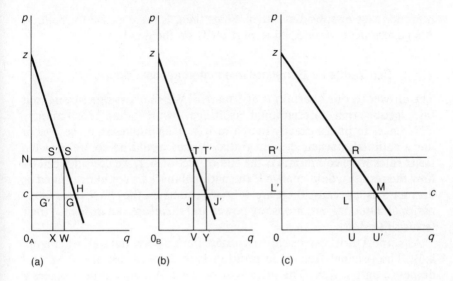

Figure 4.2   Two-country triopoly.

in A's firm's profits. A's firm would not just suffer a loss in profits per unit of output: it would cut back on its level of output too.

In figure 4.2 there are three firms, one in A and two in B. Demand conditions are similar. World output is again $0U$, which this time is three-quarters of its optimal value $0U'$. The equilibrium world price R is one-quarter of the way up from c to z, so that $L'R' = \frac{1}{4}L'z$. As before, LRM represents the world's deadweight loss, but this is a smaller triangle than in figure 4.1 because we now have three rather than two firms. The formula for the deadweight loss can be inferred from (4.2) and (4.3): it is $[(z - c)/(n + 1)]^2/2b$, which decreases as n rises. Since demands are similar in A and B, consumer purchases in the two countries are equal ($0_AW = 0_BV$). But because A has only one of the three firms, production is half that in B. Each firm produces the same, but because B has two firms and A only one, two-thirds of the world's production is in B. So B is a net exporter (VY) and A is a net importer (XW).

4.2 Oligopoly and Trade Policy

Having set up the Cournot model of oligopoly in an international setting which assumes no government intervention, let us now consider the effects of government action. So far we have been assuming that policies of free trade are pursued by both countries' governments, and there have been no taxes or subsidies either. First, then, is there a case for country A's government to place an import tariff on the good?

4.2.1 Can Tariffs be Beneficial in an International Oligopoly?

The answer to our question is affirmative. We shall assume throughout this section that international arbitrage ensures that cross-country differences in prices exactly match tariffs. This implies that the two or more national markets are integrated. Prices would be common if the tariff rates were common. At the end of section 4.2, we consider briefly how the results would change if the national markets could be treated as distinct. Also, because there are only two countries, they have some international monopoly/monopsony power and therefore can influence their terms of trade.

An import tariff can be shown to increase A's potential welfare (Figure 4.3). The original free trade position is at S, with demand $0_A W$ and domestic output $0_A X$. The price is at N. Then A's government places a tariff on the imports of the good at the rate $N'N''$. The domestic price goes up from N to N' and the price in B falls to N''. The reason why the

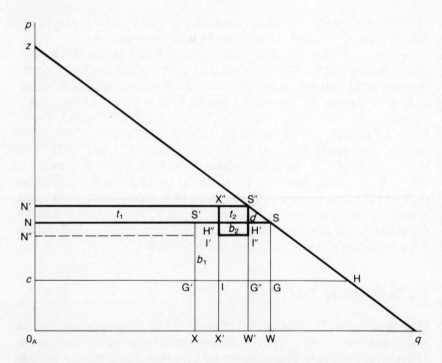

Figure 4.3 International oligopoly: the benefits and disbenefits of a tariff on imports in country A.

price in B falls is twofold. First, the markets are integrated: consumers in A are assumed to be able to arbitrage themselves, so that the price in A has to equal the price at which they could buy in B plus A's tariff. Second, because there are only two large countries involved, the home country can influence prices in the rest of the world. The price in the rest of the world falls after A's demand is cut by the tariff. In the circumstances of figure 4.3, it turns out that the home price rises by five-eighths of the tariff and the foreign price falls by three-eighths. Domestic demand drops to S", or $0_A W'$ units. The domestic firm benefits from a price increase, while its overseas rivals suffer from a fall in the price they receive. So the domestic and foreign firms now produce different amounts. The home firm raises its output by XX', to earn profits of N'X"IC in place of NS'G'C.

The volume of imports shrinks to X'W', on which the government earns a tariff revenue of X"S"I"I'. Consumer surplus shrinks by the area N'NSS", a quadrilateral which consists of two rectangles t_1 and t_2 and a triangle d. The first of the two rectangles, t_1, is a transfer from consumers' surplus to the profits of the home firm. The second, t_2, is a transfer to government revenue. The remaining area d is not offset by any gain to the other agents, and so it is an unambiguous disbenefit. The increase in the home firm's profit is, as we saw, partly accounted for by a transfer from consumers' surplus (area t_1) but area S'H"IG', labelled b_1, is in fact transferred from foreign firm's profits. So b_1 is a clear net gain to country A, although not of course to the world as a whole. The other unambiguous benefit to the domestic economy is the rectangle labelled b_2, which is that part of A's government revenue not transferred from domestic consumers' surplus. The rectangle b_2 is also obtained at the expense of the profits of B's firms. The net gain to country A, if we set aside problems over income distribution and possibly different marginal evaluations of money by the different domestic agents, is $b_1 + b_2 - d$. As long as the tariff rate is low enough, there is no denying that $b_1 + b_2$ exceeds d. Thus A's potential welfare increases with a sufficiently modest tariff.

There are two elements to the story leading to this result. One is familiar from the traditional large country case considered in chapter 3. If a country has monopsony power in international markets, it can gain from improved terms of trade that follow from imposing a tariff. A small country is a price taker for its imports. But not so country A in figure 4.3. By reducing its imports, it drives down their world price, and the surviving shrunken import volume can be acquired more cheaply. The gain from monopsony power is shown by area b_2 in figure 4.3.

The second element is special to imperfect competition and did not arise in the examples considered in chapter 3 where perfect competition was assumed throughout. This is the profit that can be earned by oligopolists benefiting from an implicit entry barrier – recall that the number n of firms is fixed by virtue of assumption (6). Anything that increases one firm's output at the expense of its rivals transfers profits too. The tariff achieves this by lifting the price received by the domestic firm and reducing the price facing its overseas rivals. Area b_1 in figure 4.3 shows the gain from the transfer of profits.

Let us now look briefly at the effects of A's tariff on B's potential welfare, and then consider whether B's government, too, has an incentive to depart from the principles of free trade. We have already seen how A secures gains, in the form of government revenue and increased domestic profits, at the expense of B's firms. This is not the end of the story for B's producers, because they suffer a twofold contraction of profits. The price they receive is driven down and, in response to that, they lower their output which leads to a further cut in total profits. Put another way, B's firms transfer profits not just to A's firm and A's government but also to B's consumers' surplus. The only good news for B is that its consumers benefit from a fall in the price of the product, giving rise to a small net gain triangle southeast of point T in figures 4.1 and 4.2. But the loss in profits will typically be much larger than this, and B's potential welfare will fall overall.

In figure 4.1, B is a net exporter because A's demand is stronger than B's. Could B's government also gain from applying protectionist policies? Indeed it could. It should subsidize exports, rather than tax them. Figure 4.4 explores this idea. B's government introduces an export

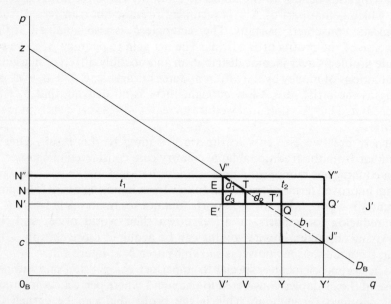

Figure 4.4   International oligopoly: the benefits and disbenefits of an export subsidy in country B.

subsidy at the rate $N''N'$. B's firms will switch sales from domestic to foreign markets to benefit from the subsidy until the domestic price exceeds the foreign price by the level of the subsidy. The price inside B climbs from N to N'', while the price in A drops to N'. B's firms increase their output from Y to Y', while domestic demand shrinks to V'' in response to the price rise. The new volume of exports is $V'Y'$ instead of VY. The firms earn N'' on all their sales, but the government export subsidy costs $E'Q'Y''V''$ and the country's export earnings are $E'Q'Y'V'$.

The profits of B's firms swell from $cJ'T'N$ to $cJ''Y''N''$. Net of the export subsidy costs, this increase in profits is equal to the sum of the six areas shown in figure 4.4: $NEV''N''$, labelled t_1; ETV'', labelled d_1 the polygon $TV''Y''Q'QT'$, labelled t_2; and the rectangles labelled d_3, d_2, and b_1. Area t_1 is a transfer from consumers' surplus to profits, and so it has no effect on aggregate potential welfare in B. Area d_1 is also lost from consumers' surplus and forms part of the transfer from B's taxpayers to its firms' profits on exports.

The polygon t_2 is a gain to profits but a loss to government revenue it is simply a transfer. The two rectangles d_2 and d_3 form part of the government's export subsidy costs and do not represent an increase in profits for B's firms, and so these two areas are a net loss. Finally, area b_1 is a pure gain for country B, since it represents that part of the rise in B's firms' profits not transferred from B's consumers or B's government. It is transferred from the profits of the firm in A. If b_1 exceeds $d_1 + d_2 + d_3$, country B will gain on balance from its export subsidy. The repercussions on country A are quite straightforward: A's firm suffers from a large profit squeeze, greater than area b_1, but its consumers gain from the price reduction and a small pure gain emerges southeast of point S in figure 4.2.

To sum up: an export subsidy of $N'N''$ cuts consumer surplus by $t_1 + d_1$, leads to government revenue loss of $d_1 + d_2 + d_3 + t_2$, but raises B's firm's profits by $t_1 + d_1 + t_2 + b_1$. For country B, the net gain is $b_1 - d_1 - d_2 - d_3$.

4.2.2 But Production Subsidies could be Better

It is clear that imperfect competition constitutes an important additional qualification to the case for free trade. Import tariffs and export subsidies can bring net welfare gains to the countries that apply them, something that is not generally true for small countries under perfectly competitive conditions. In a world of oligopolies, import tariffs can increase the welfare of the country imposing them, relative to free trade. This point is worth stressing. It has emerged from relatively recent research, well summarized, and represented, by Helpman (1984) and Helpman and Krugman (1985).

Yet this result also prompts further questions:

1   Can countries in international oligopoly gain more by combining protectionist policies with other measures, and, if so, what does that imply for the character of protection?
2   What happens when both (or all) countries have the freedom to apply protectionist policies and other measures?

In a nutshell, the answer to question (1) is that countries can do better by combining production subsidies with tariffs on imports or subsidies on exports, and, if they do, the optimal values of these import tariffs or export subsidies will in fact typically be negative. The answer to question (2) is that at least under simple conditions, when all countries can employ both production subsidies and protectionist trade policies, they will do best by adhering to free trade. The answers to the two questions, taken together, go a long way to dispelling the newly fashionable belief that imperfect competition somehow 'justifies' protection. We turn now to a demonstration of why these answers are valid.

We shall continue to retain the framework of two-country Cournot oligopoly, with the convenient simplifications of undifferentiated linear demand and horizontal and constant marginal costs for the firms. Demands will be the same for the two countries as in figure 4.2. We shall continue to assume that each country's welfare W can be defined as home consumers' surplus plus net home government revenue plus profits of home firms.

As before, each country has a protectionist policy instrument t. Here t represents either a tariff on imports or a subsidy on exports, so that the domestic price p always equals the foreign price p^* plus t if the country is alone in employing protection. If both countries' governments employ tariffs and/or export subsidies, this condition becomes

$$p = p^* + t - t^* \tag{4.4}$$

where t^* denotes the foreign country's tariff and/or export subsidy. The one novel feature we add at this stage is the device of a subsidy applied to production by a domestic firm. The home country's production subsidy is s, and s^* denotes that of the foreign country.

To answer question (1), assume that the home country sets s and t to maximize W, home welfare. B's government is non-interventionist, so that $s^* = t^* = 0$. Let n_A represent the number of firms in A and n_B the number of firms in B. Each of these firms is a Cournot oligopolist. The price of the good in country A will be[1]

---

1   Equation (4.5) can be shown to emerge from demand curves of the form $p = z - bD_A$ and $p^* = z - bD_B$, (4.4) with t^* set to zero, and the fact that each domestic firm i chooses its output q_i to maximize $q_i(p - c + s)$ and each foreign firm sets q_j to maximize $q_j(p^* - c)$ in each case believing all other firms' output levels to be given.

$$p = \frac{z + c(n_A + n_B) - n_A s + t(n_B + \frac{1}{2})}{n_A + n_B + 1} \qquad (4.5)$$

Equation (4.5) is a generalization of (4.3) to take account of the government's two types of intervention and the more precise assumption about the number of firms. A subsidy on production will lower the home price, while a tariff on imports (or subsidy on exports) will increase it.

Suppose that the home government sets s and t together to maximize welfare w. Their combined impact is such as to bring the domestic price down to the level of marginal cost c. Country A therefore reduces its price to point H in figure 4.2 or 4.3.

The sum of producers' and consumers' surplus is always maximized where price equals marginal cost. This is true in all market forms, not just oligopoly, and holds true whatever the shapes of demand and marginal cost curves are, provided only that the former crosses the latter from above. An import tariff or export subsidy cannot achieve this optimum when the economy is open, for the simple reason that such instruments increase the price to domestic consumers. An import subsidy or export tax, on its own, would succeed in lowering domestic price, but it would increase foreign producers' surplus at the expense of domestic firms' profits and therefore fail to maximize national welfare. Thus what the country needs to do is to combine the import subsidy and export tax with a generous subsidy on production limited to the domestic firm or firms.[2]

We now turn to the second question. This asks what both countries will seek to do when we allow both of them, not just the home country, to employ production subsidies and taxes or subsidies on trade. In this case the domestic price of the product will no longer be given by (4.5): we have to incorporate the effects of the production subsidy and import tariff and/or export subsidy applied by the foreign government. The resulting expression will be

$$p = \frac{z + c(n_A + n_B) - n_A s - n_B s^* + t(n_B + \frac{1}{2}) - t^*(n_A + \frac{1}{2})}{n_A + n_B + 1} \qquad (4.6)$$

Equation (4.6) shows that the foreign production subsidy tends to lower the domestic price (since it stimulates additional world production) but also that the same effect is produced by the foreign tariff t^*. The reason is that t^* increases the foreign price p^* and, at the same time, reduces country B's excess demand (or increases its excess supply) and therefore exerts downward pressure on the price in country A. There is an analogous expression for the domestic price in country B:

---

2 The production subsidy is set at $3(z - c)/4n_A$, and the negative import tariff (or export subsidy) at $-(z - c)/2(2n_B + 1)$.

$$p^* = \frac{z + c(n_A + n_B) - n_A s - n_B s^* + t^*(n_A + \frac{1}{2}) - t^*(n_B + \frac{1}{2})}{n_A + n_B + 1} \quad (4.7)$$

which displays symmetry with (4.6) and can be confirmed by combining (4.6) with (4.4). The next stage is to let A's government select s and t to maximize A's national welfare subject to (4.6), and to let B's government choose s^* and t^* to maximize B's national welfare subject to (4.7). We assume that each country selects its optimum values of the production subsidy and import tariff and/or export subsidy independently, taking the other's as given. The upshot is that A's government will introduce a production subsidy of $(z - c)/2n_A$ and B's a production subsidy of $(z - c)/2n_B$. The country with more firms will have a lower production subsidy; if the number of firms is equal, so will the subsidy rates be. More strikingly, each country will set its import tariff and/or export subsidy instrument at zero. So the outcome will be that $n_A s = n_B s^* = (z - c)/2$ and $t = t^* = 0$. Incorporation of these results into (4.6) and (4.7) reveals that $p = p^* = c$. Thus both countries will bring down prices to the common level of marginal cost.

This optimum free trade equilibrium is entirely cheat-proof. Neither country has an incentive to tax imports, or tax or subsidize exports, as long as both employ their optimum production subsidies. The message to be gleaned from this analysis is that imperfect competition certainly calls for policy intervention by the national governments – *laissez-faire* will fail to deliver the best results – but that this intervention should involve production subsidies rather than tariffs on imports or taxes or subsidies on exports. The case for departing from free trade is essentially second best. Only if the superior instrument of production subsidies is for some reason ruled out will protectionist trade policies be advantageous. It is simply false to maintain that imperfect competition provides a general justification for protection.

Throughout this section we have assumed that the two national markets were integrated. This meant that prices in the two economies were linked by the equation $p = p^* + t - t^*$. International arbitrage kept price differences equal to tariff differences. Our results change somewhat if the two markets can be treated as distinct and unrelated. When each country has one firm and identical linear demand and marginal cost conditions, tariffs are set at $(z - c)/3$ and production subsidies at $7(z - c)/24$. This happens when each country sets these instruments independently, taking the other's as given. The two countries do better still by setting tariffs at zero and production subsidies at $(z - c)/3$, so that prices are brought down to marginal cost.

The results in this section have been obtained from an analysis of Cournot's model of oligopoly, cast in a two-country setting. Section 4.3 consists of a brief scrutiny of what can happen if assumptions underlying Cournot's approach to oligopoly are relaxed.

4.3 Relaxing Cournot's Assumptions

In sections 4.1 and 4.2 we explored two-country oligopoly within the framework of Cournot's approach to that market form. The present section is devoted to looking at what can happen if Cournot's assumptions are replaced by others. We proceed to relax assumptions (1)–(7) made in section 4.1.1. Assumption (8) was relaxed in section 4.2.

4.3.1 Non-profit-maximizing Behaviour

Relaxing assumption (1) leads to differentiated products and monopolistic competition, explored in detail in section 4.4. Relaxing assumption (2) introduces many possibilities. Firms may be interested in total sales revenue or growth. They may have a 'utility' function, which depends on two or more 'goods', and may aim for the most desirable trade-off between sales revenue and profits, for example. The separation of ownership (the shareholders) from control (the managers) could give management freedom to pursue their own objectives, subject perhaps to the threat of takeover or dismissal, especially when shareholders cannot see what their managers do. Finally the costs of gathering information and taking decisions may make the firm's managers 'satisficers' who adopt rules of thumb, repeating their previous actions or imitating their rivals, for example, unless some crisis forces them to reexamine their environment and decisions.

Such alternatives to profit maximization have no simple implication for the firm's decisions. A firm which aims to maximize total revenue will produce more than a profit maximizer if marginal costs are positive. The sales maximizer is like a profit maximizer who ignores his costs. If this is true for all oligopolists, industry output will be higher than under profit maximization. Price will come down closer to marginal cost – it could even fall beneath marginal cost. The benefits from government intervention will generally be smaller.

Qualitatively, allowing firms to maximize sales revenue rather than profits will be similar to introducing more firms in the Cournot setup. If one oligopolist is a sales maximizer and his rivals aim to maximize profits, the first firm actually ends up with more profits than the others! This paradox, first examined by Vickers (1985), is explained by the fact that the sales maximizer produces more and has the same profit margins as his rivals, so his total profits must be higher. In an international oligopoly, a firm's shareholders, and indeed its national government, have some incentive to see that its managers aim for high sales volume. It is interesting to note that nationalized companies operating in international oligopoly are sometimes encouraged to pursue aggressive selling policies. Renault, the French state-owned car concern, and British Leyland, a UK automobile producer which was publicly owned from 1975 to

1988, may be instances of this. Counterexamples are provided by state-owned international airlines, which have long participated in a multi-country cartel, the International Air Transport Association (IATA), which has held prices far above marginal costs.

4.3.2 Price Setting

An alternative to output-setting behaviour (assumption (3)) is price setting. At one extreme we could have Bertrand competition (Bertrand, 1883) which could bring price down to marginal cost. This would be ideal from a world efficiency standpoint, but large exporting countries could gain by taxing the exports of Bertrand firms. At the other extreme, firms could set their prices in unison, so as to maximize joint profits, behaving like a multi-plant monopolist. Price is now much higher than in Cournot's model. Industry output is reduced. What essentially happens, in Cournot's terms, is that the number of 'firms' shrinks to unity. So the benefits from government intervention to reduce the price are magnified. If all the firms inside one country collude, domestic output is squeezed, but their ability to raise price is tempered by competition from abroad.

Most dangerous of all will be the possibility of international collusion by both domestic and foreign firms. IATA is an instance of this. Against an international monopoly the government of a single country, even a large country, may be quite powerless. Governments will need to collaborate in such conditions to ensure that competition is enforced. In the West European context, it is this thinking that underlies the counter-monopoly provisions of Articles 85 and 86 of the Treaty of Rome.

Overt or tacit collusion is not the only possible outcome. Other situations can occur. Collusion can be threatened by the incentive that individual firms will have to break ranks and increase output or trim their selling prices to poach business from others. The Organization of Petroleum Exporting Countries (OPEC) experienced growing difficulties in maintaining prices after the two price hikes of 1973–4 and 1979–80. Smaller oil producers, such as Iraq or Nigeria, were tempted to increase output above the quotas assigned to them or enter secret bilateral trade deals at lower prices. By 1984, Saudi Arabia, the leading producer, had become impatient with the large output cuts it had to enforce on itself to keep world prices up. Successful collusion requires a great deal of information about individual producers' decisions and a credible punishment mechanism to deter double crossing, conditions which rarely apply, especially at the international level.

Collusion can also be undermined from outside. The higher the price is, the greater is the incentive for new firms to enter the market. Incumbent firms will then be forced to accept lower prices to stop market share dwindling. In the oil case, the price increases of the 1970s were followed by the development of new oilfields in non-OPEC countries such as Mexico, Norway, and the UK, whose additional production did much to drive OPEC's share of world oil output down from over 80 per cent in 1973 to barely 40 per cent by 1988, excluding the Eastern bloc.

4.3.3 Beliefs about Rivals' Outputs

We have just seen what can happen if firms collude. This amounts to relaxing assumption (4), that firms bahave independently taking their rivals' decisions as given. If we return to the concept of output setting, we are confronted with the limiting case of monopoly, where $n = 1$ and all firms set their output levels together to reap the maximum benefits of collusion. One ironical feature of Cournot's model is that, although firms aim to maximize their profits, they do not in fact do so: his assumption (4) prevents them from exploiting their collective monopoly power. They have a shared interest in acting in concert, but any attempt to do so will be bedevilled by the incentive that each firm has to break ranks and produce more.

The idea that firms treat their rivals' output levels as given is somewhat unappealing, because any experience of disequilibrium must show that rivals do react. Firms that operate according to Cournot's principles actually lower their output somewhat in response to a rise in the output by others. One oligopolist, having learnt or understood this, could increase his output, expecting the others to retreat a little. Such a firm would then act as a 'leader'. If the others do behave as Cournot says they will, the leader will gain higher profits, and the resulting equilibrium for the industry will display an overall rise in total output and some reduction in the price charged. This case, first explored by Stackelberg (1934), is closer to the perfectly competitive ideal than is the Cournot solution. A duopoly with one leader and one follower resembles a Cournot triopoly. However, if both firms try to act as leaders, the resulting equilibrium will be disastrous for both: profits will vanish, and price will tumble to marginal cost.

In our international context, with just a single Stackelberg leading firm, the country in which the firm resides is likelier than not to be a net exporter. An equilibrium with a Stackelberg leader is more favourable for social welfare at the world level than the Cournot case, because the price is lower; the country in which it produces will gain more, both from higher profits and the lower consumer price, than the rest of the world where profits will be depressed. If firms are price setters rather than output setters, however, Stackelberg leadership has anti-competitive, not pro-competitive, implications: the price leader will impose a high price, expecting his rivals to raise theirs somewhat in response.

4.3.4　Marginal Costs are Dissimilar or Non-horizontal

Turning to assumption (5) if oligopolists' marginal cost curves are horizontal but not common, firms' output levels will differ. The lower its costs are, the more a firm will produce. A country with higher cost firms will tend to produce less and, all else equal, will tend to import the commodity. If the cost differences and the number of firms are small, higher cost producers can survive. But if low cost firms are numerous, price will be close to their low marginal cost level, and firms with sufficiently high costs will be unable to survive without production subsidies or tariffs to restrict imports. The government of a country with one or more high cost firms may be tempted to impose such policies. It will of course face intensive lobbying to do so by the threatened firms. But should it? If the import price that would result if such firms were allowed to close was below those firms' marginal cost, only externality arguments would justify keeping them alive and, in that case, production subsidies would be the optimum policy, not tariffs on imports. At the world level, efficiency suggests that production should be transferred from higher cost to lower cost firms, thereby reducing total costs. Any adverse implications for competition that would ensue from the disappearance of some firms could be countered by appropriate production subsidies.

If they are non-horizontal, firms' marginal cost curves could have several different shapes. Cournot's simple formulae for industry output and price ((4.2) and (4.3)) cease to apply, but (4.1) is valid provided that the firms' cost curves are similar; it therefore remains true that the number of firms plays the same critical role in determining the size of the gap between price and marginal cost. If marginal cost curves slope downward, the best policy for the world as a whole is to concentrate production in just one firm and then to ensure that price is set at, not above, marginal cost by an appropriate production subsidy. This will presumably entail that production occurs in just one country, although it could be dispersed across different countries if the phenomenon generating increasing returns related to the company rather than to its plant or plants.

Another consequence of downward-sloping marginal cost curves is that collusion in oligopoly is even likelier to be undermined by aggressive price cutting by individual firms hoping to enlarge their output; however, the threat of entry is reduced.

4.3.5　Allowing for Entry and Exit

Assumption (6) fixed the number of firms. Relaxing this introduces the possibility of entry and exit. In perfectly competitive and mono-polistically competitive markets, it is customary to allow the number of firms to adjust so as to eliminate (supernormal) profits. The idea can be applied to oligopoly, although it relies upon a notion of free entry which may be less than plausible. What would free entry imply? If firms had no fixed costs, and new entrants enjoyed the same cost conditions as incumbents, entry would continue until price was driven down to marginal cost: the number of firms would be infinite. But suppose that all firms, incumbents as well as entrants, have a total cost function of the form

$$C = F + c \times \text{output} \tag{4.8}$$

where F represents fixed costs. Let the numbers of firms increase or fall until each firm (approximately) receives zero profits, net of fixed costs. In Cournot oligopoly, (4.2) and (4.3) imply that each firm's profits will tend to

$$\begin{aligned} \text{profits} &= \text{output} \times (p - c) - F \\ &= \frac{[(z - c)/(n + 1)]^2}{b} - F \end{aligned} \tag{4.9}$$

As before, z is the vertical intercept of the demand curve for the product, and $-b$ is the slope of the demand curve. If profits are to vanish, (4.9) implies that $n + 1 = (z - c)/(bF)^{1/2}$ and hence, from (4.3),

$$p = c + (Fb)^{1/2} \tag{4.10}$$

Price will exceed marginal cost, by a margin which increases with F and decreases with b. A rise in F implies that the number of firms will fall, and that in turn leads to a higher price by (4.3). A fall in b, in contrast, represents a rise in market demand, and this creates room for additional firms. The industry supply curve implied by (4.10) is therefore downward sloping. However, the entry mechanism can often be sluggish or even blocked, for reasons that will be discussed in section 4.3.6.

When fixed costs F are large relative to the size of world demand, the market for the product in question is said to be a 'natural oligopoly'. In the limit, with really large F, it will be a worldwide natural monopoly. There is room for only very few firms, perhaps just one. The market for wide body jet airframes provides an example. Virtually all the world's production of these goods is confined to just three producers: Boeing, MacDonnell Douglas, and the consortium of West European aircraft companies (Airbus Industrie). In this instance, the massive fixed cost of research and development, design, training, prototype production, and setting up a specialized production line ensures that entry by newcomers is prohibitively expensive. The governments of particular countries are often tempted to encourage domestic production of such goods. There are considerations of national prestige, military security, the possible unreliability of foreign suppliers, and potential spillover technological benefits that might be reaped by other sectors in the domestic economy. One policy that offers particular appeal consists of government subsidies to defray fixed costs. But there are persuasive counterarguments. Worldwide productive efficiency calls for concentration, not needless duplication of the heavy fixed costs. The profits earned by incumbent firms in such industries are rarely high for long periods, and are often low or negative. The chronicle of the involvement of some governments with projects of this nature, well told by Henderson (1977), makes depressing reading.

4.3.6. Introducing Dynamic Considerations

We come now to Cournot's penultimate assumption of a static one-period framework. Three important issues are raised once we allow for dynamic considerations, for the passage of time:

1   the implications of concerns about the future for the likelihood of tacit cooperation, as opposed to competition, between incumbent oligopolists;
2   the relevance of the future for an incumbent's (or incumbents') reactions to entry, and hence the likelihood of entry, in monopoly and oligopoly;
3   the future benefits that firms may reap from their experience of production now and in the past, or 'learning by doing'.

We examine each in turn.

In Cournot's model of oligopoly, firms decide on their output levels independently, treating rivals' outputs as given. This is a form of competition. It falls short of perfect competition, but establishes a market price far below what would happen under monopoly. Profits are less than they could be, and would be, if the firms exploited their common interest to the full and behaved like a multi-plant monopoly. Cournot's analysis suggests that a cartel of that type could not last, because of the strong incentive its members would face to cheat the others and produce more.

In a dynamic setting, Cournot-type objections to the collusive outcome are less appealing. If one duopolist cheats the other and lowers his price or raises his output in the current period, the injured party can retaliate by doing the same in the next. As long as firms do not discount their future profits too much, strategies of 'tit for tat' may sustain a form of tacit collusion between oligopolists in the long run.

Tit for tat means punishing your rival by reducing price, or raising output, in the subsequent period whenever he does this, but keeping price up when he has adhered to the unwritten rules and done the same. This type of tacit collusion is easiest to maintain in duopoly. As the number of firms increases, it becomes progressively harder: it is often difficult to identify who has broken ranks; punishment means hurting innocent as well as guilty parties; and individually injured parties, firms which kept their output down let us say, have a much weaker incentive to conduct the punishment themselves rather than hoping that another firm will do so. But the fact remains that, in a dynamic oligopoly, what a firm hopes to gain by competing in the current period must be set off against the possible future losses from doing so, and that some form of cooperation will be likelier than in a one-period setting. Cooperation, whether formal or tacit, will often be harder to achieve at an international level than within the confines of a single country, however.

Turning to the issue of entry, an incumbent's threat to fight an entrant is empty in a static model, unless the incumbent has sunk costs in a form which pays him to fight: he will do better to accommodate an entrant, and the entrant will know this (Dixit, 1982). In a dynamic context, fighting off an entrant now can be an investment in a reputation for toughness that scares off others later. Entry can also be blocked if there is a tiny chance that the incumbent could go crazy and slash his prices (Kreps and Wilson, 1982) or if the entrant suffers from a cost disadvantage, has to incur sunk costs, or provokes immediate matching cuts by the incumbent (Schwartz, 1986).

This section concludes with a brief mention of the significance of learning by doing. The idea here is that productivity now increases with past output experience. It was Arrow (1962) who first studied the phenomenon in detail, though Dasgupta and Stiglitz show in the epigraph to a recent paper (1988) that the concept was known to Aristotle. When the fruit of experience by one firm can be transmitted to all, learning by doing has no direct implications for market structure. But if it is specific to the firm, it may well result in monopoly. The capitalized value of such a firm's profits can be held to zero in the absence of entry barriers, with profits typically negative in the learning phase and positive thereafter. Entry barriers mean that early losses can be overcompensated by subsequent profits. In an international context, Dasgupta and Stiglitz show that insulating a firm from overseas competition at the learning stage could be in everyone's interests, provided that there is no forward market in which it can pre-sell its future output at this point. They go on to argue that learning by doing provides a powerful case for each country to specialize, and that countries could gain by subsidizing imports of goods not produced at home. This is a particularly attractive idea in the context of monopolistic competition, where each country can concentrate on the production of one type in a set of differentiated goods. Monopolistic competition is the form of imperfect competition to which the next section is addressed.

4.4 Monopolistic Competition

4.4.1 Definitions and Questions

Monopolistic competition is a market form where firms offer their customers differentiated products. The goods may be physically similar but differ in geographical position, so that customers face transport costs that depend on how far they are from suppliers. The retail markets for bread and gasoline are examples of this. Alternatively, the products could be differentiated according to some quality or set of qualities. Wines can be ranked on a spectrum from dry to sweet; computers differ by size of memory, cars by top speed, pullovers by colour. As its name implies, monopolistic competition combines elements of monopoly and competition. Monopoly arises in so far as an individual firm may be the only one to sell a good with a precise set of qualities and characteristics. Competition comes in because there will often be another product, not quite the same but similar, to which a customer will switch if it is cheap enough.

Like oligopoly, monopolistic competition provokes a number of questions. Answers to these questions define the type of model to be explored. Generalizing is difficult; results depend very much on the facts of the case considered. Such questions include the following.

1 What do firms' cost curves look like?
2 Do products differ according to location or physical characteristics?
3 In how many dimensions, or respects, do these products differ?
4 Do consumers like variety, or do they tend to pick the single product that suits them best? If the latter, what do individuals' demand curves for particular goods look like, and how are market demands derived?
5 How many firms are there?
6 How many different products can a firm make and sell?
7 Are the prices of the products chosen by the firms, independently or together, or determined in some other way?
8 Are the characteristics of products chosen by firms?
9 Are customers perfectly informed about the prices and characteristics of the goods on offer?
10 What do firms try to maximize?
11 How many time periods are we considering?

4.4.2 Hotelling and Chamberlin

There are numerous models of monopolistic competition, too many to mention here. The classic analyses were conducted by Hotelling (1929) and Chamberlin (1933). Hotelling looked at spatial duopoly. Two firms chose where to produce and sell otherwise identical products in a market represented by a straight line between two points. One might imagine two theatres, located in a city stretched out along a straight road, or icecream sellers on a beach. He showed that, if the prices of the products were exogenously imposed, the duopolists positioned themselves at the same point, the centre of the market. They did this because any firm that went elsewhere would do less business and earn lower profits than its rival. Chamberlin looked at a case where there were many firms, all offering customers different products, each of which was an equally close substitute for another. Free entry would drive price p to average cost AC. However, because the products were not perfect substitutes for each other, each firm would have a slightly downward-sloping average revenue curve: this meant that price would exceed marginal cost MC since under profit maximization $AC = p = MC(1 - 1/e)$, where e, defined as a positive number, is the high but finite elasticity for a particular firm's product.

4.4.3 The d'Aspremont and Salop Models

Among more recent studies, three stand out. They are those by d'Aspremont et al. (1979), Dixit and Stiglitz (1977), and Salop (1979). The Dixit and Stiglitz paper bears close resemblance to Spence (1976) and less resemblance to later work by Lancaster (1979), itself based on an earlier analysis by Gorman (1980), and Salop's resembles that of Eaton and Lipsey (1975) and Hay (1976). The three studies give common answers to some of the questions listed above. They assume unity in answer to (3), (6), and (11), yes to (9), and profits to (10). On (7), they agree in modelling firms as setting prices independently, taking the other firms' prices as given. The remaining assumptions differ and are summarized in Table 4.1.

The major results of these models are as follows. d'Aspremont et al. showed that the two firms will go to the opposite ends of the market, which is represented, like Hotelling's, by a straight line. They will charge a price equal to the marginal cost plus a transport cost term h. The length of the market is defined as unity, if transport costs H are quadratic in the customer's distance from the nearer seller ($H = dh^2$) and if the whole market is covered, so that everyone buys from one of the sellers. Their extreme differentiation result is in marked contrast with Hotelling's. For

Table 4.1   Assumptions in monopolistic competition models

Questions	d'Aspremont et al. (1979)	Salop (1979)	Dixit and Stiglitz (1977)
1	Common, horizontal MCs	Common, horizontal MCs, with common fixed costs F	
2	Location	Location	A physical characteristic
4	Individuals differ in location; they buy either one unit or nothing, from the cheapest source, allowing for transport costs		Individuals share common preferences; they like variety and buy a little of everything
5	Two, no entry	n, free entry	n, free entry
8	Yes	Exogenously imposed, with maximum differentiation	Yes

Hotelling, it is customers towards the edge of the market who get the worst deal; for d'Aspremont et al., the people in the middle fare worst. Both the d'Aspremont et al. and Hotelling outcomes differ from the social optimum, which locates the firms at one-quarter and three-quarters of the distance along the line.

Salop's firms locate along a circle. The market resembles the capital beltway surrounding Washington, DC, the M25 around London, or the *autoroute périphérique* around Paris. The distance between any two neighbouring firms is $1/n$ if the circumference of the circle is unity. Each firm sets a price equal to marginal cost plus h/n, where h represents the (linear) cost of transport per unit distance. The number of firms n depends in turn on the size M of the market and the level F of fixed costs: $n = (hM/F)^{\frac{1}{2}}$. Here M is the number of consumers at each point. Hence price exceeds marginal cost by a gap equal to $(hF/M)^{\frac{1}{2}}$. Customers lucky enough to live next door to a firm face a price of $c + (hF/M)^{\frac{1}{2}}$ where c equals marginal cost; those furthest away have to pay $c + \frac{3}{2}(hF/M)^{\frac{1}{2}}$ including transport costs.

The key features of this model, for our purposes, are as follows.

1   A more populous economy will enjoy more firms, lower prices, and lower transport costs, so that on average people will be able to buy something that comes closer to their personal needs, since location can be interpreted as a metaphor for a physical characteristic of the good.
2   An economy with higher fixed costs suffers the opposite to (1).
3   If the economy is closed to trade with the rest of the world, it will have twice as many firms as it should if it were to minimize the sum of total fixed costs Fn plus total transport costs $Mh/4n$, since this would imply $n = \frac{1}{2}(Mh/F)^{\frac{1}{2}}$.

4.4.4 The Dixit–Stiglitz Model

In the d'Aspremont et al. and Salop models, almost everyone opts to buy from only one producer; a few people, in the middle, are indifferent about which of the two (or two nearest) suppliers they buy from. They buy at most one unit of the good. The Dixit and Stiglitz model is very different in these respects. Here, everyone has the same preferences. They all like variety, such as green, yellow, red, and blue pullovers. The more the merrier. A mauve pullover is assumed to be an equally close substitute for a red or a green one. Pullovers are perfectly divisible, and people will choose more than one of each colour type if they are cheap enough. In the d'Aspremont et al. and Salop stories, they buy at most one pullover, and always one that comes closest to their ideal colour. The Dixit and Stiglitz consumers spend a given fraction of their incomes on other goods (for which there is no product differentiation) and the remainder on pullovers. There are two-tier preferences: overall utility is modelled as a weighted geometric mean of each of the other goods and what one may call 'pullover sub-utility' v. v is related to the consumption g_i of each pullover by

$$v^r = g_1^r + g_2^r + \ldots + g_n^r$$

if there are n pullovers on offer in all. Here r is defined as unity minus the reciprocal of the elasticity of substitution between any pair of pullovers:

$$1 - 1/\sigma$$

The elasticity of demand for any particular pullover which is produced by a single firm will equal $\sigma + (1 - \sigma)/n$. This tends to σ if n is large. As in Chamberlin's model, the ratio $(p - c)/p$ is equal to $1/e$. If y represents national income and b the proportion of it devoted to spending on pullovers, $pQ = by$, where Q is the total output of pullovers. The assumption of free entry (question (5)) ensures, as under Chamberlin and Salop, that the price–marginal cost margin has to balance average fixed costs per firm, so that profits vanish: $p - c = Fn/Q$.

Rearranging these results establishes the equilibrium number of firms, or pullover types:

$$n = by/F\sigma + r \tag{4.11}$$

The price–marginal cost margins, relative to price, will be

$$\frac{p - c}{p} = \frac{1}{\sigma}\left[1 + \frac{F(\sigma - 1)}{by}\right] \tag{4.12}$$

The key results to notice here are as follows.

4   A richer economy produces more types of pullover and not just a larger volume of pullovers; the increased variety is associated with lower prices and greater consumer utility. Similar results follow from an increased budget share devoted to pullovers.
5   An economy with higher fixed costs experiences effects opposite to (4).
6   An economy closed to trade may produce either too many or too few types of pullover from the standpoint of social welfare. An additional producer increases consumers' total utilities by more than he can recover in sales revenue or profits. In contrast, a new producer will deflect business from existing producers. The first effect taken by itself suggests that there will be too few producers, the second that there will be too many.

4.4.5 The Monopolistic Competition Models in an International Context

We now examine what implications these models may have for international trade. It should be stressed at the outset that the models are highly restrictive, since they are based on specific assumptions which do not permit ready generalization. The crucial questions to which one would like answers include the following.

1   **Net trade**   What features will an economy tend to display, if it is to be a net exporter of goods produced under monopolistic competition?
2   **Intra-industry trade**   How can we explain two-way trade or 'intra-industry' trade in monopolistically competitive products?
3   **Gains and losses from trade**   Does monopolistic competition qualify or extend our notion of gains from trade?

We examine these questions in turn.

Net Trade
Net trade is influenced by the same three principal considerations that were seen to govern it under perfect competition in chapter 2: relative factor endowments, taste patterns, and technology. Before elaborating, one point should be clarified. The Salop and Dixit–Stiglitz models both suggested that the prices of goods produced under monopolistic competition will be lower in large economies than in smaller ones, all else equal. It is therefore tempting to infer that larger economies are likelier to be net exporters of such goods once international trade is allowed. Unfortunately this does not follow. Firms in small economies will have just the

same access to the big world market as those in larger ones, if trade barriers such as tariffs and international transport costs are eliminated. Provided that firms in all economies have common cost functions, and this presumably means that factor prices and technologies are common, the size of the national economy within which production occurs is irrelevant.

For concreteness, assume that there are two economies A and B. There are two goods, bread and computers. Bread is a homogeneous good produced under constant returns to scale; computers are a motley collection of objects with product differentiation. Let A and B differ in factor endowments, A being relatively well endowed with labour and B with capital. Let computers be relatively capital intensive. Assume that countries A and B exhibit common homothetic preferences. Firms' technologies in the two countries are the same.

The Heckscher–Ohlin model examined in chapter 2 would predict that the labour-rich economy A will export the labour-intensive good bread. Under the conditions given, this will be exactly what happens under monopolistic competition too. Measured in units of bread, A's wage rate will be lower than B's in autarky and its rental on capital will be higher. Factor endowment differences will determine the pattern of net trade: A will be a bread exporter, B a net exporter of computers. This result will follow even if country A is larger than B – and to the extent that the autarky relative price of computers could be lower there, by virtue of its larger size. The reason for this lies in the fact that, once computer manufacturers have access to the still larger world market, the relative abundance of capital in B ensures that it will concentrate on production of the capital-intensive good.

It is not just factor endowments that govern net trade patterns. Suppose we take the Dixit and Stiglitz model and introduce international differences in demand patterns. Suppose that b, the fraction of incomes devoted to the products of the monopolistically competitive industry, is higher in A than in B. All else equal, that should ensure that A is a net importer of computers. Had the countries been of equal size, and with common factor endowments, A would have had a lower relative price of computers than B in autarky. Again, pre-trade price ratios would be a misleading predictor of trade direction: A would still import computers, despite having been able to buy them more cheaply in terms of bread before trade than the residents of B. The new world price of computers, after trade, would of course be still lower, because the expansion of the total market would drive it down even further. In contrast, if A's computer manufacturers enjoy a relative technological lead over B's, as against bread, this would predispose A to export computers and to display a lower pre-trade price as well, all else equal.

Intra-Industry Trade

The above has sketched out an answer to our first question, on net trade. What of the second question which concerns 'intra-industry' trade or two-way trade in computers? If countries A and B do not differ too much in their factor endowments, and if we return to assuming common homothetic preferences and common technology, we find that the two countries should engage in reciprocal trade in computers. This result should follow under both the Dixit and Stiglitz interpretation (where everyone likes variety) and the Salop model, where one person likes one type and a second person another. The reason here is that there will be some demand in B for the type of computers made in A, even if country B is a net exporter of computers. If there is a really pronounced difference in factor endowment ratios, however, country A will specialize exclusively in the production of bread, and all the world's computers will be made in B.

A sufficiently small difference in factor endowments, however, will permit two-way trade, however unbalanced. Many Frenchmen enjoy the occasional glass of hock, even though Germany is a large net importer of wine from France; the addition of hock to the wine list enlarges the choice set the Frenchman enjoys. This is the Dixit–Stiglitz effect. A few Germans will prefer a British Mini or Rolls Royce because the characteristics they offer come closer to their preferences than the wide range of domestic cars produced, despite the fact that the UK is a massive net importer of cars from Germany. This is the Salop effect. A few Americans will watch programmes transmitted by Canadian television stations in preference to their homogenized local products, Hotelling's arguments might suggest. d'Aspremont could argue the opposite, so that Canadian television filled a neglected niche between the highbrow output of at least one US station and the downmarket glitz and advertisements of US commercial networks.

Gains from Trade

Answers to the first two questions are provided in greater detail and rigour by Helpman (1981), Helpman and Krugman (1985), and Helpman and Razin (1983). For further details on our third question, the gains from trade, the reader is advised to consult Krugman (1981) and chapter 9 of Helpman and Krugman (1985). What follows summarizes and amplifies some of the results presented there.

In aggregate welfare terms, a country will not lose from international trade if two conditions hold:

1 the change in variety provided for consumers is beneficial;
2 the country can still buy the bundle of goods it enjoyed under autarky.

All else equal, consumers would benefit on average from greater variety. In the Dixit and Stiglitz framework, this comes about as a result of an addition to the list of differentiated products that the representative consumer purchases; in the Salop story, it comes about from a reduction in the interval between products along the circle, so that the average consumer pays a lower delivered price, inclusive of transport costs. So condition (1) reduces to the requirement that international trade increases variety. In an environment with several industries each producing differentiated sets of products, it is possible that trade does not increase the variety of all of them. Autarky might imply fewer varieties of car, but more of beer. When variety increases in one product range and falls in another, the net effect of trade, as far as condition (1) is concerned, is likelier to be beneficial if the consumers regard the goods for which variety increases as less good substitutes for each other than for the set of goods where variety falls.

The second condition is met if firms produce more, on average, under free trade than in autarky. Average productivity needs to increase. This might fail to hold if the economy were to specialize in the production of homogeneous goods produced under constant returns and perfect competition and switch away from the production of differentiated products with increasing returns. Monopolistic competition depends crucially on the existence of some form of increasing returns: if there were constant or decreasing returns in the output of every other type of good, so many firms could produce it that perfect competition would prevail. In a framework with more than one set of differentiated products, gains from trade could be threatened for an economy which abandoned to foreign importers the production of goods where average costs were falling particularly steeply. Raising the production of other differentiated goods industries where returns to scale increased more gently could lead to an overall fall in productivity. The issue of how trade could lead to a decline in an economy's average productivity if it switched output away from industries with increasing returns is explored further in section 4.5.

The gains from trade also depend crucially on the gains to individual consumers and owners of factors of production. Consider the Salop model first. Take the example of the market for pullovers. Before trade, the economy's consumers had a choice of just two colours, red and blue. Both are priced at marginal cost plus half the transport cost term x if the market is covered, and even those who would ideally like yellow or green pullovers reluctantly buy a red or blue one. Suppose three otherwise identical countries decide to trade with each other. The nearest approximation to breakeven may mean that there is room for five or seven types of pullover in the integrated three-country market, not six. The equal spacing assumption for firms' locations means that at least three firms have to adjust and modify their colour specification somewhat. Someone who was lucky enough to get his ideal shade of red pullover could lose, now, because the nearest approximation was scarlet or pink. But the majority will gain from the new range of colours available.

Turning to the prices of factors of production, Krugman (1981) showed that there can be increases in the rewards to all factor owners under increasing returns. The Stolper–Samuelson results, explored in chapters 2 and 3, showed that scarce factors, employed intensively in importables industries suffer a fall in real income when the economy moves from autarky to trade. Krugman showed that when factor endowment differences are small enough, and returns to scale increase enough, the gains from specialization which trade permits could conceivably raise prices of all factors of production in both countries.

Essentially imperfect competition and increasing returns provide additional avenues along which gains from trade could arise. These avenues are perilous. The welfare effects of trade, so straightforward under perfect competition, become much more complicated. Numerous examples can be constructed to suggest that gains from trade could be reversed. In the oligopoly model considered in section 4.1, for example, the move from autarky to trade will tend to reduce prices because the domestic firm or firms face additional competition. But the overall welfare effect of the gain in consumers' surplus could be qualified, even reversed, by a transfer of the profits of home producers to foreign producers. Empirical evidence, surveyed by Hutchinson (1989), frequently reveals that imperfect competition *increases* the estimates of the welfare gains from freer trade. This gives some suggestion that imperfect competition may be likelier than not to reinforce the social superiority of free trade over no trade that should normally arise under perfect competition. In the current context of monopolistic competition, the gains from trade are suspect if variety falls, especially for a range of goods which consumers treat as relatively poor substitutes for each other and/or the economy is induced to concentrate on exporting goods where returns to scale are constant or only slightly decreasing. The next section explores the question of increasing returns in more detail.

4.5 Increasing Returns

4.5.1 Increasing Returns External to the Firm

The simplest form of increasing returns is the only kind which is compatible with perfect competition. This is returns to scale which are perceived as constant by individual firms, but which increase *externally*. There are three possibilities here. Returns to scale in a particular industry could increase with the total output of that industry in the economy in question. They could also rise with the output of another industry in the domestic economy, or with worldwide output of that good or other goods. In the first two cases, the externally increasing returns to scale are country specific; in the third, they are international. In each case they are also sector specific. We could have combinations of the three cases: for example, returns to scale in one domestic sector might increase with the economy's total output of all goods. The appeal of externally increasing returns is their consistency with perfect competition: individual firms will not observe them, and so they can remain small and continue to employ factors of production to the point where the value of their marginal products balances their rewards. Price will continue to equal marginal and average cost, as observed by the firms themselves.

To see the effects of external scale economies in action, consider the following model. Here, externally increasing returns will be industry specific and country specific. Two goods x and y can be produced in each of the four countries A, B, C, and D. All countries have given and equal endowments of labour N. Labour is the only factor of production, and so the model resembles Ricardo's framework discussed in chapter 2.

In industry x the average product of labour (APL) is unity and returns to scale are constant with no externalities. In industry y, each firm regards its APL as a constant but this increases with the size of the output

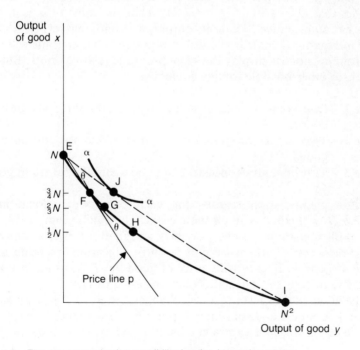

Figure 4.5 The convex production possibility frontier, increasing returns.

of the industry of that economy. To be precise, let $\text{APL}_y^i = L_y^i$, where L_y^i denotes employment in industry y in economy i. All consumers in each country have the same preferences. They devote three-quarters of their incomes to expenditure on good x and the remainder to good y. Good x is numeraire, with a price of 1.

These assumptions generate common production possibility frontiers (PPFs) for the four countries given by

$$Q_x + Q_y^{1/2} = N \tag{4.13}$$

where Q_x denotes the output of industry x. These PPFs are convex to the origin, as depicted in figure 4.5. The vertical intercept of the PPF, with good x on the vertical axis, is N. That on the horizontal axis is N^2.

If these countries do not engage in international trade, demand and supply for each good will have to balance within the boundaries of each. Both goods will be produced in every country. Given perfect competition, firms in industry x will pay labour the value of its marginal product. This will be unity, so the money wage is unity. Firms in industry y will do the same. This implies that the price p_y of good y will equal $1/Q_y^{1/2}$. The assumption that consumers will devote three-quarters of their incomes (which add up to $Q_x + p_y Q_y$) to good x tells us that in equilibrium $Q_x = 3p_y Q_y$. Thus $Q_x = 3Q_y^{1/2}$ and the equation for the PPF therefore implies that $Q_x = \frac{3}{4}N$ and $Q_y = (N/4)^2$. Thus the value of p_y is $4/N$. No firm has an incentive to alter its output, and both markets clear.

If international trade is allowed, it is possible that no trade will occur. All four economies display the same pre-trade relative prices. But there are three other possible trading equilibria.

Case 1   One country specializes in good x and three produce both goods.

Case 2   Two countries specialize in good x and two produce both goods.

Case 3   Three countries specialize in good x and the fourth in good y.

A little manipulation reveals that each country's national income $Q_x + p_y Q_y$ will equal N in all these cases. The equilibrium money wage rate is also common, to every country and in every case, at unity. The differences come in the pattern of resource allocation and trade and the price of good y. In case 1 the price of good y is $3/N$, as against $4/N$ in autarky. In case 2 it falls to $2/N$ and in case 3 to $1/N$.

The allocation of resources also changes and differs. In autarky each country produces and consumes at point F. Here an indifference curve, labelled Θ, is tangent to a straight line P from E which crosses the PPF at

F. In case 1, one country produces at point E and the other three at G, where one-third of their labour forces are now devoted to the production of good 2, instead of the one-quarter under autarky. In case 2, two countries produce at E and two at H, where the latter's labour forces are split half and half between the two industries. In case 3, three countries produce at E and one at I. Specialization is universal and complete. In this third case, each country consumes at point J on the broken line between E and I, attaining indifference curve α.

In this example, every country gains equally from trade. The greatest gains come in case 3, the least in case 1. Nobody loses. If utility displays constant returns to scale in consumption, everyone in each country is nearly 19 per cent better off in case 1 than in autarky. In case 3, they are 41.4 per cent better off than under autarky. Increasing returns therefore provide an additional reason for trade, and for the gains that come with it. We saw in chapter 2 that differences in technology, tastes, or factor endowments could all lead to mutually gainful trade. To this list we must now add increasing returns, which can constitute a further reason for beneficial trade even when autarkic prices are common to the economies involved. The only doubts in the context of this example centre around the question of whether any of these beneficial alternatives to autarky will in fact come about. There is nothing to ensure this. When autarkic prices are common, as they will be in this instance, no one has an incentive to start trading and commence the process that could establish any of the trading equilibria we have identified.

The example we have been examining is a special case. The assumptions on technology, factor endowments, and preferences were kept deliberately simple, to permit relatively straightforward solutions. Had we made the sizes of the countries' labour endowments differ, one immediate result would have been that pre-trade price ratios would have diverged. Good y, which enjoys increasing returns, would have been cheapest in the largest economy since, in autarky, $p_y = 4/N$, which is inversely proportional to the size of the country's labour force.

So differences in sizes of economy could have provided the trigger for trade. We would probably have seen the largest economy exporting the increasing returns commodity. Interestingly, had that not happened, had it been a small economy which concentrated on producing and exporting the good subject to increasing returns, it is conceivable that the larger economy which specializes in the constant returns good could end up, after trade, with a consumption bundle yielding lower utility than in autarky. In that event, the larger economy would have lost by trade, principally as a result of the fall in labour's average productivity that comes about from transferring labour away from good y (where returns are increasing) towards good x (where they are not). Helpman and

Krugman (1985) provide an example where this can happen. So the conclusion that increasing returns may lead to gainful trade among all participants cannot be universalized.

4.5.2 Increasing Returns Internal to the Firm

The type of increasing returns assumed in this section so far has been *external* economies of scale. These are compatible with perfect competition if returns to scale to the firm are constant. Suppose now that they had been internal to the firms in industry y, the sector enjoying them. We would observe a sudden scramble between the producers of good y which would end up, unless impeded by government regulations, with monopoly. Consider what an autarkic equilibrium would look like. With sector x's production function $Q_x = N_x$ unchanged, and its firms perfectly competitive, the wage rate would still be unity. But p_y would now be under the control of the single producer of that good. He would presumably choose his employment level N_y to maximize the utility he could enjoy from his profits. His maximand would be $(p_y Q_y - N_y)/p_y^{1/4}$, where $Q_y = N_y^2$ and $p_y Q_y = \frac{1}{3}(N - N_y)$. The solution to this problem is $N_y \approx 0.086N$ and $p_y \approx 41.3/N$. The economy in autarky would produce much less of good y than under perfect competition with external scale economies and the price of the good would be more than ten times higher.

Now suppose that each of the four economies A, B, C, and D is in this position, and trade is suddenly introduced. There are now four oligopolists in the market for good y, instead of four natural monopolists. Aware of their increasing returns to scale and decreasing marginal costs of production, each of our firms would race to exploit them. A likely final outcome would be a monopoly. Three of the four national firms would close, and we would be left with just one company producing for the enlarged market.

Suppose that it is country A which retains its producer of good y. A will now export the good to B, C, and D, and import x in return. B, C, and D will specialize in the production of good x. If A's monopolist acts as before, assuming that all four countries have the same labour endowment N he will set p_y and N_y at about 10 and $0.35/N$ respectively. The wage rate will remain equalized at unity. All four countries will gain from trade in this example, but A will gain much more than the others. With utility displaying constant returns to scale, A's utility rises 120 per cent, compared with less than 20 per cent for B, C, and D. In this example, it pays to buy your goods more cheaply from a foreign monopolist, but it pays much more to be that foreign monopolist yourself. Workers in all four economies are equally well off, since they have a common money wage and face the same prices for the goods they buy. It is the monopoly firm's owner or owners who really benefit most.

4.6 Market Imperfections: Some Further Implications

This section explores a set of further issues, linked by the general theme of market imperfections and how they impinge on the open economy. The first of these is concerned with missing markets and how, when these markets are incomplete, trade could conceivably bring losses to everyone. The second looks at quantitative trade barriers under imperfect competition, and the third examines the phenomenon of lobbying and what it suggests about the welfare effects of trade restrictions in general.

4.6.1 The Second Best Theorem

The theorem of second best, due to Lancaster and Lipsey (1956), states that Pareto conditions for efficiency are liable to modification in the presence of an ineradicable distortion which stops them being applied in every context. We saw in chapter 3 that Pareto efficiency requires consumers and producers in all countries to face the same relative prices of traded goods when conditions are ideal. What 'ideal' means in this context is that no other market should suffer from distortions and that the set of markets should be complete. What follows demonstrates that, if one or more markets are missing, it no longer follows that free trade is best. In fact a particular case has been constructed by Newbery and Stiglitz (1984) under which everyone can be worse off under free trade than under autarky.

4.6.2 The Newbery–Stiglitz Model

Consider a world of two countries where each of two goods can be produced. One of these has a fixed production function where the output from a set of inputs is predictable and determined. The other displays a random output level affected, let us say, by the weather. The weather has the property that it is certain to rain in only one of the two countries. It is equally likely to rain in either. If it rains in one economy, it rains everywhere there, and all the producers of the random good find the productivity of their land enhanced; a drought entails lower output for every firm. Consumers have identical Cobb–Douglas preferences, so that their expenditure on each good is a fixed fraction of their incomes. The resulting demand curves for each of the two goods are unit elastic to their price. Producers are averse to risk and cannot get weather insurance, the missing market. Under autarky, the local demand curve for the risky good gives its producers perfect income insurance: drought prices are higher than rain prices in such a way that the producers' total receipts from selling the risky good are independent of the weather.

If trade is opened up and the two economies are of equal size and identical factor endowments, the price of the risky good is uniform in the two countries and fixed, independent of the weather. Producers of the risky good no longer have constant incomes. If it rains, they get large sales revenue; a drought brings low total receipts, when output is correspondingly higher in the other country. Producers' utility is reduced, since they do not like risk. Thus they react by switching production into the safe product, where there is no income risk. This has an efficiency cost, because the price ratio consumers face no longer equals the mean marginal rate of transformation, since the PPFs are concave. If consumers dislike volatility in the price of the risky good, the stability of price provided by free trade will be beneficial for them. But since consumers derive their incomes from the sale of factors of production, the efficiency loss from overproduction of the safe good will entail an income loss for them. Under free trade, it is possible that this adverse effect dominates the gain from greater price stability, especially if consumers' aversion to price risk is small. If that is so, everyone in both economies is worse off under free trade than under autarky. Consumers and producers are worse off because of the instability in their incomes which they are assumed to dislike. A modest departure from autarky, involving restricted trade, could bring gains to everyone if compensation to the producers were allowed. But if the two countries proceed to completely unrestricted trade, everyone could be worse off.

The ideal policy in these circumstances is to allow free trade but to introduce insurance against the weather for producers of the risky good. It remains true that free trade is best if markets are complete. But there may be difficulties with providing insurance: compensating individual producers for low output could induce them to work less hard and claim that poor weather was responsible for a fall in production, if the insurance agency could monitor neither the state of the world (the weather) nor the producers' inputs. Moral hazard under asymmetric information is the central reason why insurance against poor crops is typically unprovided in practice.

4.6.3 Import Quotas under Imperfect Competition

We turn now to the issue of quantitative trade barriers under imperfect competition. Suppose we consider a small open economy, facing an exogenously given world price of a particular imported good. The good is homogeneous, and there is one domestic manufacturer who manufacturers the product. Under free trade, the domestic firm is a price taker and, if it maximizes profit, will produce where marginal cost crosses the world price line from below. If a tariff is imposed at anything less than a prohibitive rate, this remains true, except that marginal cost is now balanced with the higher domestic price which includes the tariff. But suppose that a quota is imposed on imports to give the same import volume as a tariff levied at rate *t*.

The domestic firm will now behave like a Cournot oligopolist. In this case, the quota ceiling on imports must bind. The firm will calculate that the average revenue curve facing it is equivalent to the domestic demand curve for the product, shifted left by the amount of the quota. Since this average revenue curve slopes down, marginal revenue must lie beneath. Profit maximization entails equating marginal (not average) revenue with marginal cost. Thus the firm will produce less, and charge more, under an import quota than under a tariff which has the same effect on the volume of imports.

This is bad news for domestic consumers, who will lose much more surplus than under a tariff. It is good news for owners of the domestic firm, whose profits will be far higher. The quota involves a huge redistribution of income from consumers to the home firm. It also leads to lower home consumption and production; the first of these has adverse welfare effects, the second beneficial, at least to the point where home output falls back to the level that it would have been in free trade. If the quota licence is auctioned on a fair market where bidders realize how valuable it will be once the domestic firm drives the price up, the home government can at least keep the revenue. If not, the whole of this large rent payment accrues to the lucky firm or firms (possibly foreign) that do the lucrative importing. Provided that the government gets the rent itself and the quota does not lower domestic output by too much, the quota could do less damage to domestic welfare than the tariff. This condition is most likely to be met if the home firm's marginal cost curve is more elastic than the domestic demand curve.

We can conclude from this that a domestic producer facing import competition in his home market will gain much more from physical barriers to imports than from tariffs that restrain imports to an equivalent degree. This will be so, at least, unless there are so many domestic producers that competition within the national boundaries remains perfect after foreign supplies have been cut back. A single firm, or small group of firms, producing import substitutes can be expected to lobby hard for physical import barriers. These could of course take the form of specifying standards which preclude many, perhaps all, foreign producers and which the home firm or firms could fulfil. Such standards could relate to the nature of the product or the conditions governing its production. Licensing import quotas for any overseas firms that meet the test will typically prove very difficult, and so such policies have the added disadvantage in comparison with tariffs, of forgoing a valuable source of revenue to the government. Voluntary export restraints on foreign importers are a similar device which has the interesting feature that it could tip the scales against Cournot competition in favour of collusion between the overseas and domestic producers (Dixit, 1984). All the firms involved could gain from the increased profits that followed the home price rise; it is more than possible that the foreign firm invited to restrain its exports could end up with higher profits as a result.

4.6.4 Rent Seeking

The last topic to be examined in this section is lobbying. Trade barriers provide opportunities for greatly increased profits for domestic producers and for importers who manage to retain access to the domestic profit. This gives such companies an incentive to lobby. Lobbying is a costly exercise. It requires personnel, premises, and organizations to provide plausible arguments in favour of the restrictions, or 'party pamphlets, the wretched offspring of falsehood and venality' (Adam Smith, 1776). Real resources are consumed in lobbying. Even when lobbying takes the ugly form of bribery to particular politicians or officials, real resources may be expended by domestic citizens keen to acquire positions that enable them to receive lucrative bribes. Either way, lobbying or 'rent seeking' is a directly unproductive activity and must entail a shrinkage of the country's genuine production opportunities. Lobbying is like a distortionary tax, or a fire, which burns up valuable resources. In the context of trade policy, it generally reinforces the arguments against protection. It has been examined at length in a number of recent papers, most notably by Bhagwati et al. (1984).

The waste of resources consumed in political activity and lobbying is a theme that has long attracted economists' attention. To Adam Smith, Edinburgh's demotion from political capital city, after the Act of Union between Scotland and England in 1707, seemed to bring it economic benefits:

> There was little trade or industry in Edinburgh before the Union. When the Scotch Parliament was no longer to be assembled in it, when it ceased to be the necessary residence of the principal nobility and gentry of Scotland, it became a city of some trade and industry. (1776, Book 2, ch. 3)

If the rents provided by trade barriers are largely gobbled up in the costs of seeking them, it may be better to impose them randomly rather than in response to political representations – better still, perhaps, to dispense with them completely.

4.7 Conclusions

When competition is perfect and markets are complete, free trade is best. It is the most efficient system in the world as a whole. Under certain circumstances a restriction on trade may bring net advantages to the country applying it but, with the single exception of the monopoly power in trade argument for an optimum tariff, some other form of intervention will secure such gains at lower cost. Market imperfections, whether in the form of oligopoly, monopolistic competition, or incompleteness, introduce new elements into the story. The profits which may accompany such market imperfections, and the increasing returns which give rise to them, provide new arguments for policy intervention at the national level: the country can gain from sharing in these profits and can lose if it does not participate in the activity in question. Subsidies on exports, or tariffs on imports, can help to achieve this. This argument loses its force if there is an entry–exit mechanism that eliminates profits, although price will still be higher than marginal cost. The ideal response to such market imperfections, however, will typically take the form of subsidies on production, and, as we saw in the context of oligopoly, trade intervention is pointless or damaging if all countries pursue these to the optimum degree.

Increasing returns provide an additional reason for thinking that trade may be gainful, possibly for all individuals in all countries. But this need not be so: examples can be constructed where a country can lose from trade. This is especially likely if it is induced to abandon to the others the production of goods where increasing returns are pronounced or, in the context of monopolistic competition with differentiated goods, if variety is reduced. Turning to the issue of incomplete markets, free trade could even be damaging for everyone in the absence of insurance (the Newbery–Stiglitz result).

Yet the possibility that trade could be harmful and the enriched set of arguments in favour of trade intervention by national governments do not add up to the general presumption that market imperfections justify taxes on trade. As under perfect competition, large countries can improve their terms of trade by restricting imports and exports. Yet if exports or imports are controlled by a single domestic firm, profit maximization will lead it to apply the optimum trade taxes itself. There is also a powerful strategic argument for being prepared to threaten or adopt trade restrictions if other countries do so, if only to achieve a better international bargain from the standpoint of national welfare. Threats of 'reciprocity' are an admirable deterrent, as long as they never have to be enforced! The only key result worth stressing is that free trade remains best, provided that the correct policies are applied to deal with the distortions to which market imperfections give rise. If you need an industrial policy to get rid of these distortions, have an industrial policy – not a policy of protection.

5

Trade Integration

In this chapter we discuss the effects of trade integration, with special reference to the European Community (EC). Trade integration means the integration of trade in goods and services across national frontiers. Depending on degree, it is possible to distinguish between four types of trade integration. A free trade area consists of member countries which agree to remove trade barriers among themselves but maintain separate national barriers against trade with the rest of the world (ROW). For example, the Canada–USA Free Trade Pact (1987) is an agreement between these two countries to introduce free trade across their national frontiers but does not cover trade barriers imposed on third countries. In a customs union (CU), members remove all barriers to trade among themselves and adopt common external tariffs and non-tariff barriers. If, in addition to the CU, factors of production are permitted to be freely mobile between countries, we have what is known as a **common market**. For example, the aim of '1992' is to establish a single European internal market by 1992. It is hoped that, by 1992, Europe will consist of a single common market with free movement of goods, services, labour, capital, and other factor inputs. The ultimate form of integration is economic union, where member countries agree to common monetary, fiscal, and welfare policies. Belgium and Luxembourg have had a monetary union since 1921, and this is an ultimate goal of the EC, for some of its members.

5.1 The Welfare Effects of Trade Integration

5.1.1 The Viner Model

To analyse the welfare effects of trade integration, we draw on the Viner (1950) model of CU formation. The key assumptions in the Viner model are as follows.

1   Two countries A and B form a CU leaving C, an aggregate for the ROW, out.
2   Commodities are consumed in the same fixed proportion, independent of the structure of relative prices.
3   Competitive conditions hold in all markets.
4   There is no monopsony power on world markets. Each country takes the world price as given.

In the Viner model, the welfare effects arising from the formation of the CU depend on the relative degree to which there is trade creation and trade diversion. The formation of the CU is said to be trade creating if it brings about an improvement in resource utilization, that is, if its formation shifts production away from a less efficient to a more efficient member of the union.

For example, suppose that, prior to the formation of the CU, country A produced part of its requirements for good Q at home but inefficiently because it was a protected industry. Country B is the most efficient producer of the good and its sole world exporter. When the CU is formed, the tariff is abolished. B's exports rise and A's production declines as it faces new competition. Trade is *created* because the inefficient producer is no longer protected.

This point is illustrated in figure 5.1 which shows the domestic demand and supply curves of country A. tt' is the price paid in country A with the tariff and pp' is the world price, the price at which country B supplies Q without the tariff. The CU lowers the price to pp', reduces domestic production of Q from 0M to 0M', increases consumption of Q in A from 0N to 0N', and expands trade from MN to MN'. There is a net gain from A's membership in the CU in this case. A's consumers' surplus increases by area $1 + 2 + 3 + 4$, A's producers lose area 1, and the government loses revenue (area 3), making for a net gain of areas $2 + 4$.

Trade diversion arises when the formation of a CU causes a deterioration in the utilization of resources because it shifts production away from the lowest cost producer to a higher cost partner.

Suppose that, before the union, country A's consumption of good Y was supplied by outsider C, the most efficient producer of good Y. B can also produce good Y but at higher cost. When the CU is formed between A and B, A switches its purchases of good Y from C to B because tariff barriers between A and B, but not those between A and C, have been lifted. This is a trade diversion because A shifts to the higher cost producer. A good example is in the field of agriculture. EC members purchase agricultural products from member countries when, in many cases, the product could be obtained more cheaply (in the absence of protectionist policies) from a non-member country.

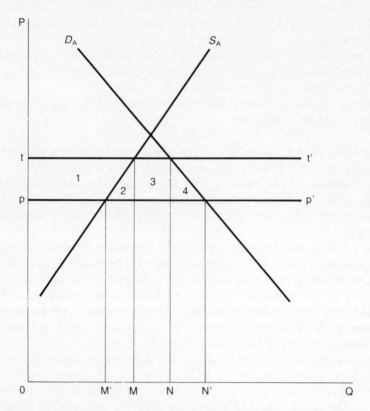

Figure 5.1   Trade creation after country A joins a customs union.

Figure 5.2 illustrates the case of trade diversion. It gives A's demand curve for good Y. p_C is the price Y on world markets and p_B is the price at which B would supply Q. Prior to the CU, both B and C are subject to the same tariff imposed by A. A imports all Q from C. When the tariff is removed for B but not C, p_B is the price charged to A's consumers and A begins to import from B, now seemingly a cheaper source of supply because C is still subject to a tariff. Thus, CU may cause a trade diversion. Whether there is a net welfare gain for country A depends on the relative sizes of the gain to A's consumers' surplus (area $1 + 2 + 3 + 4$), net of loss in producers' surplus (area 1) and the loss to A's government (area $3 + 5$). There is a net gain if area 2 + area 4 is greater than area 5, that is, if the gain in surplus to consumers (consumption effects) is greater than the loss from trade diversion (switching to a less efficient source of supply). There is a net welfare loss if area 5 is greater than area 2 + area 4.

We have demonstrated that whether member countries of a CU experience a welfare gain or loss will depend on the extent to which net

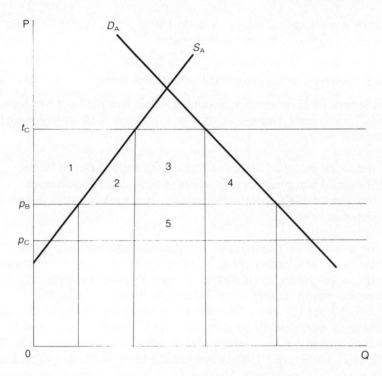

Figure 5.2   Trade diversion after country A joins a customs union.

gains from trade creation are offset by net losses arising from trade diversion. Note that it is possible to have no trade creation and a net gain if the consumption effects outweigh the trade diversion effects.

In our simple model, trade diversion reduced ROW sales in country A. A CU will harm the ROW if the supply curve for the ROW slopes upward: lower sales would entail lower prices, reducing the ROW's terms of trade.

However, the formation of a CU does have the potential of increasing trade with the ROW. This will occur if C's goods are complementary to goods whose internal consumption is increased after the formation of the CU. For example, after the formation of the original EC, UK and US capital exports increased in response to the investment boom in member countries.

A CU is a step on the road to free trade, and so it might seem superior, from a welfare standpoint, to a regime where every country imposes a tariff against all the others. But this is not so. Figures 5.1 and 5.2 have shown that a country may gain or lose from joining a CU, compared with an initial equilibrium with common tariffs against all countries. We now wish to probe more deeply and ask what the optimum trade policy for a country consists of. Could it ever do better by joining a CU than by adopting a policy of unilateral free trade?

5.1.2 Optimal Trade Policy and the Customs Union

In otherwise ideal conditions, a country will do best for itself by choosing a total import level, and source of import purchases, to try to equate the following:

1   the social marginal utility of consuming importables at home;
2   the social marginal cost of consuming importables at home;
3   the social marginal cost of importing from each country or from the cheapest source.

In the absence of externalities or market imperfections, (1) will be measured by the demand curve for importables, and (2) by the domestic supply curve. When, as in figures 5.1 and 5.2, the home country faces horizontal supply curves from other countries, the marginal cost of importing from any one of them is given by its supply curve. The ideal policy is to purchase all imports from the cheapest source and to set domestic prices for consumers and producers at this level. The CU achieves this in figure 5.1, since partner B is the lowest cost source. But it violates the rules in figure 5.2 in two respects: first, a tariff is imposed on imports from the excluded country C, ensuring that (1) and (2) both lie above (3); second, the absence of a tariff on B diverts trade and violates the condition for the optimum sourcing of imports.

Imports are optimally sourced when they are bought most cheaply. If countries' supply curves are horizontal, optimal sourcing means buying from the lowest cost source, for example from the country C in figure 5.2. If foreign countries' supply curves are upward sloping, the marginal cost of importing lies above them. Importing more means driving up the price, and not just on the additional units but on the intramarginal units too, assuming that there is no discrimination. If B's and C's supply curves are equally elastic with elasticity e, country A does best by applying a common tariff of $1/e$ on both of them. In figures 5.1 and 5.2, e is infinite, and so the optimum tariff is zero on both of them. Only if B's supply curve is horizontal and C's is upward sloping could country A do best by putting a tariff on imports from C and not on those from B. These results are optimal for country A from its national standpoint rather than world welfare, and they ignore the possibility of retaliation.

Analogous conditions hold for exports. Acting purely in its own interests, and assuming that there are no distortions in any relevant market, a country should select a total export volume, and export destinations, to achieve equality between the following:

4   the social marginal utility of domestic consumption of exportables;
5   the social marginal cost of domestic production of exportables;
6   the social marginal revenue from exporting to each country or the most lucrative market.

If all the countries' demand curves for its exports are horizontal, this means setting the home price equal to the highest attainable export price. There should be no tax on exports. If countries' demand curves slope down, marginal revenue lies below the price obtained: the country has monopoly power. Exports should be taxed. The export tax should be non-discriminatory and set at a common rate for every overseas market, if foreign demand curves have the same price elasticity. Only if B's demand curve is horizontal and C's slopes down should an export tax be confined to exports to C.

We have seen that there can be conditions when it pays a country to impose different rates of tax on trade with different countries. But it will only be in a pure fluke that it is best to exempt some trading partners from such taxes. If the home country is small, it is best advised to trade freely with all countries. Furthermore, looking at the issue from the standpoint of world efficiency, there can be nothing but harm from a CU. Global free trade is best, where necessary supplemented by other types of intervention to remedy any distortion (such as an externality, missing market, or instance of imperfect competition) that may be present.

Is a CU ever an ideal device for a group of countries acting on their own? Despite the fact that it must infringe conditions for efficiency at the world level, it could be. Suppose that these countries have similar patterns of trade with the ROW. None on its own will be able to exert much influence on the terms of that trade. But if they are in concert and set their import tariffs and export taxes in unison, they can exploit their common monopsony and/or monopoly power to the full. One may think of the Organization of Petroleum Exporting Countries (OPEC) as a kind of CU which harmonizes its export taxes (on oil) to maximize joint 'profits' from oil sales. This type of CU will do much damage to excluded countries, except those that also sell oil. A CU may also be a convenient staging post on the road to free trade, where its members plan to bargain together for the removal of remaining trade barriers with other countries.

It might seem as if countries excluded from a CU can only lose from it. This is not so. They could even gain when the CU has adverse welfare effects on its own members. Suppose that C exports three goods before the CU is formed: x_1, produced under conditions of rising cost, and sold to both A and B; and x_2 and x_3, produced under constant returns, and sold to A and B respectively. In the CU, A buys x_2 from B instead; B is a much dearer source of supply, with a horizontal supply curve almost as high as A's pre-union tariff-inclusive price of x_2. Exactly the same is true of B with x_3. Both A and B suffer substantial trade diversion losses and negligible efficiency gains from lower home prices of x_2 and x_3. Thus they are both worse off in terms of overall welfare. C's exports of x_2 and x_3 vanish but it continues to sell x_1 to A and B (they cannot produce x_1 themselves).

For C to gain from improved terms of trade, all we need is a reason why A and B might buy more of x_1 after the CU is formed. There are several: x_1 could be inferior; it could be an input in the union's home industries producing x_2 and x_3, which expand their output; it could be complementary in demand with x_2 in A and x_3 in B; or the union's x_2 and x_3 industries might be intensive in a factor with a strong demand preference for x_1. So it is quite possible for a CU to be disadvantageous for its members and yet beneficial to the ROW. This is hardly likely, but it is conceivable. If that could happen, literally any pattern of national gains and losses is possible.

We turn now to consider four further points. These relate to complications introduced by

1 upward-sloping supply curves,
2 imperfect competition,
3 dynamic effects,
4 moving from partial to general equilibrium.

5.1.3 Customs Unions when Supply Curves Slope Up

In figures 5.1 and 5.2 B's and C's supply curves were drawn horizontal. Suppose that they are upward sloping and, for simplicity, identical. A, B, and C are the only three countries in the world. The good in question is not consumed in B or C, and not produced in A. Neither B nor C taxes or subsidizes its exports. Three regimes are compared: free trade, when A places no tariff on the good; a non-discriminatory tariff imposed at the specific rate t on imports from B and C; and a CU where A trades freely with its partner B and levies a tariff of t on imports from C.

The situation is illustrated in figure 5.3. The downward-sloping demand curve D_A is A's demand curve for imports. The steeper solid line represents the supply curve of B, and also C. Under free trade (FT), their combined supply is given by J_{FT}; p_0 will be the equilibrium price, and M_0 the total level of imports. The regime of non-discriminatory tariffs (NDT) levies a common tariff on imports from B and C. As A's residents see it, their supply curves are shifted from S_B (equivalently S_C) to S'_B (equivalently S'_C). The equilibrium price inside A is p'_1 and p_1 $(=p'_1 - t)$ is the price received by the exporters in B and C. The two countries'

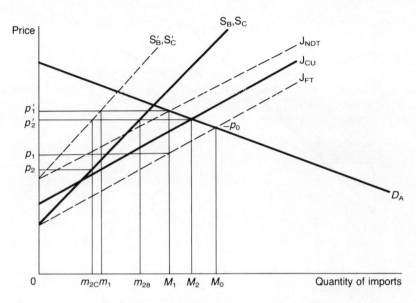

Figure 5.3 A customs union (CU), compared with regimes of free trade (FT) and non-discriminatory tariffs (NDT): price and trade effects.

combined supply curve, including the tariff, is J_{NDT}. Each country exports m_1; A's total imports are M_1.

With a CU the combined supply curve is J_{CU}. This adds S_B and S_C' horizontally. The price inside A and B is p_2'; C's exporters earn p_2. C's exports fall to m_{2C}, while B's advance to m_{2B}. A's total imports are M_2. Figures 5.4 and 5.5 show the effects that the move from non-discriminatory tariffs to CU will bring. Area a is a gain to A's consumers' surplus. Area b represents the gain to producers' surplus in B, and c is the loss in C's producers' surplus.

In figure 5.5, d is the transfer from A's government tariff revenue to A's consumers' surplus, while the triangle e represents the reduction in the deadweight loss associated with the fall in price from p_1' to p_2'. Area e is an unambiguous gain to potential welfare in A. Area f shows that part of the loss in A's government tariff revenue is attributable to the fact that the tariff is no longer levied on imports from B, while g is added to government revenue on the surviving imports from C. A's government therefore gains g and loses d ($= a - e$) and f. A's potential welfare increases by e and g, but falls by f. Since $e + g$ may exceed or fall short of f, the net welfare effect of the move is ambiguous. In this case, B gains and C loses. Both A and B could gain overall, of course, if we extend the analysis to consider a good which A exports to B: what B gains in figure 5.5 would then provide a measure of what A would gain, mostly in the form of increased producers' surplus, on that commodity.

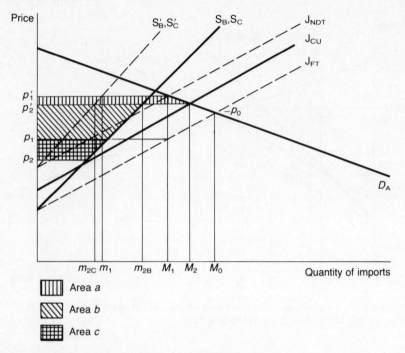

Figure 5.4   Effects of a move from non-discriminatory tariffs to a customs union on consumers' surplus at home and producers' surplus in the foreign countries.

5.1.4   Imperfect Competition and the Customs Union

In this section we explore some consequences of introducing imperfect competition. The CU offers new threats and opportunities once imperfect competition is allowed for. For a good produced under sharply increasing returns there is room for only one country to produce it after the union is formed. Corden (1972) provided the classic analysis of customs unions under conditions of increasing returns.

The chief threat for a CU member is that it may be forced to switch resources out of sectors with returns which increase relatively rapidly and, instead, export goods to its partner(s) where costs are constant or only slowly falling. Opportunities are provided by the increase in affordable varieties to consumers which are likely to emerge once the tariff on imports from its partner(s) is lifted. There is no simple way of resolving these effects a priori. If imperfect competition takes the form of oligopoly, consumers should gain from lower prices when partner firms gain easier access to the domestic market, and domestic firms' profits should improve as a result of increased sales in other parts of the CU. However, the CU governments lose tariff revenue when tariffs

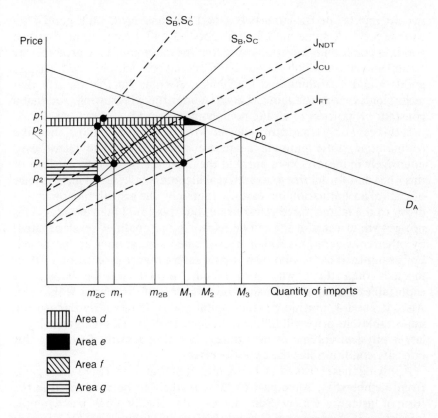

Figure 5.5 Effects of a move from non-discriminatory tariffs to a customs union on tariff revenue and the domestic deadweight.

against partner imports are removed. The net welfare change depends on the relative magnitudes of these effects. It is quite possible that the drop in tariff revenues swamps the gains to domestic consumers and firms' profits. Venables (1987) presents a thorough analysis of the factors at work here.

5.1.5 Dynamic Effects and General Equilibrium

We turn now to the possible dynamic effects of joining a CU. These are primarily of two kinds: learning by doing effects of the kind explored by Dasgupta and Stiglitz (1988), summarized in chapter 4, and other trade on growth effects. We shall discuss the second type here. What follows is a brief account of a most ingenious model due to Corden (1971), and a sketch of how it can be applied in the context of the CU.

Consider first a closed economy which produces four goods. The first two are inputs into the latter two. Good 3 is consumed, while good 4 is a capital good. Assume initially that goods 3 and 4 employ the first two goods in common proportions, and that the latter goods are produced by capital and labour alone. Goods 1 and 2 could be electricity and steel, and goods 3 and 4 clothing and machinery. Assume for the moment that technologies are unchanging, that the labour force is growing, and that a constant proportion of all the net incomes is saved.

If this economy is suddenly allowed to trade in goods 1 and 2, there is a comparative static jump in aggregate real income. The factor used intensively in imports loses out, but the other factor gains more. Part of this once and for all rise in overall real income is invested. Thus the pace of capital accumulation increases. Ultimately, the growth rate of capital drops to the labour force growth rate, but this could take decades. This pro-growth effect of trade can be reinforced or qualified (even negated) by other considerations which emerge when assumptions are modified. For example, if those who own capital save a higher proportion of their incomes than those who own labour, growth will be boosted if exportables are capital intensive and weakened if the reverse is the case. Also, if good 4, machinery (the capital good), is relatively intensive in importables, its price will fall, and the same level of real savings will buy a larger physical volume of investment, boosting growth. Reversing this intensity condition has the opposite effect.

Applying these ideas to a CU, we note first that, if there are static gains from membership, some part of these is likely to be dynamized in the form of faster investment. Static losses will probably show up as dynamic losses too: if the economy is impoverished by joining the CU, it cannot afford to save so much. If CU membership lowers the relative price of investment goods (likely if they, or key inputs into their production, are imported from partners), there will be a further boost to growth. If CU membership entails exporting more investment goods (or key inputs in their production) to partners, the opposite happens. Then there are income distribution effects to allow for, if the different groups in the population whose incomes are altered by CU membership differ in their marginal propensities to save.

We conclude this part of the chapter with a few qualifications relating to general equilibrium. Much of the analysis we have presented in this chapter has been based on partial equilibrium. For the most part, just a single market for importables has been examined. The concepts of trade creation and trade diversion emerge very clearly in this framework. They become buried in a welter of complex cross-effects once additional sectors are introduced. A reasonably full three-country model of a CU really calls for a minimum of six goods: three potential exports from the excluded country C plus one 'natural exportable' from both A and B, together with a non-traded good in each country. The resource allocation implications of the formation of a CU between A and B are much more intricate in a framework of this kind; analysis becomes difficult and results opaque. Nevertheless, there has been some excellent applied work in a general equilibrium setting. Miller and Spencer's (1977) study of the UK accession to the EC is probably the finest. They find that the welfare effects are dominated by the impact of the EC's Common Agricultural Policy (CAP), which is particularly adverse for the UK with its traditional reliance on imports of food from non-European sources.

5.2 The European Community

We begin with a brief review of the background to the formation of the EC. The European Economic Community (EEC) was established after France, West Germany, Italy, the Netherlands, Belgium, and Luxembourg, the original six members, signed the Treaty of Rome in 1957. The EC embraced the EEC and two other bodies, the European Coal & Steel Community (ECSC) and the Atomic Energy Community (Euratom), founded in 1952 and 1958 respectively. The UK, Ireland, and Denmark joined the EC in 1973, and were followed by Greece in 1980, and Spain and Portugal in 1986. At the time of writing, Turkey has applied to join, and Austria and Norway are expected to follow.

The structure of the EC is as follows. The Commission comprises 14 members appointed by member states for a four year term. It represents the EC at world meetings and initiates and executes EC policy. The Council consists of heads of state from all member governments. It shares executive power with the Commission. It can choose to adopt proposals made by the Commission in which case they become law but, in general, it cannot amend them. Each country had a right of veto, but, at the time of writing, it is being replaced by qualified majority voting. The Court of Justice interprets Community law. Its findings are binding, even on member governments. The judges are appointed by member states but cannot be removed by them. The European Parliament, first directly elected for five year terms in 1979, must be consulted by the Commission and the Council on most issues. It has the authority to dismiss the Commission *en masse*, and its consultative role is of growing importance.

The EC's share of world trade is 29 per cent if intra-EC trade is included and 17.5 per cent if intra-EC trade is excluded. Shares for the USA are 11.5 per cent and 13.5 per cent on these definitions. EC countries trade almost as much with each other as with the ROW.

Attempts have been made in a number of studies to measure the amount of trade creation and trade diversion arising from the formation of the EC. If we assume that trade created is $10 billion and trade diverted $1 billion at current 1989 prices, then the net gain would be $\frac{4}{3}$ per cent of the combined EC imports or some 0.4 per cent of Community gross national product (GNP). But this is *not* of course a satisfactory measure of net gains in the welfare sense: so many other factors need to be taken into account, as our discussion of the CAP, below, will make clear.

Estimates of the welfare gains suggest that they are less than 1 per cent of EC GNP, which is, of course, a large denominator, surpassing US national income at current exchange rates. These welfare estimates may appear low because the net gains from the formation of a CU primarily arise in connection with that part of its production which is traded internationally; less than one-sixth of total production actually leaves the EC. Also, there are few examples of very costly protection (in the efficiency sense) before the EC was formed: really large welfare gains would emerge only if the previous tariff regime was highly distortionary. Finally the measure is static, and ignores possible dynamic gains and the benefits of a larger market in stimulating further exploitation of economies of scale. It is also argued that the expansion of firms may promote research and development and strengthen their ability to compete in world markets. Other sources of gain include the enhanced mobility of factors of production and the fact that firms subject to greater competition from rivals in other member countries may be forced to lower prices and costs.

The Common Agricultural Policy

EC revenue comes mostly from its shares of receipts of value-added tax (up to 1.4 per cent) levied by member governments. Over two-thirds of the EC annual budget of some £25 billion goes to agriculture. The CAP was established in 1958 in order to protect the European farmer and to stimulate greater integration of Europe's economies. Most of the £25 billion meets the cost of buying up surpluses of products in excess supply, the prices of which are fixed, often above world levels. The welfare cost of these policies is large: studies reviewed by Winters (1987) give estimates in the region of £20 billion at current prices, representing some 0.7 per cent of the area's gross domestic product (GDP). The EC's CAP also entails redistribution between member countries. Those with above average shares of agriculture in GDP are most favoured. The heaviest burden falls on the UK and West Germany.

A simple partial equilibrium analysis of the welfare effects of the EC's CAP is shown in figure 5.6. The European authorities set an internal price of p_2 for domestic consumers and producers alike, although consumers will pay more because of distribution costs, a point ignored in this analysis. In figure 5.6, this is pitched at a point where domestic production outstrips domestic demand, as has been the case in many recent years for a wide range of foodstuffs including beef, dairy products, grain, and wine. We assume that European countries could buy

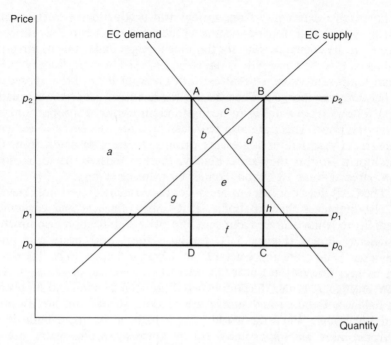

Figure 5.6   The welfare effects of the Common Agricultural Policy.

the good on international markets at a given price p_1. In the absence of policy intervention, figure 5.6 suggests that the EC area would have been a net importer.

The 'intervention' price of p_2 creates excess supply AB. This is stored and then destroyed or dumped on outside markets, such as the Soviet Union. In figure 5.6, the average price obtained from sales of intervention purchases is assumed to be p_0. Thus the rectangle ABCD represents the total financial cost of the scheme, to which, as we saw, the lion's share of the EC budget is devoted. If we contrast the CAP with a policy of free trade, consumers lose a surplus of $a + b + e + g + h$, while producers gain a surplus of $a + b + c$. In the short run, the producers' gain shows up in the form of improved employment or pay prospects for agricultural labour and farmers' incomes. Ultimately, much of it will be absorbed in higher rents on land. The consumers' surplus losses fall disproportionately on the poor, since the income elasticity of demand for food is low.

If we treat social welfare as the sum of consumers' and producers' surplus, net of financial costs, the total net cost of the policy equals $b + d + 2e + f + g + h$. In figure 5.6, this is approximately the same as the area of the revenue loss rectangle ABCD. This measure may exaggerate the true real resource cost of the policy if we argue that there is a favourable externality from agricultural production in Europe, or a social gain in transferring income to the poor or meritorious farmers. But there are cogent reasons for thinking it might understate it. First, the financial loss rectangle ABCD has to be financed by distortionary rather than lump sum taxes, so that extra deadweight losses are imposed on other domestic markets. Then there is the increased economic inequality that follows from a policy of taxing food purchased disproportionately from the poor. There are also rent-seeking costs, the costs of lobbying incurred by agricultural pressure groups, to be subtracted from the additional surplus they gain. Finally, there is massive fraud, recently estimated at some £8 billion, connected with the system.

The CAP does not just impose prices that usually exceed world levels, it also stabilizes them at home. Risk averse farmers and consumers benefit, to some degree, from this. But price stabilization also involves efficiency losses (Figure 5.7). Suppose the world price can jump anywhere, and quite unpredictably, in the range from p_2 to p_0. The CAP, let us say, freezes the European price at the average of these, p_1. For convenience, p_1 is also the point where European demand and supply are in balance. Demand and supply are random abroad but are assumed fixed at home. When the world price is high, at its upper limit of p_2, Europe loses an opportunity for producers' surplus gain, net of

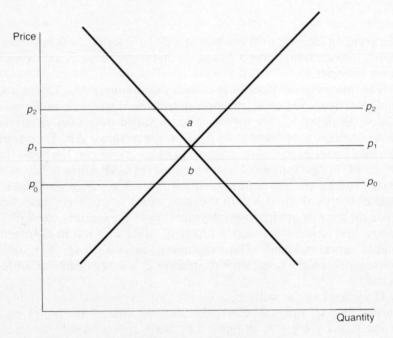

Figure 5.7   The simple welfare effects of price stabilization.

consumers' surplus lost, equal to area a. This is a simple partial equilibrium measure of the welfare cost of not letting domestic agents face the high world price. When the world price is at its lower limit p_0 Europe misses out on the chance of boosting consumers' surplus net of producers' surplus by area b. This figure suggests that European price stabilization can only do harm. While there are factors that qualify this, such as the welfare gains from more predictable prices if domestic consumers and producers are risk averse, there are others that reinforce it, such as the fact that prices outside the EC swing more violently because it refuses to align its domestic prices on them.

Finally, the CAP has increased world production and reduced world consumption of agricultural products. The EC is a 'large' country, which can and does influence its terms of trade. The effects of the CAP were reviewed in a recent IMF Report (1989). It was calculated that removal of the CAP would raise agricultural prices outside the EC by from 0.1 per cent for rice to 28 per cent for dairy products.

The European Community Internal Market, 1992

The Single European Act (SEA) was adopted by the governments of the EC in 1985. Its aim is the creation of a true common market with the free movement of goods, services, and factors of production within Europe by 1992. The key to this is the adoption, by 1992, of some 300 directives (identified by Lord Cockfield). A directive becomes European law once it is agreed by member states, and it is binding. All directives are to be implemented by 1 January 1993. By the end of 1988, about one-third of these directives had been agreed.

The 1992 programme as a whole is designed to remove all barriers to trade and to permit equal access in all European markets. The directives may be divided into three categories. The first group aim to remove physical barriers to trade, such as frontier formalities and lack of mutual recognition of qualifications of labour. A second group focuses on the removal of technical barriers, such as differences in product standards and requirements, patent law, and company law. Fiscal directives form a third group: the aim is to harmonize (but not equalize) rates of indirect taxation. There are also ancillary proposals to abolish remaining foreign exchange controls on the movement of capital, and open up public procurement of all EC firms.

The SEA is an attempt to succeed where the Treaty of Rome (1957) failed. Internal trade within the EC area is free of tariffs but frequently restricted by non-tariff barriers. Germany has traditionally banned imports of beer on the grounds that these did not meet its strict purity conditions, the French authorities require French degrees for senior positions and treat foreign ones as worthless, and all governments bias their purchases in favour of local suppliers. The SEA's directives, except those relating to fiscal matters, are to be adopted by a 'qualified majority' of ministers, rather than by unanimity. Individual member states no longer have the power of veto. The voting system is weighted by country size. Another change is the emphasis on 'mutual recognition' rather than 'harmonization' of laws within the EC. Until the SEA, changes in the Community were based on European legislation that attempted to achieve a harmony of member state laws. Each member state was required to enact identical laws that had been agreed at Community level. Proposals for change could be blocked by veto or threatened by obstruction in national parliaments.

The directives required to achieve a single internal market will be passed on the basis of mutual recognition. There will be basic standards set for all EC countries. Mutual recognition implies that goods legally produced in one member state will be given free access to markets in others, even though countries differ in standards applied in addition to the harmonized basic standards. For example, in the case of financial services, while there will be basic standards such as rules on capital adequacy, a firm recognized and supervised by the monetary authorities in one member state will be free to operate in others. Thus countries within Europe may have different laws and Europe's businesses and individuals will be able to choose the country with the most appealing set of regulations.

The shift in emphasis to mutual recognition is not without its problems, because it relies on a high degree of trust among member states. For example, in the case of regulation of financial services, the UK has expressed concern over the less stringent supervision of securities firms in certain EC countries. Yet firms licensed to operate in one state may set up and operate in London, where domestic firms must conform to tighter regulations.

Cecchini (1988), in a study funded by the Commission, estimated that the completion of the internal market will give rise to a gain of about 4.5 per cent in EC GDP. This includes:

1.5 per cent from freer trade in financial services,
0.5 per cent from the removal of frontier controls,
2 per cent from improved competitiveness, economies of scale, and general supply side effects.

The Cecchini Report consisted of ten detailed volumes of research. Its findings are summarized in a short volume (Cecchini, 1988). A more detailed account is provided by Emerson et al. (1989), while Pelkmans and Winters (1988) and the Economic Policy Symposium (1989) offer the benefit of independent scrutiny and assessment of the issues involved. Although the Cecchini Report's claims about the GDP effects of the SEA programme have been disputed (we incline to the view that they are more likely to be in the 2–2.5 per cent range), it is important to explain them.

The gains in the area of financial services come largely from the beneficial output effects expected to follow the removal of the present controls on the movement of capital within the EC region. France, Greece, Italy, Spain, and Portugal currently use a battery of devices to discourage exports of capital by domestic residents. The UK also did this for 65 years until 1979, and the Belgium–Luxembourg monetary union has long employed a separate exchange rate for capital movements (the 'financial' Belgian franc) that has some similar effects. If capital is not allowed to move between countries, it may earn higher returns in some places than in others. Under ideal conditions, letting it migrate should even up the rate of profit. Output should rise more where capital expands than it falls in regions that export capital, as chapter 6 illustrates in more detail.

Hand in hand with gains of this kind come the more specific benefits claimed to follow from allowing cross-border intra-European trade in financial products. For example, mortgages, large scale equity transactions, and life insurance are relatively cheap in the UK, company overdrafts and loans in West Germany, and personal loans and house insurance in France. The authors of the Cecchini Report assumed that introducing genuinely free trade in such products would 'even down' prices to the average cheapest four of the current 12 members of the EC. This would bring large gains to households and companies that purchase financial products and force the less efficient financial intermediaries currently insulated from international competition to reduce their costs or quit.

Our doubts about these claims centre on three points. First, current prices of financial products in particular markets may be distorted by credit rationing and regulatory controls, and serve as an unreliable basis for predicting trade patterns and prices in their absence. Second, borrowers and lenders build up long-term relationships of trust with their financial institutions. This makes entry by newcomers, especially foreign newcomers, a slow process. A bank accepting loan applications in an unfamiliar environment is all too likely to attract dud business from potential borrowers whom existing local banks knew enough to turn down! Third, even if financial intermediaries succeed in penetrating each others' home geographical markets, it is far from clear that they will necessarily compete effectively, rather than evolve some form of tacit collusion at higher prices.

Some of the benefits from the removal of border controls are easier to quantify. Real resources are wasted in the form of labour and capital expended in maintaining customs offices, for example. More important, border delays mean idle time for trucks and drivers; there are time-consuming customs documents to fill in; and potentially beneficial trade opportunities between EC countries are sacrificed as firms decide that it is easier to sell at home. Sceptics would point out that, if border controls are retained on trade with non-EC countries, trade may be as much diverted as created when they are removed on internal frontiers. The UK government is alarmed that it will be harder to monitor or prevent the movement of an assortment of unwelcome undesirables, such as criminals, terrorists, rabid animals, and illegal migrants.

The Cecchini Report suggested that the largest source of gain is in the areas of public procurement, increased competition deemed to follow from the imposition of mutual standards recognition rules, and the elimination of non-tariff barriers on intra-EC trade. As in financial services, the Report assumed that the prices of affected goods will fall to the average of the lowest currently prevailing in the EC, generating large gains in consumers' surplus. Firms with unit costs above this level are assumed to increase productivity and cut their costs in line, implying further real resource gains. There is also a third effect, as the structure of European industry is rationalized to permit greater exploitation of economies of scale. Public procurement will be opened up by the adoption of rules to ensure that firms in other EC countries get equal access to tendering opportunities issued by public agencies anywhere in the EC.

However, one must have doubts over the enforceability of new rules on public procurement and the complex and vexatious issue of how to treat imports by, and affiliates of, non-EC companies. Car imports from Japan, for example, are currently limited to 3 per cent of the French market and barely 1 per cent of the Italian market. These countries' governments are worried that other EC countries such as Denmark and the Netherlands impose no quota or 'voluntary restraint' on Japanese car imports. The Mediterranean governments are therefore pressing for tight EC quotas to protect (or continue to protect) their domestic producers, while smaller north European members complain that choice and surplus for their consumers will be reduced. There is pressure to adopt 'reciprocity' conditions in the treatment of non-EC companies. That could mean subjecting US banks or Japanese electronics companies to non-EC restrictions similar to those operating in the USA on European banks or in Japan on European electronics companies. These issues have yet to be resolved. There are widespread fears that the EC could adopt a posture of 'Fortress Europe' that could entail large welfare losses from reduced trade with North America and Japan and a fall in European exports to these countries. What the EC could gain, on balance, from freer internal trade could easily be offset if extra-EC trade were cut back.

Smith and Venables (1988) used a trade model with imperfect competition to evaluate the effects of a reduction in trade barriers between EC member states and the effects of an end to price discrimination by firms in EC markets. The model carried out simulation exercises for 11 industries in six EC countries for each policy change. Various assumptions are made about the entry and exit of firms and the degree of product variation. They reported that the ratio of welfare gain to trade created ranges from 0.8 to 22 per cent when the number of firms is variable. The second policy, that of forcing firms to behave as if Europe were a single market (elimination of price discrimination), showed large welfare gains, ranging from 0.02 to 1.31 per cent depending on the industry.

Butt Philip (1988) identified many obstacles to the achievement of a single European market by 1992. While the Council of Ministers may be able to speed up its decision making with the introduction of a qualified majority vote, its decisions may not be implemented if the national governments are reluctant to accept them. There have been many problems related to **implementation** of directives, well documented in the Butt Philip paper. In the period 1982–6, the Commission issued 2,097 letters of formal notice to member governments indicating that breaches of EC law were suspected and 325 references to the European Court of Justice were made in pursuit of offenders. Butt Philip identified Italy, France, Belgium, and Greece as the worst offenders between 1981 and 1985. Also, even though member states may adopt an EC law, they may give it a low enforcement profile with minimal sanctions for non-observance. Butt Philip found that the policy areas essential to the creation of a single integrated market (liberalization, competition policy, and harmonization) are those where implementation is particularly difficult.

Finally, the SEA is aimed at removing all barriers to trade in goods, services, and factors within Europe, but it does not address several important issues within the EC which, if not resolved, may inhibit the achievement of a single European market. These include the CAP, the debate about the size, contribution, and control of the European budget, and competition policy.

5.3 Other Trade Organizations and Trade Agreements

While the EC is the most important form of trade integration observed since the Second World War, there are other trade organizations. These include the Latin American Integration Association (LAIA), which embraces Argentina, Bolivia, Brazil, Chile, Colombia, Ecuador, Mexico, Paraguay, Peru, Uruguay, and Venezuela, and Sovjet Ekonomicheskoi Vzaimopomoshchi (SEV), known in English as the Council for Mutual Economic Assistance or COMECON, comprising the USSR, Bulgaria, Cuba, Czechoslovakia, East Germany, Hungary, Mongolia, Poland, Rumania, and Vietnam. There is also the European Free Trade

Association (EFTA), comprising Austria, Finland, Iceland, Norway, Sweden, and Switzerland, and, until they joined the EC, Denmark, the UK, and Portugal; the Association of South East Asian Nations (ASEAN), including Indonesia, Malaysia, the Philippines, Singapore, and Thailand; the Central American Common Market (ODECA), including El Salvador, Guatemala, Honduras, and Nicaragua; and the Caribbean Community (CARICOM), with 12 former UK territories in the region. Mention should also be made of the extensive set of bilateral trade agreements between the EC and many African and other primary producing and developing countries (most of them former British and French possessions) ratified at the Yaounde and Lome Conventions.

The General Agreement on Tariffs and Trade (GATT) was formed in the immediate post-war period with the objective of liberalizing trade between nations party to the agreement. The Kennedy Round (1962–7) saw large cuts in tariffs, averaging about one-third, in non-socialist countries. The Tokyo Round (1973–9) ended in an agreement to reduce tariffs further (by 34 per cent on manufactures by 1987) and deal with the problem of non-tariff barriers. GATT has succeeded in reducing tariffs on complex manufactured goods and raw materials in developed countries. The average level of nominal tariffs (as opposed to effective rates, discussed in chapter 3) on manufactured trade fell dramatically in the post-war period, from 40 per cent in 1947 to less than 10 per cent in 1974, to between 5 per cent and 6 per cent in 1979, and to about 4 per cent by 1988. However, there are still substantial barriers to trade in agriculture, services, and textiles. For example, the Multifibre Arrangement is a bilateral trade agreement involving country by country quotas on textile imports.

It is hoped that the current Uruguay Round (to 1990), in which 105 countries are participating, will tackle some of these trade barriers. The current negotiations are hampered by differences in opinion over agricultural subsidies and trade in intellectual property. It should also be stressed that progress in reducing tariffs has been far less marked in many developing countries than in developed Western Economies and that, for every two steps forward in tariff cuts, there has typically been one step backward in the form of covert non-tariff barriers.

The Canada–USA Trade Pact was reached in October 1987 and is a bilateral free trade agreement. Either country can withdraw from the agreement after notification of six months. The agreement does not exempt Canada from the Comprehensive Trade Act passed by the US Congress in 1988, designed to permit swift retaliation to any government policy that discriminates against US exports. However, the Pact will allow for arbitration on trade disputes between Canada and the USA. Its objective is to dismantle trade barriers between the countries. Specifically, it is to discourage government purchases of national products and liberalize trade in farm products and services, and Canada is to relax its foreign direct investment rules.

5.4 Conclusions

Economic integration occurs when a group of countries removes barriers against trade between them. When they set common restrictions against imports from excluded countries, the free trade area becomes a CU. A country *may* be better off in a CU than if it applies non-discriminatory tariffs against all other countries: trade is created with partner countries. But trade is also diverted from lower cost sources outside the union. If the country and the union are small, it must be better off trading freely with everyone than retaining barriers against non-union imports. CUs typically violate optimum sourcing of imports for large countries, and must do so for small ones. If countries A and B form a CU and C is excluded, all combinations of welfare gain and loss are possible: a case can be found where C gains and A and B both lose!

The most thoroughgoing CU today is the EC. This union seems to have created more trade than it has diverted, at least in the realm of manufactures. Agricultural policy has been highly protectionist and wasteful, however. Internal trade in manufactures and services is still impeded by various remaining barriers, despite the fact that tariffs have disappeared; the SEA is designed to ensure their removal by 1992.

A CU affects resource allocation within its borders in many ways. There may be significant changes in technology or migration of factors of production. The next chapter is devoted to exploring the effects of changes in factor endowments and technology in an international context.

6

Trade, Factor Movements, and Technical Change

In previous chapters we looked at trade and resource allocation in economies endowed with given supplies of factors of production, and whose firms employ a given technology. What happens when the supply of these factors changes? In this chapter we examine the effects of this, first in the context of purely domestic developments (section 6.1) and then when factors migrate from one country to another (section 6.2). How are trade, factor prices, output patterns, and welfare affected by changes in technology? This is the subject matter of section 6.3. While earlier chapters established how a country's terms and volume of trade are determined at a single point in time, this chapter addresses the broader long-run setting, and immediately raises the question of what determines the **time path** in the prices of the countries' exports and imports. Some countries import raw materials and export manufactured commodities and services produced, in part, from them; other countries do the opposite. So both sets of countries will be concerned with the trends of prices of primary products, and particularly the price of oil. Section 6.4 is devoted to investigating these.

6.1 Factor Endowment Changes

6.1.1 Capital Increases in a Small Economy

What happens to a country's pattern of production if its factor endowments change? Consider the simplest case: the country is small, so that the prices of the goods are fixed by conditions in the rest of the world; it produces two goods a and b using two factors of production K and N; production functions for the two goods are given and display constant returns to scale. There is perfect competition. The factors K and N are mobile between the domestic industries but not across international boundaries, and their total supplies are given. Suddenly the endowment of the factors, K let us say, rises, while the other is unchanged. What effects will this have?

Rybczynski (1955) showed that under these circumstances more of the relatively capital-intensive good will be produced. This is hardly surprising. However, Rybczynski also demonstrated that the output of the labour-intensive good will go down absolutely. Put another way, a small country which loses some of its labour force will experience an absolute increase in its output of the relatively capital-intensive good. How and why do these consequences follow?

The key idea is that neither industry's capital–labour ratio k_i, i = a, b changes. So k_a and k_b remain the same. This is because the wage–rent ratio w/r does not change and so producers have no incentive to alter the proportions in which capital and labour are hired. Given constant returns to scale and perfect competition, k_a and k_b depend on w/r and on nothing else. The reason that w/r remains the same is that the country is small: thus the price ratio p_a/p_b for the two goods is unchanged. Only changes in supply and demand conditions abroad can alter it; because the home country is a price taker in world markets, changes in domestic factor endowments have no impact on it. Provided that p_a/p_b is unchanged, and given no change in firms' production functions in the two industries (we are not considering the consequences of technical progress, for example) k_a and k_b are unchanged.

How is the extra capital endowment in the economy to be accommodated? The additional total stock of capital, dK^e let us call it, has to equal the sum of increases in the capital stocks employed in the two sectors:

$$dK^e = dK_a + dK_b \qquad (6.1)$$

Now the increase (or fall) in capital employed in a (or b) will be related to the increase (or fall) in labour employed in a (or b):

$$dK_a = k_a dN_a$$

$$dK_b = k_b dN_b \qquad (6.2)$$

Equations (6.2) hold because k_a and k_b are unchanged, for reasons already discussed. Since the economy's labour force has not changed, the rise in employment in one sector must be offset by a fall in employment in the other:

$$dN_a = - dN_b \qquad (6.3)$$

Putting (6.1), (6.2), and (6.3) together, we find that

$$dK^e = (k_a - k_b) dN_a \qquad (6.4)$$

This tells us that employment in industry a goes up if and only if k_a exceeds k_b, that is, if and only if a is more capital intensive than b. Furthermore, given constant returns to scale, the two industries' production functions can be written as

$$Q_a = N_a f(k_a)$$

$$Q_b = N_b g(k_b)$$

(6.5)

Since k_a and k_b are locked, (6.5) implies that

$$dQ_a = dN_a f(k_a)$$

$$dQ_b = dN_b g(k_b)$$

(6.6)

Now (6.4), (6.3), and (6.6) yield

$$dQ_a = \frac{f(k_a)dK^e}{k_a - k_b}$$

(6.7)

$$dQ_b = \frac{-g(k_b)dK^e}{k_a - k_b}$$

Equations (6.7) establish our results: if k_a exceeds k_b (so that a is relatively capital intensive), an increase in the economy's total endowment of capital raises the output of a and cuts the output of b. The output of the capital-intensive sector rises, and that of the labour-intensive sector falls absolutely.

Figure 6.1 illustrates these findings geometrically. An addition to the economy's capital stock elongates the dimension of its factor endowment Edgeworth box. The origin for sector b shifts up from 0_b to $0_b'$. The ray $0_a ED$ shows the capital–labour ratio in sector a; the steeper rays from the top right-hand corners 0_b and $0_b'$ of the box have gradients equal to the capital–labour ratio in industry b (k_b). In figure 6.1, it is b which is assumed to be relatively capital intensive. $0_b D$ and $0_b'E$ are parallel, reflecting the fact that k_b is unchanged.

Perfect competition entails the full utilization of the available factor endowments K^e and N^e. So point D gives the allocation of factors before the rise in capital; after capital jumps by dK^e, the new allocation point is E. The labour-intensive sector a shrinks its employment, capital, and output in equal proportions. Industry a retreats from D to E. Figure 6.2 illustrates these changes in commodity space. The original production

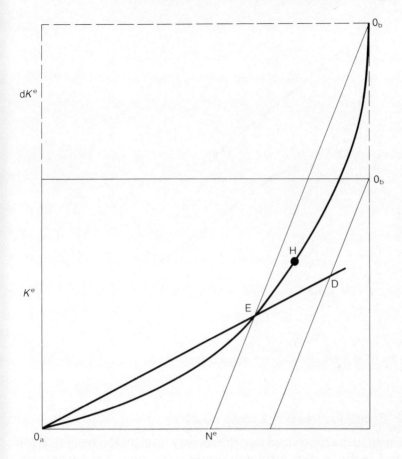

Figure 6.1   The Rybczynski effect in factor space.

possibility frontier (PPF) is XY. The increase in the economy's endowment of capital raises the maximum amount of a that could be produced (the horizontal intercept) from Y to Y', and the highest possible output of b rises from X to X'. The second increase is proportionately larger than the first, reflecting the fact that capital is a more important factor of production in capital-intensive industry b than in a. The pattern of production shifts from R to S, on the new PPF $X'Y'$. R corresponds to D in figure 6.1, and S to E. The shift from R to S leads to a large rise in the output of b and an absolute decline in the production of a. If the home country exports good a, these developments will reduce its trade: if it imports a, its foreign trade will increase sharply.

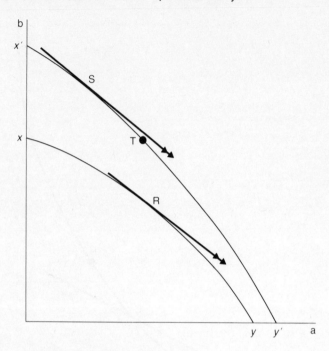

Figure 6.2   The Rybczynski effect in commodity space.

6.1.2   Capital Increases in a Large Economy

Up to now we have assumed that the country is small, too small to affect its terms of trade. We also have assumed that capital and labour are internally mobile. These two assumptions will now be relaxed separately, in this section and the next. If a large country accumulates additional capital, there will be a worldwide fall in the price of its capital-intensive product (good b in figures 6.1 and 6.2). The price of a will rise in terms of b. So there will be a southeastward movement along the new PPF $X'Y'$ towards a point such as T. The net result could involve higher output of a than before: this will happen if there is a large enough fall in p_b/p_a. In figure 6.1, the allocation of factors of production moves northeastwards along the new contract curve from 0_a through E to $0_b'$. For example, the new equilibrium corresponding to T might well be at H. Notice that both industries a and b have become more capital intensive than they were at E or D. What this tells us is that there must be a fall in the rental on capital, and a rise in the wage rate, as the economy shifts along the new contract curve from E to H. The terms of trade will improve if the country exports good a and worsen if it exports b.

6.1.3 Labour Increases with Sector-specific Capital

How will the analysis change if the assumption of perfect internal factor mobility is relaxed? Suppose now that it is the economy's endowment of labour which increases. Let labour be freely mobile between the two industries, but suppose that capital is not. The two sectors a and b both have arbitrarily fixed allocations of capital. What will happen in these circumstances is that the extra labour will find employment in both industries at the cost of a fall in the wage rate. Rates of profit on the sector-specific capital stocks in each sector will be bid up. Both industries will increase output, and in the same proportion if their elasticities of

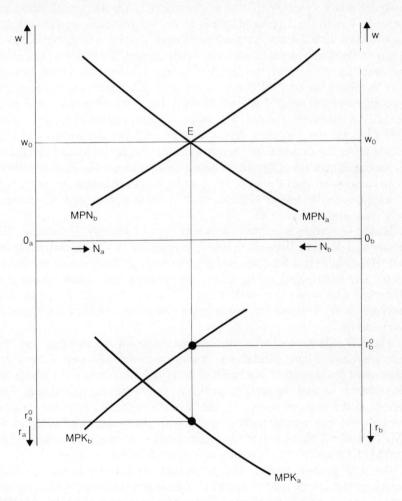

Figure 6.3 Employment and factor prices when capital is sector specific.

supply are the same. If the country's export industry has a lower (higher) supply elasticity than its import competing industry, its volume of exports is likely to go down (increase). If the country is large, its terms of trade will then tend to improve (worsen); if it is small, the terms of trade will of course remain unchanged. The ideas on which the argument of this section is based have already been encountered in chapter 2. They owe much to Neary (1978).

The effects on employment, wage rates, and capital rentals of an increase in the economy's labour force are shown in figure 6.3. The upper half of the diagram depicts the labour market before the labour force rise occurs. Employment in sector a is measured rightwards from 0_a, and that in b leftwards from 0_b. Total employment is the horizontal distance between 0_a and 0_b. The wage rate is measured vertically upwards. Each sector has a diminishing marginal product of labour curve (MPN), based upon its fixed allocation of sector-specific capital. Since labour is mobile between the two sectors, the forces of competition establish a single wage rate w_0 where the two MPN curves cut at E. The vertical axes below the two employment origins 0_a and 0_b show the rates of profit, or capital rentals, in the two industries. The two marginal product of capital curves (MPK) slope the way they do because an increase in employment in a sector raises the demand for, and reward to, the capital stock fixed there. Since the allocation of capital between the two sectors is arbitrary, there is no reason why the rates of profit r_a and r_b will be the same. In figure 6.3, r_a happens to be higher than r_b, just because it has been allocated a relatively low capital stock.

If the economy's labour force is now suddenly increased, the horizontal distance between 0_a and 0_b is enlarged. This is shown in figure 6.4. Here, the origin for b, 0_b, is shifted to the right from its old value at 0_b to $0_b'$. The MPN_b and MPK_b curves are repositioned rightwards by this distance. The wage rate falls from w_0 to w_1. The MPN curves now intersect at E'. The rates of profit in the two sectors climb from r_a^0 and r_b^0 to r_a^1 and r_b^1.

The key differences between the sector-specific capital case and the previous case where capital was mobile between the two sectors are illustrated in figure 6.5. We begin at an initial equilibrium E_0, where the wage rate is w_0 and the rates of profit on capital are equalized at r_0. The labour force then increases by the distance $0_b0_b'$. With sector-specific capital, the new equilibrium is at E_1, with the wage rate falling to w_1 (MPN_b and MPK_b shift from the solid curves to the broken lines MPN_b^1 and MPK_b^1 respectively). Employment in both industries rises.

But with mobile capital, and given that the country is small, factor prices remain unchanged at w_0 and r_0. The new equilibrium is at E_2 for the labour market and F_2 for capital. Industry a loses capital (shifting MPN_a left) and labour (shifting MPK_a left), reflecting an assumption for the

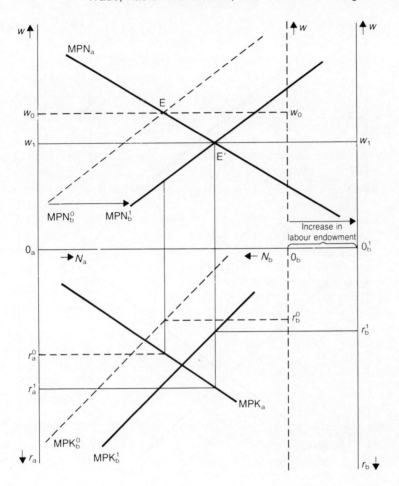

Figure 6.4   The effects of an increase in the labour force in the sector-specific capital model.

purposes of this figure that a is capital intensive. Capital and labour both transfer towards sector b, the labour-intensive industry, which also of course absorbs the additional labour $0'_b0_b$. The MPN and MPK curves are interdependent and are propelled leftwards to MPN^2_a and MPK^2_a. There is no downward pressure on wage rates; nor any upward pressure on rates of profit. Such developments are negated because the economy adjusts to the additional labourers by expanding its labour-intensive industry and contracting its capital-intensive one.

Few economies provide historical examples of very large sudden changes in capital or labour endowments. The exception to this is afforded by the instance of Portugal, which received nearly 700,000

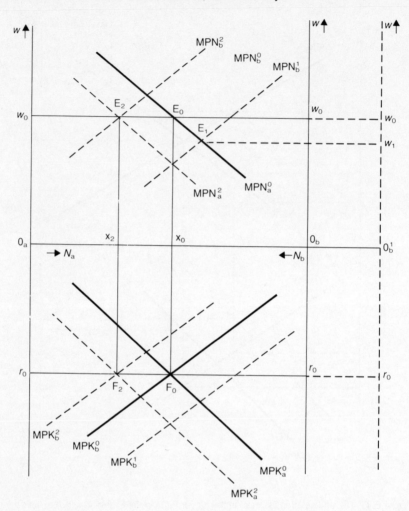

Figure 6.5   The effects of more labour: sector specific and mobile capital compared.

'retornados' from its former African colonies in 1974–5. This represented a large increase of a tenth or so in its potential labour force. Although there could be other explanations, the Portuguese economy suffered a massive jump in unemployment shortly afterwards. This suggests that a wage cut would have been required for the retornados to have gained employment. It accords with the predictions of the sector-specific model if the reduction in wage rates that was required for full employment was obstructed by trade unions or legal restrictions.

6.2 International Capital Movements

In section 6.1 we examined the effects of an increase in an economy's capital stock or labour force. The change in its factor endowments was treated as a single isolated event. It is the purpose of this section to study what happens when capital moves from one economy to another, and also to explore why this could happen and what reasons the governments of the two countries might have to welcome or prevent it. For a more detailed treatment of the analysis readers are referred to MacDougall (1969) or Sinclair (1983). Although this section examines the effects of international migration of capital, very similar consequences would follow if it were labour, rather than capital, that moved between countries: all we would need to do would be to replace 'capital' by 'labour' and 'rate of profit' by 'wage rate'.

6.2.1 A Simple Model

We begin by stipulating a number of assumptions.

1   Each economy produces a single good.
2   Each country's output Q_i increases with its capital stock K_i and its labour force N_i. There are constant returns to scale, and the marginal products of the two factors are diminishing; an increase in one factor raises the marginal product of the other. There is no depreciation.
3   There is perfect competition: factors are rewarded by their marginal products, there are no externalities, prices adjust instantly to clear all markets, and there is perfect information and perfect foresight.
4   There is no tax, such as corporation tax, on capital.
5   The levels of technology in each country are given, and the labour forces are given.
6   Each country's social welfare is captured simply by its national product, that is, by its domestic output plus any net income from overseas net assets.
7   International capital movements are initially prevented and then suddenly allowed to proceed costlessly and unhindered.

Before capital is allowed to move across international boundaries, rates of profit on capital will only be equal in the different countries by fluke. If one country's residents have repeatedly saved more than another's, they are likely to have accumulated more capital. All else equal, a capital-rich country will have a low rate of profit. Perfect competition ensures that the rate of profit on capital in each country will equal its marginal

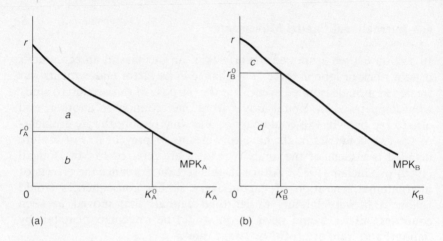

Figure 6.6   Initial capital stocks and rates of profit in two countries.

product. Since there is no depreciation, the rate of profit in a country will also equal the (real) rate of interest there. The fact that the marginal product of capital is diminishing (assumption 2) means that a larger volume of capital must imply a lower rate of interest. This point is illustrated in figure 6.6. Figure 6.6(a) shows the capital stock K_A^0 in country A and the rate of profit r_A^0 ruling there; corresponding values for country B are shown in figure 6.6(b). The downward sloping curves MPK_A and MPK_B represent the marginal products of capital in the two countries. The areas b and d show the total earnings of capital in A and B. Areas a and c represent incomes accruing to labour in the two countries; the areas under the MPK curve ($a + b$ for A, $c + d$ for B) will equal the levels of domestic output.

What happens if the barrier to international capital mobility is suddenly removed? Capital must flow from A, where it earns less, to B, where it is paid more. International capital movements continue in this two-country case until a common rate of profit, or interest, is established at r^1, illustrated in figure 6.7. Country A exports capital until K_A, the capital stock located in A, shrinks to K_A^1. Country B imports it until K_B has swelled to K_B^1. The fall in A's stock, $K_A^0 - K_A^1$, matches the rise in B's, $K_B^1 - K_B^0$. What effects does this have?

Domestic output in A falls by the areas $g + k$. Domestic output increases in B by the areas $n + q$. Since $q = h + g + k > g + k$, world output goes up. The increase in total output, in the two countries combined, is equal to $n + h$. But A's national product does not go down. Its residents own the new capital in B ($K_B^1 - K_B^0$) and earn r^1 on it. So area q represents the flow of income they will receive in the form of interest,

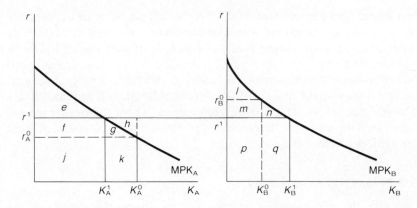

Figure 6.7   International capital movements: rates of profit equalize.

profits, and dividends on their overseas assets. Consequently A's national product rises by q, less the fall in domestic output $g + k$: area h represents the rise in A's national product. In B, national product also increases but only by n because area q is paid abroad.

The capital located in A, now K_A^1, earns the same rate of profit as it would abroad, and so total profits on this will be $f + j$. What is left out of the value of A's domestic output (area e) is paid to labour. So labour loses out in country A. It suffers a fall in income of areas $f + g$. By contrast, the capital-receiving country B sees a gain to its workers of areas $m + n$. B's domestic capitalists are the losers here: they suffer an income loss of m. Since each country's social welfare simply equals its national product (assumption 6), we can say that both countries gain unambiguously from this international relocation of capital. Welfare rises in A by h, in B by n.

The transfer of capital from A to B could take either of two forms. There could be direct investment by A's residents in B. Firms in A would set up plants in country B: factories, processing and distribution centres, buildings, and infrastructural assets such as railways, highways, electrical and telephone networks. Alternatively residents in A could acquire title to existing assets in B – shares and bonds for example, which could drive up their price, cutting the cost of capital faced by residents in B. B's firms and households would respond by adding to their stocks of capital, now that the cost of capital was lower. They would face an incentive to adopt more capital-intensive techniques of production since capital was cheaper (and labour there would become more expensive). In this second case, it would be portfolio investment by residents in A which would provide the vehicle of capital transfer. In country A in the meantime, upward pressure on the cost of capital would discourage investment; asset prices would fall; there would probably be a protracted phase during which capital would be allowed to wear out without being replaced (once depreciation is allowed for), or at least the capital stock would grow more slowly than population. Country A's investment goods industries would not necessarily suffer a dramatic loss of business, however: they might find that the investment boom in B provided a new overseas market for their products to compensate for the weaker market at home. The economic determinants of foreign direct investment form the subject of chapter 7.

6.2.2 Relaxing Assumptions

Consider the consequences of relaxing the assumptions made at the beginning of section 6.2.1. If we introduce more than one product in each country, relaxing assumption (1), we notice that the Heckscher–Ohlin trade model could allow for equalization of capital rental and rates of profit and interest without the need for international capital movements. B could compensate for its low endowment of capital by concentrating on the production of labour-intensive goods, while A did the opposite and used its plentiful supply of capital to export capital-intensive ones. Under rather restrictive conditions, we saw in chapter 2 that free trade could equalize factor prices. However, even a cursory glance at international statistics reveals huge international discrepancies in wage rates and often large ones, too, in rates of profit and capital rentals. So there still seems to be room for worldwide production gains from allowing international migration of capital.

Assumption (2) could be relaxed to introduce depreciation, the only effect of which (in a one-product competitive world) would be to drive a wedge between the marginal product of capital and the rate of profit on one side, and the real rate of interest on the other. The cost of capital would have to include depreciation as well as interest. Nothing else of substance would change. Introducing a third factor, such as land, could introduce the possibility (not perhaps a large one) that the marginal product of either labour or land (not both) could be reduced, not increased, by a rise in the supply of capital. In this event, labour in A might not suffer a fall in its equilibrium wage, and labour in B might not experience a rise.

It is relaxing the third assumption which opens up the largest set of alternative possibilities. If market imperfections broke the link between factors' marginal products and their rewards, the equalization of rates of profit to which international capital mobility should lead would not bring capital's marginal products together. World productive efficiency calls for an equalization of the marginal product of capital (given that it is declining); therefore free international capital movements would fail to achieve their desirable outcome. If there were externalities which created a gap between the private and social marginal products of capital, free capital movements would equate the private but not the social marginal product, unless the externalities happened to be similar in the two countries. In both these circumstances, a policy of allowing unimpeded international capital movements on their own would not be ideal; other measures would have to be taken to rectify the market imperfections, and without these measures welfare could be even lower than before. If prices adjust sluggishly and fail to clear markets instantly, the spectre of unemployment raises itself in the capital-exporting country A. If the real wage paid to labour is stuck at its old high value, the fall in the demand for labour will be registered in rising unemployment. The unemployment may be reinforced by the adverse aggregate demand implications of a period of protracted disinvestment.

Assumption (3) also stipulated perfect information. Repealing this feature of perfect competition introduces the important possibility that investors can make mistakes. Capital might move so as to equate *expected* returns in the two countries, but there is nothing now to ensure that these expected returns materialize. A's investors who form or buy capital in B may get it wrong. Their investments may prove unlucky. In this event they will not earn a profit flow of area q in figure 6.7, but something less than that. So A's national product could fall, not rise. Furthermore, once risk and uncertainty are allowed for, attitudes to risk matter too. Expected returns on capital in A and B are only equalized if investors (or enough of them) are neutral to risk. Risk aversion would suggest higher expected returns in one country if investment there were thought to be riskier. Moreover, imperfect information may mean asymmetric information. B's residents may know more about the economic prospects in their own country than A's. An owner of a particular firm in B may have private information about what is likely to happen to it, for example. This will make him keen to sell his business to those who are less informed. The companies that come up for sale in B to A's residents may be 'lemons'. If the buyers in B do not realize this, they will not earn as much as q on their investment. If they appreciate the risks of this, they will be wary of transferring capital to B in the first place, and the seeming gains from international capital movements simply will not occur.

The introduction of any tax on capital, such as corporation tax, also complicates matters. The significance of taxes levied by A's and B's governments is that capital should flow to equalize net of tax expected rates of return. Unless the tax rates are the same, this will not imply equality of gross of tax returns, and it is to the latter that marginal products of capital will be linked. There is also a further point. A's residents will not care much, as individuals, which government levies tax on their income: the net income is what will interest them. If capital transfers from A to B, the proceeds of the tax on the yield on that capital are likely to travel with them. This gives B's government a greater benefit from attracting capital: some of the area q will stay at home. But A's government will lose revenue.

Capital is often sunk. Commitments are irreversible. What this means is that governments may have an incentive to spring surprise increases in tax on investors once they have committed themselves. Assets could even be expropriated. Governments' promises not to do this may not be credible. This suggests that internationally mobile capital may gravitate towards countries with a long-established reputation for light taxes and where governments keep their word. This may well not be where capital is most needed.

Relaxing assumption (5) introduces the possibility that migrating capital could take technical knowhow or workers with it. Such effects, especially the prospect of technology transfer, could make foreign capital more attractive to the country that imports it, although overseas technology might be inappropriate in local conditions. If social welfare is no longer synonymous with national income (relaxing assumption 6), the international movement of capital would be less beneficial, or even harmful, to the capital exporter who weights wages more heavily than profits – recall that the wage rate in A is bid down as the capital stock shrinks. B will treat it as a mixed blessing, or even a curse, if B's social welfare function is tilted in favour of domestic capitalists.

6.2.3 Long-term Dynamics

Up to this point we have not explored the forces governing the evolution of capital stocks in either of our economies. The initial stocks of capital, at the moment before capital movements were introduced, have been assumed to be given. The time has come to examine why they are, what they are, and to see what may happen subsequently to each country's net assets.

Continue to assume that technology and the labour force are given. Let us focus attention on the evolution of consumption and capital in each economy before the movement of capital between them is permitted. Consumption displays an upward trend over time if the rate of interest exceeds the rate at which utility from postponed consumption is discounted – the rate of 'impatience'. If impatience exceeds interest, consumption will be high to start with but falling; if interest exceeds impatience, consumption will be growing from a low initial base. Capital will be growing if income exceeds consumption, and falling if the opposite is true. Consumption and capital will rise or fall together, because the rate of interest will rise if the capital stock shrinks and fall if it grows. Changes in consumption and capital will eventually stop. Capital and consumption will stop climbing when the capital becomes plentiful enough to bring the rate of interest down to the rate of impatience.

Suppose economies A and B are in long-run equilibrium at the point where international capital movements are allowed for the first time. If this is so, and the rate of interest is higher in B than in A, that can only be because A's citizens are less impatient than B's. B's residents discount utility from future consumption more highly than A's. The residents of B may have consumed a great deal in the past, but their current levels of consumption, capital, and output will all be low. Capital will be scarce and expensive.

To make matters simple, assume that there is a positive subsistence level of consumption, z, where consumption is so low that the marginal utility of consumption is infinite. There is also a high satiated consumption level y at which it is zero. When consumption is between its ceiling of

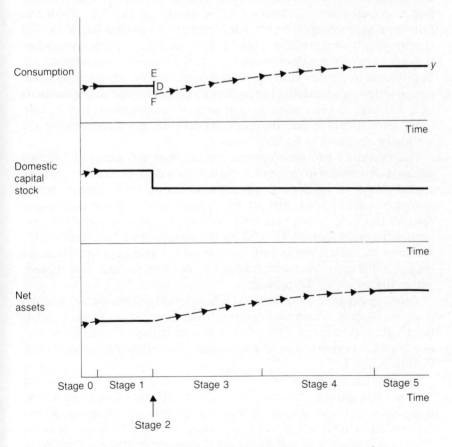

Figure 6.8 The evolution of consumption, capital, and net assets for country A.

y and its floor of z, the marginal utility of consumption is positive. Let us suppose that these floor and ceiling levels of consumption are the same for each citizen in both countries. The only respect in which the two sets of individuals differ is that B's residents always discount the utility from future consumption more highly than A's.

Now allow capital to move between countries. A's economy will lose capital to B's, where it earns more. A new rate of interest gets established, somewhere between the interest rates (and hence impatience rates) previously prevailing in A and B. Both countries can increase their consumption levels because national income per head jumps in A and B.

Previously interest rates had come to rest at levels equal to the two countries' impatience rates. Now that they are equalized, A's residents will want to add to their assets and B's will wish to run their assets down. The new common rate of interest exceeds the impatience rate in A. But it is less than that in B. So consumption in A will rise by less than the rise in its national income; indeed, it could initially fall. Faced with the new higher interest rate, A's residents will want to increase their wealth and substitute into cheaper future consumption. Consumption in A will climb slowly from its relatively low base. It will only stop increasing when it has reached y, the consumption ceiling. B's residents, by contrast, will be attracted to the new lower interest rate to borrow, raising their initial consumption substantially. But as they go deeper into debt, the residents of B will have to keep reducing their level of consumption from its high initial level, if only to meet the mounting debt charges. Consumption will gradually slip down to its floor value z.

The evolution of consumption, capital, and net assets in the two countries is depicted in figures 6.8 and 6.9. In stage 1, both countries have settled down to a long-run equilibrium before international capital movements are allowed. The previous phase, stage 0, shows adjustment towards this long-run equilibrium: consumption and capital might have been rising (as in figure 6.8) or falling (as in figure 6.9). In stages 0 and 1, the domestic capital stocks and the levels of net assets are equal because capital is the only asset and capital can only be formed, and owned, within the countries' boundaries.

Then, at stage 2, international capital movements occur. Capital transfers from A, where the interest rate has been low, to B, where it has been higher. If each countries' residents were happy to consume at their new higher national income levels, consumption would jump from D to E in both A and B.

A's residents will not wish to consume at E. They would rather consume less and save, because the rate of interest they face is above their impatience rate. So instead they lower their consumption to F and accumulate claims against B's residents who are keen to borrow. Throughout stage 3, A's residents are 'immature creditors'. They run a

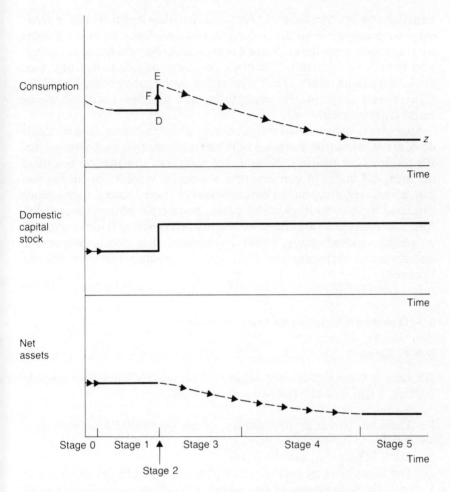

Figure 6.9   The evolution of consumption, capital, and net assets for country B.

surplus on trade, lending more than their growing interest charges. But as their claims on B mount, the point is eventually reached where they start to run a trade deficit and start to enjoy the fruits of their earlier abstinence. This initiates stage 4. Consumption and net assets keep climbing through stages 3 and 4, levelling off once consumption has attained its ceiling value y.

Meanwhile, B's residents really enjoy themselves early in stage 3, consuming at a high rate. They do this because they face an interest rate which is now below their rate of impatience. They run a trade deficit in stage 3, going deeper into debt, and consumption, though still high, is falling. The switch from stage 3 to 4 marks their transformation from immature to mature debtors. At this point they begin to run a trade surplus, because the charges on accumulated debts to A's residents overtake their fresh loans. Stage 4 is also marked by declining consumption and falling net assets. Eventually consumption falls to its floor value z. At that point their debts stop rising and consumption stabilizes. Convergence to point z is asymptotic, and so stage 4 will be almost infinitely protracted.

Stage 5 is in many ways a tragic point at which to end up. The residents of A are satiated: the marginal utility of consumption for them is zero. B's residents are paupers, living on the margin of subsistence. For them the marginal utility of consumption is infinite. Were it not for the fun that B's residents had had in the early days of stage 3, and the abstinence practised by A's residents at this point, an external observer would call for an income redistribution from country A to country B in the interests of justice. Indeed many would recommend that policy despite the circumstances that gave rise to it, on the grounds that bygones are bygones.

6.3 Technical Change in an Open Economy

6.3.1 Model 1

We turn now to explore the effects of technical change. To simplify matters, begin with the following assumptions.

1　There are two countries; the rest of the world (ROW) is very large relative to the home country.
2　There is no growth in the ROW.
3　The home country produces two goods a, b and has exogenous and constant endowments of two factors K, L which are perfectly mobile between the two industries.
4　The home country has a given homothetic community indifference map expressing aggregate preferences between a and b; indifference curves are continuous and convex to the origin.
5　Each of the home country's industries has constant returns to scale production functions, with isoquants convex to the origin.
6　There is perfect competition.
7　There is free trade.
8　Technical progress occurs at the same rate in both the home economy's industries.
9　Technical progress is Hicks neutral, that is, isoquants are simply relabelled with a common equiproportionate increase in output, and not repositioned: any combination of factors produces x per cent more than before.

This set of assumptions constitutes model 1. What does it imply? The first assumption ensures that the home country's terms of trade are independent of any domestic developments. In combination with assumption (1), assumption (2) tells us that these terms of trade will be constant over time. The third assumption expresses the standard Heckscher–Ohlin two-good, two-factor setup considered in earlier chapters. Assumption (4) means that growth had no particular implications operating through the demand side, and assumptions 5–7 are self-explanatory. Taken together, assumptions (8) and (9) imply that the country's PPF (concave to the origin if a and b employ K and L in different proportions) is subject to homothetic expansion. It is blown out radially as a result of technical progress by the same proportionate amount along any ray from the origin, and in such a way that the marginal rate of transformation, the slope of the tangent to the PPF, is unchanged along that ray (figure 6.10).

Assumptions (1), (2), and (7) imply that the commodity price ratio p_a/p_b which domestic producers face will be unaffected by the technical

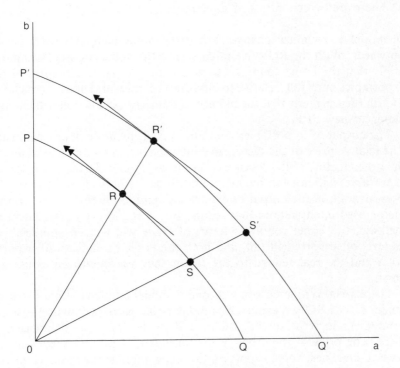

Figure 6.10 The homothetic expansion of the production possibility frontier in model 1, with Hicks-neutral technical progress at the same rate in both industries: PP′/OP = RR′/OR = QQ′/OQ = SS′/OS, and the marginal rates of transformation at R and R′, S and S′, P and P′, Q and Q′ are the same.

progress. Assumption (6) ensures that this price ratio will equal the slope of the tangent to the PPF. Our assumptions (8) and (9) imply that there will be an equiproportionate rise in the output of the two industries. The prices of both factors of production will go up by the same proportion. Since preferences are homothetic, all domestic citizens spend their higher incomes on the two goods in the same proportion as before. The income elasticities of demand for both goods are unitary. So aggregate demand and output of each good, as well as both factor prices, all rise by x per cent, the rate of technical progress. The absolute volumes of exports and imports also go up by x per cent: the home country's offer curve is expanded at all terms of trade by x per cent, but since the ROW is so large, there is no effect on the terms of trade.

6.3.2 Model 2

Consider the effects of relaxing some of the assumptions made in model 1. Model 2 replaces the first assumption with

1* There are two countries of similar size.

In model 1, technical change shifted the home country's offer curve outwards. With the ROW a similar size to the home country, this must imply that the home country's terms of trade worsen. The price of its exportables must fall, relative to importables, for world markets to clear. This in turn suggests that the pattern of domestic production will change along the new PPF.

The output of importables goes up, overall, by more than x per cent. The relative price of the factor used intensively there goes up in terms of the other factor. If the foreign offer curve is quite elastic, the price of exportables will not fall by much, and there is still likely to be absolute rises, overall, in the output of exportables and in the real reward to the factor used intensively in that sector. But if the ROW's offer curve is inelastic, the home country's terms of trade will worsen appreciably, its level of imports will fall, and both the home production of exportables and the real reward to the factor they use intensively could go down.

There are also repercussions abroad in model 2 which did not occur in model 1. The ROW's exportables industry increases production, with a consequent increase in the real reward to the factor used intensively there. The price of the other factor must fall. If the ROW consists of several countries, some exporting the same good as the home country, this group will suffer a terms of trade deterioration too, without the compensation of technical progress.

6.3.3 Model 3

Assumption (8) is relaxed next, to be replaced by

8* Technical progress is confined to sector a.

Retaining all the other assumptions made in model 1, we obtain model 3. The fact that technical progress is now restricted to one of the two goods implies that the PPF is no longer blown out equiproportionately. If good a is placed on the x axis as in figure 6.11, the PPF will be expanded horizontally. There is an equiproportionate increase in the output of a, for any given output of good b.

When the output of b is given at 0W, for example, the economy can produce 0Y units of a with the new PPF, and 0X with the old. But model 3 retains assumption 1, that the home country is small. This means that the world price ratio of the two goods is given, and will not be affected by the technical changes in the home economy. Since there is perfect

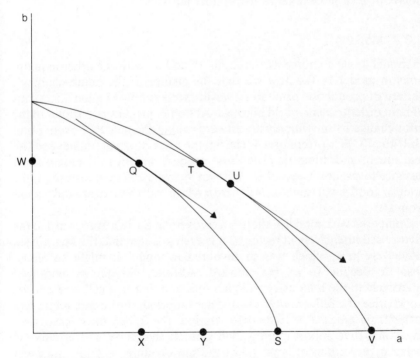

Figure 6.11   An equiproportionate horizontal expansion of the production possibility frontier, with Hicks-neutral technical progress confined to good a. QT/QW = SV/0S: output of a rises and that of b falls, shown by the movement from point Q to U.

competition and free trade, the marginal rate of transformation is unchanged. Since the new PPF is flatter than the old PPF, the results of this kind of technological change will always be to increase the output of a good experiencing technical progress (in this case, good a) and reduce the output of the other good. If the economy was in equilibrium at Q before the change in technology, the new production pattern will be at U. The output of b falls; that of a increases sharply.

What implications will this have? The prices of both factors of production will rise but the factor used intensively in the expanding sector a will gain more. So if good a is labour intensive, real wages will rise more than the rental on capital. This change in factor price ratios is due to the southeastwards movement along the new PPF from T to U. As far as trade is concerned, the home country's offer curve will move outwards, implying a greater volume of exports and imports if good a is exportable. The opposite happens if good a is importable. Indeed, trade could be contracted so much that the pattern of trade could even be reversed, with the home country starting to export good a instead of importing it. These results follow if the home country is small enough, compared with the ROW, to be a price taker in its product markets.

6.3.4 Model 4

In model 4, we combine assumptions 1* and 8* with the other assumptions in model 1. We now see that the change in the home country's pattern of production generates a world excess supply of good a, in terms of b, in order to clear world markets. At home, producers respond to the price change by moving northwestwards along the new PPF from point U. If the ROW's offer curve is elastic, the price of a will not have to fall that much, and domestic producers' production will shift only a short distance to the northwest of U. With an inelastic offer curve abroad, the price of good a will tumble, and there is a large northwestward movement from U.

Compared with model 3, there is a recovery in the relative reward to the factor used intensively in sector b. It is even possible that the factor used intensively in a, which was so favoured in model 3, might suffer an absolute decline in its real reward. Abroad, the factor employed intensively in the b industry will gain too, and that in a will suffer if the world price of a falls enough. If good a is exported, the home country will suffer from a terms of trade deterioration; the ROW, or at least those parts of it that import good a, will gain. If the ROW's offer curve is inelastic, the volume of imports into the home country will fall, and it will rise if the offer curve is elastic. The volume of exports must rise, however. If the foreign offer curve is inelastic, the adverse effect of the terms of trade improvement may be large enough, in welfare terms, to swamp the benefits from the improvement in technology, and the home country as a whole may be worse off. This is the case of 'immiserizing growth' first studied by Bhagwati (1958). Growth is likeliest to be immiserizing when technical change is confined to a country's export industry and foreign demand is inelastic.

Technical progress in the importables industry, however, brings the large home country substantial gains: a terms of trade improvement, to add to the gains from the productivity increase itself. It follows from this that large countries' governments may perceive an advantage in directing research and development spending into import replacement rather than export industries. Suppose a country is lucky enough to engineer a new strain of coffee tree which grows much more than the old one. Small coffee producers, such as Costa Rica or Jamaica, might apply our invention with alacrity. Brazil, with a dominant world market share for the production of this inelastic demand commodity, may be horrified. The biggest potential welfare gains might accrue to a large coffee importer, such as the USA, especially if our miracle coffee tree can be induced to grow there successfully.

6.3.5 Relaxing Assumptions

These are the results obtained from our simple models with different assumptions about the relative sizes of the home and foreign countries and about where the technical progress occurs. It remains to consider briefly what may happen when the other assumptions we have retained in all four models (2-7, 9) are relaxed.

Introducing growth in the ROW (relaxing assumption 2) adds few new insights, since the effects of this are just a mirror image of growth in the home country. One point is worth emphasizing, however: the home country is likeliest to suffer when the other countries advance their technology in the product(s) it exports.

Suppose the home country's endowments are endogenous (relaxing assumption 3). For example, because the labour supply responds to the real wage rate, there will be Rybczynski effects of the induced endowment changes to integrate into the story. Technical progress in a small country's labour-intensive industry could have far reaching repercussions if subsequent rises in real wages stimulate immigration and/or higher female participation. Technical progress in a capital-intensive industry could lead to an inflow of foreign capital in the same way. Internal factor immobility would bring gains to the owners of factors specific to expanding sectors.

If the home country's community indifference map is given but not homothetic, technical progress is likelier to boost trade and worsen the terms of trade the greater the income elasticity of demand for importables is. The community indifference map may not, of course, be given: if labourers and capitalists differ in tastes, and factor price ratios change, the change in income distribution will have to be allowed for. A pro-trade bias is likeliest when favoured groups have a relatively high propensity to spend on importables. The relaxation of assumptions (5) and (6), to allow for increasing returns and imperfect competition, has been discussed in chapter 4.

If there are tariffs (relaxing assumption 7), technical progress in a large country's exportable industry will be likelier to lead to immiserization than under free trade. This is especially so if the home country was already applying an optimal export tax or import tariff. The outward shift of its offer curve will resemble the consequences of an export tax cut; the new optimum tariff will have to go up.

If technical progress is not Hicks neutral (relaxing assumption 9), it will not just relabel isoquants. It will reposition them. Consider this in the context of model 3, so that technical progress is confined to industry a. There are two possible cases. In the first case, it will narrow the differences in factor intensities between the two industries. The new contract curve linking tangencies between isoquants for goods a and b, drawn as an Edgeworth box whose sides are the economy's capital and labour endowments, will be brought closer to the diagonal than before. The new PPF will be more elastic than before (it would be linear, of course, if the factor intensities were the same). At constant relative commodity prices, the output of a will go up even more than in model 3 as a result of this, and that of b will fall even more. This is the straightforward case in which all the effects explored in model 3 are qualitatively unchanged, although quantitatively amplified. But in the second case technical progress in a makes the two industries' factor intensities less alike. The contract curve is driven away from the diagonal. The new PPF is more sharply curved than before. This will mean that, at constant relative commodity prices, we can no longer be sure that the output of b goes down. It could rise. So the directions of effects for export volume and domestic factor prices now become ambiguous.

This concludes our analysis of changes in an open economy's factor endowment or technology, and their effects on trade and other variables. We have seen that growth can have a variety of effects on trade. Trade can affect growth, too. An excellent model that studies this is due to Corden (1971). Chapter 5 contained a summary of the key features of Corden's model, extended to the case of customs unions; it need not be repeated here. Historical evidence on the association between growth and trade is mixed. Although strong export performance and rapid growth often go together (for example Japan after the Second World War) the opposite is sometimes seen also. The UK's ratio of exports to national income rose fastest in 1900–14 and 1973–9 when output growth was at its weakest.

6.4 Terms of Trade Trends

Will the long-term trend of prices favour exporters of primary products? Or will primary commodities display a falling price trend relative, let us say, to manufactures? These are the questions to which this section is addressed.

6.4.1 Why Primary Product Prices can Fall

The short answer is that, as with so many other issues in economics, the key variable in question can go either way. Arguments for expecting an adverse long-term price trend for primary products include the following.

1   The income elasticity of demand for foodstuffs is less than unity. As people's incomes grow, the proportion of their budget that they devote to purchasing food goes down. Evidence suggests that the income elasticity of demand for food, taken as a whole, is about 1/2 in most economies. The past 200 years have witnessed rising living standards in most economies.
2   Advanced countries have adopted protectionist policies in agriculture. Self-sufficiency in foodstuffs was seen to be a crucial military objective for natural food importers such as Japan and the UK. Agricultural support measures were increased sharply during the Second World War, and if anything have grown in generosity since then.
3   There have been rapid technological advances in agriculture, and recent developments in biotechnology look like maintaining or even improving this trend.
4   New discoveries of metals and fossil fuels occur continuously and are especially large after any period in which their prices have risen.
5   There has been a continuing tendency for machinery to become smaller. Electrical engineering developments overtook mechanical engineering in the period from 1875 to 1950, to be succeeded by an electronic revolution from then on. The process of miniaturization of machinery reduces the demand for metals.
6   Synthetic substitutes have reduced the demand for, and squeezed the prices of, primary products such as rubber. This trend may continue, and could be explained by the particular terms of trade and strategic benefits from research activity conducted by advanced countries.

6.4.2 Why Primary Product Prices can Rise

There are also arguments pointing in the opposite direction, suggesting that primary product prices should on average rise over time in real terms. Here is a selection.

7   Increasing returns are most pronounced in manufacturing industry, and much less so in the extractive or agricultural sectors. As the world economy gets larger, and the demand for manufactures increases, their relative price should tend to drop.

8   Labour productivity usually increases fastest in manufacturing. Yet within a country's borders, at least, there is no tendency for wages in manufacturing to advance faster than for other relatively stagnant sectors. Thus the relative price of non-manufacturing is bid up.

9   Rapid industrialization in the Far East, first in Japan, and then in South Korea, Taiwan, Malaysia, Thailand, and China, is forcing down the worldwide relative price of what these countries export.

10   Population tends to grow, and capital accumulates still faster; but the stock of land is (approximately) fixed. Were it not for land-augmenting technical progress, which is usually erratic, the price of land must rise relative to labour and capital. This can only push up the relative price of land-intensive products, primarily foodstuffs.

11   The stock of metals in the earth's crust is given at any moment. Valuable metals tend to be recycled, but long-run total supply must shrink. This must imply a rising relative price of metals, in the absence of sufficiently fast technical progress to economize on them.

12   Metals can be recycled, but not fossil fuels. The laws of thermodynamics prohibit this. Thus the price of oil should display a positive time trend, probably steeper than that for recyclable metals.

6.4.3   Evidence

The two sets of arguments are nicely balanced. There is much to be said in favour of each of the 12 propositions. So what does the evidence suggest? The prices of individual primary products are subject to large and violent movements. Sometimes these occur when the prices of other primary commodities are steady; sometimes they all go up or down together. The periods from the mid-1920s to the late 1930s, from 1951 to the mid-1960s, and since the mid-1970s saw quite large slides in the real prices of most primary products. The 10–12 year periods ending in 1951 and 1974 witnessed sharp jumps. Meretricious proponents of the view that there are negative or positive time trends can support their claims by judicious selection of dates. It is much harder to find reliable evidence of very long-term time trends (stretching over a century or more) in relative prices of primary commodities as a group. One reason for this is that though primary commodities are homogeneous and have well recorded prices, the quality and range of manufactures and services against which they are to be compared keeps changing. An uncontroversial trustworthy relative price index is unavailable over a very long time span. So primary exporters and importers can both continue to moan that there is some iron law which makes their terms of trade move unfavourably in the long run, without fear of being convincingly disproved!

6.4.4 Oil Prices

In the 1970s and 1980s the international economy has been buffeted by enormous swings in the price of oil. Oil price changes have had profound effects on all countries, exporters and importers alike. The oil price quadrupled in 1973–4, and then, in the next five years, fell by nearly a quarter in real terms. In 1979, the price doubled. The subsequent ten years saw it retreat by some 60 per cent in real terms, much of this decline occurring in 1984–6 with some recovery in 1988–9. In what follows, we present brief answers to three questions.

1 What should govern the long-term trend in the real price of oil?
2 Why should oil prices be subject to sudden violent changes?
3 What effects do oil price changes have on countries' trade patterns and other key economic variables?

To answer question (1), consider what happens in a simple case. Suppose the costs of extracting oil are negligible. Imagine that there is no uncertainty, no tax on oil extraction, and no market imperfections, so that all oil sellers are perfect competitors. Under these circumstances, an oil well owner will want to extract all the oil now if he expects the price of oil to increase more slowly than the rate of interest r available on an alternative asset. He does better to sell oil now, and invest the proceeds to earn r, than to wait. But if r is less than the rate at which prices are expected to rise (call this x), it is better to postpone extraction. Oil under the ground gives better return than above it! Consequently, if all oil well owners keep extracting some of their oil and leaving most of it in the ground until later, they can only be in portfolio equilibrium if $x = r$. This is the Hotelling rule, first proved by Hotelling (1931). It follows that oil prices should rise by the rate of interest if conditions remain tranquil. The real price of oil should rise by the real rate of interest, the nominal price by the nominal rate of interest.

With positive but constant real extraction costs c, it is the gap between the price of oil p and c that should rise by r. Under an oil monopoly, portfolio equilibrium tells us that the marginal revenue should increase by r, which implies that p will rise faster or slower than r according as the price elasticity of demand for oil falls or rises over time. If oil extraction is taxed, it is the expected net of tax price that rises with r. These results, and others (relating to oligopoly, the Organization of Petroleum Exporting Countries (OPEC), and entry by fringe producers such as Norway and the UK), are established and discussed in a paper by Newbery (1984).

The second question is concerned with why oil prices should be subject to violent changes. Three possible explanations offer themselves at once. One is the discovery of new large scale oil reserves. This should imply a lower price path, for all time. The moment the new discovery is made the oil price should collapse, and it should then adjust to resume its normal rate of increase. Another explanation is technical breakthroughs in the development of alternative energy sources. They should have similar effects. The development of nuclear energy in the 1950s, first in the UK and then in the USA, Canada, France, Japan, and West Germany, helped to explain why real oil prices actually declined between 1951 and the late 1960s. Nuclear fusion, if it ever becomes feasible and cheap enough, will have the same consequences. A third factor is sudden changes in the structure of the oil market. Oil producers acted like Cournot oligopolists in the years before 1973, setting output independently and constrained by the oligopsony power of the western oil companies. In 1973–4, many of them colluded to exert their latent monopoly power. The sudden swing from Cournot to collusive behaviour saw the price quadruple. The subsequent downward drift in prices, briefly interrupted in 1979–80, owed much to the entry of new producers and to the difficulties (see chapter 4) of making the cartel's members adhere to the strict output quotas that are necessary to make the high price stick.

Hotelling's rule also suggests other positive causes of dramatic changes in the level of oil prices. Suppose that everyone comes to expect that the real rate of interest will be lower than they previously anticipated. This must mean, by Hotelling's rule, that the future rate of ascent of oil prices will be lower. But as soon as the expectation of lower real interest rates comes about, the price of oil must jump. This has to happen, under rational expectations at least, for the total stream of oil demands over time to match the stock that can be supplied. Oil must become more expensive now if its price has to climb more slowly thereafter. If current and expected real interest rates suddenly go up, the opposite happens: oil prices tumble, to make room for their steeper subsequent rate of increase. This seeming paradox resembles the 'overshooting' of exchange rates under rational expectations, discussed in chapter 9. A fuller account of it is furnished by Sinclair (1988). It is worth noting that the 1970s saw an unparalleled reduction in real interest rates, to negligible, sometimes even negative, levels, just at the time that oil prices went up. The 1980s have witnessed falls in oil prices and exceptionally high real rates of interest.

Now for our third question: how do oil price swings affect trade patterns and other key economic variables? A rise in the price of oil improves the terms of trade of countries exporting it, and worsens them for importers. It entails a major redistribution of world income, and wealth. In oil-importing countries in particular, equilibrium real wages should fall, except for particular groups such as coal miners and geologists whose scarcity value increases. If real wages are prevented from falling there, unemployment results. The relative prices of certain goods go up: substitutes for oil in the productive process (such as coal); energy-intensive products (such as steel); goods for which oil exporters have relatively strong demand (such as real estate in Texas or Aberdeen). Non-traded industries in oil-exporting countries thrive, but non-oil traded goods industries suffer a squeeze in those economies, handicapped by a rising exchange rate.

Similar results follow in countries which discover valuable reserves of oil or metals. This phenomenon is known as Dutch Disease, after the curious malaise that befell manufacturing industries in the Netherlands when that country began to develop and export its large reserves of North Sea gas. The resource allocation effects of Dutch Disease are explored in detail in a number of recent papers, including that by Corden (1984). Natural resource exporters do not suffer a fall in overall real income when they benefit from price increases or discoveries, but there are adverse effects on some other industries which qualify the gains secured.

6.5 Conclusions

When an open economy experiences an increase in the endowment of one of its factors of production, it is likely to see a rise in the output of the industry which uses that factor intensively and a decline in output in its other sector. This is the Rybczynski effect which occurs in a simple two-good two-factor case of a small open economy where both factors of production are mobile within its national boundaries. Trade increases if the expanding sector exports some of its output, contracts if it competes with imports. These effects formed the subject matter of section 6.1.

In section 6.2, it was shown that international capital movements tend to increase national income for both the exporting and the recipient countries, given appropriate conditions. Wages tend to rise in the second country but fall in the first. Output rises in the recipient country and falls in the country from which the capital is exported. If the recipient country's initially low stock of capital is explained by the fact that its residents are impatient, allowing them to borrow will lead to a jump in consumption followed by a slow slide back into poverty. Section 6.3 explored the effects of technical progress, both at home and abroad. A large economy experiencing a technical advance in its export industries could even suffer a loss in welfare. Section 6.4 illustrated the complexity of the analysis of trends in primary product prices, and focused particular attention on the causes and consequences of changes in the price of oil.

7

The Multinational Enterprise

In previous chapters in this book we have explored key concepts in trade theory and policy, under conditions of perfect and imperfect competition. Firms engaged in international trade, but they produced their output only at home. In this chapter, we turn attention to the phenomenon of the international company. Traditional trade theory offers few reasons why companies should become international and conduct foreign direct investment. We seek to address these issues here. Economics has much to say on the subject. In section 7.1 we provide some brief background. Section 7.2 defines the multinational enterprise (MNE) and discusses general principles governing location, production, and sales decisions by multiplant firms. We then explore the main characteristics of the MNE. Section 7.3 examines the empirical evidence relating to these.

7.1 Background

The growth of international companies has been a marked feature of the twentieth century. The world's largest 200 private sector companies, defined by sales, today enjoy a combined turnover approaching one-third of the world's gross domestic product (GDP). Most of these firms operate on an international scale. In the 1920s, 1950s, and 1960s, foreign direct investment was dominated by US firms. In the 1980s, Japanese firms have made much of the running, most often in the form of new plants in foreign countries rather than foreign acquisitions. Large parts of US business are now owned by Japanese, British, Canadian, and German concerns. Foreign ownership is still more marked in Australia, Canada, and Latin America, but much less so in Japan. Most large European companies have tended to confine production to their home base or to other continents. Cross-border mergers or acquisitions are comparatively rare in Europe. The Anglo–Dutch giants, Shell and Unilever, the recent Volkswagen–SEAT link, and the strong Swiss presence in food products and pharmaceuticals are not typical. It seems likely that this may change with the European Communities' 1992 programme, discussed in chapter 5. But at present most large foreign subsidiaries operating in Europe are American owned. France, the UK and West Germany are countries where foreign direct investment by domestic companies roughly balances inward investment by foreign firms. The USA and Japan have been major net exporters of capital in this sense, with Japan increasingly overhauling the USA. Many developing countries have hosted inward direct investment by foreign firms, but several have recently started to spawn international companies of their own. This new phenomenon is explored by Lall (1983).

Yet international companies are not new. By the end of the nineteenth century, many of Britain's leading firms had spread tentacles over large parts of her overseas empire, particularly in the fields of banking, confectionery, engineering, insurance, mining, shipping, and tobacco. The sixteenth and seventeenth centuries saw the emergence of great Portuguese, Dutch, and English trading companies, with vast networks of offices, trading posts, and factories spread around the globe. They were preceded on a smaller scale by Genoa, Venice, and the Baltic Hansestaedte, and long before that, the Carthaginians, the Phoenicians, and the Greeks. The phenomenon usually begins with trade. But the trading company moves swiftly to establish a strong physical presence in the host country to preempt supplies from competitors.

The host country's residents have always had varied reactions to foreign companies. Some welcome them as a channel to technological knowhow and wealth. Others see them as latter-day Vikings bent on pillage. These complex attitudes persist. The hope of lucre is tinged with fear for sovereignty. Opinions in the capital-exporting country, whose companies internationalize their operations, are similarly mixed. The prospects of higher and steadier profits, and considerations of national prestige, are qualified by apprehension for exports, wages, jobs, and dissemination of advanced domestic technology. Governments everywhere are as excited by the thought of attracting foreign capital as they are fearful that tax revenues will be lost if the prices on intra-firm international transactions are warped with the aim of minimizing global tax payments.

In the USA, the traditional home base for most of the world's largest MNEs, there have been growing worries about the scale of recent inward direct investment and acquisitions by foreign firms. Some are concerned at the thought that foreign companies are buying up US businesses to drain off superior US technology. Research suggests, however, that such fears may be unjustified (Arpan et al., 1981).

7.2 Analysis of the Multinational Enterprise

A company can be a multinational in at least three senses. It can sell in more than one country; it can run plants or own subsidiaries in two or more countries; and it can be owned internationally, with quotations on more than one national stock exchange, for example. Many large companies are multinational by all these definitions. But for our purposes the most important test of multinationality is production. Let us define an enterprise as multinational if it owns or runs production facilities in two or more countries. MNEs on this definition are responsible for much of the foreign direct investment undertaken throughout the world.

7.2.1 Location, Production, and Sales Decisions

National or international, a firm has three major decisions to take:

1　where to produce;
2　how much to produce in each location;
3　how much to sell where, and at what prices.

These decisions are essentially interdependent. They also turn on the firm's objective. Suppose this is to maximize profit. That means minimizing the total of production and distribution (transportation) costs of any given global output level.

One aspect of the location decision is the question of how many plants it should have. Some considerations point to many plants, others to few. The key factors favouring many plants and geographical dispersion are transport costs and convexities in costs at plant level. Transportation costs are most simply modelled as proportional to distance and volume transported, though there could be scale economies here. Plant level cost convexities arise chiefly through the problems of controlling and providing incentives to personnel. If workers' pay is related to the value of what they produce together in that plant, the link between the effort and reward that an individual employee faces gets steadily weaker as the number of employees per plant increases. The major influence favouring fewness of plants is plant level indivisibilities of certain inputs, particularly on the capital side.

This idea can be captured by supposing that each plant has a fixed cost, of f say, which has to be incurred whatever its output level. The firm's total output Q is given; the average plant size q defined in plant units is inversely proportional to the number of plants n because $nq = Q$. The optimum value of n is where the marginal gain in operating and transport cost savings balances the additional fixed cost f. For example, suppose that transport costs are trivial but that the incentive problem outlined in the previous paragraph means that each plant's total costs are quadratic and convex in its output:

$$C = f + c_1 q + c_2 q^2 \tag{7.1}$$

where f, c_1, and c_2 are positive. Since $q = Q/n$, a firm will minimize its total costs

$$TC = Cn = nf + c_1 Q + c_2 Q^2/n \tag{7.2}$$

by setting n equal to $Q\,(c_2/f)^{1/2}$. The latter is an approximation since n must be a whole number. This result tells us that the optimum number of plants is proportional to total output and rises with the square root of c_2, the term governing the convexity of (7.1). It is inversely proportional to the square root of fixed costs f. So the number of plants depends critically on the relative strengths of the two opposing forces, fixed plant costs, favouring fewness, and plant cost convexity, favouring the opposite.

Turning to the transport costs case, suppose now that the firm's transport costs for each consignment of output are proportional to the distance travelled s, the cost of transportation per unit distance (x), and the volume carried. Suppose, as in Salop's (1979) model discussed in chapter 4, that customers are evenly distributed along a circle of unit circumference. Unlike Salop's case, here it is the firm that incurs delivery costs. The firm optimizes by spacing its plants equally around the circular (world) market. Suppose we delete c_2 in (7.1), so that variable production costs in each plant are proportional to its output. Each plant transports output a distance of up to $1/2n$, and let us suppose that it sells the same volume of output to its nearer and more distant customers. Total plant costs will then be

$$C = f + c_1 q + 2q \int_0^{1/2n} xs \, ds = f + c_1 + \frac{qx}{4n^2} \tag{7.3}$$

Its total costs for all plants, summed together, are

$$TC = fn + c_1 Q + \frac{Qx}{4n^2} \tag{7.4}$$

It will now wish to select n to minimize (7.4) for given Q. The resulting expression is

$$n = \left(\frac{xQ}{2f}\right)^{1/3} \tag{7.5}$$

Equation (7.5) tells us that the number of plants is positively related to the cube root of its total output Q and of the transport cost term x. It is negatively related to the cube root of fixed costs f. Equation (7.5) resolves the conflict between fixed costs, which favour fewness of plants, and transport costs, which encourage spatial diversification.

Having seen how the firm can decide on how many plants it should have and, in the second case, where they should be placed, we should now turn to answer questions (2) and (3) with which this section began. How much should it produce in each plant? How much should it sell where, and at what prices? Fortunately these questions are rather easier to handle. The answers to both, given profit maximization and, for convenience, monopoly (so that we can ignore the behaviour of other firms) will be implicit in the following rule:

marginal revenue in each market (MR_i)	=	marginal transport costs to market i (MTC_i)	+	marginal production costs in plant j (MC_j)	(7.6)

Equation (7.6) should hold for all markets and all plants. One implication is that output should be assigned between plants so that their marginal production costs are equalized, setting transport costs aside for the moment. If marginal costs are higher in the Birmingham plant than in Toledo, transfer some production from Birmingham to Toledo. Another implication is that output should be assigned between different destinations so that marginal revenues, net of transport costs, should be equalized. If marginal revenue is higher in Halifax than in Richmond, sell more in Halifax and less in Richmond. That can only boost total receipts. In any market i, $MR_i = p_i(1 - 1/e_i)$, where e_i (defined positive) is the price elasticity of demand. So the rule tells us to charge more where demand is less elastic.

There are qualifications to the rule embodied in (7.6). First, we need to ensure that it maximizes, rather than minimizes, profits. This means ensuring that marginal costs in each plant are non-decreasing and that marginal revenues in each market are non-increasing. Transport costs aside, downward-sloping marginal cost curves would mean that the firm should concentrate its productivity in just one plant, while upward-sloping marginal revenues would imply that it should choose just one market. Second, some important qualifications are particularly relevant to the case of the MNE. The market that we have been looking at could easily be the world market as a whole, but, if it is, it is more than likely that marginal operating costs will differ across countries.

All else equal, the MNE is likely to locate in a country where marginal costs are relatively low. It is at this point that we see how valuable the principles of comparative advantage are: they act as a guide for efficient location and trading patterns for the MNE, in a much more direct and graphic way than in the simple model of small perfectly competitive firms restricted to operating in a single country. A country well endowed with a factor employed intensively in this industry will probably display a low price for that factor. So production costs are likely to be lower than elsewhere and it should be a favoured location. The choice of where to produce does not just turn on factor prices, of course: unit labour costs, for example, are the ratio of the wage rate to the productivity of labour. The effort, consistency, skill, and assiduity with which labour works are just as important as pay.

A location decision is also highly sensitive to government policy. A country which levies a tariff on imports of the good will be a more attractive place to produce, all else equal, because its domestic price will be lifted above its levels elsewhere. As we saw in chapter 4, what matters here is the effective rate of protection. That involves a comparison of the tariff on the final product with tariffs imposed on importable inputs used in its production. The ideal location may have a large nominal tariff on the final good and very little tariff on the inputs that go into it. Indeed, many countries deliberately employ a structure of tariffs, low on raw inputs and high on final output, to entice foreign business to set up there.

The chosen location may be a base for export production and not just domestic sales. Plus points here will be easy access to neighbouring markets, or government subsidies on export and production. To the extent that domestic markets matter, the MNE will be keener to select a richer or more populous economy than a small one, especially if there is little domestic competition in the industry already. Then there is the question of a more realistic treatment of geography. The one-dimensional Salop-type model is excessively simplified here. Generalizing to a two-dimensional plane of one unit area (but retaining the other assumptions) gives rise to the phenomenon of hexagonal market areas around each plant, and the optimum number there will be approximately $0.8(xQ/f)^{2/3}$. Generalizing to the surface of a sphere, like the world, could point to the MNE choosing 4, 6, 12, or 20 plants (depending again on the sizes of x, Q, and f) located at the centre of each face of the smallest optimal regular polyhedron in which the world can be enclosed. For the case of the cube, with its six faces, locations at Johannesburg, London, Los Angeles, São Paulo, Sydney, and Tokyo are tolerably good approximations!

A final point in this connection concerns the nature of foreign direct investment. As noted in chapter 6, this takes the form of a commitment. It is hard, perhaps impossible, to undo. Once committed, the MNE is vulnerable. The host government could make its life uncomfortable by unexpected taxes, or withdrawing fiscal or commercial privileges. There is an ultimate threat of expropriation. The host government will not pursue such strategies if it values the gains from preserving a good reputation with foreign business highly enough. But if it discounts such gains heavily, or deems them small, it could. The risks of this happening are greatest in poor countries with unstable or myopic governments, but may not be confined to these.

The MNE can protect itself to some degree by employing local residents in senior positions, establishing a good record on exports and on pay and conditions, or by hinting that future investment plans in the country could be jeopardized if the climate turns sour. Best of all, it can try to retain flexibility and show that it has an 'external option', such as moving to another location. The interactions between the MNE and the host governments with which it deals are essentially game theoretic in nature. It is curious that the rich insights provided by games theory have yet to be registered in the voluminous literature devoted to multinational companies.

In this section we have examined a number of factors that govern the MNE's choices of location, production, and trade. But the very fact that it is the MNE, and not a domestic firm, that is carrying out the production testifies to the existence of some market imperfection. The next section examines this idea in detail, and demonstrates its importance in explaining why MNEs exist and why they take the form that they do.

7.2.2 Essential Characteristics of the Multinational Enterprise

Previous chapters looked at the question of why countries trade with each other. The concepts and theories discussed there clearly serve to explain trade patterns. However, they take a very limited local view of companies' production behaviour. Does the fact that we observe MNEs mean that these theories are of no use? The answer is no. Just because a theory does not explain every real world phenomenon does not mean that it should be discarded. The principle of comparative advantage is extremely important, whether or not there are MNEs. If the theories are found to be deficient because they do not explain an important phenomenon, the assumptions made in the model must be examined: this is usually the source of the deficiency. When discussing the notion of comparative advantage in chapter 2, for example, we assumed that all firms were *perfectly competitive* and had *equal access* to the international markets, independent of their country of location. We have to relax these assumptions if we wish to identify and explain the economic attributes of the MNE. In fact, we shall see that MNEs do not undermine the concept of comparative advantage. They underline it. For comparative advantage plays a vital role in the MNE's location and trading decisions.

The MNE exists precisely because these assumptions (perfect competition and equal access) may not hold. One can explain the existence of the MNE by acknowledging the existence of certain types of market imperfection in the international economy. Before we study the market imperfections that give rise to the establishment of overseas plants two points should be noted.

First, we note that MNEs are typically oligopolists, that is, the output and pricing decisions of firms in a particular industry are interdependent. Empirically, we observe that all MNEs enjoy market power. The market form in which they operate is usually one of international oligopoly, with elements of monopolistic competition. One possible reason for this is the sizeable setup costs that are involved in establishing an overseas plant. Only larger firms will be willing to incur these. Firm size obviously correlates with market power. In a recent British study, Dunning (1985) identifies oligopoly as a distinguishing feature of markets in which MNEs operate, confirming what many other investigators have found.

The establishment of overseas subsidiaries is hardly compatible with the strict conditions of perfect competition. In a perfectly competitive industry there are many independent small firms enjoying common access to knowledge. The element of oligopoly power provides some insight as to why certain firms choose to establish cross-border plants. Entry barriers are crucial in maintaining high profits. If these come to be eroded in the domestic market, then the firm may find it best to set up plants overseas. This argument is false in a world of full information: firms will go overseas anyway, regardless of domestic developments, if there are profits to be had by doing so. But it becomes appealing when information and decision-making costs are taken into account. The expected adverse trends in home profits, due perhaps to increased competition from rivals, will shake a firm into scrutinizing its options carefully, something it would be less likely to do had conditions been tranquil. The outcome could be the discovery that costs are low enough abroad. Foreign direct investment (FDI) would follow.

In the discussion that follows, it is assumed that, in the decision to set up a plant overseas, locational efficiency conditions have been met. Considerations of locational efficiency, that is, comparative production and distribution cost considerations, obviously help to explain where production occurs. But it cannot be the only factor at work. If it were, one would have to ask why a host country firm is not producing and exporting the good. The MNE has to have some firm-specific advantage that gives it an edge over potential indigenous producers. A recent study by Michalet and Chevalier (1985) cited over 30 reasons given by French MNEs for setting up overseas plants. Prominent among these were the importance of gaining access to a particular market, the desire to spread risks, and adverse trends in the home market. There is obviously no single factor at work.

There are any number of explanations for why firms may choose to establish an overseas plant, all of them essentially related to some form of market imperfection. Such imperfections in turn cause the firm to internalize the market, a concept which will be explained below. The **market imperfections** include the following.

Barriers to International Trade

Tariffs and other barriers to trade mean that not all firms have equal access to the same markets. Provided locational efficiency conditions are met, the establishment of the plant in the protected country is one way of overcoming these barriers.

Market Imperfections in the Supply Markets

Market imperfections arise from imperfect competition or imperfect information. Suppose that the supplier of a crucial factor input in a firm's production process has some monopoly power. Then the purchasing firm may confront problems such as price discrimination and it will certainly pay a higher price for the input than it would have done under conditions of perfect competition. In these conditions it may pay the firm to internalize the supply network by buying up the supply source: making the supplier a part of the buying firm's production process. If the supplying firm happens to be located in another country, then the purchasing firm becomes a multinational.

Product differentiation may also lead to internalization. Suppose that some crucial factor input is supplied by a number of firms but the products of each of these firms are slightly differentiated. Then the buyer of the product will face a large fixed cost in switching from one supplier to another, because of the costs of testing or adapting to new varieties and/or differences in the organizational structure of the selling firms. In the presence of switching costs, it is in the interest of buyer and seller to enter into a long-term 'arm's length' contract (a contract formed between separately owned firms) with terms specified in advance to take account of every possible contingency. But negotiating such a contract will prove very costly. The alternative is internalization of the intermediate product market.

Less than perfect information regarding supply is a problem if the supplier of the factor input is external to the production process. Suppose the buyer has less than perfect information on the price and future availability of the input and the supplying firm does not provide all the information (for example, on future price volatility). If such behaviour is potentially very costly for the buyer then internalization will ensure that the firm has the most information available. It may be especially important for firms relying on raw materials in the production process, where prices are highly volatile and accurate information on price changes is very important.

Presence of Increasing Returns

A further explanation is the presence of increasing returns for the MNE which transcend any scale economies at the level of individual plants. There could be monopsony power in the market for raw materials and cost savings for coordinating inventories and research and development activity, or economies in the transportation network when the shipment of goods extends beyond the output needs of a single plant. Finally, there may be scale economies from the pooling of the capacities of the different national plants to meet local demand fluctuations. All these are examples of positive externalities between plants, which only an integrated firm, the MNE, is in a position to exploit.

Difficulties in Trading Intangible Assets

Difficulties in trading a firm's intangible assets may explain the establishment of plants across national boundaries. Knowledge is one example of an intangible asset. The firm may possess knowledge of how to produce a cheaper or better product at given input prices which permits production at lower cost. It may take the form of a patented process or design or it may be less formal, involving the knowhow shared among the employees of the firm. Marketing skills permit a firm to differentiate its product from those offered by competitors. Managerial skills lead to more cost-effective production.

Why is a firm unable to trade some of its intangible assets? The answer is that the traditional market concept may break down in this case. The market fails because there is an important characteristic of intangible assets which prevents them from being traded in the usual way: the one-sided or asymmetric information aspect of intangible assets prevents there being an efficient market in them.

Intangible assets have some attributes of a public good because knowledge or informational advantages are important features. If a piece of information can be used to the firm's advantage at one location, it can be deployed profitably at another without a reduction in knowledge at the original location. The marginal cost of using the knowledge in the production process is zero. Attempts to trade the intangible asset on the open market are likely to fail. For example, suppose a firm tries to sell its intangible asset to another firm. The intangible nature of the asset will mean that the potential buyer is unable to assess the true value of the proposed purchase. If the selling firm reveals the details of why the asset is valuable, the buyer obtains knowledge that has not been paid for. A further problem is the fact that the commercial value of the information, even if it could be established, depends on how many firms are to purchase it, and when.

So a firm may be endowed with an intangible asset it might like to sell some of but cannot. It may have, for example, an excess capacity in managerial skills. It may then be profitable to 'internalize' the market for intangible assets by setting up other plants, if they meet the test of locational efficiency. If conditions point to an overseas location, then the firm becomes an MNE.

The firm has three choices: it can serve a foreign market by exports from its domestic production base; it can license other firms to produce abroad; or it can set up production facilities of its own overseas. Asset intangibility does not always give rise to the third option of FDI. If the intangible asset can be embodied in the product without adaptation and if plant level returns are strongly increasing and international trade barriers weak, then exporting is the best method for penetrating the international market. It is worth stressing, however, that multinational production is not necessarily a substitute for exports from the home base. This is especially true in the case of vertically integrated MNEs. Bergston et al. (1978) found that FDI can have a modest pro-export effect for the country conducting it.

If the intangible asset takes the form of knowledge of a specific process or product technologies that can be written down and transmitted, then foreign expansion is likely to take the form of licensing: a local firm is licensed to manufacture the company's product in return for royalties and other forms of payment. But the firm may find that such a strategy eventually leads to the growth of competitors.

If the intangible asset is inseparable from the firm itself because of a strong public goods element in it, then the market fails and the firm finds it is unable to unbundle these skills: the answer is FDI. The choice between FDI and licensing also depends on other considerations, above all the 'market solution', bedevilled, as we have seen, by the difficulties in drawing up appropriate contracts. The non-market solution of FDI can suffer from other disadvantages. How is the foreign subsidiary to be monitored and controlled? How much latitude should its managers be given? Should their rewards be related to results, or should the parent company offer them some form of implicit income insurance against risks?

Reduction of Risk

One advantage of FDI is the reduction of risk through international diversification. Much of the systematic or general market risk affecting the corporation is related to the business cycles in a firm's national economy. By diversifying across countries the economic cycles of which are not perfectly phased with the home country, the variance in the firm's overall earnings and cash flows can be reduced. However, many of the political and economic risks specific to the MNE are unsystematic. Diversification cannot really help here.

More important, various market imperfections may deny individual investors full access to the international capital markets. Information barriers, and legal economic considerations (tax regulations, currency controls) may prevent individuals from fully diversifying their portfolios. Investment in the stock of a multinational is a means by which these imperfections can be overcome. By setting up foreign subsidiaries, the MNE gives investors a geographical spread of risks on their assets more cheaply than they could obtain on their own. Asymmetric information is also relevant here: the MNE can be thought of as an institution, rather like a bank, which specializes in exporting private unmarketable information about the particular set of products and markets with which it is involved.

To summarize, MNEs, the predominant form of FDI, are the response of the oligopolistic firm to

1   market or international capital markets, or imperfections which can arise in the intermediate product markets; because of market failure associated with intangible assets
2   the need to achieve economies of scale that extend beyond national plants; and
3   government barriers to international trade that deny equal access to markets.

Further discussion of the economic determinants of the MNE may be found in Caves (1982).

MNEs tend to fall into one of three categories. Horizontally integrated MNEs are firms with national branches of an enterprise producing largely the same product. American car companies and fast food chains are examples. In vertically integrated MNEs, the output from one national plant provides an intermediate input to another national plant, all under common ownership and control. Until recently, MNEs in the oil industry were an instance of this: crude oil is extracted in one country, refined in another, and marketed in a third. Diversified MNEs are firms with national plants the outputs of which are neither vertically nor horizontally integrated. The Nestlé Corporation is Swiss owned but 95 per cent of its production is outside the country: it is involved in foods, restaurants, wine, and cosmetics. The number of diversified MNEs is growing rapidly. In the next section, we examine some of the econometric evidence on FDI.

7.3 Empirical Evidence

A variety of studies have attempted to identify the variables that are statistically significant when it comes to explaining why a company has foreign plants. We report on a sample of important results below.

Caves (1974) and Meredith (1984) employed similar methodology. From an econometric and statistical viewpoint, these are the most comprehensive of the empirical work available. In these studies, the dependent variable is the market share of the host country manufacturing industry i held by US-controlled multinationals. For Caves, data for two host countries, Canada and the UK, were used while Meredith employed data for Canada only. In Caves, the Canadian data consisted of a dependent variable, the average share of sales accounted for by foreign-owned firms in 1965–7 for 64 industries. The computation for the UK was more problematic but in the end the data were similar to those for Canada. In the Meredith study the dependent variable was the market share of Canadian manufacturing industry i held by US multinationals. The data covered 50 industries, half of which produced consumer goods and half of which produced industrial goods for the period 1972–5.

Employing multiple regression techniques, both studies tested a range of independent variables. They suffered from the problem of multicollinearity, when the right-hand side variables are not in fact independent of each other. Multicollinearity is a potentially serious problem because it makes the results sensitive to the sample and deprives one of an accurate estimate of the relative importance of the independent variables.

Variables found to be statistically significant in Caves's study were as follows.

(1) Intangible assets, as proxied by advertising as a percentage of sales, and research and development expenditures as a percentage of sales were found to be significant.

(2) The absolute size of firms in an industry: Caves argued that larger firms are more able to bear the higher relative cost of setting up a foreign plant rather than exporting or licensing. Also, if there are entry barriers due to the size of the capital costs, these are more likely to be overcome by the larger firms. Caves used the percentage of shipments in the US market accounted for by firms with assets of US$100 million or more. It was found to be statistically significant with the right sign.

(3) Economies of scale across national boundaries were measured by the percentage of shipments in the US industry accounted for by multi-plant firms. It was found to be statistically significant for Canada but not for the UK, probably because of the geographical proximity of Canada to the USA.

(4) As a separate determinant Caves tested for the influence of what he called 'entrepreneurial resources'. One can think of these as being intangible assets. He used the following variables as proxies for entrepreneurial resources: non-production workers as a percentage of total employees in the host country industry, payroll per employee in the host country industry, wages per production worker in the Canadian industry, and the percentage of shipments in the US market accounted for by firms with assets of US$100 million or more. The latter variable, the only one found to be statistically significant, was included on the grounds that the greater the absolute size of the firm is, the greater should be the quality of entrepreneurial resources.

Meredith (1984) tested some important new marketing variables in addition to many of the variables tested by Caves. She found the proportion of research and development personnel in each US industry and the proportion of wages and salaries devoted to non-production employees had positive signs and were statistically significant. Large plant, the proportion of shipments accounted for by firms with assets of more than US$100 million, and multi-plant scale economies were statistically significant with a positive sign. Effective rates of tariff protection for Canadian manufacturing industries (1970) were also significant but only for a few of the regressions.

The marketing variables tested by Meredith included the spillover effects of advertising, found to be statistically significant. This may demonstrate the desire on the part of US firms to capture the economic rents of advertising budgets arising from the fact that their advertising spills over across the border through TV, radio, and magazines. The ratio of advertising to sales had the right sign and was statistically significant. It may be interpreted as a measure of the relative attractiveness of alternative market development. Marketing management expertise was also positive and statistically significant.

Finally, Meredith tested for the importance of *relative* market conditions. Relative market growth rates, relative market risk, proxied by the relative variance of the market growth rate, and relative market concentration (if concentration in one market is lower than in the other, entry barriers are lower) were all found to be statistically significant with the right sign.

Maki and Meredith (1986) attempted to test for the importance of tariff barriers as a factor explaining FDI and to use empirical evidence to compare and contrast the 'portable' and 'non-portable' technology models of FDI. Both models start from the premise that a firm decides to enter a foreign market and the question is whether the firm should export to the market or set up production facilities there.

The non-portable technology model states that FDI will be chosen when $R(FDI) > R(EX)$:

$$R(EX) = Q(1 - T)P - C^* \qquad (7.7)$$

$$R(FDI) = QP - C \qquad (7.8)$$

where R is revenue, Q is the quantity sold in the host country market, P is the selling price of a unit of the product, T is the nominal rate of tariff levied on imports by the host country, C is the production cost in the host country, and C^* is the production cost in the foreign country, that is, the firm's home base. Thus FDI is chosen if

$$T + \frac{C^*}{QP} - \frac{C}{QP} > 0 \qquad (7.9)$$

In words, FDI is positively related to the tariff rate and the ratio of foreign production costs to sales revenue and negatively related to the ratio of host country production costs to sales revenue.

The portable technology model assumes that any unique production advantages enjoyed by the domestic firm are fully portable, so that the firm can produce in the foreign country at domestic costs. Thus

$$R(FDI) = QP - \min(C, C^*) \qquad (7.10)$$

Equation (7.10) is compared with (7.7). If $C > C^*$ the model predicts that FDI is positively related to the ratio of host country production costs to sales revenue and negatively related to the ratio of domestic production costs to sales revenue. This counter-intuitive prediction is based on the following reasoning. If a firm in one country has a technological advantage over firms producing the same product in the foreign country such that their production costs are lower, then FDI will be positively related to the ratio of C/QP and the firm will undertake FDI in order to exploit the production cost differences.

In the portable technology model, FDI is positively related to the tariff rate but only for firms for which $C < C^*$. Otherwise, it is hypothesized, tariffs are irrelevant to the FDI–export decision. Maki and Meredith tested these propositions using cross-section regression on data from US investment in Canada in 41 manufacturing industries. FDI was measured at two time points, 1975 and 1980, and all the independent variables were measured as of 1975. Their results strongly supported the portable technology model. High production costs in Canada relative to the USA have *not* been a factor discouraging entry of US multinationals. On the contrary, they have been a source of attraction. They also found that tariff levels did not appear to be important influences on FDI in the presence of production cost differentials. But it may be that the production cost differentials are partly explained by tariffs that have protected Canadian firms from the need to increase productivity.

Horst (1972) compared the characteristics of domestic firms with those of MNEs. The market share of the firm in the domestic market was found to be the only significant variable, suggesting that firms will only go overseas when their success in the domestic market is exhausted. Servan-Schreiber (1968) found that the managerial skills of US corporations were the sole explanation for foreign investment by US firms. But he was looking at the immediate post Second World War period: this intangible asset has declined in value since.

Poulsen (1986) looked at the determinants of US activities of Japanese banks. She found that tight credit conditions in Japan increase the use of US markets. Loans issued in the USA and funds returned to Japan increase under the above conditions. This example points to regulations as one factor that can influence the character of FDI. Japanese customers using US offices of Japanese banks were found to be an important source of custom and, as Japanese trade increased, Japanese banks in the USA increased their loans.

7.4 Conclusions

Companies have become multinational for many reasons. Transport costs favour international dispersion of production facilities. Although increasing returns at the plant level make for geographical concentration, there are numerous reasons why they may relate to the firm and not just to its individual plants. If they do, the international company will be admirably placed to exploit them. Tariffs set by individual governments play a key role too. Also, individual investors will often find that stocks in MNEs give a better risk–return trade-off in their portfolios than an assortment of shares in different national firms in different countries. Asymmetric information issues are one aspect of this. They also explain why companies often choose to set up overseas subsidiaries rather than licence production by foreign firms, and at the same time, why such firms structure their worldwide operations in the different ways that they do. Asymmetric information considerations, and associated game-theoretic concepts, lie at the heart of every facet of the MNE: its internal operations and transactions; its external dealings with customers, suppliers, rival firms, and national governments; even the reasons for its existence. It is also to be regretted that the existing literature on multinational companies by and large ignores them. Many of the ideas summarized in section 7.2 receive confirmation from the econometric evidence, as is clear from the sample surveyed in section 7.3. Others wait to be tested.

Like the great international trading monopolies of earlier centuries, today's MNEs are almost states in themselves. Some generate turnover far in excess for the GDP of smaller countries. This is an appropriate point, therefore, to turn from the microeconomic analysis of international activity to the macroeconomic. The remaining chapters of the book are concerned with how the broad aggregates of trade and capital flows interact with countries' exchange rates, national incomes, and prices.

Part II

The Macroeconomics of the Open Economy

8

Concepts in Open Economy Macroeconomics

There are many questions which open economy macro-economics seeks to answer but two stand out. First, what determines a country's balance of payments (BOP) and exchange rates? Second, what are the effects of monetary and fiscal policy changes in an open economy? That is, what impact (if any) do these policies have on real output, employment, inflation, the BOP, and the exchange rate, if the latter is flexible?

Answers to these questions involve a number of concepts used in open economy macroeconomics. The aim of this chapter is to review these concepts (section 8.1), to introduce the reader to the monetary and Keynesian approaches to the BOP under fixed exchange rates (sections 8.2 and 8.3), and to present a general framework of equations that will be used in subsequent chapters (section 8.4). In section 8.5 we review general trends in the inter-national economy, and in our conclusion we discuss the main objectives of the next three chapters.

8.1 Key Concepts in Open Economy Macroeconomics

As background to the next three chapters we must explore the BOP, the exchange rate, and the links between them. Below, we explain these terms with reference to the UK and US economies, but the main ideas apply to all open economies.

8.1.1 The Balance of Payments

A country's BOP is defined as the record of transactions between domestic residents and residents in foreign countries over a given period of time, usually quarterly and annually.

A country's BOP accounts have three components: the current account, the capital account and official financing items. The **current account** consists of

1   the visibles or trade account, that is, exports and imports of goods, and
2   invisibles, including (a) the exports and imports of services such as shipping, insurance, tourist, and banking transactions, (b) net interest payments (interest payments made from abroad less interest payments made to foreigners), net profits, net dividends, and (c) private and official transfers (POT).

POT includes the remission overseas of the earnings of foreigners working in the home country, net of foreign earnings remitted home and certain government transactions such as payments to and from the European Community budget and government aid to other countries. Referring to table 8.1, which reproduces the UK BOP, these parts of the current account are found in columns 1–4. As will be observed from the table, the UK has run a visibles or trade deficit in every quarter since the second quarter (Q2) of 1983. Revenues from net oil exports allowed the UK to run a trade surplus from 1980 Q3 to 1983 Q1. Prior to this, the UK ran a trade deficit. Although net transfers (column 4) are negative, the surplus from trade in services and interest, profits, and dividends means that the UK runs a surplus on its invisibles account. The seasonally adjusted current account fluctuates between deficit and surplus. A deficit has persisted since 1987 Q2 and grew rapidly in 1988.

The **capital account** consists of all flows of capital, classified by the maturity date of the assets involved. An outflow of domestic capital (direct or portfolio) is recorded as a debit, shown in table 8.1 column 7, that is, transactions in assets. Portfolio capital exports include all purchases by domestic residents from foreign residents of titles to wealth, such as equities, bonds, and real estate. An inflow of foreign capital (direct or portfolio) is recorded as a credit shown in table 8.1, column 8 (transactions in liabilities). From column 9 it will be observed that the capital account is sometimes in deficit, sometimes in surplus. Short-term capital flows (with a maturity of less than one year) are highly volatile, while the UK is traditionally a net exporter of long-term capital.

Official financing items consist of net transactions with the International Monetary Fund (IMF), net transactions with overseas monetary authorities, plus any foreign borrowing by the government and drawings on/additions to official reserves. It is shown in table 8.1, column 10. Column 11 shows the 'balancing item', that is, the amount required to make the overall account balance. It reflects errors and omissions (strictly speaking net errors and omissions) elsewhere in the accounts. International capital movements, in particular, are often hard to identify and measure accurately.

The BOP accounts are an integral part of the national income and expenditure accounts. A BOP deficit (surplus) on current account is identically equal to the excess (shortfall) of national expenditure over national income and hence to the reduction (increase) in the net external assets owned by UK residents. It is possible to incorporate the BOP into the income and expenditure relationship of the closed economy. In a closed economy, aggregate demand consistency requires that real national output y equals real national expenditure a. If a exceeded (were less than) y, domestic investment would outstrip (fall below) domestic saving, making aggregate demand and national income inconsistent.

In an open economy, y and a do not have to equal each other. Any gap between them will be bridged by external trade:

$$y - a = \text{ex} - \text{im} \tag{8.1}$$

where ex and im denote the real values of exports and imports. If exports exceed imports, and hence output exceeds expenditure, domestic savings will outstrip domestic (private and official) investment. This is so because

$$y = c + I + g + \text{ex} - \text{im} \quad \text{and} \quad y = c + S + t \tag{8.2}$$

Therefore

$$\text{ex} - \text{im} = S - I + t - g \tag{8.3}$$

where c is private consumption, I is private domestic investment, g is government spending, S is private domestic savings, and t is taxes, all expressed in real terms.

If exports exceed imports, so that the home country runs a current account surplus, it must be adding to its stock of net overseas claims, including reserves. Examples of a countries adding to their stock of net overseas assets are Germany and Japan. If $\text{ex} - \text{im} < 0$, there is net foreign disinvestment at a given exchange rate. A current account deficit will mean that the country is running down its net foreign assets, as has been the case for the USA in recent years.

8.1.2 The Exchange Rate

The exchange rate E is defined as the price of foreign currency in units of home currency. If free to float, it is determined by the supply and demand for foreign exchange (forex). The demand for forex arises from debit items on the BOP, and the supply of forex from the credit items on the BOP. Suppose the UK's BOP, current and capital accounts combined, is in deficit. Then the demand for forex will exceed the supply of forex in the UK and sterling will depreciate in value on the forex markets, if exchange rates are flexible. In this case the exchange rate has risen, that is, the price of foreign currency rises relative to sterling.

Table 8.1 The United Kingdom's balance of payments (£ million)

	1	2	3	4	5	6	7	8	9	10	11
		Seasonally adjusted					Not seasonally adjusted				
		Invisibles (balance)					UK external assets and liabilities				
Year	Visible trade (balance)	Services	IPD	Transfers	Total	Current balance	Trans-actions in assets[a]	Transactions in liabilities[a]	Net transactions	Allocation of SDRs and gold subscription to IMF	Balancing item
1977	−2,324	3,037	265	−1,128	2,174	−150	−13,844	9,952	−3,892	–	4,042
1978	−1,593	3,542	806	−1,791	2,557	964	−4,377	1,506	−2,871	–	1,907
1979	−3,398	3,907	1,205	−2,210	2,902	−496	−40,189	39,446	−743	195	1,044
1980	1,353	3,949	−196	−1,984	1,769	3,122	−43,439	39,567	−3,872	180	570
1981	−3,350	3,923	1,210	−1,547	3,586	6,936	−50,793	43,398	−7,395	158	301
1982	2,218	2,762	1,446	−1,741	2,467	4,685	−31,381	29,053	−2,328	–	−2,357
1983	−1,075	3,721	2,847	−1,661	4,907	3,832	−30,120	25,810	−4,310	–	478
1984	−4,580	3,941	4,433	−1,772	6,602	2,022	−31,953	24,289	−7,664	–	5,642
1985	−2,346	5,962	2,800	−3,079	5,683	3,337	−53,282	44,208	−9,074	–	5,737
1986	−8,716	5,618	5,079	−2,180	8,517	−199	−95,037	80,837	−14,200	–	14,399
1987	−10,162	5,638	5,523	−3,503	7,658	−2,504	−75,094	74,055	−1,039	–	3,543
1980 1	−440	953	−62	−483	408	−32	−14,401	13,026	−1,375	180	1,546
2	−183	924	−186	−597	141	−42	−8,157	7,941	−216	–	519
3	865	1,002	−45	−572	385	1,250	−4,695	4,350	−345	–	−1,077
4	1,111	1,070	97	−332	835	1,946	−16,186	14,250	−1,936	–	−418
1981 1	1,703	1,044	251	−52	1,243	2,946	−15,113	10,815	−4,298	158	1,461
2	1,302	971	373	−588	756	2,058	−8,535	6,055	−2,480	–	756
3	33	948	281	−671	558	591	−13,845	13,141	−704	–	23
4	312	960	305	−236	1,029	1,341	−13,300	13,387	87	–	−1,939

Year	Qtr												
1982	1	336	881	88	125	1,094	1,430	−11,568	11,375	–	−193	–	−959
	2	221	694	423	−743	374	595	−21	1,247	–	1,226	–	−1,361
	3	626	530	402	−647	285	911	−18,409	16,483	–	−1,926	–	963
	4	1,035	657	533	−476	714	1,749	−1,383	−52	–	−1,435	–	−1,000
1983	1	8	996	815	6	1,817	1,825	−10,706	8,468	–	−2,238	–	761
	2	−511	929	361	−713	577	66	−187	508	–	321	–	61
	3	−210	839	1,003	−397	1,445	1,235	−11,455	11,885	–	430	–	−1,828
	4	−362	957	668	−557	1,068	706	−7,772	4,949	–	−2,823	–	1,484
1984	1	−118	1,017	896	−356	1,557	1,439	−14,120	13,048	–	−1,072	–	207
	2	−1,304	877	872	−676	1,073	−231	−8,862	6,949	–	−1,913	–	2,591
	3	−1,613	998	965	−619	1,344	−269	−554	−563	–	−1,117	–	929
	4	−1,545	1,049	1,700	−121	2,628	1,083	−8,417	4,855	–	−3,562	–	1,915
1985	1	−1,394	1,288	918	−862	1,344	−50	−17,244	13,270	–	−3,974	–	4,642
	2	−149	1,590	678	−674	1,594	1,455	−6,841	5,563	–	−1,278	–	300
	3	−590	1,639	814	−846	1,607	1,017	−16,126	9,966	–	−6,160	–	4,735
	4	−213	1,445	390	−697	1,138	925	−13,071	15,409	–	2,338	–	−3,940
1986	1	−1,403	1,463	1,018	3	2,484	1,081	−15,578	12,746	–	−2,832	–	2,176
	2	−1,667	1,317	1,234	−560	1,991	324	−16,012	11,365	–	−4,647	–	4,832
	3	−2,996	1,364	1,419	−756	2,027	−969	−42,839	41,971	–	−868	–	1,760
	4	−2,650	1,474	1,408	−867	2,015	−635	−20,608	14,755	–	−5,853	–	5,631
1987	1	−1,292	1,433	1,552	−849	2,136	844	−15,443	16,143	–	700	–	−1,231
	2	−2,390	1,455	1,350	−770	2,035	−355	−24,743	24,132	–	−611	–	1,408
	3	−3,202	1,652	1,424	−978	2,098	−1,104	−25,058	20,981	–	−4,077	–	5,225
	4	−3,278	1,098	1,197	−906	1,389	−1,889	−9,850	12,799	–	2,949	–	−1,859
1988	1	−3,953	931	1,246	−1,067	1,110	−2,843	−3,449	4,421	–	972	–	2,162
	2	−4,433	907	1,509	−897	1,519	−2,914	−17,554	16,031	–	−1,523	–	5,021

IPD, interest, profits, dividends; SDRs, special drawing rights.

[a] Prior to 1979 foreign currency lending and borrowing abroad by UK banks (other than certain export credit extended) is recorded on a net basis under liabilities.

Source: Central Statistical Office, Economic Trends (419), September 1988

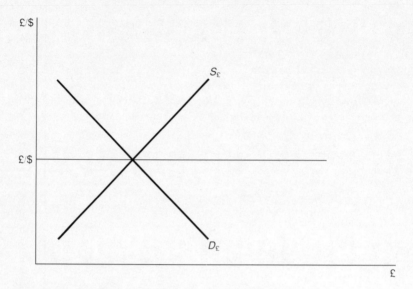

Figure 8.1   The sterling-to-US dollar exchange rate.

Alternatively, the government can prevent depreciation by selling forex from its own central bank's reserves to match the shortfall, as we shall see below.

Consider figure 8.1. Here we are looking at the US$ price of sterling exchange rate: the amount of dollars that can be purchased by a unit of sterling. In the diagram, $D_£$ is the demand for sterling by non-UK residents and $S_£$ is the supply of sterling by UK residents.

Suppose the demand for sterling declines because fewer exports are being purchased by the rest of the world (ROW). For an unchanged capital account, this puts a downward pressure on the sterling exchange rate because it costs fewer dollars to purchase one unit of sterling. The dollar exchange rate rises and the value of sterling depreciates on world currency markets.

However, if the exchange rate is **fixed** or **managed**, the government may intervene because it wishes to support sterling at the original exchange rate. In this case the central bank (in the UK, the Bank of England) will purchase sterling to offset the falling demand. Intervention by a central bank in the foreign exchange markets has implications for a country's money supply. To see this, consider the liability and asset definitions of the money supply:

$$M = \text{MBp} + \text{Dep} \tag{8.4}$$

$$M = F + \text{Sec} \tag{8.5}$$

where M is the supply of money, MBp is fiat money in public circulation, Dep is deposits, F is gold + forex reserves, and Sec is domestic credits, that is, securities held by the consolidated banking sector (domestic banks and the central bank).

Equation (8.4) is the liability definition of the money supply: these are the banking system's liabilities. Equation (8.5) is the assets definition, where the money supply is defined in terms of the assets of the consolidated (public and private) banking sector. Using the second definition, the relationship between the money supply and foreign exchange reserves can be readily seen. If a central bank has to purchase (sell) sterling in order to support sterling (or some other currency), it does so by selling (buying) forex. In the absence of any other actions, the money supply must fall (rise). Therefore, any management of an exchange rate by a government is liable to affect the domestic money supply.

8.1.3 The Link between the Balance of Payments and the Exchange Rate

From an accounting viewpoint the BOP must always balance in total because each external item is effectively entered twice, once to indicate the original transaction (for example the import of a commodity) and again to indicate how the transaction was financed. Table 8.1, column 11, shows the balancing item, which ensures that the BOP does balance: it compensates for net errors and omissions in other items.

BOP equilibrium is often defined as a situation in which, at the existing exchange rate, credits are equal to debits and no official transactions are required. If the exchange rate is allowed to fluctuate freely with no interference, then the forex markets will always clear and the BOP will be in continuous equilibrium, that is, the *ex post* BOP will sum to zero. An *ex ante* deficit or surplus on the current or capital account will cause a change in the exchange rate which will ensure that the *ex post* BOP will sum to zero. If the exchange rate is managed, forex reserves can be manipulated to make the overall accounts balance.

8.2 Fixed Exchange Rates and the Monetary Approach to the Balance of Payments

In the next two sections we examine the links between the money markets and the BOP under fixed exchange rates. In this section, there is continuous full employment and perfect flexibility in the domestic wage rate and in prices. By contrast, section 8.3 will freeze certain prices and allow explicitly for different types of disequilibrium. Section 8.2 is a sketch of the oldest theory of open economy macroeconomics, the monetary approach to the balance of payments, which goes back to Hume (1752). Section 8.3 introduces other possibilities; in particular the Keynesian view of the open macroeconomy is introduced, although it is examined in more detail in chapter 9 under floating exchange rates. To keep matters simple, in both sections capital movements are ignored and we concentrate on a small open economy with no power to influence the foreign exchange prices of its exports and imports.

Many, perhaps most, of the goods produced and consumed within the nation's boundaries are traded internationally. If trade barriers are negligible, their domestic prices in home currency will equal their foreign prices abroad, converted at the relevant exchange rate. But there will be other goods and services (such as bricks, haircuts, restaurant meals) which cannot be bought and sold overseas because of high international transport costs. These goods are non-traded. If both sets of goods, the traded and the non-traded, are produced under perfect competition, profit maximization will ensure that the money wage rate w equals the value of labour's marginal product, where the latter is diminishing as output rises. Consequently, traded sector output will rise when w falls or p_T, the home price of traded goods, increases. Non-traded sector output and employment will go up as w falls or there is a rise in the index of prices of non-traded goods (p_N). On the demand side, assuming the two sets of goods are substitutes, the demand for traded (non-traded) goods will rise (fall) after a rise in p_N or a fall in p_T. Demands for each will also rise following an increase in the supply of money, M_s.

The country may run a surplus or deficit on trade in the short run. It will run a surplus when the output of traded goods outstrips the domestic demand for them. Essentially, this will happen if there is a domestic excess demand for money. A deficit on trade will reflect an excess supply of money, since all capital flows have been banished. The exchange rate is fixed and there is no reason why the money market has to clear continuously. Eventually, however, the current account surpluses or deficits will tend to disappear, if we rule out growth in population and technical change. This is because a surplus implies a rise in reserves; a rise in reserves implies a rise in the domestic money supply, and that in turn will put an upward pressure on w and p_N; traded sector output will fall, while the demand for traded goods rises, and so the trade surplus must tend to decline. In the end, the domestic money supply and the demand for money are brought into balance.

If the central bank increases the money supply in this model, the following happens. If we begin in equilibrium, money will now be in excess supply. People will try to switch into goods. Higher traded goods demand can be satisfied by imports rising or exports falling, so that the trade balance swings into deficit. Higher non-traded goods demand pushes up p_N; and labour market equilibrium calls for a higher money wage w. We now enter a phase of protracted payments deficits where reserves, and hence the money supply, are gradually reduced. So w and p_N fall back until eventually monetary equilibrium is restored. In the end, all the additional money will have been exported. A policy-induced monetary contraction leads to the opposite: falls in w and p_N, external surpluses, and a gradual recovery in the money supply which slowly brings w and p_N back up again.

If the authorities devalue their currency then the price E of forex is raised once and for all by the direct action of the central bank. The domestic currency value of p_T goes up. Both exportable and importable goods will cost more in units of home currency: since the country is small, their foreign currency prices will be given independently. The money wage will be bid up somewhat, as traded goods producers react to the incentive to increase output and employment. Non-traded goods prices p_N will also go up, but by less than the wage rate, and this sector must release labour. On the demand side, a jump in p_T stimulates a switch in favour of non-traded goods. Thus the trade balance improves because traded output rises and trade demand falls, or, put another way, because devaluation has created an excess demand for money. But, assuming trade was initially balanced, the new trade surplus will imply rising reserves and hence rising money supply, and so there will be a sequence of further rises in p_N and w. The process stops when the trade surplus vanishes; that, in turn, requires the money market to be reequilibrated. This happens when the total changes in w and p_N just match the devaluation-induced increase in p_T. In this model, the exchange rate is 'neutral' in the long run: real variables such as relative prices and levels of output and employment in the various sectors are ultimately unaffected by it and nominal variables (p_T, p_N, and w) respond, sooner or later, one to one with it. In contrast, the money supply has no long-run effects at all, on either nominal or real variables.

There are two qualifications to all this. One is the fact that we have abstracted from any trends in national income. Suppose one country keeps growing faster than the rest of the world. The model discussed above suggests that the faster grower should run a surplus on its current account. Why? Because its demand for money and its demand for reserves will be rising quickly. Presumably it will wish to hold a rising share of the world's reserves, such as gold. The only way its share can keep rising is for it to keep running payments surpluses. It is noteworthy that West Germany and Japan, the fastest growing of the world's major economies for most of the post-war period, have shown the strongest tendency to current account surpluses. The USA and UK, relatively slow growing by contrast, have often run deficits.

The second qualification is the assumption that domestic prices (p_N and *w*) are perfectly flexible, ensuring continuous clearance in the markets for labour and non-traded goods. In section 8.3 we explore what happens if p_N and *w* are not free to move.

8.3 Fixed Exchange Rates: The Sticky Price Case of the Balance of Payments

In this section we adhere to every aspect of the model in 8.2 except one. There was perfect price flexibility. Here, by contrast, we shall assume that the money wage rate *w* and the price index p_N for non-traded goods are both frozen. Both this section and section 8.2 provide a simple account; the interested reader is recommended to consult Neary (1980) for a more detailed technical discussion.

Suppose we begin at a point where the labour market and the non-traded goods market both clear. Then we revalue the currency. This is the opposite of devaluation: *E* is cut and a unit of foreign currency now buys less of the home currency than before. Since the overseas prices of exportables and importables are given, p_T must fall at home. Measured in terms of traded goods, the real wage rate has risen: *w* is of course frozen. Thus employment in the traded sector contracts, and so does the domestic output of importable and exportable goods. Now that p_T is lower, demand switches away from the now relatively dearer non-traded goods in favour of traded goods. These changes suggest that the trade balance swings into deficit. In the domestic market there is an excess supply of non-traded goods. Unable to sell so much of their output, the non-traded sector producers release labour. There is a fall in employment in both traded and non-traded industries, and matters do not end there. With their reduced labour incomes, workers spend less on traded and non-traded goods. The reduced demand for traded goods implies that the trade deficit will be lowered, possibly reversed. The fall in demand for non-traded goods triggers a multiplier reaction of falling sales and employment in this domestic industry. The end result, one of excess supply in both labour and non-traded goods markets, is an example of Keynesian unemployment.

A rather different kind of unemployment would have emerged had the money wage rate *w* been increased and imposed at a higher value. Again, there would have been a squeeze on output in the traded sector as firms reacted to a rise in the real wage rate. But this time there would be a real wage jump in the non-traded sector too. Employment would go down there, not because demand was insufficient but because labour was now simply too expensive to hire at its previous higher level. So the economy suffers from an excess supply of labour: employment levels are squeezed in both sectors. But in the non-traded goods market there will be excess demand. This state of affairs is known as classical unemployment.

Other disequilibrium regimes can also arise. A rise in the money supply or an exchange rate devaluation, starting at full equilibrium, would very probably induce a situation of repressed inflation if both w and p_N were pinned down at their old values. We saw in section 8.2 that both these changes would put upward pressure on w and p_N if they were free to move to clear markets; if these price changes are banned, excess demand will arise both for labour and for non-traded goods.

The determination of the trade balance, and the levels of output, employment, and demand in both sectors, is a complex matter which depends on agents' expectations of the future as well as current interrelationships between these and other variables. But it is quite clear that all these regimes are very different. It is most unwise to discuss the effects of policy changes, for example, without stipulating which regime they refer to. Take the case of monetary expansion. This will have no effect on output or employment levels under conditions of classical unemployment. Non-traded production and jobs are held down because labour is too expensive, not because demand is in need of a boost. Under repressed inflation a money supply increase could make matters worse because it would drive the equilibrium money wage–non-traded goods price nexus further away from their imported market-clearing values. But under Keynesian unemployment, monetary expansion would raise employment and output directly in the depressed non-traded sector. A fiscal stimulus would do the same, unless it took the form of increasing state purchases of traded goods, when the only effect would be a cut in the trade surplus. Looking at the trade balance, we can see that the effects of monetary or fiscal changes, and exchange rate changes, differ from those expected under perfect price flexibility (section 8.2). When wage rates and non-traded goods prices are locked, exchange rates exert less net effect on the trade balance and monetary policy changes more. This is especially true of Keynesian unemployment, where it is not even clear that devaluation improves the trade balance. For example, it could set off such a strong boom that domestic demand in the traded sector rises by as much as supply.

The argument so far can be depicted geometrically (figure 8.2). The vertical axis shows the money wage rate, the horizontal axis the price of the non-traded good, p_N. To the left of the origin, the horizontal axis gives the price of an aggregate basket of traded goods, p_T. For the small open economy, p_T is determined by the overseas foreign exchange price of traded goods, p_T^*, and the exchange rate E (defined as the price of foreign currency in units of local money). In the absence of trade barriers $p_T = p_T^* E$. A devaluation of the home currency is a rise in E.

Point A in figure 8.2 is a position of long-run equilibrium, where trade is balanced and the labour and non-traded goods market clear. The

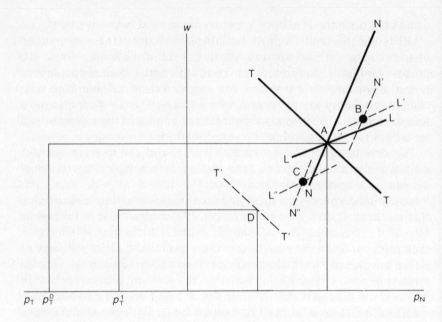

Figure 8.2   The effects of money supply and exchange rate changes in a model with non-traded goods.

flatter line LL shows the combinations of w and p_N along which the labour markets clear. A higher money wage rate reduces employment in the traded sector since p_T is given and a rise in labour costs there squeezes the profit-maximizing level of employment. So full employment calls for a large rise in p_N, in order to generate enough extra jobs in the non-traded sector to compensate for the fall in traded sector employment. Points to the left of LL correspond to an excess supply of labour, points to the right to excess demand. The steep line NN gives the combinations of w and p_N for the non-traded market to clear. A higher p_N will create an excess supply of non-traded goods, and so a large rise in w is required to reduce firms' output enough to match the fall in the demand for these goods. To the right of NN there is excess supply of non-traded goods; to the left, excess demand. The locus TT shows the combinations of w and p_N that yield balanced trade. Above TT there is a trade deficit; below, a surplus on trade. The reason why the TT locus has a negative slope is this. A rise in w worsens the trade balance by lowering traded goods production. So, for trade to remain in balance, p_N has to be lowered to reduce the demand for traded goods in line; consumers switch away from traded goods when they become more expensive relative to non-traded goods.

Now consider the effects of a money supply rise when w and p_N are perfectly flexible and trade is initially in balance. There is upward pressure on p_N (because the new excess supply of money forces up the demand for non-traded goods). This leads to a higher demand for labour in that sector, and so w rises to some extent to clear the labour market. Thus the economy jumps from A to a point such as B. There is now a deficit on trade: traded sector output falls as a result of the higher w, and the demand for traded goods is boosted by the higher money supply and the higher level of p_N. The trade deficit leads to a loss of reserves, and this implies a continuous process of monetary contraction. The economy moves slowly back to point A.

A revaluation of the currency, by contrast, causes an immediate fall in p_T, from p_T^0 to p_T^1. With w and p_N perfectly flexible, w falls, reflecting the drop in traded employment, and p_N drops a little too. A short-run equilibrium at C is established. At C there is a trade deficit, since traded output is squeezed while the domestic demand for now cheaper traded goods is increased. This leads to losses in reserves and continuing falls in the domestic money supply. Eventually, a new long-run equilibrium is reached at D. Here w, p_T, and p_N have all fallen by the same proportion from the initial pre-revaluation equilibrium at A. At D, trade is in balance again.

These are the results when w and p_N are perfectly flexible. If, instead, they are arbitrarily imposed, and frozen, various types of disequilibrium can arise. The Keynesian unemployment (KU) region lies northeast of the full market-clearing equilibrium at A. Both labour and non-traded goods are in excess supply. The KU region is actually larger than the wedge-shaped area between the LL and NN curves: points on NN above A will correspond to effective excess supply of non-traded goods, because the unemployment there will lower workers' effective demand for them. Northwest of A lies a region of classical unemployment (CU) and, to the south, regions with excess demand for labour. If we start with full equilibrium at A and revalue the currency when w and p_N are locked, the result will be Keynesian unemployment. The sharp jump in unemployment which Britain experienced after 1979 can be put down in large part to the substantial appreciation of sterling which occurred at this time.

In these conditions, then, revaluation will be 'contractionary'. In the circumstances of Keynesian unemployment, devaluation is expansionary. Employment and output rise in both traded and non-traded sectors. Here, an import tariff resembles a devaluation to some degree, but will typically be less powerful: devaluation raises labour demand and output directly in exportables industries as well as importables, while import tariffs do not. As argued in chapter 3, import tariffs are all too likely to introduce new damaging distortions; they are not even a second- or third-best device as an instrument for reducing unemployment. Exchange rate devaluation is rather more appealing but is still not fool-proof.

There are several conditions where devaluation could reduce aggregate employment. First, it could induce or aggravate repressed inflation, where labour and non-traded goods are in excess demand. Second, employment could fall if devaluation led to such a large rise in money wage rates (reflecting a high share of spending by workers on traded goods, for example) that real wage rates in terms of non-traded goods actually went up. Third, if the country had large foreign-currency-denominated debts and its residents were forced to lower their effective demand for goods, it is possible that the demand for labour could decline in non-traded industries in the presence of Keynesian unemployment. Another perverse case, considered by Jones and Corden (1976), could arise where capital was perfectly mobile between the traded and non-traded sectors (assumed fixed up to this point) and the non-traded goods sector was labour intensive. In this case, devaluation would have perverse effects: it would raise the relative price of non-traded goods and, instead of reducing a trade deficit, would increase it if wages were held constant. Other cases where devaluation could exert perverse external balance effects are discussed in chapter 11, section 11.2.

When all prices are perfectly flexible, a payments surplus signifies an excess demand for money, or, in a dynamic context, that the home country's growth trend is relatively fast. With price wage stickiness, this no longer follows. There are numerous possible causes, and generalization across the different possible regimes is difficult. The longer the time period under study, the more the monetary approach to the balance of payments has to offer us. Persistent long-term overall payments imbalances probably do betray some form of monetary disequilibrium, or the monetary consequences of differences in long-term growth rates, but for short periods of perhaps a year or less we are better able to rely on a story which recognizes wage stickiness and types of non-monetary disequilibria, such as in the labour markets. Big swings in a country's trade balance in periods as brief as this will usually testify to changes in domestic demand and, underlying them, changes in monetary and fiscal policy. Money wage rates and non-traded goods prices are neither perfectly flexible nor absolutely rigid. In practice they often rise more quickly in states of excess demand than they fall in excess supply, and non-traded goods prices are typically more flexible than wage rates. This suggests that the economy will often be on, or close to, the borderline between Keynesian and classical unemployment. Labour is in excess supply here, but the non-traded goods market clears, or nearly so. These are exactly the conditions that the traditional IS/LM/AS/AD macroeconomic system was devised to explore, in the context of a closed economy. In section 8.4 we look briefly and formally at how this system is adapted to an open one, and the topic is continued in chapter 9 where complete models of exchange rate determination are explored. Discussion of the internal and external balance problems examined above is reviewed in chapter 11, in the context of international policy coordination.

8.4 A General Open Economy Macroeconomic Model

This section provides a general framework for exploring open economy macroeconomics and presents most of the equations used in the models presented in chapter 9. Unlike the previous two sections, which were informal summaries of micro level approaches, this section broadens the analysis to introduce explicit roles for interest rates and international capital mobility. It provides a simple model based upon the principles of the Keynesian paradigm, which dominated macroeconomic thinking for three or four decades after 1936 when Keynes's great work, *The General Theory of Employment, Interest and Money*, was published. However, the framework is flexible enough to encompass rivals. It suppresses the distinction in the previous sections between traded and non-traded sectors, but allows the home country's aggregate price level to deviate from the domestic currency value of foreign price levels.

The general framework consists of a number of equations. Starting with the money market, we have

$$
\begin{matrix}
\text{nominal} \\
\text{money} \\
\text{demand} \\
M_{\mathrm{d}}
\end{matrix}
=
\begin{matrix}
\text{home} \\
\text{price} \\
\text{index} \\
P
\end{matrix}
\times F'
\begin{pmatrix}
\overset{+}{\text{real}} & \overset{-}{\text{nominal}} \\
\text{national} & , \text{interest} \\
\text{income} & \text{rate} \\
Y & i
\end{pmatrix}
\qquad (8.6)
$$

$$
\begin{matrix}
\text{nominal} \\
\text{money} \\
\text{demand}
\end{matrix}
=
\begin{matrix}
\text{nominal} \\
\text{money} \\
\text{supply} \\
M_{\mathrm{s}}
\end{matrix}
\qquad (8.7)
$$

$$
\begin{matrix}
\text{nominal} \\
\text{money} \\
\text{supply}
\end{matrix}
\quad \text{is a given parameter, } M_{\mathrm{s}}
\qquad (8.8)
$$

The plus sign above real income in (8.6) states that money demand rises with incomes, and the minus sign above i indicates that it is lowered by a rise in the nominal rate of interest. Equation (8.6) is a conventional money demand equation. Equation (8.7) states that the money market clears: this is only a *long-run* equilibrium condition in the monetary approach, discussed in section 8.2 above, but becomes a continuous requirement in some other models, especially if exchange rates are floating freely. Equation (8.8) treats the money supply as a policy parameter but can allow for possible feedback from changes in forex reserves of the kind noted in section 8.2 and equation (8.5). It also conceals the forces determining the levels of bank deposits, and the behaviour of financial intermediaries if the money supply is defined more widely than the monetary base.

Together (8.6)–(8.8) provide an LM curve depicting the combinations of i and y where the money market clears for given values of M_s and P. There is also an IS curve, providing an expenditure link between y and i:

$$
\begin{matrix} \text{real} \\ \text{aggregate} \\ \text{demand} \\ \text{for} \\ \text{home} \\ \text{goods} \end{matrix} = \begin{matrix} \text{real} \\ \text{domestic} \\ \text{product} \\ y \end{matrix}
$$

$$
= F^2 \left(\begin{matrix} \text{real} \\ \text{rate of} \\ \text{interest} \\ r \end{matrix} , \begin{matrix} \text{parameters} \\ \text{affected by} \\ \text{fiscal, monetary} \\ \text{policy} \end{matrix} , \begin{matrix} \text{current} \\ \text{account} \\ \text{balance} \\ \text{CAB} \end{matrix} \right) \quad (8.9)
$$

$$
\text{CAB} = F^3 \left(\overset{+}{\text{competitiveness}} , \overset{-}{\begin{matrix} y - \text{productive} \\ \text{potential} \end{matrix}} - \begin{matrix} \text{interest} \\ \text{payments on} \\ \text{net overseas} \\ \text{debt} \end{matrix} \right)
$$
$$(8.10)$$

$$
\text{Competitiveness} = \frac{\begin{matrix} \text{nominal forex} \\ \text{price index } (P^*) \text{ of} \\ \text{foreign goods} \end{matrix} \times \begin{matrix} \text{exchange rate} \\ E \end{matrix}}{\text{home goods price index } P} \quad (8.11)
$$

$$
\begin{matrix} \text{real} \\ \text{rate of} \\ \text{interest} \\ r \end{matrix} = \begin{matrix} \text{nominal} \\ \text{rate of} \\ \text{interest} \\ i \end{matrix} - \begin{matrix} \text{expected} \\ \text{inflation} \\ \dot{P}^e \end{matrix} \quad (8.12)
$$

There are several points to note about (8.9)–(8.12). First, while it is the nominal rate of interest on which money demand depends, since this is the opportunity cost of holding it (using a narrow definition at least), expenditure is sensitive to the real rate of interest. The difference between the two, if one looks forward, is the expected rate of inflation, as (8.12) states. Second, once the economy is opened up to international trade, the concept of aggregate expenditure underlying the IS curve is not total expenditure by domestic residents (for which the symbol a was used in (8.1)) but total worldwide demand for home-produced goods. The former can be identified with the sum of the first two terms on the right-hand side of (8.9); to obtain the latter, we add the current account balance CAB. CAB depends partly on competitiveness (defined in 8.11)) and partly on the gap between real domestic product and productive potential. It also includes net interest payments from overseas, as seen earlier, and here, defined negatively.

The next stage is to allow for inflation. The simplest way of modelling this is to introduce a Phillips curve:

$$\dot{P} = F^4 \left(\begin{matrix} + & + \\ y - \text{productive} & \text{expected} & \text{socio-} \\ \text{potential,} & \text{inflation } \dot{P}^e, & \text{political} \\ & & \text{factors} \end{matrix} \right) \tag{8.13}$$

In (8.13) the speed of a price increase depends on the gap between output and productive potential, a proxy for the difference between the natural and actual levels of unemployment. The Keynesian tradition is to treat expectations of inflation as given in the short run, reacting slowly, if at all, to previous forecasting errors, and perhaps rather unimportant in determining actual inflation. It also regards actual inflation as rather insensitive to real domestic product, particularly when unemployment is high; and it is the socio-political factors governing wage demands, for example, on which greatest emphasis is placed. By contrast, in the rival monetarist tradition (see, for example, Friedman, 1968) the actual rate of inflation responds one to one with expected inflation; the socio-political factors are unimportant except in so far as they include the all-important growth of the money supply; and actual inflation is highly sensitive to the gap between domestic product and productive potential.

The final elements in the story concern international capital movements and the forex reserves–exchange rate relationship. Call the capital account KAB and define it as in surplus, the excess of capital imports over capital exports. KAB is held to depend on the gap between domestic and foreign nominal interest rates $(i - i^*)$ and the expected rate of depreciation of the home currency $(\dot{E}^e)$:

$$KAB = F^5(i - i^* - \dot{E}^e/E, \text{net overseas debt}) \tag{8.14}$$

If international capital mobility is perfect, KAB is so sensitive to $i - i^* - \dot{E}^e/E$ that the gap between these variables actually vanishes. If not, a KAB surplus will be higher the greater is $i - i^* - \dot{E}^e/E$. The level of net overseas debt may exert a negative influence on KAB.

If the exchange rate is floating freely, if there is no intervention by the authorities, and if reserves are constant then

$$CAB + KAB = 0 \tag{8.15}$$

Continuous balance in external payments is achieved at the cost of exchange rate volatility. The exchange rate absorbs all the pressure from shocks of sudden unexpected changes in any of the above equations. Under managed exchange rates, however, both (8.8) and (8.15) are modified to become

$$\begin{matrix} \text{rate of} \\ \text{change in} \\ \text{nominal} \\ \text{money} \\ \text{supply} \end{matrix} = F^6 \begin{pmatrix} \overset{+}{\text{rate of change}} & \text{, other variables} \\ \text{in forex} \\ \text{reserves} \end{pmatrix} \tag{8.8'}$$

and

$$CAB + KAB = \text{rate of change in forex reserves} \tag{8.15'}$$

8.5 Trends in the International Economy

The twentieth century has witnessed sporadic periods of rapid growth in international trade, large international capital movements, and relatively tranquil financial conditions. Most of these characteristics are evident for the period 1900–14 and again for 25 or 30 years after the Second World War. The years between the wars displayed sluggish world trade: in the early 1930s with the impact of a major worldwide recession and the protectionist policies which many countries adopted to export unemployment, world trade actually declined. This period was also one of turbulence in exchange rates and reduced capital movements.

The period after 1973 has seen a reduction in the growth of world trade from its high levels of the 1950s and 1960s. Primary commodity prices have swung violently. In real terms, most have fallen sharply, but erratically, from peaks in 1973–4. The most spectacular and significant changes have been in oil. 1974 saw a quadrupling of oil prices, as the

Organization of Petroleum Exporting Countries (OPEC) exploited its latent monopoly powers to the full. After marking time in money terms, and slipping back by a half in real terms, the oil price doubled again in 1979–80. By contrast, the 1980s have witnessed a fall in real oil prices of nearly 75 per cent, much of it in 1984–6. OPEC's share of free world oil production had dropped from 80 per cent in 1973 to 40 per cent in 1985 as dearer oil prices provoked exploration, discoveries, and conservation measures in countries outside the organization. 1988 and 1989 have seen oil prices (in US dollars) recover.

A trend towards greater international capital mobility which began in the early 1960s has continued. The OPEC countries were large net exporters for almost a decade after 1974, but the falling real oil price has squeezed their current account surplus sharply in the 1980s. In the 1980s the USA has been the world's largest capital importer, borrowing up to 3 per cent of its national income annually. Japan, West Germany, and for six or seven years after 1979 the UK have been large net capital exporters. In the late 1970s and early 1980s there was a major flow of capital to the Third World, particularly to Latin American countries. Explanations for this phenomenon, and an analysis of its effects, are presented in chapter 11. The trend to greater international capital mobility is reflected in section 8.4, equation (8.14).

In marked contrast with the 1950s and 1960s, exchange rates have become highly volatile. The formal lynchpin of the 'Bretton Woods' system of largely fixed exchange rates which prevailed until 1971 was the free convertibility of the US dollar into gold at a fixed price of US$35 per ounce, which held also for private free market transactions until 1968. However, in August 1971 President Nixon broke the dollar–gold link. This initiated a period of free floating between the world's major currencies (the US dollar, the German mark, the Japanese yen, and sterling) which has continued ever since, with one exception: at Christmas 1971, an experiment with new fixed parities began but it broke down 15 months later.

The major swings in exchange rates since the early 1970s are as follows. The US dollar fell by some 40 per cent against a basket of the world's leading currencies from 1973 to 1980. It then rose by about 70 per cent until January 1985, only to fall to its 1980 level in 1988. The dollar's jump in the early 1980s is widely attributed to the combination of tight money and lax fiscal policy which increased US interest rates. Its subsequent decline owes much to the burgeoning, and clearly unsustainable, US trade deficits to which the fiscal boom and loss in competitiveness gave rise. The large overseas borrowings which are counterpart to these must imply a need for subsequent trade surpluses (and hence improved competitiveness) to meet overseas debt charges.

The Japanese yen has climbed unevenly between 1973 and 1988 by about 120 per cent against the average of other currencies. The key factors underlying this have been Japan's relatively fast growth rate: this has given it a sharp competitive edge in its export markets, boosting export receipts and the trade surplus, to which currency appreciation is the only possible long-run reaction. The fast rate of economic growth has also propelled Japan's real demand for money upwards, which again induce exchange rate appreciation given that its monetary policy remained relatively tight. Much of the increase in the yen's external value came in 1986-7.

Sterling fell sharply between 1972 and late 1976. It then climbed until 1981 (especially quickly in 1979 and 1980). Since 1981 its movements have been smaller, slipping gently against many major currencies in the mid-1980s and climbing back somewhat in 1988. The falls in sterling from 1972 to 1976-7 can be put down in part to the UK boom between 1971 and 1973 and the rapid inflation that came in its wake, peaking in 1975. The surge in the late 1970s and 1980 is attributable to a combination of tight monetary policy and oil-related developments, which included the prospect of net exports from North Sea oil and the 1979-80 oil price hike. Chapters 9 and 10 are devoted to analysing the possible explanations for these exchange rate swings, and seeing how well the theories fit the evidence.

There are signs of renewed interest in returning to fixed exchange rates. Of the nine member countries in the European Community in 1979, all but Britain agreed to a system of fixed parities and narrow fluctuations for their currencies, the European Monetary System's exchange rate mechanism. There have been 13 occasions when parities have altered since then, and so exchange rates have not been permanently frozen. In practice the system looks much like a Deutsche mark bloc: West Germany is the dominant country in the group. The issue of global macroeconomic policy coordination is also receiving attention as we near the close of the decade. For example, in 1987, Japan and the USA joined Germany, the UK, and other European countries in an attempt to coordinate their exchange rate, monetary, and fiscal policies. It is too early to see whether this will prove a precursor to a new system of fixed exchange rates and improved coordination of policies between countries. These issues are discussed in chapter 11.

8.6 Conclusions

This review of key concepts and basic models in open economy macroeconomics provides the reader with a background to the rest of the material in this book. Chapter 9 presents three theoretical models of the BOP and exchange rate determination. The variables which influence

BOP and exchange rates are identified. The models also provide some insight into the question of the effectiveness of monetary and fiscal policy in an open economy. Chapter 10 reviews the empirical evidence on exchange rate determination, and in chapter 11 we discuss a number of controversies in open economy macroeconomics, such as how to deal with volatile exchange rates, the debt problem in developing countries, and global macroeconomic policy coordination.

9

Models of Exchange Rate Determination

The purpose of this chapter is to present key models of the macro open economy with the objective of answering the two questions raised at the beginning of chapter 8. At least two of the models have strong roots in their respective closed economy versions. The purpose of closed economy macro models is to explain how the economy of a given country works at the aggregate level. By modelling aggregate demand and aggregate supply, it is possible to draw policy conclusions about the ability of government intervention to affect variables such as aggregate output, the rate of inflation, and unemployment. When these models are enlarged to take account of a country's position in the world economy, attention focuses on the balance of payments (BOP), the foreign exchange (forex) markets, and the feasibility of government policy intervention.

In this chapter, theoretical aspects of four models of the open economy are explored. These are the simple Keynesian model (KM), modern versions of KM referred to as the Dornbusch model (DM), the monetarist model (MM), and the portfolio balance model (PBM). For further background on these models, readers are referred to, for KM, Meade (1951) and Purvis (1985). The work by Mundell (1962) and Fleming (1962) was an outgrowth of the simple KM. Modern versions of the simple KM are explored by Dornbusch (1976, 1987), Dornbusch and Fischer (1980), and Buiter and Miller (1981). Expositions of the MM may be found in Bilson (1979), Frenkel (1976), Minford (1981), and Mussa (1982). Recent contributions to the development of the PBM include Branson and Henderson (1985), Driskell (1980), and Lee (1983). MacDonald and Taylor (1989) provide a good theoretical and empirical survey of the MM and PBM.

Each of the models uses a different set of assumptions to identify the key determinants of the exchange rate and/or BOP and to assess the extent to which monetary and fiscal policy can be effectively employed in an open economy. After these models are reviewed, we turn to a recent attempt to model more than one type of exchange rate expectations formation, and the implications that this has for the determination of exchange rates.

9.1 The Keynesian Model of the Open Economy

9.1.1 The Basic Model

The KM of the open economy involves extending the closed economy IS/LM framework to include an additional market: the forex market. The derivation of aggregate demand in a Keynesian closed economy is based on the LM curve, which gives the combinations of r (the real rate of interest) and y (real output) for which the money market is in equilibrium for a given rate of expected inflation, and the IS curve, which gives the combinations of r and y for which aggregate expenditure is consistent with aggregate output (y). In an open economy, it is necessary to derive a curve which gives the combinations of r and y for which the BOP identity is met and the forex market is in equilibrium.

Essentially, there are two modifications to the IS/LM model once the economy is opened.

Modification 1
Compared with a closed economy, the IS curve is steeper. The introduction of exports and imports changes the condition that injections equals withdrawals from

$$S + T = G + I$$

to

$$S + T + \text{IM} = G + I + \text{EX}$$

where S is the aggregate nominal savings, T is the aggregate nominal taxation, IM is the aggregate nominal imports of goods and services, G is the aggregate nominal government expenditure, I is the aggregate nominal investment, and EX is the aggregate nominal exports of goods and services. There are three main influences on ex − im, that is, the visible and invisible components of the *real* current account balance. These are domestic real income y, foreign real income y^*, and the degree of competitiveness of the home economy. Competitiveness is defined as the difference between the prices of foreign and domestic goods, expressed in a common currency. In the simple KM, only y is an important influence. As domestic real income rises, ex $-$ im falls because imports are an increasing function of y. Hence, there is an additional withdrawal via the rise in imports but no corresponding increase in injections.

Therefore, compared with the closed economy, withdrawals are greater for a given rise in income. To maintain consistency in aggregate demand, the rate of interest r has to fall by more (than in the closed economy) in order to stimulate investment so as to raise injections to the point where equality is restored between injections and withdrawals. This makes the open economy IS curve steeper than its closed economy counterpart.

Modification 2

As was noted earlier, we need a relationship which gives the combinations of r and y for which the forex market is in equilibrium. It is called the BP curve and its derivation requires us to link the forex market with the BOP.

In chapter 8 we identified the two main components of the BOP, the current account and the capital account. Ignoring the third component (the official financing item), we can say that, under flexible exchange rates, for the forex market to be in equilibirum the sum of the current account balance (CAB) and the capital account balance (KAB) must be zero. Thus

$$D \text{ for Forex} = S \text{ of Forex when CAB} + \text{KAB} = 0$$

This condition is used to derive the BP curve, that is, the combinations of r and y for which CAB + KAB = 0 and therefore the forex market is in equilibirum. To simplify its derivation, two further assumptions are made. First, the CAB varies with domestic income. If income rises, imports increase relative to exports and the current account deficit widens or the CAB surplus falls, raising the demand for forex. The converse is true for a fall in domestic income. Second, the size of the capital account varies directly with levels of differential interest rates between countries. A higher real rate of interest r is likely to be associated with a higher nominal interest rate i. Provided that higher r is not offset by an increase in foreign interest rates (i^*, r^*) or a sudden increased expectation of depreciation, the higher r generates an inflow of capital and the size of the capital account, if in surplus, gets larger.

The simple Keynesian model has capital flows responding to any interest differential that exists such that interest parity will be restored. If $i > i^*$, capital flows into the home economy, increasing (reducing) the size of the capital account surplus (deficit). For an unchanged current

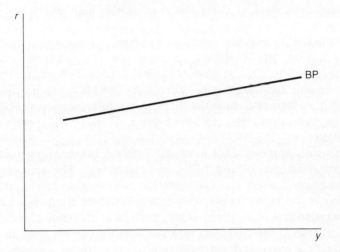

Figure 9.1   The BP curve. There is foreign exchange market equilibrium when an economy is on its BP curve. If the economy is at a point above the BP curve it is running a balance of payments surplus; for points below the BP curve it is running a balance of payments deficit.

account, this causes the value of the domestic currency to appreciate. If $i < i^*$, then capital flows from the domestic economy, reducing (increasing) the size of the KAB surplus (deficit).

Derivation of the BP Curve

With these modifications it is possible to derive the BP curve, that is, the combinations of r and y for which CAB + KAB = 0 and the forex market is in equilibirum. Figure 9.1 shows r on the vertical axis and y on the horizontal axis. In the derivation of the BP curve and the subsequent discussion of policy in the simple KM, the real rate of interest r is used interchangeably with, the nominal rate of interest i because expectations of inflation are assumed to be zero.

The BP curve has a positive slope. To see this, assume that r^* is constant. If r rises, the size of the capital account surplus increases, putting an upward pressure on the value of the currency. To maintain equilibrium in the forex market, the size of the current account deficit must increase and this will occur if there is an increase in y (which increases imports). If r falls then y must fall to maintain equilibrium in the forex markets.

The BP curve is illustrated in figure 9.1. If the economy is at a point below the BP curve, there is a BOP deficit. An economy at a point above its BP curve is running a BOP surplus. The BP curve is horizontal if there is perfect capital mobility and vertical if capital is immobile between countries. In contemporary conditions, a country's BP curve is likely to be flatter than its LM curve because of the high degree of capital mobility.

Shifts in the BP curve are caused by exogenous changes in the level of exports and imports. If there is an exogenous rise in exports (imports) then the size of the current account deficit is reduced (increased) at every level of income and the BP curve shifts right (left). Exogenous changes in net capital inflows also cause the BP curve to shift. Suppose that the level of net capital inflows rises (falls) at every r. Then the BP curve will shift down (up).

In the open economy IS/LM model, internal balance may exist at the point at which the IS and LM curves intersect.[1] The economy is in external balance when the forex market is in equilibrium, that is, the economy is on its BP curve. For internal and external balance to be achieved simultaneously the economy must be at the point where all three curves intersect. Internal and external balance can be used as policy targets. If internal and external balance are to be achieved simultaneously, two independent policy instruments are required. More generally, to achieve n independent targets, it is necessary to use n independent instruments.

9.1.2   Government Policy in the Keynesian Model

The analysis below is largely based on various papers by Mundell and Fleming, including Mundell (1962) and Fleming (1962). In some of their work, these authors assumed perfect capital mobility across national frontiers, implying a horizontal BP at the world rate of interest. It is assumed here that there are some imperfections in the capital markets, enough to make the BP curve slightly upwards tilted. The basic results of the Mundell–Fleming analysis remain unchanged.

To examine the effectiveness of monetary and fiscal policy in this open economy, two further assumptions are made. First, it is assumed that the government uses monetary and fiscal policies to achieve output objectives, that is, to restore y to its full employment level. The economy is initially at a point of external balance but IS and LM intersect at a level of output that is below full employment. The government can achieve its full employment objective in one of two ways (or both).

1   **Through expansionary monetary policy**   An increase in the money supply will shift the LM curve to the right (figure 9.2). Internal balance is achieved at E' but this creates a BOP deficit.

---

1   Internal balance is defined as the point where output and employment are at their natural rates or, in the original definition, where there is full employment. If it exists where IS and LM intersect, then the level of income y is consistent with some form of equilibrium in the labour market and hence with a predicted or constant (possibly zero) level of inflation.

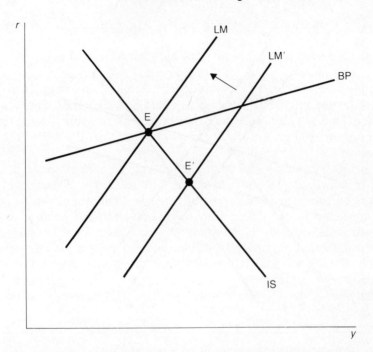

Figure 9.2 Expansionary monetary policy under a fixed exchange rate: LM shifts right to LM'. Balance of payments deficit at E'. The government must sell forex reserves to maintain the exchange rate. Using the assets definition of the money supply (M = forex + gold + securities), the sale of forex reduces the money supply. LM shifts left (see arrow) to its original position and deficit is eliminated. Therefore expansionary monetary policy is ineffective under a fixed exchange rate.

2 **Through expansionary fiscal policy** An increase in government expenditure or a reduction in taxation will shift the IS curve to the right. Internal balance is achieved at E' (figure 9.4) but the policy results in a BOP surplus.

Second, it is assumed that prices are unaffected as a result of these policy actions.

With reference to figures 9.2–9.5, it is possible to draw the following conclusions about the effectiveness of monetary and fiscal policy in an open economy. First, **expansionary monetary policy**, shown in figures 9.2 and 9.3, is only effective (that is, achieves its output objectives) under a regime of flexible exchange rates.

Under fixed exchange rates, the government must intervene in the forex markets to preserve the exchange rate in the face of the BOP deficit (at E') created by the expansionary monetary policy. The buying up of the home currency to support the exchange rate runs down forex reserves which exactly offsets the original increase in the money supply. The LM

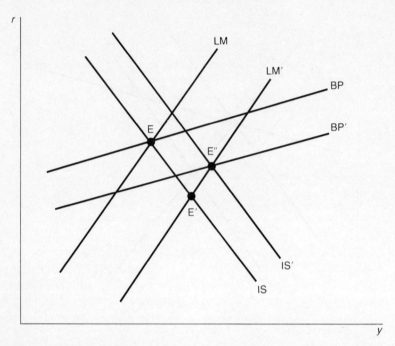

Figure 9.3   Expansionary monetary policy under a flexible exchange rate: LM shifts right to LM'. Balance of payments deficit at E'. The value of the domestic currency depreciates. Exports increase and imports decline, shifting IS and BP to the right (IS' and BP') until the deficit is eliminated at E". Therefore the policy is fully effective.

curve returns to its original position. The only way to avoid this result is through sterilization policy: the money supply is increased by the amount of the decline in forex reserves, keeping LM at LM'. But such a policy does not eliminate the BOP deficit.

Second, **expansionary fiscal policy**, shown in figures 9.4 and 9.5, is fully effective under a regime of fixed exchange rates but under a flexible exchange rate regime its effects are modified: the surplus created on the BOP (at E') will cause the currency to appreciate, reducing exports and raising imports, and thereby shifting the IS and BP curves leftward until the surplus is eliminated at E".

9.1.3. Relaxation of Assumptions in the Keynesian Model

It is possible to relax some of the assumptions used in the simple KM. First, domestic prices were assumed to be fixed. If prices are flexible, it is important to consider the impact of a change in the exchange rate on the domestic price level. Consider the case of flexible exchange rates and expansionary monetary policy. The rightward shift in the LM curve

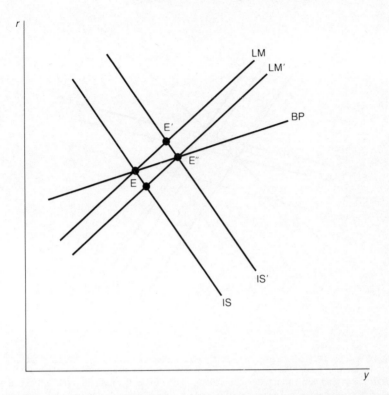

Figure 9.4 Expansionary fiscal policy under a fixed exchange rate: IS shifts to IS'. Balance of payments surplus at E'. The government must buy forex reserves to keep the exchange rate constant. The assets definition of the money supply is M = forex + gold + securities, and so the money supply increases as forex reserves are increased. LM shifts to LM' and the surplus is eliminated at E". Therefore expansionary fiscal policy is fully effective.

(caused by an increase in the domestic money supply) is neutralized and offset by the rise in domestic prices that the money supply increase engenders. The competitiveness gain from the depreciation in the home currency is offset by the domestic price increase and so the rightward shift in the IS curve is also cancelled. In short, the money supply increase is neutral, with real variables (r, y, and the real exchange rate) unchanged. However, if prices adjust slowly, the fall in r and rise in y do occur but they are gradually offset by the subsequent price increases.

Expansionary fiscal policy may have some impact on demand if prices are permitted to vary. The currency appreciates after the policy initiative creates a surplus. The overall price index will decline if foreign goods are an appreciable proportion of aggregate expenditure. A fall in the price index induces the LM, IS, and BP curves to shift to the right, thereby enhancing the effects of the original policy.

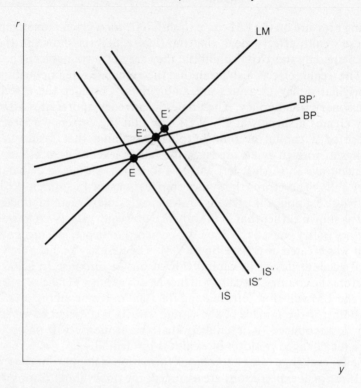

Figure 9.5 Expansionary fiscal policy under a flexible exchange rate: IS shifts to IS'. A balance of payments surplus at E'. The value of the domestic currency appreciates. Exports decline and imports rise. The IS and BP curves shift left to IS" and BP'. The deficit is eliminated at E". Therefore expansionary fiscal policy is only partly effective under a regime of flexible exchange rates.

Second, the simple KM excluded the impact of changes in an economy's aggregate wealth. A persistent current account deficit, balanced by capital inflows, will ensure overall BOP equilibrium (the economy will be on its BP curve) but the situation is not sustainable over the long term. In the case of a current account deficit, the country's net wealth is gradually reduced by the inflow of foreign capital. The impact of the reduced wealth is to cause agents to reduce consumption and increase savings (thus the IS curve shifts left) and to reduce their money holdings (causing the LM to shift right): as the demand for money falls, a higher income is required to absorb the given money supply.

If exchange rates are flexible, there is a third wealth effect. A depreciation of the domestic currency raises the value of assets denominated in foreign currencies but lowers those denominated in the home currency. If domestic residents are net holders of foreign-currency-denominated assets, domestic wealth will rise, increasing the demand for money and exerting pressure on the LM curve to shift left, for a given money supply.

These wealth effects mean that the final equilibria shown in figures 9.2–9.5 are only short-run equilibria: they are not sustainable in the long run. The wealth effects also mean that the exchange rate implications of the original policy measures are ambiguous. Consider the effects of expansionary fiscal policy. The domestic currency appreciates after the policy creates a surplus at E′. We know that the currency appreciates because of a capital account surplus. Assuming that residents' net holdings of foreign assets are zero, the falling level of wealth over time will encourage IS to shift left and LM to shift right as the demand for money falls. Therefore, the policy implications of the simple KM (an effective fiscal policy if exchange rates are flexible) are ambiguous.

It was shown earlier that in the absence of wealth effects expansionary monetary policy caused the domestic currency to depreciate after a BOP deficit was created at E′ (see figure 9.3). The deficit was due partly to a capital account deficit as capital flowed out in response to a lower r. Therefore the country's wealth will increase over time. Hence IS will shift right and LM will shift left, making the final outcome ambiguous. One final point: if the impact of the wealth effects is anticipated when the policy is announced, it is unlikely that the economy will move to E′ before the changed position in wealth is influential.

Finally, exchange rate expectations formation is not part of the simple KM. If rational expectations are assumed, the policy implications of the original Mundell–Fleming analysis are modified because, as soon as the policy is announced, agents react at once to the anticipated change in the exchange rate, thereby generally mitigating any impact on output.

9.1.4 Modern Versions of the Keynesian Model – the Dornbusch Model

Dornbusch (1976, 1987) formally incorporated the points raised in section 9.1.2, thereby presenting a modern version of the simple KM. The 1976 model formally incorporates sluggish price adjustment and rational expectations formation, while his 1987 extension includes wealth effects. We choose to focus on the 1987 model with reference to the 1976 model where necessary.

As in the simple KM, capital is perfectly mobile across countries and productive potential is exogenous, but, in the goods markets, prices are no longer fixed. There is a sluggish response to excess demand and supply. Asset markets adjust immediately to any changes in demand and supply. Asset market participants are assumed to form expectations rationally.

The difference in price adjustment in the goods and assets markets reflects the Hicksian notion (Hicks, 1974, pp. 23–6) that while asset markets are 'flex price' because they respond instantaneously to 'news' (unanticipated events) and excess demand or supply, goods markets are 'fix price' because, at best, they respond only sluggishly to excess demand or supply. The difference in the rate of price adjustment in the goods and asset markets means purchasing power parity (PPP) (the price of a homogeneous good is equal across countries, with prices converted at current exchange rates) holds, if at all, only in the long run. As will become apparent, this is a fundamental difference between the DM and the MM and PBM. In common with the MM and some PBMs, Dornbusch assumes that agents form expectations rationally, that is, they utilize all available information and do not make systematic forecasting errors. In the DM, future shocks apart, the expected rate of currency depreciation is equal to the actual rate of depreciation.

With these assumptions, the simplest 1987 version of the DM of exchange rate determination is summarized as

$$m - p = hi \tag{9.1}$$

$$i = i^* + \dot{e} \tag{9.2}$$

$$\dot{p} = A[a(e - p) + g + b(i - \dot{p})] \tag{9.3}$$

All variables except the interest rate are in logs: g is a variable representing fiscal policy, m is the log of the nominal money stock, i is the nominal interest rate, p is the log of the nominal price level, e is the log of the nominal exchange rate ($\dot{e}$ is positive when the currency is depreciating and negative when the currency is appreciating), and an overdot indicates a change in the log of a variable over time.

Equation (9.1) represents the LM schedule (therefore equilibrium in the money markets) and is a simplification of the 1976 model, where an income term was included. Equation (9.2) says that assets are perfect substitutes (there are no risk premia), with an adjustment for anticipated depreciation. It is a statement of the uncovered interest parity (UIP) condition. Readers are referred to appendix 9.1 for derivation of this condition, covered interest parity and the efficient markets hypothesis. Equation (9.3) states that price adjustment is linked to excess demand which in turn is a function of the real exchange rate ($e - p$), fiscal policy (g) and the real interest rate ($i - \dot{p}$). In Dornbusch's 1976 paper, inflation was related to the difference between output and productive potential. In turn, output was linked to competitiveness (the IS curve shifts right if competitiveness increases as a result, say, of a depreciation in the currency) and the interest rate.

The key feature of this expanded Keynesian model is the difference in flexibility between the asset and goods markets. Any news will cause the exchange rate to adjust instantaneously to the level where the expected capital gains or losses precisely offset the nominal interest rate differential between the home country and the rest of the world (ROW). But price adjustment in the goods market is sluggish.

Dornbusch (1976) explored the impact of an unexpected change in the money supply. Suppose the money supply figures announced by the Bank of England (the central bank) are unexpectedly high and the change in the money supply is expected to be permanent. All agents, with rational expectations and complete knowledge of how the economy works, will sell sterling in anticipation of the higher price level. Thus, within a few moments of the announcement, sterling depreciates to a point below its new long-run equilibrium as dictated by the new money supply figures, that is, it overshoots. To see why sterling must overshoot the new equilibrium exchange rate, consider what would happen if it merely depreciated to its new equilibrium long-run level. In the short run, after the Bank's announcement, i must fall to induce agents to hold increased money balances – prices are sluggish in the short run. Therefore i is less than i^*. If $i < i^*$, sterling will have to appreciate to ensure equal expected returns on home and foreign assets. But it cannot possibly appreciate *above* the new long equilibrium exchange rate; it must do so from below. Therefore the overdepreciation, which occurs immediately after the announcement of money supply figures, ensures compatibility between the need for appreciation brought about by the interest differential and the need for depreciation dictated by expectations of a higher price level at home.

These points are illustrated in figure 9.6. On the horizontal axis of all four parts is time. Figure 9.6(a) shows an initial improvement in competitiveness c immediately after the increase in the money supply but before this increase affects prices. Between t_0 and t_1 c falls, returning to its original level in the long run. Note the large deviation from PPP between t_0 and t_1. Figures 9.6(b) and 9.6(c) show what happens to y and i over time. y rises above y' (y prior to the unexpected increase in the money supply) in transition because of the improvement in the country's competitiveness, i eventually returns to i^* as y falls back to its original level. Figure 9.6(d) shows how the exchange rate E initially rises to match $i < i^*$ and then appreciates over the long run: since E is the price of foreign currency, appreciation of the home currency is a fall in E.

Consider the following numerical example. Real money demand is proportional to income, and both it and aggregate demand have a semi-elasticity to the rate of interest i of $-\frac{1}{2}$. Aggregate demand is barely affected by competitiveness. The Phillips curve (parameter A in (9.3)) has a slope of 2 in output space, so that inflation equals twice the gap between aggregate demand and natural output. The foreign rate of interest is 10 per cent and foreign prices are constant. In these circumstances, and starting at full equilibrium, an unexpected permanent rise in the home country's nominal money supply of 5 per cent will cut the domestic rate of interest from 10 per cent to 5 per cent at once. There is an immediate depreciation of 10 per cent and a 2.5 per cent increase in domestic output. As time goes on, domestic prices rise, the domestic rate of interest climbs back to 10 per cent, and the exchange rate appreciates gradually to reach a new long-run equilibrium where the currency's external value is 5 per cent lower than before. The reasoning behind these results is given in appendix 9.2.

Therefore, DM 1976 confirms the key findings of Mundell and Fleming illustrated in the KM. That is, under conditions of perfect capital

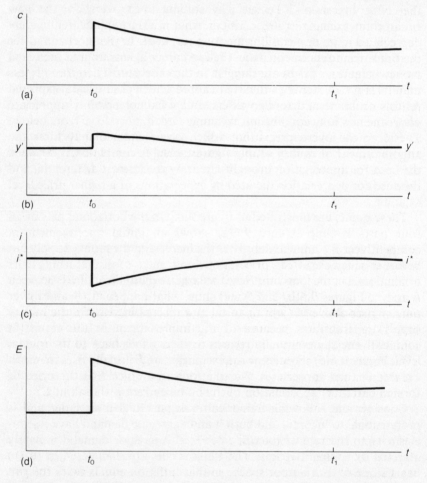

Figure 9.6   The effects of unexpected expansionary monetary policy in the Dornbusch model.

mobility and flexible exchange rates, it is possible to operate an effective monetary policy, although, unlike in the KM, the impact on output is transitory and the exchange rate overshoots because of domestic price sluggishness and perfect international capital mobility, combined with rational expectations formation. The higher price level caused by the unexpected monetary expansion will reduce real balances so that i, relative prices, y, and E return to their original levels.

The DM 1987 considers the impact of fiscal policy on wealth effects and the current account. As in the simple KM, the initial impact of fiscal expansion is appreciation of the home currency but also cumulative current account imbalances. Expansionary fiscal policy gives rise to an inflow of capital as the domestic interest rate rises. As capital flows in, the country increases its external indebtedness. For example, the USA became a net debtor in 1985. The increase in external indebtedness has current account implications because of debt servicing charges. To restore current account balance, the currency will have to depreciate but by more than would be required to return the country to the original equilibrium real exchange rate that existed prior to the fiscal expansion. In this sense, the currency will have to overdepreciate. This type of adjustment is not captured in the simple KM.

The simple KM assumed that assets are perfect substitutes, that is, there is no risk premium or discount attached to assets denominated in different currencies. To allow for a risk premium, equation (9.2) is modified to

$$i = i^* + \dot{e} + a(F - F^* - e) \tag{9.2a}$$

where F and F^* are the supplies of domestic and foreign debt in the national currencies.

Suppose a current account imbalance is financed by an increase in the supply of domestic debt. For example, in the USA in the 1980s the current account deficit was financed by an increasing fiscal deficit which raised domestic rates of interest and stimulated capital inflows. In the DM 1987 the cumulative imbalance requires an increase in the relative yield on domestic securities or a depreciation of the currency. This would correct for the increase in the relative supply of domestic securities denominated in the domestic currency by reducing their value in the foreign currency, restoring portfolio balance with an unchanged yield differential.

To summarize, Dornbusch extends the IS/LM model to include rational expectations, explicit sluggish price adjustment in the goods market, and wealth effects. The implications for policy is as follows. Depending on the unexpected policy change, the exchange rate overshoots its equilibrium real rate because of the immediate impact of the unexpected policy change. For example, in the case of a change in fiscal policy, the initial effect may be appreciation and overvaluation of the currency, but over the longer term the value of the currency must depreciate below its original equilibrium level.

9.2 The Monetarist Model of the Open Economy

The MM of the BOP and exchange rate determination is a logical extension of the closed economy model, where the flexibility of price adjustment in markets is the key to understanding monetarist policy prescriptions. With perfectly flexible prices, markets adjust instantaneously to restore equilibrium.

9.2.1 The Basic Model

In the MM, two fundamental relationships are assumed to hold. First, the fundamental inflation equation holds at home and in the ROW, that is

$$p = m - l \tag{9.4}$$

$$p^* = m^* - l^* \tag{9.4*}$$

where p is the log of the price level, m is the log of the nominal money supply, l is the log of the real money demand, and an asterisk denotes an ROW variable. These equations are merely money-market-clearing conditions. To proceed further, the determinants of real money demand must be specified. In a simple case, these might be

$$l = k + ny - ai \tag{9.5}$$

$$l^* = k^* + ny^* - ai^* \tag{9.5*}$$

where y is the log of national income and the parameters a and n are both positive. When these equations are inserted into (9.4), we observe that income and interest rates drive money demand, which in turn affects the price level. For example, if the growth rate in the money supply exceeds that of money demand, inflation ($\dot{p} > 0$) is the result. Equation (9.5*) is written on the assumption that real money demand is equally elastic to income, and semi-elastic to the interest rate, at home and abroad.

Second, the purchasing power parity (PPP) condition is assumed to be satisfied. PPP is said to hold when, adjusted for the current exchange rate, the price of a good in one country is equal to the price of the good in another country. There must be perfect instantaneous cross-border arbitrage in product markets if PPP is to hold. Thus

$$P = P^*E$$

or, in log form,

$$p = e + p^*$$

or

$$e = p - p^* \qquad (9.6)$$

or

$$\dot{e} = \dot{p} - \dot{p}^*$$

where E is the spot exchange rate (the price of foreign currency in terms of the domestic currency) and e is the log of the exchange rate (for $\dot{e} > 0$, the home currency depreciates).

Combining the equilibrium conditions implied by these two fundamental relationships we have

$$e = (m - m^*) + (l^* - l) = p - p^* \qquad (9.7)$$

or

$$e = (m - m^*) + (k^* - k) + n(y^* - y) + a(i - i^*) \qquad (9.8)$$

Equation 9.8 shows that, *ceteris paribus*, the home currency appreciates (e falls) if the domestic level of income rises relative to the foreign level of income. Also, the home currency depreciates in value if, *ceteris paribus*, i rises relative to i^*. Finally, the inflation rate and the exchange rate cannot both be controlled simultaneously by the authorities if foreign prices (p^*) are varying. To see this suppose that the government is committed to a fixed or stable exchange rate. Normalizing E to unity and setting $e=0$, by equation (9.6) we have

$$e = p - p^* = 0 \quad \text{or} \quad p = p^*$$

It is clear that, if the government is committed to $e = 0$, it must import inflation or deflation ($\dot{p}^* > 0$ or $\dot{p}^* < 0$) from abroad. Also, the growth rate in the domestic money supply must be controlled so that $\dot{m} - \dot{l} = \dot{p}^*$.

It is straightforward to introduce the interest parity condition (see appendix 9.1 for details on interest parity):

$$f = s + d \qquad (9.9)$$

$$d = i - i^*$$

where f is the forward exchange rate and d is the forward premium on the forex rate, or the difference between the log of the forward (f) and spot (s) exchange rates. Inserting the expression for d into equation (9.8) we have

$$e = (m - m^*) + (k^* - k) + n(y^* - y) + ad \qquad (9.10)$$

Thus a rise in d, the forward premium on foreign exchange, implies a lower level of the value of the domestic currency (e is higher).

9.2.2 Government Policy in the Monetarist Model

The MM has several policy implications. First, if the government is committed to a fixed exchange rate then it loses its control over its domestic money supply growth rate and imports inflation (or deflation) from abroad. Second, under flexible exchange rates, monetary policy has negligible effects on real output because the product market will adjust immediately (as it does in the closed economy) given a vertical aggregate supply curve. The same may be said for fiscal policy, though if the policy affects the supply side it could have output effects. The instantaneous price adjustment will in turn be fed through to the forex markets, leading to a currency adjustment and satisfaction of PPP, which rules out any effects on real output arising from trade in the international economy. It is worth stressing, however, that the MM does not depend on PPP: as we saw in the DM, the crucial assumption for monetarist results is perfect price flexibility.

The monetarist prediction about how international capital flows respond to changes in interest differential is very different from the KM. The MM asserts that differences in international nominal interest rates between countries reflect expectations of changes in exchange rates which in turn reflect expectations of differential inflation rates, and hence of differential monetary growth rates (and other variables). For example, if $i - i^* > 0$ there are expectations of higher domestic inflation than foreign inflation and therefore, in the short run, depreciation of the home currency: expectations of a higher domestic inflation rate than foreign inflation rate will raise the demand for forex as agents attempt to reduce their domestic money holdings.

9.3 The Portfolio Balance Model of the Open Economy

9.3.1 The Basic Model

The PBM of exchange rate determination is an extension of the MM. In the MM exchange rates are determined by the relative demand and supply of money at home and in the ROW. The PBM modifies this idea by introducing foreign money and foreign bonds as substitutes for the bonds and money of the home economy. If foreign and domestic bonds are perfect substitutes, then provided the condition of interest arbitrage holds, PBM reduces to the MM and exchange rates are determined solely by activity in the money market. But in the PBM they are not perfect substitutes in the short run. Therefore, exchange rates are determined not only by the relative demand and supply of money but also by the relative demand and supply of other assets.

The differences between the PBM and the MM are summarized as follows. First, the PBM concentrates on the short-run effects on exchange rates of changes in the supply of financial assets. In the monetary approach the determinants of exchange rates are identified in a long-run steady state model. Second, in the PBM, agents are allowed to hold international portfolios of assets denominated in different currencies. This makes the demand for money functions more complex than in the MM and an additional determinant of exchange rates is the presence of imperfect substitution between assets. Finally, in the PBM there is a wealth effect: changes in exchange rates affect the wealth of holders of foreign-currency-denominated assets.

The main assumptions of the PBM are as follows:

(1) The public use their domestic wealth W to hold a combination of three assets, domestic money M, domestic bonds B, and foreign bonds B^*. This assumption contrasts with the MM where residents of a country could hold domestic money or domestic securities but there was no explicit home demand for foreign assets. In the PBM, residents of the home country can hold assets denominated in the currencies of the ROW, while overseas residents can hold assets denominated in the home currency. However, to keep matters simple, it is sometimes assumed that domestic bonds may not be traded internationally and, further, that foreign bond holders exchange B^* for goods; their demand for B and M is not specified. Hence, in aggregate, B^* may only be accumulated by domestic residents through a current account surplus.

Compared with the MM, the introduction of asset substitution across currencies means that the demand for money functions (l, l^*, as given in equations (9.5) and (9.5*)) are more complex and will include both interest rates (i, i^*), expected foreign and domestic inflation, and the forward premium on forex. Foreign and domestic income are additional independent variables, entering, respectively, the domestic and foreign demand for money functions.

Once the demand for money functions are modified and inserted into the exchange rate equation (9.10), the effects of changes in variables such as the growth rate of income, money supply, or interest rates on the exchange rate will depend on the relative sensitivity of *l* and *l** to changes in these parameters, which in turn will depend on the extent to which these different assets are substitutes. The equation for the exchange rate can be reduced to $E = f(M, B, M^*, B^*)$.

(2) The domestic economy is a price taker in all markets including the international financial markets.

(3) Foreign interest rates are assumed to be kept at a constant level by the foreign monetary authorities.

(4) In some PBM's expectations with respect to the forward rate and the rate of inflation are assumed to be formed in an adaptive way, that is, agents revise their forecasts of these variables in the light of past forecasting errors. In others, expectations are assumed to be formed rationally.

The implications of PBM assumptions are illustrated in figure 9.7 which shows the financial markets. The figure is adapted from Girton and Henderson (1977) and Lee (1983). Lee (1983) assumed adaptive expectations for the forward rate and the inflation rate. The vertical axis of figure 9.7 shows the nominal interest rate *i*, and on the horizontal axis is

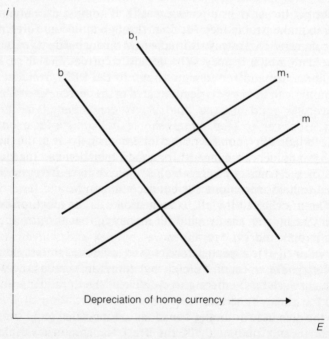

Figure 9.7 The portfolio balance model of exchange rate determination.

the exchange rate, defined as the price of foreign currency: as the exchange rate rises, the value of the home currency depreciaties. Curve b gives the combinations of interest rates and exchange rates for which the bond market is in equilibrium. It has a negative slope, by the following reasoning. If interest rates in the home country rise, residents will wish to hold more domestic bonds in their portfolios. If the supply of these bonds is fixed, then an excess demand for domestic bonds emerges and the only way to eliminate the excess demand is by a fall in the domestic currency value of their foreign bonds. Thus the home currency must appreciate (that is, the exchange rate falls) in value, reducing the real wealth of the portfolio holders (since their foreign bond holdings are now worth less) and, through this income effect, eliminating the excess demand for domestic bonds. Therefore, with a fixed supply of domestic bonds, equilibrium in this market is maintained by the indirect relationship between the exchange rate and the domestic interest rate or the direct relationship between the value of the home currency and the interest rate.

Curve m gives the combinations of interest rate and exchange rate for which the domestic money market is in equilibrium. It has a positive slope, meaning that, as interest rates rise, the exchange rate must rise (the value of the home currency depreciates) in order to maintain money market equilibrium when the money supply is held constant. An increase in interest rates reduces the demand for money, but with a constant money supply the only way to eliminate the implied excess supply of money is to make people feel wealthier through an income effect which raises the demand for money. It is achieved through depreciation of the home currency which increases the domestic currency value of foreign bonds.

9.3.2 Government Policy in the Portfolio Balance Model

Referring to figure 9.7, consider the effects of an increase in the supply of domestic bonds. The b curve shifts right to b_1 because the domestic residents of the country require higher interest rates if they are to be persuaded to hold more domestic bonds, less money, and fewer foreign bonds. The m curve shifts left to m_1 because, as the stock of bonds is increased, the money supply will fall, assuming that the government is engaging in open market operations.

The combined effect of these shifts is to raise the interest rate in the home country. The effect on the exchange rate is ambiguous and depends on which curve shifts by more and on their relative gradients. In figure 9.7, curve b shifts by more, resulting in a depreciation of the home currency: in this case domestic bonds and money are closer substitutes than domestic and foreign bonds, and hence the drop in the demand for foreign assets is less than the drop in the demand for money. If the m curve had shifted by more (assuming equal absolute gradients), the exchange rate would have fallen in value, that is, the domestic currency would have appreciated; in this case domestic and foreign bonds are closer substitutes than domestic bonds and money, and hence the decline in the demand for foreign bonds is greater than the decline in the demand for money.

An increase in the money supply, resulting, for example, from a monetized budget deficit, causes the m curve to shift right. As individuals find that they are holding an excess of money balances, the resulting readjustment in their portfolios is reflected in an excess demand for foreign and domestic bonds. Thus the domestic rate of interest declines (the price of bonds rises), resulting in a higher exchange rate or depreciation of the home currency. An increase in the stock of foreign bonds held at home is generated by a current account surplus in the home country and raises wealth at any given exchange rate. With domestic money and bond supplies fixed, wealth must be reduced to its original level to restore equilibrium. This is achieved by an appreciation of the domestic currency which lowers the value of foreign bond holdings.

9.3.3   Wealth Effects in the Portfolio Balance Model

The PBM has a wealth effect because residents of a country can hold foreign currency assets, the value of which is affected by changes in the exchange rate. The wealth effect means that, in the short run, changes in monetary and/or fiscal policy can have an effect on the real sector of the economy. For example, the increase in the money supply which lowers the domestic rate of interest and depreciates the value of the home currency increases the real wealth of portfolio holders because their foreign bonds increase in value. Consumption rises through the wealth effect, investment is stimulated by a fall in the interest rate, and the demand for exports increases because of the depreciated currency.

All three of these effects raise the level of aggregate demand. For an unchanged aggregate supply, prices rise, thereby damping real wealth effects. In the long run, the PBM reduces to the MM if money is neutral and all the non-money assets are perfect substitutes for each other. Proportional shifts in the price and exchange rate variables eventually eliminate any of the effects on real output described above.

9.4 Models of Exchange Rate Expectations Formation

Expectations formation is an important component of any macroeconomic model. Begg (1982) reviewed its history and argued that Keynes treated expectations as exogenous in the short run to avoid difficulties of modelling endogenous expectations formation and to simplify intertemporal analysis. The immediate post-Keynesian contribution was to incorporate adaptive expectations formation into macroeconomic models, where information on past forecasting errors are used to revise current expectations. But this hypothesis has never been universally accepted, because of the narrowly focused and backward-looking nature of the rule: agents rely on past values in order to form expectations about future values of a variable. If an economic variable such as the exchange rate is *not* determined just by its own history, how could rational agents ever believe that it was? Rational expectations was offered as an alternative hypothesis by Muth (1961) and emphasizes forward-looking behaviour, where agents form expectations about the value of a variable on the basis of all available information. A central claim of the rational expectations hypothesis is that individuals cannot make systematic forecasting mistakes.

Many scholars have focused on the difficulties of modelling exchange rate expectations, with rational expectations receiving most of the attention (for example, see Begg, 1982). Evans (1986) and Meese (1986) also address the question of speculative bubbles. As may be observed from the earlier sections of this chapter and appendix 9.1, rational expectations formation is a key part of the DM and MM and the efficient markets hypothesis.

In a recent paper de Grauwe (1988a) argued that the forward-looking rational expectations behaviour common to the DM, MM and some PBMs should be combined with a specification for backward-looking behaviour. Modelling near rational behaviour is justified by the failure of the other models to explain certain statistical properties of exchange rate movements since the early 1970s. The idea is that, in times of economic uncertainty when no economic model appears to explain exchange rate behaviour, agents resort to backward-looking rules based on technical analysis.

Begin with an equation for the spot exchange rate at date t:

$$E_t = aZ_t + b\dot{e}_t^e \tag{9.11}$$

where Z_t is the vector of exogenous variables that affect the demand and supply of forex. These differ according to the economic model adopted, for example, KM/DM versus MM/PBM. $\dot{e}_t^e$ is the expected rate of currency depreciation. In a perfect foresight rational expectations world, $\dot{e}_t^e$ is determined using a forward-looking rule based on the future values of the exogenous variables Z_t.

The near rational model says that expectations formation is based on backward-looking rules (BLRs) and forward-looking rules (FLRs). The BLR or technical analysis drives expectations when the exchange rate is not deviating significantly from 'fundamentals'. Technical analysis consists of the extrapolation of systematic tendencies observed in past and present exchange rate behaviour. For example, agents might use moving averages or more complex time series analysis to predict future movements in an exchange rate. Such a rule is 'near rational' behaviour because it recognizes that economic models do not provide reliable information to forecast the future. In the absence of such a model, technical analysis takes over.

An FLR is used once agents recognize that an exchange rate has been driven outside the 'agnostic range' (when the BLR is in force) and it becomes clear that it is deviating from fundamentals.

The two rules may be summarized in the following equation:

$$\dot{e}^e = k \left(\sum_i c_i \dot{e}_{t-i} \right) + (1 - k) (e_t^* - e_t) \tag{9.12}$$

The first term on the right-hand side of the equation is the BLR. The expected depreciation of the exchange rate is some average of past and present rates of depreciation. The type of technical analysis depends on the values of the coefficients c_i. If $c_i > 0$, the agent extrapolates past and present rates of depreciation. If $c_i < 0$ the agent expects regression, that is, depreciation after appreciation and vice versa. If $c_i = 0$ exchange rates are expected to follow a random walk, so that only the current exchange rate is relevant. The parameter k is the weight given to the BLR; if k approaches unity, little weight is given to economic rules, and much weight is given to technical analysis.

The second term on the right-hand side of the equation summarizes the FLR. Economic agents respond to a significant deviation of the current exchange rate e_t from the current equilibirum exchange rate e_t^* as determined by the underlying model. If k approaches zero, the FLR dominates.

For example, suppose that there is a shock at date t (that is, a shock to Z_t) which gives rise to an excess demand for forex. The home currency depreciates but, if this is within the range of agnosticism, technical analysis dominates. If the technical analysis is based on extrapolation, the currency will depreciate further and will be moving away from the equilibrium rate. The process continues until the exchange rate leaves the band of agnosticism and the FLR component takes over. At this point, the exchange rate is driven back to its equilibrium rate.

As the near rational model stands, there are two problems. First, what determines the band of agnosticism? Second, the model says nothing about the correct components of Z. If these were known, there would be no need for a BLR. The model avoids the issue of what determines the exchange rate and concentrates on how it may move as a result of expectations formation. However, the model raises the whole question of how expectations are formed, an issue which is discussed further in chapter 10.

9.5 Conclusions

There are a number of important differences between the three models of exchange rate determination. The key variables and assumptions of each model are summarized in table 9.1.

This chapter has demonstrated the increased convergence of theoretical models of exchange rate determination. While there is a marked contrast in the assumptions underlying the simple KM and the MM, there are many assumptions common to the DM and PBM such as rational expectations formation and sluggish price adjustment. The difference relates largely to what policy or market is emphasized. For

Table 9.1 Summary of models of exchange rate determination

Variables and assumptions	KM	DM	MM	PBM
PPP	No	No	Yes	Yes
CAB	Yes	Yes	No	Yes
Effect of				
$i - i^*$ on e	–	na	+	na
UIP	na	Yes	Yes[a]	No
Risk premium	na	Yes, 1987	No	Yes
Goods price				
flexibility	No	Slow	Perfect	Various
International				
K mobility	Some	Perfect	Perfect	Some
Expectations	na	FLR	FLR	FLR/BLR
Impact of policy changes on y?				
(1) dg, fixed e	Yes	na	No[b]	na
dg, flex e	No	Yes[c]	No[b]	Yes[c]
(2) dm, fixed e	No	na	No	na
dm, flex e	Yes	Yes[c]	No	Yes[c]

KM, simple Keynesian model; DM, Dornbusch model; MM, monetary model; PBM, portfolio balance model; PPP, purchasing power parity; CAB, current account balance; e, log of the exchange rate (the domestic currency depreciates if $\dot{e} > 0$; i, i^*, domestic and foreign nominal interest rates; na, not applicable; UIP, uncovered interest parity; FLR, forward-looking rule; BLR, backward-looking rule; dg, change in fiscal policy; dm, change in monetary policy.

[a] Long run only.
[b] Not via demand effects but supply effects can occur.
[c] Yes, but a transitory effect only, and only if the policy change is unexpected.

example, the DM focuses on the impact of unexpected changes in policy and consequences for the exchange rate (overshooting its equilibrium value), while the, PBM highlights the effects of asset substitution on the exchange rate. Unlike the KM and MM, both the DM and the PBM consider certain implications of wealth or asset market effects for the real sector of the economy. Finally, de Grauwe stresses the importance of specifying two types of exchange rate expectations formation, though the problem of specifying the underlying model remains. Can empirical evidence shed any light on which model comes closest to identifying the determinants of exchange rates? This question is addressed in chapter 10.

APPENDIX 9.1 Uncovered Interest Parity, Covered Interest Parity, and the Efficient Markets Hypothesis

The **forward market in foreign exchange** is a market where agents purchase or sell forex for delivery at a specified date in the future, at a price agreed upon at the time of the agreement. The **forward exchange rate** is the price at which the forward forex is traded. It differs from the **spot exchange rate**, the price of forex quoted for delivery of a currency within two days, and the **future spot rate**, the spot exchange rate which prevails at some future date.

For example, suppose an agent agrees to sell 90 days sterling for delivery in July. In April the sale date is set and at the same time the rate at which the sterling will be sold is agreed upon. The seller must have the sterling available in July. Agents purchase forex forward in order to eliminate currency risk. The use of the forward markets permits agents to **hedge** against the forex risk. **Speculators** are the other side of this market, taking long (a net asset position in a foreign currency) or short (a net liability position in a foreign currency) positions.

There are two kinds of interest parity. **Uncovered interest parity** (UIP) states that expected future spot rates should differ from spot rates only by an amount reflecting interest differentials in the relevant currencies for the relevant time interval. If this condition did not hold, risk neutral speculators would speculate by taking open positions in the spot exchange market until the parity was restored. An implicit assumption of UIP is that the expected rates of return open to investors are independent of the currency composition of their portfolios.

It is this condition which is behind the equation

$$\dot{e}^e = i - i^*$$

where $\dot{e}^e > 0$ is the expected rate of currency depreciation, i is the domestic nominal rate of interest, and i^* is the foreign nominal rate of interest. By UIP, if the foreign rate of interest previously equalled and now rises above the domestic rate of interest the domestic currency is expected to appreciate against the foreign currency. For example, if US interest rates are expected on average to be 2 per cent higher per year than rates in the ROW for a period of four years, then the spot dollar rate should be some 8 per cent higher than the rate expected to prevail in four years' time.

Covered interest parity (CIP) states that the difference between the forward exchange rate and the spot exchange rate should reflect the relevant interest differentials over the same holding period.

To see what we mean by a covered interest differential, suppose there are two countries, the USA and the UK. The associated currencies and interest rates are as follows:

i^* 90 day interest rate in the USA
i 90 day interest rate in the UK
E spot price of the pound
Ef 90 day forward price of the pound

It is assumed that there are no transactions costs. An agent who wishes to convert current dollars into future dollars in three months and is averse to forex risk has one of two alternatives.

1 The agent can invest his current dollars in the USA giving him $1 + i^*$ future dollars for every current dollar.
2 He can sell dollars for pounds in the spot market and invest these pounds in the UK at interest i. To avoid any exchange rate risk, the agent sells pounds in the 90 day forward market (when the US dollars are needed). Every current dollar invested in this way yields

$$(1 + i)\frac{Ef}{E} \text{ future dollars}$$

The choice made between the two alternatives will depend on the **per dollar covered interest differential**, that is

$$CD = (1 + i)\frac{Ef}{E} - (1 + i^*)$$

If $CD > 0$, alternative (2) is chosen; If $CD < 0$, alternative (1) is chosen. Rearranging terms we have

$$CD = \frac{Ef}{E} + i\frac{Ef}{E} - 1 - i^*$$
$$= \frac{Ef}{E} - 1 - i^* + i\frac{Ef}{E}$$

$$= \frac{1}{E}(Ef - E) - i^* + i\left[\frac{1}{E}(Ef - E) + 1\right]$$

$$= \frac{1}{E}(Ef - E) + i - i^* + \frac{i}{E}(Ef - E)$$

The third expression on the right-hand side of this equation can be set to zero since it is the product of two very small fractions. Thus

$$CD = \frac{1}{E}(Ef - E) + i - i^*$$

The first term on the right-hand side ($(1/E)(Ef - E)$) is the premium or discount on forward pounds relative to spot pounds and the second term ($i - i^*$) is the interest differential that prevails over the period.

If $CD > 0$ then alternative (2) is chosen over alternative (1): the agent can profit by buying a country's spot and selling it forward, profiting from the higher interest rates in the country and/or any forward premium in the country. But all agents will do this until profitable opportunities are eliminated by the adjustment of the forward premium to ensure that the interest differential is zero, that is

$$\frac{1}{E}(Ef - E) = i^* - i \Rightarrow CD = 0$$

Therefore, if CD is anything but zero, arbitrage will restore CIP in the two markets.

To take a numerical example, suppose that i (UK) = 11 per cent per annum and i^*(US) = 10 per cent. E is £1 = \$1.70. If Ef is such that £1 > \$1.6830 (approximately) in the 12 month market, the agent chooses alternative (1). He chooses alternative (2) if £1 < \$1.6830. If £1 = \$1.6830, the forward discount (1 per cent) matches $i = i^*$, and so $CD = 0$.

Given these parity conditions it is possible to explore the relationship between the forward rate and the future spot rate, assuming that CIP holds. CIP implies that $f = s + d$ where f is the log of the forward exchange rate, s is the log of the spot exchange rate, and d is the interest differential on assets maturing at the date for which the forward exchange contracts are made.

UIP implies that

$$s^e = s + d$$

where s^e is the log of the expected future spot rate.

These two equations show that UIP will hold if and only if $f = s^e$, that is, the forward rate is equal to the expected future spot rate. The **efficient markets hypothesis** may be stated as follows. If agents have rational expectations, then the forward rate f is an unbiased predictor of uncertain future spot rates.

APPENDIX 9.2 How to Find the Exchange Rate Response to News in the Dornbusch Model

Consider figure 9.8. Competitiveness c and real money $m - p$ are in logarithms. Set the foreign price level at unity so that $c = e - p$.

A locus for constant liquidity (CL) must slope down. Liquidity rises (falls) when aggregate demand lies below (outstrips) natural output, and increases in c and $m - p$ both raise aggregate demand. Beneath the CL locus, aggregate demand is below natural output, prices are falling, and liquidity is rising. So the CL locus exerts a horizontal force of attraction.

If the Phillips curve is flat enough (domestic prices are very sluggish),

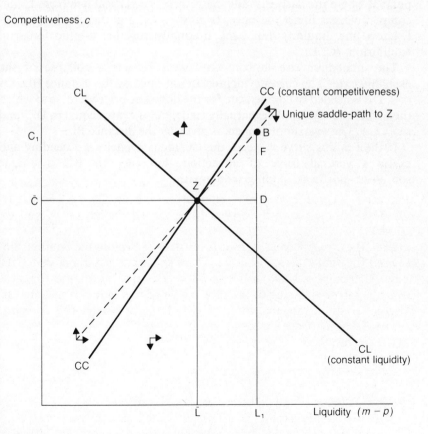

Figure 9.8 Constant competitiveness and liquidity loci, and the saddle-path to long-run equilibrium.

the locus for constant competitiveness (CC) slopes up. Keeping competitiveness steady depends chiefly on maintaining an unchanged exchange rate, and this means keeping the domestic rate of interest equal to the foreign rate. While higher liquidity lowers the home rate of interest, higher competitiveness raises it, since that increases aggregate demand and the demand for money. Below the CC locus the home rate of interest is low, and so the exchange rate must be appreciating, in conformity with UIP. Hence competitiveness is falling. The CC locus exerts a vertical force of repulsion.

The long-run equilibrium Z is defined by the point where the CC and CL loci intersect. There is a unique path, known as the saddle-path, along which this equilibrium is approached. The saddle-path will slope southwest–northeast, and in fact a little more steeply than that. An unexpected permanent rise in the domestic money supply, beginning in long-run equilibrium, raises liquidity temporarily above its long-run value: in figure 9.8, L rises from $\bar{L}$ to L_1. The rise in competitiveness consistent with this unique approach to long-run equilibrium is given by the point B where the dashed saddle-path crosses a vertical line from L_1. So competitiveness jumps, at once, from $\bar{C}$ to C_1, and then both competitiveness and liquidity fall back gradually together to the long-run equilibrium ($\bar{C}$, $\bar{L}$).

The immediate rise in competitiveness reflects a collapse of the exchange rate. The currency depreciates at once by the distance BD. Of this, DF is needed to compensate for the domestic price increase to which the higher money supply eventually leads; DF is drawn equal to DZ (and to $\bar{L}$, L_1). The overshoot element is given by the distance BF.

If the Phillips curve is steep, the CC locus is backward bending and exerts a vertical force of attraction, but there is still a unique southwest–northeast sloping saddle-path.

10

Empirical Evidence on the Determinants of Exchange Rates

This chapter examines a selection of empirical evidence on the determinants of exchange rates. The review provides some insight into the validity of the theoretical models studied in chapter 9. Rather than present a comprehensive review of the literature (which would be out of place in this type of textbook), we have chosen to focus on some key empirical studies. For broader literature surveys, readers are referred to Levich (1985), MacDonald (1988), and MacDonald and Taylor (1989).

In the theoretical models of exchange rate determination, several variables and/or interactions between variables were identified as important determinants of movements in exchange rates. In addition, a number of key concepts were introduced. These are summarized under five headings:

1 purchasing power parity
2 the role of the current account
3 interest differentials
4 interest parity, risk premia, and portfolio preferences
5 expectations formation: forward- and backward-looking rules

Our selective review of the literature is approached in two ways. Section 10.1 surveys the empirical evidence related to the five influences listed above. In section 10.2 we turn to empirical tests of the models themselves and we also report on the performance of a number of US and UK forecasting firms.

10.1 Empirical Evidence on Variables and/or Assumptions in Models of Exchange Rate Determination

Based on a survey of 12 empirical studies, we report on evidence relating to the five concepts that are important components of the theoretical

Table 10.1   Empirical evidence on determinants of exchange rates

Variables and assumptions	Evidence For	Evidence Against
PPP		(2) (3) (5) (7) (11)
Current account	(7)	(7) (12)
+ Short-term correlation between $i^* - i$ and $\dot{e} > 0$	(7)	(7)
− Long-term correlation between $i^* - i$ and $\dot{e} > 0$		(7)
Constant r		(13)
Risk premium	(5) (6) (8) (9)	(2) (4) (5) (10)
UIP	(3) (5) (11)	(1) (2) (4) (5) (6) (8) (10) (11)
FLR		(4) (6) (10)
BLR	(6)	

i, i^*, home and foreign nominal interest rates; $\dot{e} > 0$, depreciation of home currency; r, real interest rate; UIP, uncovered interest parity; FLR, forward-looking rule; BLR, backward-looking rule.

(1) Chrystal and Thornton (1988)	(6) de Grauwe (1988a)	(10) Koromzay et al. (1987)
(2) Driskell (1981)	(7) Hacche and Townend (1981a)	(11) MacDonald (1988)
(3) Edison (1985)	(8) Hansen and Hodrick (1980)	(12) Meese and Rogoff (1983)
(4) Frankel and Froot (1987)	(9) IMF Annual Report (1981)	(13) Mishkin (1984)
(5) Frenkel (1981)		

models presented in chapter 9. The findings and empirical studies from which the evidence is drawn are summarized in table 10.1. The reader should note that most of the studies are selective, that is, they tend to focus on certain propositions but do not embrace all the five concepts listed above. This makes our review a partial one, looking at the importance of each of these explanatory variables one at a time rather than testing for their relative significance simultaneously in a 'nested' econometric model.

Since we have chosen to report on empirical evidence relating to certain critical elements in the story rather than the performance of the models as a whole, such findings fall short of a comprehensive explanation of exchange rate determination. Table 10.2 summarizes empirical studies which have tested full models and we return to a discussion of this table in section 10.2.

10.1.1 Purchasing Power Parity

The concept of purchasing power parity (PPP) is straightforward. It says that the exchange rate will adjust to compensate for any differences in inflation rates between countries so that PPP is maintained. It is an important assumption in some versions of the monetary and portfolio balance models but not in the Keynesian/Dornbusch models.

Of the 12 empirical studies reviewed here, five report on the performance of PPP. Hacche and Townend (1981a) looked at the period first quarter 1972 (1972 Q1) to fourth quarter 1980 (1980 Q4) for eight currencies: the US dollar (US$) the Canadian dollar (C$), sterling (£), the Deutsche mark (DM), the French franc (FF), the Norwegian krone (NK), the Dutch guilder (DG), and the Japanese yen (Y).

Hacche and Townend studied the movement in the real value of the eight currencies, using the real effective exchange rate (RER) and an index of relative normalized unit labour costs (RNULC). An effective exchange rate is the weighted average of the value of a currency against those of its most important trading partners. A RER is the effective exchange rate adjusted for the inflation rates of the home country relative to those of its key trading partners. The inflation differential was measured as the gap between rates of increase in retail or consumer price indices; alternatives would have been differences between wholesale price index changes or gross domestic product (GDP) deflator changes. If PPP is satisfied then the RER should be constant.

Hacche and Townend found the RER for Germany and the Netherlands relatively stable and constant. But in other cases there was no evidence that the real exchange rate was near constant even in the medium term. For example, the period as a whole showed real exchange rate movements of at least 0.5 per cent per quarter in four of the eight currencies, exceeding the nominal movements in three of these cases. Sterling appreciated by more than 1 per cent per quarter in two of the last subperiods studied.

The RNULC was obtained from the International Monetary Fund's (IMF's) index of *relative* normalized unit labour costs in manufacturing and used as a measure of price competitiveness in trade. The effective exchange rate and the RNULC should move together if PPP is to hold. But the change in the RNULC was numerically larger than the change in the effective exchange rate for most of the five subperiods examined by Hacche and Townend. In half of the 40 observations, the change in the RNULC exceeded the change in the RER.

A study by Frenkel (1981) looked at the US$/DM, US$/FF, US$/£, £/DM, and FF/DM relationships for the period June 1973 to July 1979, using monthly data. Two versions of PPP were tested: a relative version

$$d \log S_t = bd \log\left(\frac{P}{P*}\right)_t + v_t$$

where

d is a first difference operator (d $\log S_t = \log S_t - \log S_{t-1}$), S is the spot exchange rate, $(P/P*)_t$ is the ratio of domestic to foreign prices at time t, and v_t is a statistical error term, and an absolute version

$$\log S_t = a + b \log\left(\frac{P}{P*}\right)_t + u_t$$

where u_t is another error term. Frenkel found no evidence to support either the absolute or the relative versions of PPP. Regression equations which excluded the US dollar showed a superior performance over those which included it.

Edison (1985), testing three asset models of exchange rate determination, finds no evidence that the long-run exchange rate supports the PPP hypothesis. Driskell (1981) did find evidence to support long-run PPP, where the long run is approximately two to three years. Details on data used by Edison and Driskell are found in section 10.2, where their work receives more attention.

de Grauwe (1988a), using 1973 as his base year, plotted the real exchange rates for the DM/US$ and the Y/US$ for the period 1973–86. Real exchange rates were not constant and exhibited very long cycles. Exchange rates persistently deviated from their PPP values. MacDonald's (1988) review of PPP cites 14 studies testing for PPP which vary in both the period tested and methodology. Of these, ten reject PPP, and only four point to some validity for it.

There are a number of factors which may prevent achievement of PPP. Perhaps the most important is the role of news and expectations in fix/flex price markets. As was noted in chapter 9, asset markets (including the foreign exchange markets) tend to be 'flex' price (prices are completely flexible) while the goods markets are 'fix' price: prices tend to move sluggishly.

The formation of expectations in flex price asset markets tends to reflect expectations about future circumstances and incorporates any 'news' (unanticipated events) rapidly. But expectations formation in the goods markets tends to reflect the past and present circumstances because agents in these markets are tied to existing contracts. In periods where there is a lot of news which affects the movement in asset market prices but not goods market prices, movements in exchange rates will not support PPP, particularly over short periods. Over the long run, one would expect exchange rate trends to match differences in inflation more closely. It may be that most of the empirical tests reported here cover too short a period.

The strictest version of PPP treats prices as exogenous with the exchange rate adjusting: the direction of causation is assumed to run from prices to exchange rates. Since causation can run either way, evidence that PPP held, if it were available, could be explained by prices adjusting to exchange rates rather than the other way round.

The choice of the price index also affects empirical results. Many investigators use a consumer price index (CPI) or GDP deflator rather than a wholesale price index, because they include prices for non-traded goods. Most wholesale goods are tradeable and homogeneous products that tend to have the same price the world over. However, if the CPI or

GDP deflator is employed, another problem arises because of the presence of non-traded goods in the index. Assume all countries have a non-traded sector (for example, haircuts, shoe shines, mortgages) in which productivity is similar in all countries. In high wage countries, such goods tend to be relatively more expensive than in low wage countries. PPP is at its most uncontroversial in the absence of non-traded goods. If the price index includes non-tradeables, then PPP may appear to be violated: rich countries appear to have overvalued exchange rates since the cost of living will be higher there.

For PPP to hold, real or structural changes must be absent from the world economy over the testing period because such changes affect relative prices. Structural changes in the world economy in the 1970s included the impact of an oil cartel (OPEC), volatility of commodity prices, and differential productivity growth rates among sectors. In addition, the presence of market imperfections arising from transport costs, trade protection, and product differentiation may distort PPP findings because they isolate certain markets and reduce the number of suppliers of a certain good.

Finally, PPP focuses exclusively on the current account. However, changes in capital flows can influence the exchange rate. As we have seen there are two views on how interest rates can affect exchange rates. But PPP assigns no role to interest rates in the determination of exchange rates since international capital flows are ignored. Nor does PPP allow for changes in portfolio preferences.

10.1.2 Influence of the Current Account

In traditional Keynesian models of the open economy, the current account plays an important role as a determinant of exchange rates. Changes in the current account may signal the need for changes in the nominal exchange rate, depending on whether it is a transitory or fundamental/structural change. In modern versions of the IS/LM model (such as Dornbusch, 1976, 1987), the current account has a cumulative effect on 'wealth' and is important because of the impact it has on expectations of the real exchange rate, that is, what the exchange rate must be to ensure current account balance in the long run. 'Surprises' contained in a stream of new information (for example an unexpectedly large move to a current account deficit or surplus) may explain movements in exchange rates.

Monetary models of exchange rate determination assign no direct role to the current account. Indirectly, however, disequilibrium in the money markets will affect the price level, and any departure from the long-run equilibrium real exchange rate is restored by exchange rate adjustment. The process by which the country reaches its long-run exchange rate will involve adjustment of the current account. In the portfolio balance model, a current account imbalance is a necessary condition for flows of foreign securities.

Hacche and Townend (1981a) tested for changes in relative (as opposed to absolute) current account positions of the main industrial countries as a determinant of exchange rates. The study looked for a link between changes in the exchange rate and current account movements by plotting the difference between an inflation-adjusted current account for each country and an inflation-adjusted aggregate current account. Their investigation confirmed that, for a number of currencies, exchange rate movements were related to relative current account developments. Examples were the rise and fall of the yen between 1976 and 1980, the weakness of the US dollar through 1977 and 1978 and its subsequent recovery, the strength of the Deutsche mark from 1973 to 1974 and after 1976, and the real depreciation of the Dutch guilder since 1976. However, the expected relationship held for the French franc up to 1976 but the subsequent improvement in the French current account did not appear to influence the real exchange rate.

For sterling, the expected relationship held for 1972–3 and from mid-1980. One interesting point observed by Hacche and Townend was the movement of the UK to oil self-sufficiency. Oil came on stream in 1976, the UK became self-sufficient in 1980, and oil prices rose rapidly in 1979–80. A rapid increase in the real value of sterling took place between 1978 and 1980. Therefore, while the expected relationship appears to hold, it points to a time displacement problem related to myopic expectations formation by agents. In addition, of all the energy-producing countries with a potential for self-sufficiency (Norway, Canada, and the Netherlands) only the appreciation of the Norwegian krone in 1973–4 approached the magnitude of the rise in the real value of sterling between 1978 and 1980.

Hacche and Townend do report evidence of **J curve** effects in operation: that depreciation of the currency initially leads to a worsening of the current account deficit rather than an improvement. The volumes of exports and imports take time to respond to exchange rate changes. Export contracts are often denominated in the home currency and import contracts in the foreign currency. Therefore, unexpected depreciation of the home currency reduces export receipts measured in the foreign currency but import payments measured in the foreign currency remain unchanged. Hence, the terms of trade (index of export prices divided by index of import prices) worsens temporarily, as does the balance of trade if volumes are initially unresponsive. This may in turn cause further depreciation and is potentially destabilizing. Hacche and Townend find a J curve effect of approximately two months. Once prices and volumes of exports and imports adjust to a fall in the value of the home currency, the negative component of the J curve will be eliminated.

If exports and imports were invoiced in the same currency, the terms of trade effect would not occur. Another possible cause of a J curve might be cost plus pricing behaviour by exporters, who reduce their foreign currency prices after devaluation when their costs are home currency denominated and given. The apparent failure of the US trade deficit to fall despite the large depreciations of the dollar which began in 1985 has renewed interest in these arguments. Possible explanations include the 'beachhead effect' (Baldwin, 1988), which is the postulated reluctance of foreign exporters to relinquish their new footing in the US market; the costs that traders sink in establishing sales networks, with similar effects (Dixit, 1989); and the fact that the dollar depreciation was accompanied by a relaxation of some of the voluntary export restraints imposed on foreign firms.

10.1.3 Interest Differentials

In chapter 9 we noted that the theoretical models of exchange rate determination posit different views as to the link between interest differentials and the exchange rate. The monetary approach predicts that the value of a country's currency is negatively related to an interest differential which favours the country. Nominal interest rates reflect inflation expectations which, in turn, are influenced by relative growth rates in the money supply. Therefore, *ceteris paribus*, a rise in the UK interest rate with interest rates in the rest of the world unchanged results in a depreciation in the value of sterling: UK real money demand falls. The Keynesian model predicts an appreciation of sterling because the value of a country's currency is positively related to an interest differential which favours the country. The portfolio balance model allows nominal interest rates to fluctuate in response to liquidity conditions independent of, or in addition to, the expected exchange rate movements.

A number of studies examine the correlation between real exchange rates and long- and/or short-term interest differentials. Hacche and Townend (1981a) found a positive correlation between short-term interest differentials and the real value of the Canadian dollar and the Norwegian Krone throughout the period 1972 Q1 to 1980 Q4, of sterling between 1977 and 1980, of the US dollar between 1974 Q2 and 1975 Q3 and from mid-1979 to 1980, and of the Deutsche mark through 1973 and from mid-1976 to mid-1977. Negative correlations between short-term interest differentials were found for the real value of sterling up to 1978 and the American, French, and Japanese currencies from 1977.

Hacche and Townend argued that, if negative correlations do exist, they are more likely to be found with respect to the real exchange rate and long-term interest differentials, if the latter reflect relative inflation expectations and are less influenced by intervention by the monetary authorities. But no evidence was found to support this proposition.

The monetary model predicts that, over the long run, the trend in the external value of a country's currency should be negatively related to the growth rate of its money supply. Hacche and Townend examined the relationship between exchange rates and movements in the ratio between an index of domestic money stock and a weighted average of indices of foreign money stocks, using both narrow and broad definitions. There was little evidence to support the monetary prediction of an inverse relationship, though relative broad money in West Germany and Canada did describe the respective trend paths of relative prices and the exchange rate.

In monetary models, expectations that the growth rate in the money supply will exceed the growth rate in output give rise to inflation expectations, which in turn will imply higher nominal interest rates to keep real rates of interest constant. A discount on the forward rate and a decline in the spot rate result from the higher nominal interest rate and inflationary expectations. Therefore an indirect test of the monetarist proposition is to look at the behaviour of the real interest rate. Mishkin (1984) tested the hypothesis of a constant real rate of interest for seven OECD countries: the USA, Canada, the UK, France, Germany, the Netherlands, and Switzerland. He used quarterly data on real three month Euro rates for the period 1967 Q2 to 1979 Q2. The hypothesis that the real rate of interest is constant over time was jointly rejected for all seven OECD countries at very low marginal significance levels. Mishkin also found a negative correlation between real interest rates and expected inflation in all seven countries.

10.1.4 Uncovered Interest Parity, Risk Premia, and Portfolio Preferences

Uncovered interest parity (UIP) is a condition assumed to be met in the Dornbusch and (long-run) monetarist models of exchange rate determination. If this condition is satisfied, then currencies are perfect substitutes. It is argued that if UIP did not hold then only the highest yield currencies would be held and the demand for all other currencies would be zero.

An alternative view is that currencies are imperfect substitutes because agents diversify their portfolios in currencies to manage exchange rate risk. Depending on relative yields, they will demand all currencies in varying amounts and a risk premium provides a measure of the differences between yields. Hence, differences in currency preferences mean that all currencies are demanded and does not necessarily imply the equalization of yields (UIP). The portfolio balance model of exchange rates assumes that currencies are imperfect substitutes, and so there is a risk premium.

Clearly, these opposing views need to be tested. However, the investigation is hampered by two problems. First, *expected* movements in exchange rates are hard to observe: proxying them by forward foreign exchange (forex) discounts is equivalent to asserting that UIP is correct. Second, data on the actual currency distribution of official and private portfolios will combine responses to possible changes in variables such as interest rates and currency preferences. It may be hard to identify the two effects separately. There are also difficulties in obtaining measures of the *ex ante* riskiness of different assets, and some of these risks, on exchange rates for example, may be avoided by forward transactions. Despite these problems, we report on several tests which try to establish whether there is evidence for UIP and/or the existence of risk premia.

In the IMF *Annual Report* (1981) an attempt was made to compare the compounded return which would have been earned (from 1973 Q2 to 1981 Q2) from an investment in particular currencies relative to a basket of currencies (the special drawing right (SDR)). The study found that the returns deviated significantly and persistently from the SDR line, that is, yields varied across currencies. For example, by 1981 Q2, the SDR value of an investment in SDRs would have risen by 96 per cent, that for sterling by 103 per cent, and that for the US dollar by 96 per cent (IMF, 1981, p. 70). In their computations, the SDR was assumed to have the same (five) currency composition throughout the test period and to have earned an interest rate equal to a weighted average of the five currency market rates of interest. The IMF findings do not prove that there is imperfect substitution among international assets, because there is always some anticipated component in exchange rate changes. But the long time span considered, eight years, suggests that there may be systematically different rates of return on different financial assets and is compatible with imperfect substitution.

Another way to test for UIP is to test the efficient markets hypothesis (EMH) and therefore covered interest parity, that is (see appendix 9.1), that the forward rate is an unbiased predictor of uncertain future spot rates if market traders are assumed to have rational expectations. While there is no direct test of whether the forward rate accurately predicts the expected future spot rate unless the latter is explicitly measured (see below), it is possible to test whether the subsequent *ex post* spot rate was well predicted by the forward rate. However, evidence of an inefficient forex market may suggest irrational behaviour on the part of agents, or the presence of a risk premium (suggesting rational behaviour by risk averse agents), or limited information sets. It will not be possible to identify which of the above factors explain the failure of EMH.

Frenkel (1981) examined the forward rate as a predictor of future spot rates and is cited here as an example of the type of investigation used to test the EMH. For a full review of the variety of approaches used, see MacDonald (1988, pp. 178–82). Frenkel used monthly data (June 1973 to July 1979) on three currency relationships: DM/US\$, FF/US\$, £/US\$. He tested the equation

$$\log S_t = a + b \log F_{t-1} + u_t$$

where S is the current spot rate, F is the one month forward exchange rate prevailing in the previous month $(t - 1)$, and u is the residual error term. If the EMH is correct then the residuals in the equation should be serially uncorrelated, the constant term should not differ significantly from zero, and b should not differ significantly from unity.

Frenkel found a small risk premium in the US\$/FF rate which goes against the EMH. In the case of the US\$/DM and US\$/£ rates, no risk premium was found: a was close to zero and b to unity; both were statistically significant at the 95 per cent level.

MacDonald (1988) reported on nine independent studies of the EMH, including the study by Frenkel noted above. The studies varied according to the type of test employed (for example, weak versus semi-strong form tests), the period of estimation (including the period 1973–80 and the interwar floating period), and the currencies tested, which covered the US dollar, the French franc, the Deutsche mark, and sterling. MacDonald concluded that, on the basis of these studies, the EMH must be rejected. His conclusion is less qualified than that reached by Levich (1985). The empirical studies reviewed by Levich supported EMH but only in the Eurocurrency markets. MacDonald also reviewed empirical studies of the UIP condition. He concluded that the evidence is mixed, citing some studies that find evidence of a risk premium (or irrationality on the part of agents) and others that support UIP.

de Grauwe (1988a) observed that movements in spot exchange rates (for the US dollar, the yen, and the Deutsche mark) are larger than the forward premia (discounts). He noted that the *systematically* lower forward premia (discounts) imply systematic underestimation of the size of the future exchange rate changes.

Koromzay et al. (1987) looked at the performance of the US dollar in relation to a weighted average of bilateral rates from 16 OECD countries for the period 1980 Q1 to 1986 Q1. The real effective dollar exchange rate was divided into two components: a deviation of the actual exchange rate from the equilibrium exchange rate that is implied by interest differentials and a residual which captured changed expectations about equilibrium exchange rates. The study observed that a long-term interest differential in favour of the dollar relative to a weighted average of foreign rates emerged in the second half of 1981, peaked at 4.5 percentage points in 1983, and then declined steadily to 1 percentage point by 1986 Q1.

However, Koromzay et al. identify a time displacement problem, inconsistent with the change in long-term interest differentials and federal monetary and fiscal policy over the period. The dollar peaked in 1985 Q1 and was some 70 per cent above its 1980 level. However, according to their calculations, real interest differentials explain only 12 per cent of the premium of the dollar over its equilibrium value. Therefore, to be consistent, the market would have had to revise its expectations of the equilibrium value of the dollar upward by 40 per cent between mid-1983 and early 1985. The subsequent fall in the value of the dollar, together with some further narrowing of interest differentials, implied a 30 per cent downward revision of the real equilibrium exchange rate.

Finally Chrystal and Thornton (1988) looked for an efficient relationship between spot and forward rates, using daily observations for the UK, France, and West Germany from March 1973 to the end of November 1983. They did not find evidence to support the EMH and the results of their study suggested that the spot rate was a better predictor of the future spot rate than the corresponding forward rate.

Frankel (1986) questioned work (including his own, reported above) that statistically rejects the hypothesis that the forward rate is an unbiased predictor of the future spot rate, on the grounds that the auto-regression coefficients in these tests were non-zero. He emphasized that these are tests of a joint null hypothesis that (a) there is no risk premium, that is, the forward rate is equal to the investor's expectations of the future spot rate, and (b) the market is efficient so that investors' expectations are equal to the mathematical expectation conditional on available information.

Frankel argued that the hypothesis of mean variance optimization implies that the risk premium, even if it does exist, must be very small in magnitude. The reasoning behind this is as follows: mean variance optimization implies a relationship between the relative variance of returns, risk aversion, and relative mean returns. If one assumes the existence of *some* risk aversion and variance in relative returns (neither very large) then the gap in expected returns (that would give rise to the risk premium) is very small.

For example, suppose the supply of foreign assets is increased by 1 per cent of world wealth, the standard deviation of international returns is 10 per cent, and therefore the variance is $0.1^2 = 0.01$ and the risk aversion coefficient is 2. Then the risk premium on these assets is very small ($2 \times 0.01 = 0.02$). i^* will rise by $i^* = i + 0.02$ assuming that $i = i^*$ before the increase in the supply of foreign assets.

Therefore, in the studies where statistically significant autocorrelation is found, a risk premium is unlikely to be the explanation *or* the hypothesis of mean variance optimization is unacceptable. Frankel's observation may well explain why evidence for a risk premium or UIP is found in some studies but not others. It may go some way to resolving the 'major dilemma' identified by Koromzay et al. (see below) but it does not explain the time displacement problem noted by them.

Recent work by Frankel and Froot (1987) measured exchange rate formation from survey data. The data came from the American Express Banking Corporation (annual, 1976–85), the *Economist Financial Report* (six-weekly since 1981), and *Money Market Services* (weekly or biweekly since 1983). Based on the median responses from these surveys, they found evidence of a discount on the forward rate. However, the same bias usually appeared in the survey data, and so the bias could not be explained by the existence of risk premia. The Frankel and Froot study also found evidence of overshooting; that is, an increase in the spot rate generated expectations of a future depreciation. While exchange rate expectations formation appeared to be subject to change, there was little evidence of bandwagon effects. On the basis of their findings, Frankel and Froot reject the hypothesis of rational expectations formation. Taylor (1989), using UK survey data, did find evidence of a sizeable risk premium. Nor could he reject the hypothesis of rational expectations.

As summarized in table 10.1, there is mixed evidence supporting and rejecting UIP and risk premia. As Koromzay et al. (1987) point out, the dilemma we confront is this: If rational expectations hold and assets are perfect substitutes, then why is the evidence for UIP weak? If assets are imperfect substitutes, why do deviations from UIP appear to be uncorrelated with the determinants of risk premia? There are a number of ways to resolve this dilemma. First, one could accept the Frankel idea that the risk premium is very small in a mean–variance optimization model with a low risk aversion coefficient. Second, one can reject the idea that the relevant expectations are formed rationally. de Grauwe (1988a) attempts to resolve the dilemma in this way, as is discussed below. Third, it can be argued that concentrating on UIP and risk premia ignores the influence of the current account as a determinant of exchange rates. Markets will recognize that a large current account deficit (surplus) sustained by capital inflows (outflows) cannot continue indefinitely.

10.1.5 Expectations Formation: Forward- and Backward-looking Rules

It was pointed out in chapter 9 that the majority of exchange rate models assume rational behaviour. Rational expectations models of exchange rates predict that any shock to one of the independent variables causes a revision of the future expected exchange rate and therefore an immediate change in the spot exchange rate. As was noted in section 10.1.4, Frankel and Froot (1987) used survey data on exchange rate formation to reject rational expectations formation. In a recent paper by Froot and Frankel (1989), rationality is rejected. As will be seen below, de Grauwe (1988a) also rejected the hypothesis that agents use a forward-looking rule. Begg (1982) reviewed the evidence on floating exchange rates and concluded that one may have to reject either the assumption that international assets are perfect substitutes or rational expectations. But he was confident that the latter need not be discarded because the presence of a risk premium resolves the dilemma. However, we have seen that the evidence on risk premia is mixed.

The 'near rational' model put forward by de Grauwe (1988a) is a supplement to the three main theoretical models because it specifies a type of near rational behaviour by agents. Confronted with the usual problem that exchange rate expectations formation is unobservable, de Grauwe relied on indirect tests to support his case.

de Grauwe compared the foreign exchange market to the stock and commodity markets where the forward-looking rational expectations model is accepted as an accurate representation of how these markets function. Over 1973–82, the monthly variability of stock prices in France, Germany, and the UK was compared with the monthly variability of the FF/US$, DM/US$, and £/US$ exchange rates. He found that, on average, the monthly variability of stock prices was twice as large as the variability of exchange rates and suggested that it points to greater inertia in the forex markets. However, the lower volatility in the forex markets may be attributed to actual or expected government intervention, or lower variability in the 'fundamentals' influencing exchange rates than in the factors governing stock and commodity prices.

The weekly variability of commodity prices was also examined. Variability in rubber (1974–9), silver (1972–80), tin (1972–80), and wheat (1977–82) prices were compared with the weekly variations in the DM/US$ and Y/US$ for the period 1977–86. He found the standard deviation of weekly price changes were two to four times higher in the commodity markets. Finally, de Grauwe compared the long-run variability of exchange rates (DM/US$, Y/US$, 1977–86) and commodity prices (rubber, silver, tin, wheat, 1977–86). The standard deviation of yearly price changes was found to be roughly the same in the forex and commodity markets, confirming that tranquillity appears to be confined to the short-run forex markets.

If the exchange rate is moving in the 'band of agnosticism', and the backward-looking rule is operative, then the expected change in an exchange rate should be negatively correlated with the risk premia. As a second test of expectations formation, de Grauwe cited two studies that find evidence of a negative correlation. For example, Fama (1984), using data for nine major currencies from August 1973 to December 1982 on spot exchange rates and 30 day forward rates, concluded that premia explain the variation in forward rates. However, he found a negative correlation between the premium and expected future spot rate components of the forward rate. However, as was noted in section 10.1.4, evidence on the existence of a risk premium is mixed and no firm conclusions can be drawn.

The near rational model predicts persistence in movements of the real exchange rate; that is, the real exchange rate will move in one direction with no tendency to return to an equilibrium value until the movements become so large that a rational expectations rule replaces backward-looking behaviour. In a third indirect test of expectations formation, de Grauwe cited the failure of real exchange rates to return to a constant value in the 1970s as evidence of persistence, consistent with a backward-looking rule.

Some authors have tested for the possibility of 'speculative bubbles'. A bubble exists when a particular asset price shows a continuing trend further and further away from the long-run equilibrium value implied by the fundamental variables determining it. The likelier it is that an asset price (agents think) will rise, the higher its current price will be, as long as the probability of the bubble bursting is sufficiently slight. Thus, we can observe asset prices (for example, exchange rates) following ultimately unsustainable trajectories. Meese (1986) looked at the monthly dollar exchange rates for the yen, the Deutsche mark, and sterling. Evans (1986) studied the US\$/£ exchange rate from 1981 to 1984. The findings of both authors were consistent with the hypothesis of speculative bubbles.

10.2 Empirical Evidence on Models of Exchange Rate Determination

In this section we turn our attention to studies which test models of exchange rate determination. It includes work by Driskell (1981), Hacche and Townend (1981b), Frankel (1984), Backus (1984), Edison (1985), Meese and Rogoff (1983), Lewis (1988), Levich (1982), and Blake *et al.* (1986). Table 10.2 summarizes the key findings from some of these studies.

The Driskell (1981) and Backus (1984) studies tested the Dornbusch idea of overshooting. Driskell used average quarterly data for the US\$/Swiss franc exchange rate from 1973 to 1977. He found evidence of overshooting in the presence of a monetary shock. A monetary disturbance in a given quarter caused overshooting of the exchange rate by a factor of 2. However, the adjustment path of the exchange rate was found to be non-monotonic. Hacche and Townend (1981b) tested the

Table 10.2   Empirical evidence on models of exchange rate determination

Model	Evidence for	Evidence against
Monetary	(3) (7)	(4)[a] (5) (7) (8)
Portfolio balance	(4)[a] (6) (7)	(6) (7)
Dornbusch	(1) (2)	(1) (5) (8)

[a] Frankel tests a 'synthesis' portfolio balance and monetary model.

(1) Backus (1984)	(4) Frankel (1984)	(7) MacDonald (1988)
(2) Driskell (1981)	(5) Hacche and Townend (1981b)	(8) Meese and Rogoff (1983)
(3) Edison (1985)	(6) Lewis (1988)	

Dornbusch model using a sterling effective exchange rate computed for the UK's five largest trading partners. The results reported were based on monthly data for the period May 1972 to February 1980. They found the money stock variable (£M3) to be significant, with evidence of overshooting. But with the exception of a monetary intervention variable, all the variables in the Dornbusch model were found to be insignificant or wrongly signed. Hacche and Townend (1981b) also tested a monetary model for the period 1972–80, using the UK effective exchange rate. The overall performance of the model was disappointing, and all the key parameter estimates were found to be insignificantly different from zero.

Backus (1984) found evidence to support a Dornbusch model using data on the C\$/US\$ exchange rate for the period 1951 Q2 to 1961 Q1 but not for the period 1971 Q1 to 1980 Q4. In a survey by MacDonald of tests on six 'sticky price' monetary models (four of which model Dornbusch overshooting, including the three cited above), MacDonald reports three studies that support this type of model, one study which finds no evidence to support the model, and two studies which report mixed results.

Meese and Rogoff (1983) tested the out-of-sample forecasting accuracy of a number of exchange rate models. All the models are versions of the monetary theory of exchange rate determination. They included a flexible price monetary model, a sticky price monetary model, and a sticky price monetary model with a current account, where the long-run exchange rate is assumed to be correlated with unanticipated shocks to the trade balance, that is, some version of the specification

$$s = a_0 + a_1 (m - m^*) + a_2(y - y^*) + a_3(i - i^*) + a_4(\dot{p}^e - \dot{p}^{e*})$$
$$+ a_5 TB + a_6 TB^* + u$$

where s is the log of the dollar price of foreign currency, $m - m^*$ is the log of the ratio of the US money supply to the foreign money supply, $i - i^*$ is the short-term interest differential, $\dot{p}^e - \dot{p}^{e*}$ is the expected long-run inflation differential, TB, TB* are the cumulated US and foreign trade balances, $y - y^*$ is the log of the ratio of home output to foreign output, and u is a disturbance term.

The models are monetary in that they posit that, *ceteris paribus*, the exchange rate exhibits first degree homogeneity in relative money supplies, that is, $a_1 = 1$. They each differ in their assumptions about price flexibility and the influence of the current account. The sticky price current account model is a very close approximation to the Dornbusch model. The parameters of each model were estimated using in-sample data and these estimates were used to generate forecasts at one to 12 month time horizons for the US\$/£, US\$/DM, US\$/Y, and a trade-weighted dollar exchange rate. Employing a monthly data series from March 1973 to June 1981, the key finding of this study was that a random walk model performs as well as any estimated model at one to 12 month time horizons. Even though realized values of the explanatory variables were used to generate forecasts from the structural models, they did not improve on the random walk model. Booth and Glassman (1986) showed that one major problem with the monetary model of exchange rates is that the evidence shows it to be misspecified. The postulated long-run proportional relationship between exchange rates and relative money supplies in fact fails to hold. As with so many macroeconomic variables, the series display non-stationarity.

MacDonald (1988) reviewed a number of econometric studies which tested the performance of the flexible price monetary model. He reported that while these models appear to perform well in the early 1970s, when the sample period extends beyond 1978 they perform very poorly.

Edison (1985) used monthly changes of the US\$/£ exchange rate from January 1973 to September 1979 to assess the long-run tendencies of the exchange rate, using three 'asset market' models of exchange rate determination. The first model was a sticky price monetary model which relaxed the fully flexible prices of the monetary model by allowing adjustment in the short run.

Second, Edison tested a Dornbusch model of overshooting. The PPP assumption was relaxed in the short run but, in addition, short-term nominal interest rate differentials were negatively related to the exchange rate and after a monetary shock there was a monotonic adjustment of the current exchange rate back to the long-term exchange rate. A synthesis model was also tested. It combined the monetary and portfolio balance models. The assumption that bonds are perfect substitutes was relaxed.

Edison drew two major conclusions from her empirical investigation. First, the augmented monetary model was supported by the empirical evidence. Exchange rates and interest rates were found to move together, supporting UIP, a fundamental part of the augmented model. Second, the long-run exchange rate behaviour did not support the PPP hypothesis.

Frankel (1984) tested the portfolio balance model for five currencies against the dollar. In the strict portfolio balance model, parameters were incorrectly signed and insignificant. A synthesis model combining the monetary and portfolio balance approaches showed (usually) significant portfolio balance parameters with the correct sign, although the monetary variables were found to be insignificant. MacDonald (1988) reports on three tests of the portfolio balance model and suggests that the results are disappointing, with serious problems of autocorrelation. Similar conclusions are drawn after a review of three synthesis monetary and portfolio balance models. These inconclusive results underline the data problems when a portfolio balance model is tested. Not only is it difficult to obtain information on holdings of financial assets by currency of denomination, but the models depend on stability of the underlying asset demand functions.

Lewis (1988) tested the portfolio balance model and improved on previous empirical tests in several ways. The most important innovation was her estimation of a multilateral portfolio balance model by decomposing the demand for foreign assets into a set of assets denominated in different currencies. Data covered the period January 1975 to December 1981. The empirical findings were mixed. The author found a significant relationship between wealth and asset demand and a correct sign for the interest rate and income level was usually found. But the expected relationship between bond demand and relative rates of return across currencies was not found, in line with evidence from earlier tests of this model, although the results were sensitive to measurement error in the rates of return.

Blake et al. (1986) took a different approach, conducting quantitative tests on exchange rate forecasts produced by six UK forecasting firms and the forward rate. The studies covered a total of 2,720 forecasts, ranging from one to 12 months ahead. The currencies included the US dollar, sterling, the French franc, the Deutsche mark, the yen, and the Italian lire (IL).

The study revealed a downward bias in the forward rate for all currencies over a 12 month horizon and for three of the currencies over a three month period. Most of the forecasting services showed an insignificant forecasting error for US\$/£ forecasts, but for other currencies, significant biases (usually negative) were found and the number of forecasting errors increased with the time horizon. Forecasting errors were also found to be serially and cross-currency correlated. Finally, more often than not, the forecasts failed to predict the correct direction of change. A similar study by Levich (1982) of 12 US forecasting services for the period 1977–81 reached roughly the same conclusions. Compared with the previous year, there was a marked deterioration in the forecasting ability of these services. In terms of accuracy, the forward rate outperformed the forecasting services. Examination of the fraction of correct forecasts by the services was slightly more promising: some of the firms demonstrated a high percentage of correct forecasts that were not due to chance.

10.3 Conclusions

In the concluding section of chapter 9 it was noted that there was a growing convergence among the theoretical models of exchange rate determination. On the one hand, modified versions of a monetary model assign an explicit role to the current account (as in the portfolio balance model) and recognize the possibility of sticky prices in product markets. Modern versions of open economy IS/LM (the Dornbusch model) recognize the importance of the asset markets in exchange rate determination, sticky but not fixed prices (as was the case in the simple Keynesian model), and rational expectations formation.

However, our review of the empirical evidence points to anything but a consensus on the significance of variables as determinants of the exchange rate. Evidence is either mixed or rejects some propositions that are of critical importance in the theoretical models.

First, real and nominal exchange rates appear to be neither stable nor constant, making it difficult to conceive of any policy of exchange rate management. Second, although most sample periods were relatively short and plagued by structural change, evidence for PPP is weak. Competitiveness does not appear to be the only factor influencing the exchange rate. Third, changes in relative current account balances seem to be influential but there appears to be a time displacement problem, suggesting myopic expectations formation on the part of agents. A similar difficulty is observed with respect to changes in interest differentials. In addition, interest differentials between countries were shown to be positively and negatively correlated with movements in exchange rates. This suggests that it may be difficult to use interest rates as a tool to meet exchange rate objectives.

With respect to the last two points, the mixed evidence on UIP, the risk premium, and rational expectations formation may be resolved in a number of ways. One may be to model backward-looking expectations formation explicitly as in de Grauwe (1988a). While some of the empirical evidence suggests that exchange rate expectations are not fully rational, we do not yet know precisely how they are formed. Hacche and Townend (1981b) concluded that their models performed poorly because of an inability to model expectations in a period of government intervention in the forex markets.

It may well be that the failure to find any conclusive evidence on exchange rate determination is due largely to difficulties in specifying and estimating the models. The dynamic properties of the equations in monetary and asset models are poorly specified in relation to the 'Hendry methodology' (Hendry *et al.*, 1984), a view supported by evidence of autocorrelation (MacDonald, 1988, p. 171). Equations critical to certain models, such as the demand for money function, have had a reputation for parameter non-constancy and poor out-of-sample prediction. MacDonald and Taylor (1989) suggest that the solution to poor model specification may be structural estimation of the models.

Finally, as was noted earlier in the chapter, the international economy has undergone a succession of large structural changes over the last two decades, and the extent and nature of exchange rate intervention by governments has been in continuous flux. In forward-looking models, exchange rates jump now to reflect future values of the relevant variables. Regressing exchange rates on contemporaneous values of the variables will never provide an adequate test.

Does the mixed empirical evidence mean that the theoretical models should be discarded as useless academic exercises? The answer is no. In chapter 2 we stressed the importance of avoiding the pitfalls of looking for unicausality. The same point applies here. Failure to identify significant variables with the right sign does not mean that they are wrong. The underlying model may be correct but, because of large structural changes in the economy, they do not perform well in empirical tests.

11

Controversies in International Macroeconomics

This chapter reviews some key controversies in open economy macroeconomics. Essentially, the main debates centre around three issues: the problem of international sovereign external debt, the degree to which foreign exchange markets should be left unmanaged, and international policy coordination. These topics are discussed in separate sections, though all three are interrelated. In the discussion, we hope to make a number of points. A goal of self-sufficiency may take the form of refusing to participate in the international capital markets, or resorting to floating exchange rates. It may appear an attractive route for a country to follow, but as a long-term objective it is questionable. On the other hand, managed exchange rates and freely flowing international capital may call for coordination of economic policies. The international economy is a game and all countries can win, if the game is played with skill and care.

11.1 The Problem of External Debt

Since August 1982 when Mexico made its inability to service its external debt public, the world has had to confront problems arising from sovereign external debt owed by developing nations. For the 'non-oil' lesser developed country group, total external debt grew to reach a total of about US$871 billion in the period 1973–83. For 1986 (World Bank, 1988), this figure was put at over US$1,000 billion for 58 less developed countries. In many of these countries, external debts amount to a sum equivalent to at least four years' exports. As will be seen in subsequent tables, much of it is in the form of sovereign debt, loans guaranteed or directly owed by the nation's government to the western private banking system.

The large debt burden has made it difficult for these countries to service their debt. But there is also a problem on the supply side of sovereign lending. Many private banks engaged in sovereign lending in the 1970s now have loans on their books that may not be repaid, or must be rescheduled over a long period in the future. The secondary loan market showed, in November 1988, that loans to the Philippines, Mexico, Venezuela, Brazil, Ivory Coast, Nigeria, and Argentina were being exchanged at less than half their face value. Chile's secondary value stood then at just over 50 per cent. Many of the banks involved are American, including Citicorp, Bank of America, Manufacturers Hanover, and Chase Manhattan Bank. Two of the big four British clearing banks are also exposed in sovereign lending.

To understand the debt problem, we require answers to three questions:

1   Why do Third World countries demand external finance?
2   What factors determine the composition of the external finance?
3   Why was the external finance, especially in the decade to 1982, often in the form of sovereign loans, that is, external debt incurred or guaranteed by the government of a sovereign nation?

After looking at these central questions, we consider some related issues: borrowers' loan repayment postponements, the roles of the International Monetary Fund (IMF) and World Bank, and implications for the future.

11.1.1 The Demand for External Finance by Developing Nations

The IMF classifies the Third World or developing nations in different ways. Key criteria are predominant export and external financial status. There are a small number of capital-exporting countries, called 'developing' because their economies rely on one predominant export (oil) in the absence of a well diversified manufacturing base. However, there are some oil exporters which import capital, such as Indonesia, Mexico, and Nigeria. The great majority of developing nations are classified by the IMF as net capital importers.

Capital-importing developing nations demand capital in excess of their own domestic capital base. As chapter 6 showed, if the expected marginal return on a country's domestic endowment of capital exceeds the rate of interest charged for the borrowed capital, it will seek to borrow (and therefore import) capital from the international markets. Borrowing capital should ensure a country a faster rate of economic growth and also smooth consumption paths over time.

What governs the composition of a borrower's capital imports, that is, its optimal foreign gearing ratio (FGR, defined as the ratio of foreign debt to foreign equity)? Foreign debt consists of loans made (or bonds purchased) by non-residents of a borrowing country and foreign equity is the sum of direct and portfolio investment undertaken by non-residents.

If it minimizes its costs of borrowing, the country's optimum FGR is set where the expected marginal cost of the debt equals that of equity.

The trends in the composition of external finance for capital-importing developing nations over the last two decades are quite startling. In the 1960s, foreign direct investment made up over a third (39 per cent) of the external finance component. The remainder came equally from official finance and commercial loans. But from the late 1960s on, the growth in the real value of foreign direct (equity) investment in developing countries was close to zero. Real commercial medium- and long-term lending rose by nearly 10 per cent per annum. Many of these loans were sovereign debt, arranged in the syndicated loan market; that is, a syndicate of western banks were party to the loan agreement.

The share of foreign direct investment had fallen to less than 15 per cent of external finance by the late 1970s, with little increase through the 1980s (table 11.1). Private net lending (most of it sovereign debt) was the dominant form of external finance from 1970 through to 1982. In the period 1982–8, the share of official finance increased to over 50 per cent. Issues of foreign bonds by developing countries have been small and countries with debt servicing problems are virtually excluded from participating on the international bond markets. 1985–6 saw a resumption of some bond lending to developing countries (by Asian investors), but it continues to make up less than 5 per cent of total external finance to developing countries (OECD, 1987, table III.1). Issues of foreign portfolio equity are negligible, although over the last two years a few (predominantly far eastern) developing nations have offered equity funds.

Thus, from the 1960s to the early 1980s, developing country FGRs rose

Table 11.1   Sources of external finance in developing countries[a]

	Annual averages, percentage share		
	1973–7	1978–81	1982–8
Official finance	45	34	62
(i) Net long-term borrowing	26	21	38
(ii) Transfers	19	13	15
(iii) Reserve-related transactions	–	–	9
Private finance	55	66	38
(i) Net borrowing[b]	42	55	20
(ii) Net direct investment[c]	13	11	18

–, specific figures for reserve-related transactions are not available for the earlier periods.
[a] 1973–81, figures are for non-oil developing countries; 1982–8, figures are for all developing countries.
[b] Net borrowing from private sources may include short-term official credits.
[c] All funds provided by the foreign direct investor: equity capital, reinvested earnings, and net borrowing from the direct investor.
Sources: IMF, January 1985, p. 4, table 1; IMF, April 1987, p. 75, table 18

as the percentage share of foreign direct investment fell and that of commercial sovereign loans and, later, official finance increased. The increase in sovereign lending coincided with, on the supply side, a rise in syndicated lending. The syndicated loan market peaked in 1982, when it provided the majority of the loans arranged for sovereign borrowers. After a decline of several years, 1987 saw a rapid increase in the volume of syndicated loans arranged but these were largely confined to the private sector. We need to explore the reasons behind the dramatic rise in developing country FGRs through the 1970s and the emergence of sovereign credit as the predominant form of lending.

Three parameters play a crucial part in the determination of a country's optimal FGR. These are risk attitudes, moral hazard, and interference costs. Exploration of these parameters will help to explain a developing nation's decision to accept most of its external finance in the form of loans.

Risk Attitudes

A borrowing nation and foreign investors possess certain risk attitudes with respect to a developing country's income: there is always a random element in this. Suppose both borrower and lender are risk neutral. An agent is said to be risk neutral (averse) if he is indifferent to (refuses) a fair bet with even odds. Then foreign debt and equity are perfect substitutes and neither party has a preference for one instrument over the other.

The outcome is quite different if either or both parties are risk averse. To isolate the role of risk attitudes, assume that there are no costs associated with moral hazard or interference. Also, both borrower and lender treat foreign equity as risky and foreign debt as safe. Suppose the returns on foreign equity are proportionate to domestic output, the size of which is subject to random disturbances. The returns on debt are guaranteed, payable at a fixed rate and independent of what happens to domestic output. Under these conditions, external finance will take the form of 100 per cent equity if the borrower is risk averse and the lender risk neutral, and 100 per cent foreign debt if the lender is risk averse and the borrower risk neutral. The risk averter gets insurance from the risk neutral party. If both are risk averse, a combination of equity and debt financing will take place – the difference in the two party's degrees of risk aversion will influence the optimal FGR. If both equity and debt are risky assets, then the optimal FGR will depend not only on relative risk attitudes but also on other factors such as the *relative degree of skewness* in returns with respect to the two assets. Loans give only downside risk to the lender; for equity, upside and downside risks are approximately symmetrical.

Perceptions of risk are a partial explanation for the rise of developing countries' FGRs over the last two decades. Lenders treated sovereign loans as safe assets. A lender's chief concern about a borrower centres on the latter's ability to repay the loan. This may be measured by the probability that the borrower will remain **solvent** (maintain a positive net worth) for the lifetime of the loan. If one accepts positive net worth as the measure of solvency, it is virtually impossible to declare a sovereign lender insolvent: doing so implies a negative net worth for the borrowing country. A country's asset growth will depend on growth of returns. These are never certain. Nor is there recourse to sovereign nation bankruptcy in international law. It is not surprising that banks were willing to grant sovereign loans, given their tendency to assess credit risk in terms of probability of default. What they failed to appreciate was that a nation could encounter a very long period of **illiquidity**: it could have a positive net worth but lack the means to meet its maturing liabilities when they came due for repayment. The accompanying debt service difficulties seriously undermine the true book value of the lender's assets.

Moral Hazard and Interference Costs

Risk attitudes were not the sole explanation for the rise in the FGRs of developing nations. The interaction between moral hazard and interference costs is also important.

Moral hazard arises whenever an agreement between two parties alters the incentive structure for either party. In a foreign loan agreement, moral hazard may arise because the borrower chooses a more risky production technique than it would otherwise have done, especially if the borrower thinks the loan agreement will be altered should debt servicing problems be encountered. The presence of foreign equity may also create a moral hazard problem because the domestic residents of the host country will not reap all the rewards of the investment. Why work hard just to boost the dividends of foreigners? Hence, production incentives may be affected by foreign direct investment. The general features of loan markets have been explored by Stiglitz and Weiss (1981, 1983), while Heffernan (1986a) has examined them in the specific context of the Third World debt problem. A moral hazard problem can also arise on the lending side if there is a lender of last resort: up to a point, banks could gamble on being rescued by a central bank.

A lender reacts to borrower moral hazard by demanding a higher risk premium on the loan or a higher yield on the equity. Ignoring the potential for lender moral hazard, the optimum mix of foreign debt to equity is guided by the principle that the marginal costs arising from the two types of 'production' moral hazard should be equalized.

Asymmetry of information explains why moral hazard may influence the FGR. The lender knows of the adverse incentive effects on the borrower's choice of production technique or level of effort. But because they are unobservable, he cannot engage in any direct action to penalize this sort of behaviour. As a result, the entire cost of the moral hazard is reflected in the premium or yield.

Alternatively, the investor may try to minimize the information asymmetry by engaging in **sighted investment**. Sighted foreign equity investment usually takes the form that managers are sent to the country to minimize the effects of reduced effort. Sighted foreign loans may involve either specification of the type of production technique (project finance) or monitoring by a third party in the event of repayment problems. In some ways, they resemble the direct investment undertaken by multinational enterprises, examined in chapter 7.

Sighted external finance reduces costs arising from moral hazard but creates **interference costs** which in turn affect the size of the FGR. Sighted foreign direct investment may infringe the host country's microeconomic sovereignty in various ways such as reduced control of natural resources, loss of remitted profits, and lack of local management control. Sighted foreign debt finance can undermine the borrower's macroeconomic sovereignty if it is forced to renegotiate the terms of the loan and, in so doing, must agree to satisfy a number of macroeconomic targets identified by a third party, such as the IMF or World Bank.

Interference costs are difficult to measure because they depend on the borrower's subjective disutility of interference by others. For example, many Latin American borrowers seem to place a heavy weight on the loss of microeconomic sovereignty associated with foreign direct investment while nations like Singapore and Hong Kong appear unconcerned by control over production passing to foreigners. During the 1970s, the majority of capital-importing developing countries favoured loans because there was no formal loss of macroeconomic sovereignty. However, the costs arising from a loss of microeconomic sovereignty were tangible and immediate.

To summarize, risk attitudes and the interaction of moral hazard and interference costs help to explain the trends in external finance over the last two decades. At first, lenders treated sovereign loans as relatively safe assets. The sovereign nature of the loan made default look very unlikely. Borrowers welcomed this form of external finance because interference costs seemed low: third party intervention in the event of debt servicing difficulties was not written into the agreement. In the 1970s, historically low real interest rates, a slump in investment in the West, and high primary product prices also played a role in stimulating lending. The growth of liquidity in the world banking system (arising from the growth of OPEC nations' deposits in the West) and the emergence of a syndicated loan market made it possible for sovereign lending to grow very quickly from the 1970s on. Sovereign lending fell back very sharply after 1982 as lenders began to assess sovereign credit risk in terms of possibly severe long-term liquidity problems, and borrowers reevaluated the interference costs associated with IMF intervention.

11.1.2 Rescheduling and Debt Conversion Schemes

Since the Mexican announcement in August 1982, many indebted countries have entered into and/or completed negotiations for the repayment of their foreign loans. Other countries have tried to reduce their FGR through debt–equity swaps and other debt conversion arrangements. Various devices to postpone loan repayments are explored in this section.

A country may attempt to ease debt servicing burdens by postponing the repayment of the original loans or by changing the nature of the loan agreement itself. Thus one observes requests to reschedule the external debt, the declaration of a moratorium on the repayment of interest, principal, or both, the placement of a ceiling on the amount of loan repaid in a given period of time, debt–equity swaps, and related agreements.

Rescheduling Agreements

As will be observed from table 11.2, rescheduling is by far the most common means by which debt repayments are postponed and loan agreements changed. Rescheduling agreements share a number of common features. These include acceptance by the debtor country of an IMF macroeconomic adjustment programme, the rescheduling of external debt, the provision of new money to enable the debtor country to

Table 11.2   Rescheduled debt, moratoriums, and debt conversion schemes

	1975–80	1981–2	1983–4	1985–6	End 1987
1 Rescheduled commercial debt by number of countries	8	9	33	29	
2 Rescheduled debt (billion US$)	5.6	6.2	40.5	166.6	
3 Moratoria[a] by number of countries	–	–	–	–	8

	1985–8
4 Debt–equity swaps by number of countries	8
5 Debt–equity swaps (billion US$)	12.94

[a] Moratoria are defined to include suspended repayments on interest and/or principal or ceilings on export earnings to service external debt.

Sources: 1, 2, World Bank, 1985, 1988; 3, *The Economist*, 14 March 1987, p. 82; 4, 5, Morgan Guaranty Trust Company, 'LDC debt reduction: a critical appraisal', *World Financial Markets*, 4 December 1988, p. 12

keep up interest payments, bridging loans, and guaranteed provision of interbank and trade facilities. Dornbusch (1988) provided an excellent analysis of how a large debtor's (Mexico) domestic policy and experience has been affected by these adjustment programmes.

Rescheduling packages are new loan agreements between borrower and lender. The IMF oversees the conditions. For the lending party, the terms of these agreements represent a form of involuntary lending. In exchange for agreeing to increase its own lending to a problem debtor nation, the IMF has required lenders not only to postpone repayment of the original loan but to provide the debtor with new money to cover interest payments. This is evident from recent figures cited by the IMF (1987). For 30 capital-importing developing countries classified as having debt servicing problems (and accounting for 50 per cent of external debt owed by developing countries), voluntary or spontaneous private lending dropped by more than 50 per cent between 1981 and 1982. Since 1983, it has been negative. Concerted lending, part of which is involuntary in the sense that banks would not have agreed to it but for IMF intervention, has been the key component of private lending since 1983 (IMF, 1987, table 17).

Debt–Equity Swaps

A debt–equity swap normally involves the sale of the debt by a bank to a corporation at the debt's secondary market price. The firm exchanges the debt for domestic currency through the central bank of the developing country (at a preferential exchange rate) and uses the currency to purchase the equity of a domestic company. Since debt is converted into local equity the country's FGR is reduced. However, as table 11.2 reveals, these swaps are not numerous. Chile is the only country to have restructured much of its commercial external debt (14 per cent) in this way. Just over 2 per cent of the commercial bank debt of participating countries is involved in debt–equity conversion.

There are other types of debt swaps. A debt–debt swap involves the exchange by a bank of one less developed country debt for the debt of another less developed country. It has no implications for the FGR of the developing country; nor does a debt–currency swap, where foreign-currency-denominated debt is exchanged for local currency debt of the debtor government.

Other Debt Conversion Arrangements

Other types of debt conversion are beginning to emerge as conditions for debt–equity swaps grow less favourable. The swap schemes depend on banks' selling off their sovereign paper on the secondary market at a large discount and the number of relatively lowly exposed banks is beginning to dwindle. Also, the swaps may be inflationary for the developing country as they tend to increase the money supply. New forms of debt conversion are emerging. For example, Exit Bonds allow lenders to swap the original loan for new long-term fixed rate bonds. In the case of Mexican Aztec bonds issued at the end of 1987, the margin on the new bonds was higher than the old debt and the principal was guaranteed by a (zero coupon) American Treasury bond. As a percentage of the total external debt, they amount to even less than the debt–equity swaps. Conversion schemes include debt reduction by private sector firms in the less developed country, where a firm buys back its foreign debt at a discount, typically in exchange for the issue of new equity or bonds. Second, debt is reduced as part of a package to privatize state-owned companies. Foreign lenders are permitted to exchange their foreign-currency-denominated debt for local currency shares in the company. Like a debt–equity swap, this type of package reduces a country's FGR. It has been more popular and successful in some countries (for example Chile's sale of its national telephone system) than in others. Finally, debt for trade swaps emerged between developing countries as a means of settling debt obligations between them. It involves a type of counter trade where, instead of repaying the debt, the borrower gives the lending country goods or commodities (for example coffee in the case of Uganda). Alternatively, a country might pay for imports by an agreement where the importing country buys some of the exporting country's external debt on the secondary markets.

The growth of involuntary private lending and official finance and the small number of debt–equity swaps and other forms of debt conversion has meant that the FGR has altered little since the 1970s. But the composition of the numerator (foreign debt) has undergone a significant transformation. From table 11.1 it can be seen that official loans have replaced private loans as the main form of external debt. Private foreign loans would make an even smaller contribution but for the growth of concerted lending, a part of the rescheduling agreements. In the context of the determinants of foreign gearing discussed earlier, the parameters influencing foreign direct investment have not altered but those associated with the type of foreign lending have. The growth of official finance as the major form of lending signals an increased awareness of moral hazard and the need for more closely monitored investments in the light of the debt servicing problems of at least 30 capital-importing countries.

The implications for the developing country debt problem are clear. First, creditors who participated in this market at the time when most of the loans were to sovereign borrowers will continue to face demands to renegotiate existing loan agreements. Given the characteristics of the rescheduling packages, these agents are likely to face increased pressure to agree to new and rescheduled sovereign loans in exchange for an IMF-monitored loan package and continued acceptance of the loans as assets on their balance sheets. There is a somewhat worrying trend: of the 11 reschedulings agreed to in principle in 1984, only three were signed in 1985 (World Bank, 1986, p. 38).

Second, new lenders are unlikely to participate in any syndicated sovereign loans to developing countries. The lessons from the early 1980s suggest that the problems of moral hazard and the uncertainty related to IMF conditionality (once the country has run into debt servicing difficulties) makes this a highly risky and unremunerative form of lending, even though the risk of insolvency is small. Developing countries may not wish to enter into these new arrangements because the interference costs associated with sovereign borrowing are now seen as potentially very high. Even countries that keep up their debt servicing, to try to protect their reputation and future access to credit, may find that overseas capital is hard to get. Bulow and Rogoff (1989) argue that many borrowers are too poor for any promises to meet large debt charges to be credible.

Third, the impact of schemes that alter the composition of external finance has been negligible. The direct or indirect (via debt conversion schemes) use of the secondary loan market provide syndicated lenders with an opportunity to remove the loans from their books, though from the standpoint of developing countries these new forms of financing do not yield any increase in real investment. These developments are unlikely to have a significant effect on the problem loans held on the books of syndicated lenders unless they are prepared to accept a substantial discount on their book value.

11.1.3 International Monetary Fund and World Bank Intervention

Creditors highly exposed in sovereign debt often speculate on the extent to which these two bodies will be able to resolve the Third World debt problem. The World Bank and IMF grew out of the 1944 Bretton Woods agreement, the objectives of which were to promote world economic growth and financial stability. The functions of each institution are outlined in their respective Articles of Agreement.

The term 'bank' in the title World Bank is a misnomer. The institution was created to encourage the economic growth of Third World countries. Unlike its commercial counterparts, the Bank's objective function is not the maximization of profits. It is a development agency formed in recognition that the social costs and benefits associated with lending to developing nations diverge from private costs and benefits. The asymmetric information problems considered above are just one reason why, if left to the private capital markets, lending may be insufficient to meet the requirements of developing countries. The World Bank has a capital base of US$85 billion (1988) and is permitted to borrow as much again from the international capital markets. It is an important lender to developing countries, with an emphasis on both project finance and lending conditional on structural adjustment programmes that promote growth. Conditionality substitutes for the more traditional collateral normally demanded by private lending agents. In its 1986 World Development Report (p. 60) the Bank indicated a desire to encourage foreign private direct investment through the provision of non-commercial risk assurance (the Bank has recently created the Multilateral Investment Guarantee Agency (MIGA)) and by acting in an advisory capacity to investors. It also stressed the need for an expanded capital base to meet the rising demand for its loans.

The IMF Articles of Agreement assign to the Fund the responsibility of assisting members with balance of payments difficulties, including the monitoring of exchange rates and policies of member countries. IMF intervention/conditionality associated with problem debtors makes demands on both the supply side (private banks must increase their exposure in exchange for increased lending from the Fund) and the demand side (debtor countries are required to implement a specific macroeconomic adjustment programme). But all of its activities on this front lie outside the scope of its Articles of Agreement, except in so far as the rescheduling packages help to relieve serious balance of payments difficulties. In its 1986 World Economic Outlook (pp. 104–5), the Fund stated that its role in dealing with the debt problem will continue in much the same way as it has since 1982, that is, it will provide appropriate conditional financing and act as a neutral third party between First World lenders and Third World borrowers in the interests of promoting private external finance. It stressed that its Articles of Agreement preclude participation in commercial financing arrangements, such as the provision of guarantees on private debt.

This brief review of the functions of the Bank and the Fund suggests that it is unlikely that either institution will assume the responsibility for problem sovereign loans currently on the books of commercial lenders. The World Bank lacks the capital base to assume an external debt burden and the official role of the IMF relates to balance of payments and exchange rate management. Neither is in a position to assume the role of an international lender of last resort, even if such a course of action was desirable.

11.1.4 Implications for the Future

While the loan market may not voluntarily increase its exposure to Third World nations, the nature of the current rescheduling agreements means that commercial bank lenders will continue to play an important part in the determination of Third World FGRs. There are some worrying features in the present situation.

First, the rescheduling packages tend to roll over the debt for a brief period, usually two to three years. Yet the rationale for developing country borrowing is based on the idea that the foreign debt or equity will be used to finance long-term growth. The inconsistency is not confined to the rescheduling agreements: it was part of the original loan agreements and continued with the rapid growth in short-term external finance after 1978. The Mexican multi-year rescheduling agreement (MYRA) signed in October 1987 is the first sign that parties are attempting to resolve this problem. Approximately US$49 billion of rescheduled debt was extended to 20 years, with a grace period of seven years.

Second, developing countries are suffering from both capital flight and a decline in savings and investment as a percentage of gross domestic product (GDP). The IMF reports that, since the early 1980s, savings per head declined from an average of just under 28 per cent between 1978 and 1980 to 17.5 per cent between 1983 and 1986. This suggests that savings were being drawn down to maintain consumption levels after cutbacks in external finance. Investment per head also fell from an average of 26.6 per cent (1978–80) to 18.4 per cent in 1983–6. The net flow of foreign savings as a percentage of GDP fell by just over half in the same period.[1] While the pace of capital flight appears to have slowed,[2] it is a source of concern. Unlike the period up to 1982 when a large part of the capital was 'recycled' via sovereign lending, this form of repatriation ceased after 1982. The implications for economic growth in developing countries manifesting these trends are serious. The decline in savings will reduce gross domestic investment (already falling), discouraging growth over the medium term, which in turn will discourage future investment and encourage further capital flight.

Third, some of the burden of the problem falls on lender countries. But who should absorb it? The shareholders of lender banks? Or their depositors? Or the central bank and, hence the taxpayer? Most observers and participants agree that, of these three, the banks' owners should bear the brunt. Many banks' own capital and reserves are insufficient to absorb the massive provisions that might be needed. The potential for widespread commercial bank failure will persist while there is a high degree of exposure of key Western banks. For example, if a number of

---

1   IMF (1987, tables 21, 22). Figures cited are for commercial borrowers with debt servicing problems.
2   A recent IMF study using a derived measure of capital flight shows that, on average, about US$26 billion of capital left developing countries each year in the period 1979–82 but this fell to about US$13 billion for the period 1983–5. The derived measure consists of the total stock of foreign assets less the capitalized value of investment income flows (Deppler and Williamson, 1987).

heavily exposed American banks were to increase their loan loss reserves by any substantial amount, a large part of their equity would be eliminated. One American money-centre bank would experience an equity loss of 131 per cent if it raised its provisioning against Third World loans to 50 per cent. Three other leading American banks could suffer an erosion of equity of over 50 per cent. Since depositor's insurance is incomplete, such concentrated exposure might precipitate bank runs and an international financial crisis.

Only the Japanese banks have taken concerted action to minimize the effect of problematic Third World loans on their balance sheets. In March 1987, 28 of the large Japanese banks agreed to create a debt clearing agency, to be owned by the 28 banks. Third World debt will be sold to the agency at a discount, enabling the banks to book a loss to offset against tax. This scheme is advantageous to the tax position of Japanese banks and also allows individual banks to avoid having to make large provisions against Third World debt, an action that has been shown to affect the share price of American banks.

One question receiving much attention of late is whether debtor nations will enter into a debtor cartel in the interest of renegotiating their debt on more favourable terms, or, if this proves impossible, defaulting on debt outright. There is little evidence of effective collusion between problem debtor countries. Mexico, Brazil, and Argentina have formed an informal 'group of three' made up of external debt netotiators from these countries who exchange information. But the variance in strategies that the countries have followed is not suggestive of collusive behaviour. In late 1987, Mexico reached the first significant long-term rescheduling agreement (MYRA) and recently attempted to swap about one-fifth of its external debt for new Mexican bonds, backed by American Treasury bonds. Argentina entered into a rescheduling agreement early in 1987 and in February 1988 negotiated a bridging loan to cover a reserves crisis associated with the repayment of interest on its BONEX bonds. In 1987 Brazil stopped paying interest and capital on different forms of debt and one of its parliamentary committees voted to ban all swaps of foreign debt into direct investments. But in early February 1988 it announced plans to clear its arrears in bank debt and to introduce a somewhat restrictive debt–equity conversion scheme. This testifies to its desire to avoid further costs arising from reduced trade credit and an inability to negotiate lower interest rates on its loans, once a moratorium was imposed. Though table 11.2 reveals that several countries have declared moratoria, there is no evidence of concerted action.

Nor is there much evidence of collusion on the supply side. Banks engage in different strategies depending on their interests. Those with relatively small exposures have been reluctant to agree to rescheduling packages, as have some of the large German banks. Large heavily exposed American banks have tended to play lead roles in restructuring negotiations and at least two have helped to arrange debt–equity swaps. The only example of concerted action was in the formation in 1983 of the Institute for International Finance, an information gathering body for member banks heavily exposed in sovereign loans.

The failure of the Baker initiative (October 1985) is evidence of an impasse between all parties involved in the sovereign debt problem. The plan stressed the need for improved collaboration between the Fund and the World Bank, increased exposure by private commercial lenders, and the use of stabilization policies to promote economic growth. While some forms of collaboration have increased, there has been no real progress on the other two points in the plan. The Brady plan (March 1988) may suffer the same fate. It explicitly recognized a need for debt reduction and called for a review of tax and accountancy rules that may hinder it. For example, accountants draw a crucial distinction between 'performing' and 'non-performing' loans. Loans perform if interest is received. Provision must be made against any loan declared non-performing.

Like Baker before him, Brady appears to place a high value on the IMF and World Bank stabilization programmes as an integral part of managing the debt crisis. More worrying, the plan says nothing explicit about which group(s) should bear the cost of debt reduction.

The seeds of the 1980s international debt problem were sown when sovereign external debt owed to private banks in the West began to grow in the early 1970s. Underlying this was a unique interaction of risk attitudes, moral hazard, and interference costs. Serious debt management problems emerged when the world economy was hit by a series of random economic shocks (Heffernan, 1986b, ch. 1) which included sharp oil price changes, volatility of interest rates and exchange rates, and, after 1978, world recession.

The absence of any long-term solution to the sovereign debt problem continues to pose a threat to international financial stability. Current management does not get at the source of the crisis, nor does it help to contain the random shocks that were responsible for precipitating it. Could greater exchange rate management or global macroeconomic policy coordination be helpful here? The answer may be yes if they help to buffer the world economy from random shocks and serve to reduce exchange rate and possibly interest rate volatility. But is either desirable in its own right? We look at these issues in the next two sections.

11.2 Should Exchange Rates be Managed?

The Bretton Woods Agreement broke down in August 1971. Since 1973, most of the world's major currencies have been free to float, albeit subject to periods of intervention and management of exchange rates by central banks and government authorities. Calls for a return to a system of fixed, or at least managed, exchange rates have occurred ever since 1973. The period has witnessed the emergence of the European Monetary System (EMS), which is really just a type of exchange rate union among member countries, a Bretton Woods in miniature. In this section, we discuss the points for and against the different types of exchange rate regime, consider various suggestions for currency reform, and review the performance of the EMS.

11.2.1 Arguments For and Against Flexible Rates

A number of points have been made with respect to the argument for and against flexible exchange rates.

Flexible Exchange Rates Promote Excessive Speculation

A common argument against flexible exchange rates claims that they cause excessive speculation on the currency markets, which in turn contributes to volatile exchange rates. Nominal exchange rates must by definition be more volatile when exchange rates are floating than when they are fixed. Evidence confirms this (see, for example, Kenyon, 1990). Real exchange rates could in principle be more volatile when nominal rates are fixed, and periodically reset, than when they float freely. In fact real exchange rates have been much more volatile in the 1970s and 1980s than in the 1950s and 1960s. However, we reported in chapter 10 de Grauwe's (1988a) finding that floating exchange rates were much steadier than prices in the stock and commodity markets.

Friedman (1953) argued that, if they destabilize prices, speculators tend to lose more than they gain because they buy when the price is high and sell when it is lower. Since agents cannot keep making losses, speculation will tend to be stabilizing. A Darwinian mechanism should ensure this. Friedman's argument is plausible but not watertight. There are three points of difficulty. First, the identity of speculators can vary. There could be a rapid unending turnover of unsuccessful speculators. Second, if the equilibrium value of the exchange rate is unique and can vary over time, profitable speculation can be destabilizing. This was proved by various authors, including Baumol (1957), Farrell (1966, 1970), and Kemp (1962). Third, the link between the activities of a central bank and the speculators may be important. Suppose the central bank intervenes in the foreign exchange (forex) markets but there is no announced policy of the circumstances that will induce intervention. If the bank's beliefs differ from the speculators', there could be scope for instability.

Speculation may also arise in managed float and fixed exchange rate regimes, caused by the development of a view that the exchange rate is deviating from its equilibrium value. In a fixed system, speculation that a devaluation or revaluation of the currency is about to take place induces sale or purchase of the currency. One-way options become available.

With managed rates, the authorities buy up the currency when it is in excess supply and sell when it is in excess demand. To do this, they hold a buffer stock of forex: the central bank's gold and forex reserves. With free floating, this task of smoothing exchange rates by intervention is essentially passed over to the private sector. It is not clear who makes a better job of it, the central banker or the private speculator. Both can and do make destabilizing interventions. What we can say is this. Floating exchange rates provide a less predictable environment than fixed rates, but exchange rate risk is easier to insure against than other risks, and speculation may on balance reduce the volatility of exchange rates.

Flexible Exchange Rates are Inflationary

Under fixed exchange rates, the burden of adjustment is usually greater for balance of payments (BOP) deficit countries than for surplus countries. The deficit countries must adjust by pursuing deflationary policies in order to bring their payments position back into line. This is borne out by the experience of Bretton Woods. Most of the comparatively few exchange rate realignments between 1950 and 1971 involved devaluation by deficit countries. As we shall see in section 11.3.4, independent policy choices by individual countries could make for a deflationary bias under fixed exchange rates.

It is often claimed that flexible exchange rates display an inflationary bias. Inflation rates for most countries have been much higher in periods of floating exchange rates (1919 to the mid-1920s and after 1971) than under the sterling-centred Gold Standard before 1914, or the Bretton Woods system. Fixed exchange rate regimes seem to keep inflation lower, more uniform across countries, and less variable within them. Two Keynesian arguments point to floating rates as a possible exacerbator of inflation. One is the idea that wages and prices rise faster when the country's exchange rate is depreciating than they drop when it appreciates. The other is that a government, once liberated from the external financial discipline of the fixed exchange rate, should try a 'dash for growth', and gamble on inflation and depreciation as a mechanism for forcing down real wages and thereby increasing output.

There are several problems here. On the historical point, it seems that countries resort to floating exchange rates because uneven inflation pressures have made fixed rates unsustainable. So floating is a symptom of financial disorder, not its cause. Furthermore, floating allows a 'sound money' country to escape inflation originating elsewhere, which it would catch under fixed rates. Empirical evidence shows that the time paths of monetary aggregates, wage rates, exchange rates, and prices are so closely interwined that causal inferences are very hard to draw.

There is no doubt that exchange rate regimes affect the policy-making behaviour of governments. Under a fixed exchange rate regime or even a managed float, government use of monetary policy is severely circumscribed. But this point does not suggest that floating regimes are inherently inflationary. Given the constraint on monetary policy under a fixed exchange rate regime, inflation is less likely to prevail as a result of purely domestic developments. But fixed exchange rates need not eliminate inflation, and as we shall see in section 11.3.6 a floating exchange rate system can also display a disinflationary bias when national governments determine policy independently.

Flexible Exchange Rates Increase Uncertainty in International Markets, Discouraging World Trade

Flexible rates increase exchange rate or currency risk. While there are forward markets that provide insurance against this risk, transactions in these markets may be costly. The markets are also incomplete. A trader may not be able to get a forward contract if the trade involves an obscure currency and a contract may not be easily available for the exact time period required, especially if the transaction extends past a 12 month period.

Have floating exchange rates since the early 1970s therefore inhibited trade? de Grauwe (1988b) found that the long-run variability in exchange rates was responsible for about 20 per cent of the slowdown in the growth rate of international trade among industrial countries in the period 1973–84. Other factors contributing to this were the decline in the growth rate of output (50 per cent) and the reduced pace of trade integration in the industrial world (30 per cent). These results were based on a cross-section of data from 10 industrialized countries for the periods 1960–9 and 1973–84. de Grauwe attributed the impact of floating to the 'political economy effect of exchange rate variability': flexible exchange rates led to long swings in the real exchange rates of major currencies, causing adjustment problems in the traded goods sector and increased demands for trade barriers. He thinks this has been more important than traders' risk aversion and the cost of forward cover, since it is not certain that the risk averse exporter will export less when uninsurable currency risks increase.

Flexible rates may well increase currency risk, but they may reduce other sorts of risk. Defending a fixed exchange rate in the presence of large international capital inflows and outflows often means being prepared to cut and raise domestic interest rates. So floating exchange rates may imply less volatility in interest rates. This is particularly likely if the disturbance originates abroad. It can be much harder to get insurance against interest rate changes than exchange rate changes. Also, if governments resort to tax changes, trade barriers, or restrictions on international capital movements in order to hold a fixed exchange rate parity, insurance against their actions will be completely impossible. We may conclude from this that floating exchange rates may inhibit trade somewhat, but any adverse welfare effects on this score are likely to be more than offset by the reduction in other kinds of risk, especially when some of the disturbance lies abroad.

J Curve Effects Arise under Floating Rates

For floating exchange rates to be stable, it is essential that the excess demand for a currency fall as its price in terms of others goes up. Day-to-day payments imbalances are dominated by capital flows across the exchanges, but flows on the current account are also important, especially as the time span lengthens. So stability is seriously threatened if a chance depreciation leads to a deterioration in a country's current account. Some opponents of flexible rates argue that this is quite possible.

Take a large country whose export prices are given in the home currency. Assume the same for its trading partners. For depreciation to raise the ratio of export receipts to import payments, import demands in one of the two need to be price elastic if they are price insensitive in the other. If foreign demand for the home country's exports is completely price insensitive, depreciation will do nothing to its export receipts in home currency. So the export-to-import ratio can rise only if the import bill falls in home currency. This requires the home import demand to be price elastic. The general condition for depreciation to raise export receipts relative to import payments, when the supply elasticities are infinite, is for home and foreign demand elasticities to sum to more than unity. This condition is widely (but incorrectly[3]) known as the Marshall–Lerner condition.

If the supply prices of home exports in home currency and imports in foreign currency are not given, a more complex condition obtains. This is the Robinson–Bickerdike condition, which can be written

$$\frac{1 + s^*}{1 + s^*/d} > \frac{1 - d^*}{1 + d^*/s}$$

where d and s denote demand and supply elasticities, both defined as non-negative, and the asterisk denotes foreign. When this holds, depreciation raises the ratio of export receipts to import payments. The

---

3 Strictly speaking, the Marshall–Lerner condition establishes when a country's terms of trade deterioration leads to lower excess supply of its importables; the relevant elasticities that need to sum to more than unity are those of the home and foreign offer curves.

Marshall–Lerner condition is easily inferred from this (set s and s^* to infinity, yielding $d^* + d > 1$). A different simplification applies for a small country which faces horizontal foreign supply and demand ($s^* = d^* = \infty$). This establishes the condition $s + d > 0$, which is bound to apply. There is no ambiguity for a small country. Depreciation has to help reduce the excess supply of its currency.

These 'elasticities' conditions for depreciation to raise the export-to-import ratio were very popular in the middle of this century, but interest in them has since waned. For one thing, they rely on a very partial view of markets: they provide no roles for factor prices, money, the price of other goods, or cross-effects. For another, they are silent on the major macroeconomic questions, such as whether the economy under consideration has perfect or incomplete price–wage flexibility and, if imperfect, whether output is being held down by unfavourable supply incentives or product demand. But what really took most of the shine off the elasticities approach was its lack of ambiguity for the small country. Ambiguous outcomes are oxygen for a concept in economics. Without them, interest in it is apt to fade.

Closer scrutiny reveals two possible reasons for ambiguity, after all, in the way an exchange rate affects a country's trade account. One centres on the possibility of non-market-clearing regimes examined in chapter 8. Take the case of a small open economy whose money wage rate and price of non-traded goods are frozen at values where there is currently excess supply in both the labour and non-traded goods markets. This is a regime of Keynesian unemployment. Depreciation would raise the price of traded goods. Production and employment would rise in this sector as product real wages were lower. Taken by itself, this would improve the trade balance. But there are indirect effects that could more than offset it. Higher incomes generated in the traded sector will boost demand for non-traded goods. So will substitution in demand, since non-traded prices are now relatively lower. A boom in the non-traded sector will be unleashed. But that will serve to raise domestic demand for traded goods too. Neary (1980) showed that it is quite possible, in the Keynesian unemployment regime, for these indirect effects of exchange rate changes on the trade balance to offset the unambiguously favourable direct effect. A good historical example could be the UK in 1980. The UK's non-oil trade balance registered some improvement at this time, despite the massive appreciation of sterling that occurred between 1977 and 1981. The chief reason for this was the domestic slump in 1980 to which appreciation had led. The slump squeezed imports and provoked producers to try to sell overseas when domestic buyers evaporated.

The other source of ambiguity concerns time-lags and currency-invoicing patterns. Suppose the US dollar falls unexpectedly on the foreign exchanges. For several weeks, even months, the goods that leave and enter the ports of Los Angeles and New York will be moving in response to earlier orders, made in the light of the then prevailing relative prices. So export and import volumes respond sluggishly to exchange rate changes, because of the delivery delays. But many of the imports that come in will be invoiced in marks or yen. America's import bill has to rise in dollars because of this. But its dollar export receipts do not change for a while, if trade volumes are lagged and exports are dollar-invoiced. The US suffers a temporary terms and balance of trade deterioration. Neither of these effects would occur if the proportions of exports and imports that were home-currency-invoiced were the same; and if imports were more dollar-invoiced than exports, the opposite would happen.

The combination of delivery delays and asymmetric invoicing patterns can therefore create a temporarily perverse trade balance effect from depreciation. This phenomenon is known as the J curve. The time path taken by the trade balance after a depreciation is thought to resemble the shape of a J: initial deterioration, followed by swift improvement. The J curve has attracted great interest in the USA in the late 1980s. The US trade deficit climbed, as expected, with the appreciation of the dollar from 1980 to early 1985. But it failed to fall back (in current dollar terms) when the dollar depreciated after that. In chapter 10 we noted arguments by Baldwin (1988) and Dixit (1989) that could explain this.

Keynesian explanations of America's large trade deficits in the 1980s, which seem almost impervious to exchange rate changes, would centre on the fact that real national income rose faster for most of this period in the USA than in many of its trading partners. They would stress the role of domestic demand in this, and emphasize the significance of US fiscal expansion, combined with fiscal tightness elsewhere. The UK (since 1987) provides another instance of large tax cuts, accompanied this time by rapid rises in monetary aggregates, leading to large trade balance effects that dwarf the impact of exchange rate changes.

What do we conclude from these observations? First, that there can be no guarantee that depreciation has to reduce the excess supply of a country's currency by immediately improving its trade balance. Invoicing patterns and slow reactions of trade volumes could make it react perversely for a while. So could the knock-on effects of depreciation on aggregate demand: indeed, depreciation in the exchange rate will never improve the trade balance if the money supply and money wage rates go up enough at the same time. In practice, in the short run, macro demand instruments seem to exert a much stronger influence on the trade balance than exchange rates do. However, if there is a J curve, speculators will come to know about it. They should not be put off buying a currency that has fallen when they see the country's trade figures worsen somewhat. The risk of massive currency collapse is only considerable if the government is seen to respond to depreciation by relaxing its financial policy instruments. A final point: it should be clear from the above discussion that the J curve effect could also occur under fixed rates if parities were re-aligned.

11.2.2 Reform of the Currency System?

The volatility of exchange rates since the collapse of the Bretton Woods system and other difficulties associated with this have given rise to a number of policy suggestions to reform the exchange rate system. We can observe from the above discussion that it is not possible to say definitively that flexible exchange rates have been harmful. Nonetheless, some suggestions for reform are as follows.

A Return to Fixed Exchange Rates

McKinnon (1984) argued for a return to a regime of fixed exchange rates on the grounds that the volatility of exchange rates can be explained by international shifts of capital in response to changes in the composition of financial portfolios. International portfolio shifts are usually due to changes in the demand for interest-bearing assets denominated in foreign currencies. Therefore, McKinnon argued, the appropriate policy is 'unsterilized' intervention: exchange rates should be fixed and monetary policy used to accommodate shifts in money demand.

However, if it is the demand for interest-bearing assets that is the source of the trouble, sterilized intervention might be more appropriate. For example, if the value of the home currency appreciates, the authorities should intervene on the bond markets, increasing the supply of home bonds and reducing the supply of foreign currency bonds. Money supplies would be left unchanged.

The problem with both of the above policy prescriptions is that they attribute the volatility of world currencies to fitful changes in the demand for bonds denominated in different currencies which cannot be justified by fundamentals. We have seen that this is a one-sided approach to exchange rates, which many observers would consider unduly pessimistic and seriously incomplete.

Multilateral Surveillance

Multilateral surveillance would consist of consultation on policies and performance among different countries with the objective of coordinating these policies. This proposal suggests that exchange rate management is part of a more general macroeconomic policy problem. Section 11.3 gives more detailed attention to the issue of global macroeconomic policy coordination.

The Tobin Tax

Rather than advocating a return to fixed or target exchange rates, Tobin (1982) proposed a uniform tax to be imposed on capital flows, levied by all countries, in order to make 'hot money' round trips unprofitable, and removing the dominance of capital account movements over the exchange rate. The idea would be to discourage capital flows arising from speculative activity but not those designed for long-term investment. But could the tax discriminate among the different reasons for capital flows and would such a tax be first best policy? The Tobin tax would favour inertia in local asset bias in people's portfolios. It would obviously infringe Pareto-efficiency conditions. If the problem is the slow adjustment of prices in the goods markets compared with the financial markets, should policy makers not be concentrating on the rigidities in the goods markets?

Finally, is such a proposal feasible in a world of complex capital flows, where many international assets are not controlled by any single authority or group of authorities? At present, many capital flows go unrecorded, despite the fact that they may not violate legal restrictions and do not represent tax evasion. How much more common would this be if Tobin's tax were imposed?

Target Zones

Williamson's (1983) position is representative of a group of economists who argue for target exchange rate zones based on a central rate. In their view, exchange rate changes are due largely to irrationality and bandwagons (as opposed to fundamentals) but interfere with macro stability, and so they should be avoided by a firm commitment to exchange rate targets. The central rates could be set either looking backwards (related to some base year) or looking forward, related to a set of rates consistent, for example, with some definition of BOP equilibrium expected to prevail in the future.

Zones permit fluctuation around central rates. For example, they could be 10 per cent on either side of the central rates. The proposal extends the idea of widening of exchange rate bands, which was agreed at the Smithsonian meeting in December 1971. Here, new dollar parities were worked out, and the margins between the ceilings and the floors were set at twice their Bretton Woods levels. The room for flexibility between two minor countries' currencies is enlarged still further if each sets a central rate in terms of the US dollar for example: one currency could be at its floor against the dollar, and the other at its ceiling. But unlike the Smithsonian agreement, Williamson's proposal does not make these widened bands statutory. Once the value of a currency moves out of its target zone, there would be pressure for policy action but no formal obligation. Zones could be adjusted to take account of differences in inflation or major shocks.

The problems with this prescription include the choice of central rates: what would represent 'equilibrium' from which all exchange rates could be determined? There is no consensus on the best definition of equilibrium. Governments may not agree to the coordination of monetary policy required to maintain exchange rates in a target zone or on whom the onus of intervention should fall. Even if changes in floating exchange rates are subject to irrationality and often divorced from fundamentals, they may be susceptible to new swings concerned with the chance and timing of possible central rate changes. Speculation and one-way options could result once a currency came close to moving out of its zone: this could lead to unsustainable pressure on the currency, a not infrequent problem under the Bretton Woods system after convertibility restoration in the late 1950s. The proposal would not obviate the need for forward cover: if floating inhibits trade, so would target zones. Opponents might claim that target zones have many of the drawbacks of floating without its central advantages – the unfettering of market forces in setting exchange rates, and the latitude of national governments to pursue their own objectives. Williamson's proposal has certain attractions, however, and, what is more, it bears strong resemblances to the *de facto* exchange rate system for the world's major currencies in force since 1987. Only history will tell us how well it works. One way of looking at the feasibility of a target rate system is to examine the performance of the EMS. Has it achieved its objectives? If not, why not?

11.2.3 The European Monetary System

The Werner report (1970) recommended achievement of a full monetary union within Europe by 1980. In April 1972 the 'snake-in-the-tunnel' agreement was reached, following the abortive Smithsonian experiment with widened exchange rate bands, and revised parities, that began in December 1971. These wider bands had played havoc with the operation of the Common Agricultural Policy. The snake in the tunnel limited the margins of fluctuation between European Community (EC) currencies, but attempts to keep three currencies in the system, sterling, the lira and the French franc, proved unworkable. Following the Bremen Conference of the European Council of Ministers in 1978, the EMS was established in March 1979. The UK is a member of the EMS system but does not participate in its exchange rate mechanism. Greece and Portugal are not members, but there are plans for them to join.

There are three components to the EMS. First, **an exchange rate structure**: each member's currency is assigned a central rate against other

EC currencies, together with a permitted band of fluctuation of 2.25 per cent either side of the central rate, higher than the 1 per cent under Bretton Woods. The central banks are obliged to keep their currencies within this margin of fluctuation. Second, the **European Currency Unit** (ECU) is a basket of EC currencies which acts as numeraire for the exchange rate mechanism. Once a central value is assigned to a currency, a **divergence threshold** is defined. The divergence threshold for each currency is determined as $+(-)2.25(1 - w_i)$ per cent, where w_i is the weight of the ith currency in the ECU basket.

A currency may not diverge from its central ECU rate by more than three-quarters of its divergence rate. The purpose of the divergence threshold is to avoid asymmetries in the burden of adjustment between weak and strong currencies. Under the operation of the snake and the Bretton Woods agreement, the weak currency lost reserves and was always under pressure to devalue and adjust its internal policies more than the country with the strong currency. The imposition of a divergence threshold means that a currency may well reach its threshold before it reaches any of the bilateral intervention limits defined by the currency grid. At the threshold, all members of the EMS consult with each other in order to decide on an intervention policy, changes in parities, and changes in internal policy. The onus is on the country which has reached its threshold but the currency may be appreciating or depreciating. The ECU is an instrument of settlement between EC central banks, and increasingly the numeraire for bonds and deposits with financial institutions. Eventually, it may become the single currency of the community.

The **European Monetary Cooperation Fund** (EMCF) is the third component of the EMS. Members deposit 20 per cent of their gold and gross dollar reserves with the EMCF on a three month renegotiable basis and in return have access to a wide variety of credit facilities to finance payments imbalances in the EC and to support the currency grid. The total available is 25 billion ECU (about £18 billion, equivalent to about three weeks' EC imports from non-EC countries) and, of this, 14 billion ECU has been allocated to short-term monetary support and the rest to medium-term credit facilities.

From the outset, the EMS was seen as a step towards the ultimate goal of European monetary union. But its primary objective has been to encourage stabilization of exchange rates among members, thereby stimulating trade and growth within the EC. Giavazzi (1987) and Giavazzi et al. (1988) confirmed that EMS exchange rates have been substantially less variable than before. In addition, the adjustment process has been shared by the central banks of both surplus and deficit countries. From its inception in March 1979 to the end of 1988, the EMS saw 13 occasions on which parities were changed. As time has proceeded, parity changes have diminished in both frequency and magnitude.

The EMS has not just succeeded in reducing the variability of its members' exchange rates with each other. The decade from 1979 has witnessed a fall in and a convergence of inflation rates. Nominal interest rates have likewise moved closer together, and edged downwards as expectations of inflation have subsided. It is difficult to see how much of these and other developments can be attributed to the EMS and how much would have happened anyway. But for the financially weakest members of the exchange rate union, France and Italy, with their records of relatively high inflation, participation in the EMS has brought one outstanding advantage. It has enabled member countries to lower inflation more quickly, or less painfully, than they could have achieved by independent policy. The promise to reduce inflation has been made more credible with the Deutsche mark exchange rate link, and something of the German Central Bank's reputation for financial stability has been acquired quite cheaply. This theme is explored in a detailed recent model due to Begg and Wyplosz (1987).

Sticking to tight exchange rate targets means having to fight off speculative capital movements, favourable and unfavourable. The obvious weapon for this is interest rates: cut them to stem an inflow; raise them to stop an outflow. The price of greater exchange rate stability could therefore be greater instability in interest rates. Giavazzi (1987) tests for this, and has mixed findings. Interest rates become much less volatile for the Netherlands (a full EMS participant) after 1979 than in the snake-in-the-tunnel period 1972–9. For the UK (which stayed outside the exchange rate mechanism) interest rate volatility fell much less. France and Italy managed to achieve lower interest rate volatility than in the earlier period, but only by retaining controls on capital movements. Short-term interest rates on offshore francs and lire, outside the central banks' control, swung around violently, especially just before expected parity changes.

The EMS is not a story of unmixed success. The record for some of the real variables is less impressive than for nominal variables. Real exchange rates have been quite noisy, and have not tended to converge (see Artis and Taylor, 1988). From 1982 to 1988, real national incomes of the countries participating in the exchange rate mechanism grew at barely 2 per cent per annum, as against about 3.5 per cent for the USA, Japan, and the UK. Linked with this, the EMS area displayed exceptionally steep rises in unemployment (Basevi *et al.*, 1985). de Grauwe (1987) showed that it also suffered from reduced growth in internal trade.

There have been divisions of opinion in the UK about whether to participate fully in the EMS exchange rate mechanism. Arguments against joining, which have carried the day so far, include the following: Britain's special position as a net exporter of oil, which has meant that sterling should move with oil prices; Britain's freedom, outside the mechanism, to pick any cocktail of exchange rate targets it likes rather than the set of fixed parities in terms of other EMS countries; and fear that capital market integration could be destabilizing by lowering real interest rates in weak currency areas and raising them in strong currency countries (Walters, 1986). Arguments for joining include the possible gains in real resource costs from the eventual monetary union to which it may lead, the fact that sterling exchange rates will be easier to defend with the combined muscle of all the EMS central banks, and the fact that the UK's inflation record in the later 1980s was clearly worse than for full EMS participants.

The experience of the EMS suggests that, while exchange rates have stabilized and inflation rates have converged, it has not succeeded in stimulating trade and growth. The price of lower inflation has been higher unemployment. Monetary policies have converged, but there has been lack of coordination of fiscal policies. These problems will have to be overcome if a policy of target exchange rates is to be successful, let alone lead to monetary union. The issue of policy coordination has arisen in many contexts in this chapter. It forms the basis for the next section on global macroeconomic policy coordination.

11.3 Global Macroeconomic Policy Coordination

Few countries in the world are so small that the economy of the rest of the world is unaffected by what happens there. In the international economy, all countries are interdependent. Frequently, national governments set their economic policies independently. But the game-theoretic character of international economic relations often gives rise to some form of cooperation between national governments. During and after the world slump of the 1930s, many governments tried to alleviate distress at home by policies of protection and competitive devaluation. World trade slumped.

Memories of these unhappy experiences with uncoordinated national economic policies gave rise to, in the post-war period, the Bretton Woods Agreement of 1944. It established a regime of fixed exchange rates, with (current account) surplus and deficit countries obliged to take corrective measures if their BOP was out of equilibrium. New international economic bodies which aimed to ensure cooperation grew out of the Bretton Woods Agreement. These included the General Agreement on Tariffs and Trade (see section 5.3), the IMF, and the World Bank (see section 11.1). In 1961, the Organization for Economic Cooperation and Development (OECD) was set up, encompassing a European body established in 1948.

In section 11.3.1 we begin by examining national economic policy and distinguishing between the outcomes of coordinated and uncoordinated international policies. Section 11.3.3 explores the ways in which the economic policy of one country can affect key variables elsewhere. Three examples of international policy games are investigated: a Keynesian model (11.3.4), a tariff game (11.3.5), and an inflation game (11.3.6). Further points are discussed in section 11.3.7.

11.3.1 Making Policy Choices

Countries' governments can decide on their economic policies in a variety of ways. To the economist, the key idea is that they have objectives which depend on 'goal variables' such as national income and financial stability; that there are constraints linking these goal variables to each other, to a wider set of economic variables, and to a set of policy instruments, and a supply of evidence on the form these constraints are likely to take; and lastly, that the policy instruments are chosen so as to maximize the expected value of the objective function.

Uncertainty about the constraints or the effects of the policy instruments add an important twist. The time dimension should be an essential feature of the story, for several reasons. For one thing, instruments rarely hit economic variables at once, but with effects phased over time. For another, governments will be concerned with the future as well as the current values of goal variables. Consumption, for example, can be higher tomorrow if some of it is sacrificed for more investment today. Often the government is faced with the problem of trading off jam today for jam tomorrow, or bad variables (such as inflation or unemployment) today against bad variables tomorrow. It is not just a question of achieving an optimal compromise between different goal variables in the near future. Lastly, the set of constraints that link the goal variables to the policy instruments reflects the behaviour of intelligent human beings. This means that the private sector's expectation formation mechanism acquires great importance. The actions of individuals depend on what they expect a government to do, not just on what it actually does. This feature, in certain circumstances, can render policy actions powerless. At the very least, the government has to allow for how its actions and pronouncements affect the way that private sector agents form their expectations.

The international dimension to policy choice brings further elements into the story. If one country's government uses a policy instrument to increase its citizens' aggregate demand, for instance, so much of this may spill over into imports that the domestic output effects are nugatory. Alternatively, participants in international capital markets may respond in a way that leads suddenly to dramatic changes in exchange rates, or interest rates, or both. But the most important aspect, for the purposes of this section, is the fact that *other* countries will also be trying to select their policy instruments to maximize their objectives, subject to their constraints.

Internationalization brings new goal variables (such as exchange rate stability or avoidance of trade imbalances), new intermediate variables (capital flows, exports, and imports), and new instruments (devaluation, different forms of trade policy, and policy-induced changes in foreign exchange reserves). These new instruments, and those pertaining to a closed economy, will exert influences abroad as well as at home. That means that foreign government's policy choices also have an important bearing on economic well-being at home.

11.3.2 Cooperative and Nash Non-cooperative Outcomes

There are two simple forms of policy decisions by national governments in an international context, although there are many other possibilities. One has the governments acting independently, taking the decisions of others as given. That is the Nash non-cooperative model (NNC) of government's behaviour. It bears strong resemblance to Cournot's theory of oligopoly, sketched out in chapter 4. A country acts as a Cournot oligopolist, because it sets its policy parameter(s), like output, independently, treating the choices (output levels) of 'rivals' as invariant.

The other simple form of solution to the 'international policy game' is cooperation (C). Here the national governments, the players, coordinate their decisions. They sink their differences and try to pursue their common interest. What they set out to maximize might be the sum or the product of the 'utilities' of the national governments concerned. One hopes, of course, that these will be strongly related to, or even inter-changeable with, some true social welfare functions capturing the real well-being of those countries' citizens.

However, governments may have preferences that diverge from their citizens', such as getting reelected; and a government may represent a majority coalition of domestic interests, or even the preferences of the median voted upon whom reelection will depend, rather than aiming to maximize some well-defined function of the welfare of everyone in the society. These qualifications apply, of course, just as much to the NNC model as to C; they are mentioned here because there are close parallels between the problem of choosing an appropriate objective function for a group of countries' governments, *vis-à-vis* those of constituent national powers, and that of deriving an objective function for a national society from the welfare levels of its citizens. Once having agreed upon their common objective, if agree they can, the countries set their policy instruments in unison to give the highest expected aggregate payoff. The oligopoly analogy is with collusion to maximize joint profits.

By its very definition, the C (cooperative) outcome must be superior to every other. It would not have been selected if it were not! Its superiority is gauged, of course, on the yardstick adopted by the group of players to measure their collective well-being, such as the sum or the product of utilities. If this yardstick is acceptable, the C outcome must be superior to the NNC. The conclusion to which this argument appears to be pointing is that countries can only gain, and never lose, by cooperation as opposed to independent action.

Such a claim would be false. Countries may be better off if their governments cooperate. But this is not inevitable. Cooperation may make no difference and it could make things worse. This turns out to be yet another question in economics to which the only correct answer is, it all depends. But that is no fault of economics. On the contrary, it demonstrates both the power and the importance of economic reasoning. Without such reasoning we could never tell whether cooperation is likely to pay in the particular case with which we are concerned.

In what follows, we shall start by briefly reviewing the welfare effect that one country's economic policy parameter changes are likely to have on another. This will provide the necessary foundations for identifying cases where cooperation pays; cases where it makes no difference whether countries' governments play C or NCC; and finally 'rogue' cases where countries do better if their governments do not cooperate. We shall be particularly interested in seeing exactly why cooperation does or does not pay, and what factors govern the size of the gains or losses that cooperation brings.

11.3.3 Foreign Consequences of Domestic Decisions

What are the policy instruments that we are considering? In the area of trade policy, there are import restrictions and taxes or subsidies on exports, as well as more indirect measures that have some commercial policy aspect such as subsidies granted to domestic firms to produce certain traded goods. Under monetary policy, we could look at the day-to-day levers of intervention, such as open market operations, or, to simplify matters, intermediate variables, such as some definition of monetary aggregate or interest rate on which such levers are designed to operate. Fiscal policy could likewise refer to the true control variables (tax rates, for instance) or one of the endogenous state variables on which they act, such as total transfer payments or some definition of the budget deficit. In the realm of exchange rate policy, we have to draw a crucial distinction between a regime of fixed but adjustable parities, such as the EMS, and floating exchange rates. In the first case the nominal exchange rate is a policy parameter. In the second it is not. The exchange rate is ultimately replaced by some money aggregate in this role. This reminds us that the money supply, whatever is meant by it, is ultimately not a policy instrument in an EMS type system.

From this list, we shall confine attention to just three instruments:

1 import tariffs;
2 the nominal supply of money;
3 government purchase of consumption goods.

We shall sidestep the problem of defining money. We shall assume, unless specified to the contrary, that there are just two countries, Home and the rest of the world (ROW, or Abroad) equal in size and symmetrical in all respects. The exchange rate between them is assumed initially to be freely floating and prices are assumed to be fully flexible; these assumptions will be relaxed in the course of discussion.

An Import Tariff

Suppose an import tariff is applied by Home. Abroad suffers a terms of trade deterioration. Income distribution changes there: although there is a net loss in its aggregate real income, the factor used intensively in ROW's importables industry will gain. The effect on ROW's social welfare function depends, *inter alia*, on the way we weight different factor incomes. If there were unemployment in ROW, Home's tariff would tend to boost it or squeeze it depending on whether the ROW's importables sector was labour intensive. All in all, the odds must be that ROW would be deemed to suffer. Tariffs, in general, are a 'negative transmission instrument', that is, if one country imposes a tariff, its trading partner suffers.

An Increase in the Nominal Money Supply by Home

Suppose Home's money supply is increased, once and for all and unexpectedly. Under simple idealized conditions, this will have no real effects on Home or the ROW. Home's prices rise and its currency depreciates. However, if we introduce sluggish prices with rational expectations formation at Home, the value of its currency in units of ROW's collapses by more than the money supply rise. This is the overshooting case, explored by Dornbusch (1976) and examined in chapter 9. What does this mean for Abroad? The ROW's real exchange rate appreciates, squeezing competitiveness. Suppose ROW also displays 'price inertia'. This could be because money wage rates are inert there, and its firms practice mark-up pricing. Under such conditions, the loss in competitiveness in ROW's traded industries must imply a slump. Employment and production fall. The only good news for ROW is that its cost of living tends to drop back, since the goods it buys from home will be cheaper.

However, if it is real wages that are sticky in the ROW, we could see output and employment rise there. A real exchange rate appreciation acts like a reduction in a tax wedge, splitting employers' and employees' perceptions of the real wage rate. Conclusion? The ROW is unaffected given full price flexibility, suffers under nominal wage inertia, and gains under real wage inertia.

What does this mean for the ROW? There is a temporary appreciation in ROW's real exchange rate. Home's money supply increase temporarily depresses Home's interest rate. But ROW's interest rate will have stayed up. So international capital mobility calls for an expectation that ROW's exchange rate will fall back a little, to offset the interest differential. This means that ROW's exchange rate has to jump to create room for its subsequent unwinding.

Price stickiness is not the only form of inertia which the ROW can exhibit. Consider the consumption real wage (CRW), defined as the purchasing power of wages in terms of the basket of goods that a worker buys. Suppose that it is CRW that is sluggish – 'CRW-inertia'. We saw that the ROW's cost of living falls a little because its imports from Home are cheaper. With CRW inertia, this points to a slight decline in the ROW's money wage, to keep worker's perception of the real wage unchanged.

Producers in ROW gain since the 'product' real wage (expressed in terms of their product) has declined. They should react by raising employment and production if factor availability permits. The loss in ROW's competitiveness means an improvement in its terms of trade; and with CRW inertia, that in turn implies a rise in output and employment. Thus the terms of trade improvement acts like a cut in a distortionary tax wedge because of the split between employers' and employees' perceptions of the real wage.

A final point to note is that the exchange rate changes consequent on Home's money supply rise can redistribute wealth between the countries. If the ROW has net claims on Home denominated in the latter's currency, for instance, those who hold them transfer wealth to home. Leaving such considerations aside, we can conclude that, under free floating exchange rates, the principal short-run effects on the ROW of a money supply increase at Home will be

1   a loss in competitiveness or, equivalently, an improvement in the terms of trade,
2   a modest decline in its cost of living, and
3   pressure on output and employment which is negative if the ROW displays price inertia and positive if it displays CRW inertia.

If there is no price inertia at Home, either because all prices are fully flexible there or, indeed, because Home has CRW inertia, these effects will be qualified to the point of extinction. Home inflation quickly gobbles up the potential real effects of the money supply rise.

How does monetary expansion in Home affect the ROW if the nominal exchange rate is fixed? Additional spending by Home's residents improves Abroad's trade balance. If Abroad is price inert, output rises, if demand constrained. The rise in the ROW's output is reinforced if there is capital mobility, since interest rates in ROW will tend to fall in sympathy with those at Home. If Home has CRW inertia, this last effect is weakened, since prices will rise in Home and trade will transmit this to the ROW as a cost of living increase.

If the ROW is CRW inert, her terms of trade will tend to improve, with consequent supply side benefits to output, when Home is price inert. But if both Home and Abroad are CRW inert, the rise in ROW's import prices spells a terms of trade deterioration and a slump there. In the longer run, one extra factor to consider is the ROW's money supply. This must tend to rise in response to its BOP surplus. Unless the ROW revalues its exchange rate, Home's monetary expansion will spread abroad. Prices everywhere must eventually go up. This follows, at least, when the two countries are similar in size, as we have explicitly assumed.

Unexpected Fiscal Expansion by Home

Begin with the case of freely floating exchange rates. Home's exchange rate jumps at once, to squeeze its trade balance by enough to satisfy the government's additional call on resources. The ROW experiences a cost of living rise because its currency has depreciated. Its terms of trade worsen, and its competitiveness improves. If ROW is price inert, output rises if factor supplies allow and output is demand constrained. If ROW is CRW inert, output falls because the terms of trade burden raises real wages perceived by firms. The direction of these effects does not depend on whether Home has price or CRW inertia. So the international transmission of fiscal policy changes, under free floating, looks simpler than that for monetary policy changes.

Unfortunately this is not really so. There are additional complexities which fiscal expansion introduces. These include the commodity composition of the government's increased demands; the timing and nature of tax increases which must be required to meet the government's intertemporal solvency conditions; and the longer-run requirement for a country that has run trade deficits in the wake of fiscal expansion to reduce its real exchange rate to service and repay the resulting debts. A proper treatment of these factors is extraordinarily difficult, as recent work by Buiter (1987) makes plain.

With exchange rates fixed, the short-run effects on ROW of a Home fiscal expansion resemble those of a Home money supply increase. The ROW experiences a trade balance improvement, and output tends to rise unless both economies are CRW inert, when it falls. One difference is that fiscal expansion raises Home's interest rates when monetary expansion reduces them. Under international capital mobility, ROW gets the back draught and its interest rates will tend to rise too. When ROW is price inert and demand constrained, it is quite possible that the upward pressure on interest rates there swamps any gains to aggregate demand channelled through the trade balance. In that case, Home's fiscal boost will be contractionary for output overseas.

This analysis has shown that supply side considerations have to be brought into the picture – it is not just aggregate demand that matters. It often makes a huge difference, when prices are less than perfectly flexible, exactly what form the stickiness takes. Inertia in money wage rates, and hence in price if firms practise mark-up pricing, can give strikingly different results from inertia in consumption real wages.

We should stress that our discussion has abstracted from the traded–non–traded goods distinction which, as we saw in chapter 8, could give valuable insights into the workings of the small open economy. Also, in regimes with price inertia, we have confined ourselves to the case of demand-constrained output, which corresponds to the phenomenon of Keynesian unemployment. Keynesian unemployment is not the only trap into which economies with imperfect price flexibility can fall, as chapter 8 emphasized. That said, empirical evidence, such as that explored by Laffont (1985), suggests that Keynesian unemployment is encountered more frequently than other types of non-clearing regime.

In a nutshell, policy decisions taken in one large economy have important effects on others. Import restrictions tend to reduce real income abroad. Monetary expansion in one country tends to raise prices elsewhere in the long run, unless offset by exchange rate changes. Monetary and fiscal measures taken to reflate demand in one country will affect trade, interest rates, and output in another in numerous ways. Sometimes foreign output is boosted, sometimes it is squeezed. It is not true that floating exchange rates insulate one country from the effects of policy decisions in another. The nature and character of transmission are not the same as under fixed exchange rates, but overseas repercussions there will be.

In the context of international economic relations between Western Europe and the USA, van der Ploeg (1989) has argued that both areas could gain substantially by altering their macro policy stance. He found that the USA displays price inertia (more strictly, money wage inertia), while most European countries are CRW inert. He infers from this that fiscal policy should tighten in the US and loosen in Europe, and monetary policy perhaps (briefly) the opposite. These policy changes would bring the dollar down *vis-à-vis* European currencies. Output and employment would be stimulated in both areas, with minimal impact on inflation rates. van der Ploeg's case is clearly one where cooperation 'pays'. Armed with our analysis of how policy in one country can affect the welfare of another, we can proceed to study the more general problem of what countries stand to gain, if anything, by coordinating economic policies. We consider a number of cases below.

11.3.4 A Keynesian Model of Coordination and Internal and External Balance

Suppose there are two countries, alike in all respects. The government of each has a single objective: internal balance. It dislikes any gap between domestic output y and its natural level $\bar{y}$. We might take $\bar{y}$ to denote a sustainable level of full employment, no doubt allowing for the inevitable margin of spare capacity and temporarily idle labour moving between jobs. To be precise, its welfare function is

$$W = -0.5(y - \bar{y})^2 \tag{11.1}$$

Equation (11.1) tells us that underproduction, $y < \bar{y}$, is just as bad as overproduction, $y > \bar{y}$. Welfare falls with the square of the gap between y and $\bar{y}$. The foreign country has the same welfare function.

In a Keynesian model, y is demand determined. Supposed that y increases with A, a domestic policy parameter, and also with A^*, the foreign policy parameter where the asterisk denotes ROW. This system has fixed exchange rates and price inertia in both countries; output is demand constrained; and we should think of A as either a monetary instrument or a fiscal variable which does not push up interest rates too far. A higher A^* raises y^*, and therefore pulls in additional imports from Home. Similarly, A raises y^* by raising the ROW's exports. The usual stability conditions mean that A has a stronger effect on y than on y^*. So we have

$$\begin{aligned} y &= y(A, A^*) \\ y^* &= y^*(A, A^*) \end{aligned} \tag{11.2}$$

with

$$1 > \frac{\partial y}{\partial A} = \frac{\partial y^*}{\partial A^*} > \frac{\partial y}{\partial A^*} = \frac{\partial y^*}{\partial A} > 0$$

It might be thought that each government will be fearful of raising its domestic demand parameter enough because of the spillover effect on the foreign country: some of the increased demand will be devoted to foreign goods. In fact, under welfare function (11.1) this would not be so. Each government sets its value of A, even if it takes its trading partner's actions as given, and acts in a Nash manner in such a way that the internal balance objective is fulfilled.[4] As Sinclair (1989a) shows, this result is not even affected by introducing asymmetries between the countries. So here is a case where NNC behaviour achieves exactly the same outcome as C.

However, the trouble starts if (11.1) is amended. Suppose that it takes the form

$$W = -0.5(y - \bar{y})^2 + aB \tag{11.3}$$

In (11.3), B denotes Home's trade surplus, and a, a positive parameter, reflects its government's strength of preference for a positive trade balance. Home's trade surplus equals Abroad's trade deficit, and is of course balanced by capital flows from Home or changes in reserves. The foreign country's welfare function is

$$W^* = -0.5(y^* - \bar{y})^2 - a^*B \tag{11.4}$$

The problem now is that each government recognizes that its own demand parameter has an adverse effect on its trade position. A boom at home raises imports, and this is undesirable. If we impose complete symmetry and assume that y, y^*, and B are linear in A and A^*, NNC behaviour gives rise to balanced trade but unemployment in both countries.

The resulting equilibrium is shown at point X in figure 11.1. The two policy parameters A and A^* are displayed on the horizontal and vertical axes. The FF line represents the combination of A and A^* that achieves internal balance at home, $y = \bar{y}$. F*F* shows internal balance in ROW, that is, $y^* = \bar{y}^*$. To the right of these loci, there is overproduction; to the left, excess unemployment. The two lines cut at Q, where full employment is achieved in both countries. The line 0T has a slope of unity and depicts a state of balanced trade, $B = 0$. Above 0T, Home has a trade surplus; beneath it, a deficit.

Home's government likes being as close as it can to FF, its full employment line. It also likes being as far above 0T as possible, since that means a large trade surplus. These preferences, generated from (11.3), make for a set of approximately U-shaped indifference curves. The line RR links the points at which these curves are horizontal. RR is Home's reaction curve. It tells us what A the Home government will select, for any given value of A^*. This reflects Nash behaviour under non-cooperation. R*R* is the corresponding reaction curve for ROW's government, linking points where its sideways U-shaped indifference curves are vertical. The

---

4   Maximizing W with respect to A in (11.1) implies $0 = -(y - \bar{y})\partial y/\partial A$ if A is given, ensuring full employment ($y = y$), and similarly abroad. So Nash behaviour maximizes the sum of home and foreign welfare levels.

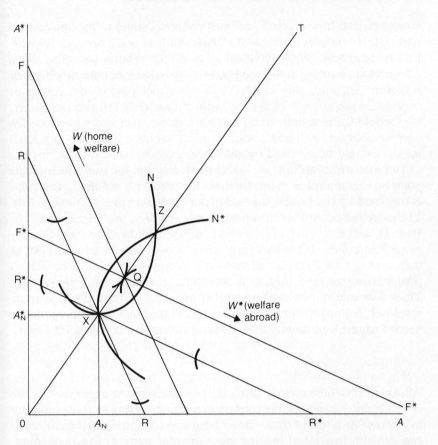

Figure 11.1 Nash non-cooperative and cooperative equilibria in a symmetrical two-country Keynesian game when governments care about external and internal balance.

two reaction curves cut at X. Here, Home's government plays A_N, because this maximizes its utility given that the ROW plays A_N^*; similarly, A_N^* maximizes W^*, given A_N. At X, both countries have balanced trade and excess unemployment.

Both countries would be as well off at Z as at X. They would still keep balanced trade, and output would exceed its natural level in both countries by as much as it falls short at X. The area enclosed by the intersection of the two indifference curves, labelled N and N*, is better for both governments than X or Z. The optimum point, where the two government's indifference curves are tangent, is Q. Q is the point of full employment in both countries and trade is balanced. Q is the equilibrium that could be reached under cooperation.

Why is the NNC equilibrium worse than C? What governs how far they are apart, and how much do the two countries stand to gain by coordinating their policies? The NNC equilibrium is at X because it yields underproduction. Nash behaviour gives a deflationary bias. Both countries are worried about the potential adverse trade balance effects of reflation. So, once they reach X, they will not pursue that course of action. Cooperation is better for both: if they only reflated in concert, they would see that both could achieve a more satisfactory outcome for domestic output, with no deterioration in their trade balance. Additional imports would be matched by additional exports.

The root of the trouble with X is the value that the two governments place on accumulating claims on the other country's residents. The value is captured by the preference parameters a and a^* in (11.3) and (11.4). The more they care about running trade surpluses, the further X will be from Q, and the worse off the two countries will be. The trade balance game is zero-sum. If the two governments could only be educated out of their mercantilist dogmas and stop loving surpluses, all would be well. Q would arise spontaneously, as it does under the welfare function (11.1). Then cooperation would be unnecessary. But if they do love trade surpluses, countries' interests will conflict to the point that cooperation is needed to resolved them. Only cooperation can bring internal balance.

11.3.5 The Tariff Game

Another case where cooperation may pay concerns the use of tariffs. We saw in chapter 3 that a large country can gain by taxing its trade, in order to improve its terms of trade. But if both large countries do this, they will end up with lower real income and potential welfare than they could. Cooperation, perhaps involving side payments if the bargaining strengths of the two countries differ, must provide opportunities for mutual gain. Markusen and Wigle (1988), for example, find an NNC equilibrium for tariffs between Canada and the USA with Canada setting a tariff at 6 per cent and the USA tariff at 18 per cent, in contrast with the cooperative equilibrium with free trade. Cooperation will call for free trade. Tariffs can also be deployed to raise domestic income in a recession, since they divert spending to home-produced goods. Many countries reacted to the severe world slump of the 1930s by restricting trade for just this reason. They adopted 'beggar my neighbour' policies. Once again, it would have been better had countries coordinated their macroeconomic and exchange rate policies under free trade, to attain internal balance.

Tariff considerations point clearly to large potential gains from cooperation and free trade. But in a dynamic context it is not obvious that individual countries will in fact seek to apply tariffs. The reason for this is that 'tit-for-tat' strategies can be optimal. Trade freely with me today and I will trade freely with you tomorrow; restrict my exports today, and I will cut back yours tomorrow. Just as we saw in chapter 4 that tit-for-tat could establish a form of tacit non-cooperative collusion between oligopolists, to their mutual long-run advantage, it can do the same here for countries in trade. What is needed for tit-for-tat to work is that nobody discounts future gains too highly. These arguments are spelt out in more detail by Sinclair (1989b). The upshot is that formal cooperation should prove unnecessary. The multiperiod NNC equilibrium should achieve the same outcome.

11.3.6 The International Inflation Game   *use*   *early*

We turn now to a context where countries' governments dislike cost of living increases, as well as internal imbalance ($y \neq \bar{y}$). Exchange rates float freely. There is price inertia everywhere. The policy parameters A and A^* are interpreted as increases in money supplies. The best of all worlds for you, in a two-country context, is when the other country increases its money supply sharply and you raise yours a little. The foreign money increase leads to a large appreciation in your currency, pushing down your cost of living because foreign goods are cheaper. The adverse output effects of your loss of competitiveness (remember that price inertia is imposed) can be offset by a modest rise in your own money supply.

Cooper (1985) showed that Nash behaviour leads to a Pareto-inefficient outcome in such a context. The analysis closely resembles that in section 11.3.4. In figure 11.2 RR is Home's reaction curve. It shows what Home's government will seek to do, for any given policy action by the ROW's. Home's indifference curves are horizontal along RR. Point B on R is the point of bliss. This is the ideal state of affairs that will hold if the ROW raises its money supply sharply and hence depreciates its currency, giving Home a welcome fall in its cost of living with adverse output effects neutralized by a small rise in its money supply. ROW's analogous bliss point is B*, on its reaction curve R*R* which links points where ROW's indifference curves are vertical. If both countries act independently, taking the other's actions as given, the resulting NNC equilibrium is at X. Both deflate in figure 11.2.

Both countries would gain by coordinating their monetary policies and moving to an equilibrium in the area enclosed by the indifference curves N*N* and NN. Point C, where indifference curves C and C* are tangent, is Pareto efficient. Reaching Q requires coordination, given that countries dislike cost of living increases. Had the government's welfare functions depended on output considerations alone, as in (11.1), Nash behaviour would take us to Q anyway. Then neither country would see any merit in monetary cutbacks to appreciate their currency and lower the cost of living.

later

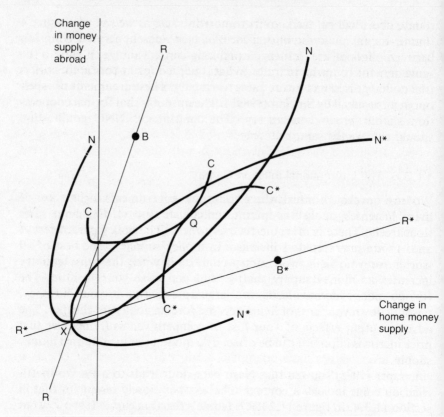

Figure 11.2   The money supply game: independent action has a deflationary bias.

So far we have only looked at cases where cooperation, C, is equivalent to NNC equilibria, or when NNC is inferior to C. Consider a situation where NNC is superior to C. We take a case similar to that proposed by Rogoff (1985). Suppose governments gain from unexpected inflation because this reduces the real value of their debts. Suppose this gain is proportional to the size of unexpected inflation. Assume too, that inflation, predicted or unpredicted, does damage which increases with the square of its speed. These assumptions were originally made for a closed economy model of inflation devised by Barro and Gordon (1983). If expectations of inflation are fulfilled, the optimal rate of inflation is zero. But with inflation expectations predetermined it becomes positive, because of the gain from an inflation surprise. The welfare of countries' residents differs from that of their governments: suppose that the former dislike inflation.

In Rogoff's model, international cooperation takes the form of an agreement to fix exchange rates. The Nash equilibrium has free floating.

Under free floating each government will be frightened of increasing its money supply on its own, because of the unpleasant cost of living hike that will follow the ensuing depreciation of its currency. But if the governments fix exchange rates and set their monetary policies in unison, the exchange rate will not collapse when its authorities raise the domestic money supply. Other countries are doing the same. Cooperation encourages the governments to exploit the gain to be had from inflation surprises, something they are inhibited from doing in NNC. So cooperation imparts an inflationary bias to the system, and citizens' welfare falls everywhere.

The Rogoff story acheives this result by making governments' welfare differ from that of their citizens. The analogy with oligopoly is helpful here. When oligopolists cooperate and collude, their profits go up. That is splendid for them. But consumers lose out, and the sum of consumers' and producers' surplus will fall. So an NNC equilibrium is better for society with C in oligopoly, despite the fact that the firms are better off than C than NNC. Exactly the same thing happens in the Rogoff case: for firms, read governments; for consumers, read their citizens.

11.3.7 Further Points

Some investigators have attempted to quantify the welfare effects of international policy coordination. A celebrated study by Oudiz and Sachs (1984) looked at hypothetical cooperation between Japan, the USA, and West Germany. Here Germany does duty for Western Europe, or at least the set of full participants in the EMS. In a model with plausible parameter values and objective functions, countries would gain from coordinating their macroeconomic policies rather than setting them independently in the Nash fashion. But the gains are modest. For the USA and Europe they amount to barely half of 1 per cent of national incomes, but more for Japan. The model is short run, and the countries' governments are assumed to know it.

Much later work has attempted to generalize these last two features of the Oudiz and Sachs study. The same authors (Oudiz and Sachs, 1985) extended their analysis to an explicit multi-period setting in the symposium on international policy coordination edited by Buiter and Marston (1985). Another pair of contributors were Frenkel and Razin, who broadened the agenda to include fiscal policy, again in a dynamic setting. Repeated games contrast quite sharply with the one-off game studied by Oudiz and Sachs. The gains from formal cooperation tend to be lower. One reason for this is that long-run macroeconomic trade-offs differ radically from their short-run values. The Phillips curve, for example, should be steeper (even vertical) in the long run, extinguishing most of the real effects associated with monetary policy in the short run.

To take a second example, taxing capital unexpectedly heavily is fine in the short run, once its owners have made an irreversible commitment which turns it into a fixed factor; but the long-run effects of doing this will be to drive capital overseas.

Another reason is the phenomenon we saw working in the case of tariffs: tit-for-tat strategies can make a non-cooperative equilibrium resemble a cooperative one. However, Levine and Currie (1987) find that there are circumstances under which cooperation pays if and only if the players act 'reputationally'. Reputational behaviour means sticking to a plan which is optimal *ex ante* and never exploiting the short-run advantages which can arise from deviating from the plan *ex post*. In the capital taxation case, acting reputationally means keeping taxes down to what had been promised.

In Oudiz and Sachs (1984) it was assumed that there is a unique model of the international economy which is known to, and agreed upon by, all the players in the game. Ghosh (1987) has explored the consequences of model uncertainty. What happens if Germany's Bundesbank thinks that the world economy conforms to the precepts of New Classical macro-economics, such as market clearing, and the authorities in the USA think it is better described by Keynesian relationships? What happens if both stories could be true in different states of the world, and nobody knows which will actually materialize next year? Such types of model uncertainty make for larger potential gains from cooperation under certain conditions, but there is plenty of room for losses from cooperation too. Frankel and Rockett (1988) found that the number of possible cases of loss from cooperation almost outnumbers those where it is advantageous. Uncertainty does not stop at the model either. Griffiths (1987) showed that countries can gain from behaving strategically and pretending to have welfare functions they do not in fact possess.

11.4 Conclusions

Self-sufficiency may be a tempting objective for a country, but, ultimately, it is a silly one. Applied to commerce in goods, it amounts to a trade ban. All the mutual benefits that trade can confer are sacrificed. This principle also holds true for three other areas of economic relations which form the subject of this chapter: flows of capital, currency links, and policy formation.

The world's poor countries need income insurance and suffer from a shortage of capital. The richer countries can supply both. Yet the trillion dollars lent to the Third World from 1973 to 1986 have generated much trouble for lender and borrower alike. Both are increasingly attracted by Polonius's maxim: 'Neither a lender nor a borrower be.'

In section 11.2 we examined how the debt crisis arose, and we surveyed and contrasted possible solutions to it. For the future, the real challenge is to devise forms of cross-border capital investment, and lender–borrower contract, where the problems of moral hazard, time inconsistency, and interference costs are kept to a minimum and all parties can share in the huge benefits that such loans can confer. The immediate task is to apportion the losses from past errors between the players, while keeping lending banks solvent and trade flows from drying up. The international authorities have so far had at best limited success in their role as umpires in this vitally important game. The twin risks of serious financial instability and a capital strike by the West remain.

In the context of currencies, economic isolationism or self-sufficiency may take the form of floating the exchange rate. In section 11.2 we investigated many of the issues at stake here. Floating is associated in the public mind with financial turbulence. We saw that the claims that floating rates were destabilizing and biased against trade and towards inflation had little foundation, but could not be entirely dismissed. Conventional opinion in most countries is moving towards the 'managed' end of the spectrum of possible exchange rate arrangements. Wild exchange rate swings are largely a reflection of inconsistent and unexpected policy actions by national governments. Volatility in currencies is not spontaneous. It reflects some underlying disharmony within national economies and their authorities' decisions.

Should governments' policy decisions be taken independently, or coordinated? This was the central question addressed in section 11.3. We found that cooperation and coordination often pays. But it does not always do so. Sometimes independent action will achieve as much as cooperation, and there are even cases when it could do better. What countries can gain from cooperating as opposed to acting independently is likely to be greater in one-off games than in repeated games and in a context where their interests are at variance. Gains become even more questionable when the model is unknown and when a distinction is drawn between a government's objectives and its national welfare. Countries that seek to beggar their neighbours usually end up beggars themselves. The international economy is a game where, with skill and care, all can win. But never with a doctrine of self-sufficiency.

References and Bibliography

Arpan, J.S., E.B. Flowers, and D.A. Ricks (1981) 'Foreign direct investment in the United States: the state of knowledge of research', *Journal of International Business* Studies, 12, 137–54.

Arrow, K. (1962) 'The economic implications of learning by doing', *Review of Economic Studies*, 29, 155–73.

Artis, M. and M.P. Taylor (1988) 'Exchange rates, interest rates, capital controls and the EMS: assessing the track record'. In F. Giavazzi, S. Micossi, and M. Miller (eds), *The European Monetary System*, Cambridge: Cambridge University Press, 185–210.

d'Aspremont, C., J.G. Gabszewicz, and J.F. Thisse (1979) 'On Hotelling's stability in competition', *Econometrica*, 47, 1145–51.

Backus, D. (1984) 'Empirical models of the exchange rate: separating the wheat and the chaff', *Canadian Journal of Economics*, 17(4), 824–46.

Balassa, B. (1963) 'An empirical demonstration of classical comparative cost theory', *Review of Economics and Statistics*, 45, 231–8.

Balassa, B. (1965) 'Tariff protection in industrial countries: an evaluation', *Journal of Political Economy*, 73, 573–94.

Baldwin, R.E. (1984) 'Trade policies in developed countries'. In R.W. Jones and P.B. Kenen (eds), *Handbook of International Economics*, vol. I, Amsterdam: North-Holland, 571–619.

Baldwin, R.E. (1988) 'Hysteresis in import prices: the beachhead effect', *American Economic Review*, 78, 773–85.

Barro, R.J. and D.B. Gordon (1983) 'Rules, discretion and reputation in a model of monetary policy', *Journal of Monetary Economics*, 12, 101–25.

Basevi, G., O. Blanchard, W. Buiter, R. Dornbusch, and P. Layard (eds) (1985) *Restoring Europe's Prosperity*, Cambridge, MA: MIT Press.

Baumol, W.J. (1957) 'Speculation, profitability, and stability', *Review of Economics and Statistics*, 39, 263–71.

Begg, D. (1982) *The Rational Expectations Revolution in Macroeconomics*, Oxford: Philip Allan.

Begg, D. (1983) 'The economics of floating exchange rates: the lessons of the 70s and the research programme for the 80s', London Business School Econometric Forecasting Unit, Discussion Paper 105, February.

Begg, D. and C. Wyplosz (1987) 'Why the EMS? Dynamic games and the equilibrium policy regime'. In R.C. Bryant and R.D. Portes (eds), *Global Macroeconomics: Policy Conflict and Cooperation*, London: Macmillan, 193–235.

Bentham, J. (1789) *The Principles of Morals and Legislation*.

Bergston, C.F., T. Horst, and T.H. Moran (1978) *American Multinationals and American Interests*, Washington, DC: Brookings Institution.

Bertrand, J. (1883) 'Théorie mathématique de la richesse sociale', *Journal de Savants*, 499–508.

Bhagwati, J.N. (1958) 'Immiserizing growth: a geometrical note', *Review of Economic Studies*, 25, 201–5.

Bhagwati, J.N. (1971) 'The generalized theory of distortions and welfare'. In J.N. Bhagwati, R.W. Jones, R.A. Mundell, and J. Vanek (eds), *Trade, Balance of Payments and Growth: Essays in Honour of Charles B. Kindleberger*, Amsterdam: North-Holland, 69–90.

Bhagwati, J.N., R.A. Brecher, and T.N. Srinivasan (1984) 'DUP activities and economic theory', *European Economic Review*, 24, 291–307.

Bilson, J.F.O. (1979) 'Recent developments in monetary models of exchange rate determination', *IMF Staff Papers*, 26, 201–23.

Blake, D., M. Beenstock, and V. Brasse (1986) 'The performance of UK exchange rate forecasters', *Economic Journal*, 96, December, 986–99.

Booth, P. and D. Glassman (1986) 'Off the mark: lessons for exchange rate modelling', *Oxford Economic Papers*, 39, 443–57.

Boughton, J.M. (1988) 'The monetary approach to exchange rates: what now remains?', *Princeton Essays in International Finance*, 171, October, 1–23.

Brander, J. and P.R. Krugman (1983) 'A reciprocal dumping model of international trade', *Journal of International Economics*, 15, 313–21.

Branson, W. and D.W. Henderson (1985) 'The specification and influence of asset markets'. In R.W. Jones and P.B. Kenen (eds), *Handbook of International Economics*, vol. II, Amsterdam: North-Holland, 745–805.

Buiter, W.H. (1986) 'Macroeconomic policy design in an interdependent world economy', *IMF Staff Papers*, 33(3), 541–82.

Buiter, W.H. (1987) 'Does an improvement in the current account or the trade balance at full employment require a depreciation of the real exchange rate?', Yale/NBER Working Paper.

Buiter, W.H. and R.C. Marston (eds) (1985) *The International Coordination of Economic Policy*, Cambridge: Cambridge University Press.

Buiter, W.H. and M. Miller (1981) 'Monetary policy and international competitiveness: the problems of adjustment'. In W.A. Eltis and P.J.N. Sinclair (eds), *The Money Supply and the Exchange Rate*, Oxford: Oxford University Press, 143–75.

Bulow, J. and K. Rogoff (1989) 'Sovereign debt: is to forgive to forget?', *American Economic Review*, 79, 43–50.

Butt Philip, A. (1988) 'Implementing the European internal market: problems and prospects', Royal Institute of International Affairs Discussion Paper 5, London.

Caves, R. (1974) 'Causes of direct investment: foreign firms' shares in Canadian and UK manufacturing industries', *Review of Economics and Statistics*, 56, 279–93.

Caves, R. (1982) *The Multinational Enterprise and Economic Analysis*, London: Cambridge University Press.

Cecchini, P. (1988) *The European Challenge: 1992*, London: Wildwood House.

Chamberlin, E.H. (1933) *The Theory of Monopolistic Competition*, Cambridge, MA: Harvard University Press.

Chrystal, K.A. and D. Thornton (1988) 'On the informational content of spot and forward exchange rates', *Journal of International Money and Finance*, 7, 321–30.

Clemhout, S. and H.Y. Wan (1970) 'Learning-by-doing and infant industry protection', *Review of Economic Studies*, 37, 33–56.

Cooper, R.N. (1985) 'Economic interdependence and coordination of economic policies'. In R.W. Jones and P.B. Kenen (eds), *Handbook of International Economics*, vol. II, Amsterdam: North-Holland, 1195–234.

Corden, W.M. (1969) *Theory of Effective Protection*, Oxford: Oxford University Press.

Corden, W.M. (1971) 'The effects of trade on the rate of growth'. In J.N. Bhagwati, R.W. Jones, R.A. Mundell, and J. Vanek (eds), *Trade, Balance of Payments and Growth: Essays in Honour of Charles B. Kindleberger*, Amsterdam, North-Holland, 117–43.

Corden, W.M. (1972) 'Economies of scale and customs union theory', *Journal of Political Economy*, 80, 465–75.

Corden, W.M. (1974) *Trade Policy and Economic Welfare*, Oxford: Oxford University Press.

Corden, W.M. (1984a) 'Booming sector and Dutch disease economics: a survey', *Oxford Economic Papers*, 36, 359–80.

Corden, W.M. (1984b) 'The normative theory of international trade'. In R.W. Jones and P.B. Kenen (eds), *Handbook of International Economics*, vol. I, Amsterdam: North-Holland, 63–130.

Courakis, A. and M. Taylor (forthcoming) *Policy Issues for Interdependent Economies*, Oxford: Oxford University Press.

Cournot, A. (1838) *Recherches sur les Principes Mathématiques de la Théorie de Richesses*.

Cox, D. and R. Harris (1985) 'Trade liberalization and industrial organization: some estimates for Canada', *Journal of Political Economy*, 93, 115–45.

Dasgupta, P.K. and J.E. Stiglitz (1988) 'Learning-by-doing, market structure, and industrial and trade policies', *Oxford Economic Papers*, 40, 246–68.

Deardorff, A.V. and R.M. Stern (1981) 'A disaggregated model of world production and trade: an estimate of the impact of the Tokyo Round', *Journal of Policy Modeling*, 3, 127–52.

Deppler, M. and M. Williamson (1987) 'Capital flight, concepts, measures and issues', *IMF Staff Studies*, August.

Digby, C., A. Smith, and A. Venables (1988) 'Counting the cost of voluntary export restrictions in the European car market', Centre for Economic Policy Research Discussion Paper 249, London.

Dixit, A.K. (1982) 'Recent developments in oligopoly theory', *American Economic Review, Papers and Proceedings*, 72, 12–17.

Dixit, A.K. (1984) 'International trade policies for oligopolistic industries', *Economic Journal, Conference Proceedings*, 94, 1–16.

Dixit, A.K. (1989) 'Entry and exit decisions of firms under fluctuating real exchange rates', Princeton NJ: mimeo.

Dixit, A.K. and J.E. Stiglitz (1977) 'Monopolistic competition and optimum product diversity, *American Economic Review*, 67, 297–308.

Dornbusch, R. (1976) 'Expectations and exchange rate dynamics', *Journal of Political Economy*, 84, 1162–76.

Dornbusch, R. (1987) 'Exchange rate economics: 1986', *Economic Journal*, 97, March, 1–18.

Dornbusch, R. (1988) 'Mexico: stabilization, debt, and growth', *Economic Policy*, 7, 231–83.

Dornbusch, R. and S. Fischer (1980) 'Exchange rates and the current account', *American Economic Review*, 70, 960–71.

Driskell, R.A. (1980) 'Exchange rate dynamics, portfolio balance, and relative prices, *American Economic Review*, 70, 776–83.

Driskell, R.A. (1981) 'Exchange rate dynamics: an empirical investigation', *Journal of Political Economy*, 89, 357–71.

Dunning, J. (1985) 'The United Kingdom'. In J. Dunning (ed.), *Multinational Enterprises, Economic Structure and International Competitiveness*, New York: Wiley, 13–56.

Eaton, J, and R.G. Lipsey (1975) 'The principle of minimum differentiation reconsidered: some new developments in the theory of spatial competition', *Review of Economic Studies*, 42, 27–49.

Economic Policy Symposium (1989) 'The Single European Act', Winter, forthcoming in *Economic Policy*.

Edison, H. (1985) 'The rise and fall of sterling: testing alternative models of exchange rate determination', *Applied Economics*, 17, 1003–21.

Eltis, W. and P.J.N. Sinclair (eds) (1988) *Keynes and Economic Policy*, London: Macmillan and National Economic Development Office.

Emerson, M., M. Aujean, M. Catinat, P. Goybet, and A. Jacquemin (1989) *The Economics of 1992*, Oxford: Oxford University Press.

Ethier, W.J. (1984) 'Higher dimensional issues in trade theory'. In R.W. Jones and P.B. Kenen (eds), *Handbook of International Economics*, vol. I, Amsterdam: North-Holland, 131–84.

Evans, G.W. (1986) 'A test for speculative bubbles and the sterling–dollar rate: 1981–84', *American Economic Review*, 76, 621–36.

Fama, E.F. (1984) 'Forward and spot exchange rates', *Journal of Monetary Economics*, 14, 319–38.

Farrell, M.J. (1966) 'Profitable speculation', *Economica*, 33, 183–93.

Farrell, M.J. (1970) 'Some elementary selection processes in economics', *Review of Economic Studies*, 37, 305–19.

Fleming, J.M. (1962) 'Domestic financial policies under fixed and under floating exchange rates', *IMF Staff Papers*, 9, 369–79.

Frankel, J.A. (1984) 'Tests of monetary and portfolio balance models of exchange rate determination'. In J.F.O. Bilson and R.C. Marston (eds), *Exchange Rate Theory and Practice*, Chicago, IL: University of Chicago Press, 239–59.

Frankel, J.A. (1986) 'The implications of mean variance optimization for four questions in international macroeconomics', *Journal of International Money and Finance*, 5, Supplement, S53–S75.

Frankel, J.A. and K.A. Froot (1987) 'Using survey data to test some standard propositions regarding exchange rate expectations', *American Economic Review*, 77, 133–53.

Frankel, J.A. and K.E. Rockett (1988) 'International Macroeconomic policy coordination when policymakers do not agree on the true model', *American Economic Review*, 78(3), 318–40.

Frenkel, J.A. (1976) 'A monetary approach to the exchange rate', *Scandinavian Journal of Economics*, 78, 280–304.

Frenkel, J.A. (1981) 'Flexible exchange rates, prices, and the role of news: lessons from the 1970s', *Journal of Political Economy*, 89(4), 665–705.

Friedman, M. (1953) 'The case for flexible exchange rates'. In M. Friedman, *Essays in Positive Economics*, Chicago, IL: University of Chicago Press, 157–203.

Friedman, M. (1968) 'The role of monetary policy', *American Economic Review*, 58, 1–17.

Froot, K.A. and J.A. Frankel (1989) 'Forward discount bias: is it an exchange risk premium?, *Quarterly Journal of Economics*, 104(1), 139–61.

Ghosh, S. (1987) 'International economic policy coordination', M. Phil Thesis, Oxford University.

Giavazzi, F. (1987) 'The impact of EEC membership'. In R. Dornbusch and R. Layard (eds), *The Performance of the British Economy*, Oxford: Oxford University Press, 97–130.

Giavazzi, F., S. Micossi, and M. Miller (eds) (1988) *The European Monetary System*, Cambridge: Cambridge University Press.

Girton, L. and D. Henderson (1977) 'Central bank operations in foreign and domestic assets under fixed and flexible exchange rates'. In P. Clarke, D. Logue, and R. Sweeny (eds), *The Effects of Exchange Rate Changes*, Washington.

Gorman, W.M. (1959–80), 'A possible procedure for analysing quality differentials in the egg market', *Review of Economic Studies*, 47, 843–56.

de Grauwe, P. (1987) 'International trade and economic growth in the European Monetary System', *European Economic Review*, 31, 389–98.

de Grauwe, P. (1988a) 'The long swings in real exchange rates: do they fit into our theories?', *Bank of Japan Monetary and Economic Studies*, 6(1), 37–60.

de Grauwe, P. (1988b) 'Exchange rate variability and the slowdown in the growth of international trade', *IMF Staff Papers*, 35(1), 63–84.

Griffiths, M. (1987) 'International policy coordination and interdependence', M. Phil. Thesis, Oxford University.

Hacche, G. and J. Townend (1981a) 'A broad look at exchange rate movements for 8 currencies', *Bank of England Quarterly Bulletin*, 21(4), 489–509.

Hacche, G. and J. Townend (1981b) 'Exchange rates and monetary policy: modelling sterling's effective exchange rate'. In W.A. Eltis and P.J.N. Sinclair (eds), *Keynes and Economic Policy*, London: Macmillan and National Economic Development Office, 201–47.

Hansen, L.P. and R. Hodrick (1980) 'Forward exchange rates as optimal predictors of future spot rates: an econometric analysis', *Journal of Political Economy*, 88, October, 829–53.

Hay, D.A. (1976) 'Sequential entry and entry deterring strategies in spatial competition', *Oxford Economic Papers*, 28, 240–57.

Heckscher, E. (1949) 'The effect of foreign trade on the distribution of income'. In H.S. Ellis and L.A. Meltzer (eds), *Readings in the Theory of International Trade*, Philadelphia, PA: Blakiston, 272–300.

Heffernan, S.A. (1986a) 'The determinants of the optimal foreign leverage ratio in developing countries', *Journal of Banking and Finance*, 3, 97–115.

Heffernan, S.A. (1986b) *Sovereign Risk Analysis*, London: Unwin Hyman.

Helpman, E. (1981) 'International trade in the presence of product differentiation, economies of scale, and monopolistic competition: a Chamberlain–Heckscher–Ohlin approach', *Journal of International Economics*, 11, 305–40.

Helpman, E. (1984) 'Increasing returns, imperfect markets and trade theory'. In R.W. Jones and P.B. Kenen (eds), *Handbook of International Economics*, vol. I, Amsterdam: North-Holland, 325–65.

Helpman, E. and P.R. Krugman (1985) *Market Structure and Foreign Trade*, Cambridge, MA: MIT Press.

Helpman, E. and A. Razin (1983) 'Increasing returns, monopolistic competition, and factor movements: a welfare analysis', *Journal of International Economics*, 14, 263–76.

Henderson, P.D. (1977) 'Two British errors: their probable size and some possible lessons', *Oxford Economic Papers*, 29, 159–205.

Hendry, D.F., A.R. Pagan, and J.D. Sargan (1984) 'Dynamic specification'. In Z. Griliches and M.D. Intriligator (eds), *Handbook of Econometrics*, vol. 2, Amsterdam: North-Holland, 1023–100.

Hicks, J. (1974) *The Crisis in Keynesian Economics*, Oxford: Basil Blackwell.

Hirsch, S. (1967) *Location of Industry and International Competitiveness*, Oxford: Oxford University Press.

Horst, T. (1972) 'Firm and industry determinants of the decision to invest abroad: an empirical study', *Review of Economics and Statistics*, 54, 258–66.

Hotelling, H. (1929) 'Stability in competition', *Economic Journal*, 39, 41–57.

Hotelling, H. (1931) 'The economics of exhaustible resources', *Journal of Political Economy*, 39, 137–75.

Hufbauer, G., D.T. Berliner, and K.A. Elliot (1986) *Trade Protection in the US: 31 Case Studies*, Washington, DC: Institute for International Economics.

Hume, D. (1752) 'Of the balance of trade'; reprinted, abridged, in R.N. Cooper (ed.), *International Finance*, Harmondsworth: Penguin, 1969, 25–37.

Hutchinson, J.D. (1989) 'Empirical research on trade liberalization with imperfect competition: a survey', *OECD Economic Studies*, 12, 7–50.

International Monetary Fund (1981) *Annual Report*, Washington, DC: IMF.

International Monetary Fund (1985) 'Foreign private direct investment in developing countries', *Occasional Paper 33*, Washington, DC: IMF.

International Monetary Fund (1986, 1987) *World Economic Outlook*, Washington, DC: IMF.

International Monetary Fund (1989) 'The Common Agricultural Policy of the European Community: principles and consequences', *IMF Occasional Paper 62*, Washington, DC: IMF.

Jones, R.W. and W.M. Corden (1976) 'Devaluation, non-flexible prices and the trade balance for a small economy', *Canadian Journal of Economics*, 9, 150–61.

Jones, R.W. and P.B. Kenen (eds) (1984, 1985) *Handbook of International Economics*, vols I and II, Amsterdam: North-Holland.

Jones, R.W. and J.P. Neary (1984) 'The positive theory of international trade'. In R.W. Jones and P.B. Kenen (eds), *Handbook of International Economics*, vol. I, Amsterdam: North-Holland, 1–62.

Kemp, M.C. (1962) *The Pure Theory of International Trade*, Englewood Cliffs, NJ: Prentice Hall.

Kenyon, A. (1990) *Currency Risk and Business Management*, Oxford: Basil Blackwell.

Keynes, J.M. (1936) *The General Theory of Employment, Interest and Money*, London: Macmillan.

Koromzay, V., J. Llewellyn, and S. Potter (1987) 'The rise and the fall of the dollar: some explanations, consequences, and lessons', *Economic Journal*, 97, March, 23–43.

Kreps, D. and R. Wilson (1982) 'Reputation and imperfect information', *Journal of Economic Theory*, 27, 253–79.

Krugman, P. (1979) 'A model of innovation, technology transfer, and the world distribution of income', *Journal of Political Economy*, 87, 253–66.

Krugman, P. (1981) 'Intraindustry specialization and the gains from trade', *Journal of Political Economy*, 89, 959–73.

Laffont, J.J. (1985) 'Fix price models: a survey of recent empirical work'. In K. Arrow and S. Honkapohja (eds), *Frontiers of Economics*, Oxford: Basil Blackwell.

Lall, S. (1983) *The New Multinationals: The Spread of Third World Enterprises*, New York: Wiley.

Lancaster, K.J. (1979) *Variety, Equity, and Efficiency*, New York: Columbia University Press.

Lancaster, K.J. and R.G. Lipsey (1956) 'The general theory of the second best', *Review of Economic Studies*, 24, 11–32.

Leamer, E.E. (1980) 'The Leontief paradox, reconsidered', *Journal of Political Economy*, 88, 495–503.

Lee, D. (1983) 'Effects of open market operations and foreign exchange market operations under flexible exchange rates'. In M. Darby, J.R. Lothian, A.E. Gandolfi, A.J. Schwartz and A.C. Stockman (eds), *The International Transmission of Inflation*, Chicago, IL: University of Chicago Press, 349–79.

Leontief, W. (1954) 'Domestic production and foreign trade: the American capital position reexamined', *Economia Internazionale*, 7.

Leontief, W. (1956) 'Factor proportions and the structure of American trade', *Review of Economics and Statistics*, 38, 386–407.

Levich, R. (1982) 'How a rise in the dollar took forecasters by surprise', *Euromoney*, August, 98–111.

Levich, R. (1985) 'Empirical studies of exchange rates: price behaviour, rate determination, and market efficiency'. In R.W. Jones and P.B. Kenen (eds), *Handbook of International Economics*, vol. II, Amsterdam: North-Holland, 979–1040.

Levine, P. and D. Currie (1987) 'Does international macroeconomic policy coordination pay and is it sustainable?: a two country analysis', *Oxford Economic Papers*, 39, 38–73.

Lewis, K. (1988) 'Testing the portfolio balance model: a multi-lateral approach', *Journal of International Economics*, 24, 109–27.

Linnemann, H. (1966) *An Econometric Study of International Trade Flows*, Amsterdam: North-Holland.

Little, I.M.D., M. Scott, and T. Scitovsky (1970) *Industry and Trade in Some Developing Countries*, Oxford: Royal Institute of International Affairs and Oxford University Press.

MacDonald, R. (1988) *Floating Exchange Rates, Theories and Evidence*, London: Unwin Hyman.

MacDonald, R. and Taylor, M. (1989) 'Exchange rate economics: a survey', *Greek Economic Review*, 11; in A. Courakis and M. Taylor (eds), *Policy Issues for Interdependent Economies*, Oxford: Oxford University Press.

MacDougall, G.D.A. (1951) 'British and American exports: a study suggested by the theory of comparative costs, part I', *Economic Journal*, 61, 697–724.

MacDougall, G.D.A. (1952) 'British and American exports: a study suggested by the theory of comparative costs, part II', *Economic Journal*, 62, 487–521.

MacDougall, G.D.A. (1969) 'The benefits and costs of private investment from abroad: a theoretical approach', *Economic Record*, 36, 13–35. Originally published 1958; reprinted in J.N. Bhagwati (ed.), *International Trade*, Harmondsworth: Penguin, 1969.

MacDougall, G.D.A., M. Dowley, P. Fox, and S. Pugh (1962) 'British and American productivity, prices and exports: an addendum', *Oxford Economic Papers*, 14, 297–304.

McKinnon, R. (1984) *An International Standard for Monetary Stabilization*, Washington, DC: Institute for International Economics.

Maki, D.R. and L.N. Meredith (1986) 'Product cost differentiation and foreign direct investment: a test of two models', *Applied Economics*, 18, 1127–34.

Markusen, J.R. and R.M. Wigle (1988) 'Nash equilibrium tariffs for the US and Canada: the role of country size, scale economies, and capital mobility', *Journal of Political Economy*, 97, 368–86.

Maskus, K. (1985) 'A test of the Heckscher–Ohlin–Vanek theorem: the Leontief commonplace', *Journal of International Economics*, 19, 201–12.

Meade, J.E. (1951) *The Balance of Payments*, London: Oxford University Press.

Meade, J.E. (1955) *Trade and Welfare*, London: Oxford University Press.

Meese, R.A. (1986) 'Testing for bubbles in exchange markets: a case of sparkling rates?', *Journal of Political Economy*, 94(21), 345–71.

Meese, R.A. and K. Rogoff (1983) 'Exchange rate models of the seventies: do they fit out of sample?, *Journal of International Economics*, 14, 3–24.

Meredith, L.N. (1984) 'US multinational investment in Canadian manufacturing industries', *Review of Economics and Statistics*, 66, 111–18.

Michalet, C.A. and T. Chevalier (1985) 'France'. In J. Dunning (ed.), *Multinational Enterprises, Economic Structure and International Competitiveness*, New York: Wiley, 91–125.

Miller, M.H. and J.F. Spencer (1977) 'The static effects of the UK joining the EEC: a general equilibirium approach', *Review of Economic Studies*, 44, 71–93.

Minford, P. (1981) 'The exchange rate and Monetary policy'. In W.A. Eltis and P.J.N. Sinclair (eds), *Keynes and Economic Policy*, London: Macmillan and National Economic Development Office, 120–42.

Mishkin, F. (1984) 'The real interest rate: a multi country empirical study', *Canadian Journal of Economics*, 17(2), 283–311.

Morgan, A. (1984) 'Protection and European trade in manufactures', *National Institute Economic Review*, 109, August, 45–57.

Morris, D.J., P.J.N. Sinclair, M.D.E. Slater, and J.S. Vickers (eds) (1986) *Strategic Behaviour and Industrial Competition*, Oxford: Oxford University Press.

Mundell, R.A. (1962) 'The appropriate use of monetary and fiscal policy for internal and external balance', *IMF Staff Papers*, 9, 70–9.

Mussa, M. (1982) 'A model of exchange rate dynamics', *Journal of Political Economy*, 90, 74–104.

Muth, J.F. (1961) 'Rational expectations and the theory of price movements', *Econometrica*, 29, 315–35.

Neary, J.P. (1978) 'Short run capital specificity and the pure theory of international trade', *Economic Journal*, 88, 488–510.

Neary, J.P. (1980) 'Non-traded goods and the balance of trade in a neo Keynesian temporary equilibrium', *Quarterly Journal of Economics*, 45, 403–29.

Newbery, D. (1984) 'The economics of oil'. In F. van der Ploeg (ed.), *Mathematical Methods in Economics*, Chichester: Wiley, 519–67.

Newbery, D. and J.E. Stiglitz (1984) 'Pareto inferior trade', *Review of Economic Studies*, 51, 1–12.

Ohlin, B. (1967) *Interregional and International Trade*, revised edition, London: Oxford University Press.

Organization for Economic Cooperation and Development (OECD) (1987) *Financing and External Debt of Developing Countries, 1986 Survey*, Paris: OECD.

Oudiz, G. and J. Sachs (1984) 'Macroeconomic policy coordination among the industrial economies', *Brookings Papers on Economic Activity*, 1, 1–75.

Oudiz, G. and J. Sachs (1985) 'International policy coordination in dynamic macro-economic models'. In W.H. Buiter and R.C. Marston (eds), *The International Coordination of Economic Policy*, Cambridge: Cambridge University Press, 274–320.

Pareto, V. (1909) *Manuel d'Economie Politique*.

Pelkmans, J. and A. Winters (1988) *Europe's Domestic Market*, London: Routledge and Royal Institute of International Affairs.

van der Ploeg, F. (1989) 'International interdependence and policy coordination in economies with real and nominal wage rigidity', *Greek Economic Review*, 11; in A. Courakis and M. Taylor (eds), *Policy Issues for Interdependent Economies*.

Posner, M. (1961) 'International trade and technical change', *Oxford Economic Papers*, 13, 323–41.

Poulson, A.B. (1986) 'Japanese bank regulation and the activities of the US offices of Japanese banks', *Journal of Money, Credit and Banking*, 18(3), 367–73.

Purvis, D. (1985) 'Public sector deficits, international capital movements, and the domestic economy: the medium term is the message', *Canadian Journal of Economics*, 18(4), 723–42.

Ramsey, F. (1927) 'A contribution to the theory of taxation', *Economic Journal*, 37, 47–61.

Rasmussen, E. (1989) *Games and Information*, Oxford: Basil Blackwell.

Rawls, J. (1971) *Theory of Justice*, Oxford: Oxford University Press.

Ricardo, D. (1971) *The Principles of Political Economy and Taxation*, Harmondsworth: Penguin.

Roberts, K.W.S. (1980) 'Interpersonal comparability and social choice theory', *Review of Economic Studies*, 47, 421–50.

Rogoff, K. (1985) 'Can international monetary policy coordination be counter-productive?', *Journal of International Economics*, 18, 199–217.

Rybczynski, T.M. (1955) 'Factor endowment and relative commodity prices', *Economica*, 22, 336–41.

Salop, S. (1979) 'Monopolistic competition with outside goods', *Bell Journal of Economics*, 10, 141–56.

Schwartz, M. (1986) 'The nature and scope of contestability theory'. In D.J. Morris, P.J.N. Sinclair, M.D.E. Slater, and J.S. Vickers (eds), *Strategic Behaviour and Industrial Competition*, Oxford: Oxford University Press.

Servan-Schreiber, J.J. (1968) *Le Defi Americain.*

Sinclair, P.J.N. (1983) *The Foundations of Macroeconomic and Monetary Policy*, Oxford: Oxford University Press.

Sinclair, P.J.N. (1988) 'Is fiscal expansion inflationary?'. In W.A. Eltis and P.J.N. Sinclair (eds), *Keynes and Economic Policy*, London: Macmillan and National Economic Development Office, 139–71.

Sinclair, P.J.N. (1989a) 'Some reasons why international policy coordination only sometimes pays', *Greek Economic Review*, 11; in A. Courakis and M. Taylor (eds), *Policy Issues for Interdependent Economies.*

Sinclair, P.J.N. (1989b) 'The economics of imitation', *Scottish Journal of Political Economy*, forthcoming.

Smith, A. (1776) *Wealth of Nations*, New York: Modern Library Edition, 1937.

Smith, A. and A. Venables (1986) 'Trade and industrial policy under imperfect competition', *Economic Policy*, 3, 621–72.

Smith, A. and A. Venables (1988) 'Completing the internal market in the European Community, some industry simulations', *European Economic Review*, 32, 1501–25.

Spence, M.E. (1976) 'Product selection, fixed costs, and monopolistic competition', *Review of Economic Studies*, 43, 217–36.

Stackelberg, H. von (1934) *Marktform und Gleichgewicht*, Berlin: Springer.

Stern, R. (1962) 'British and American productivity and comparative costs in international trade', *Oxford Economic Papers*, 14, 275–96.

Stern, R. and K. Maskus (1981) 'Determinants of the structure of US foreign trade, 1958–76', *Journal of International Economics*, 11, 207–24.

Stiglitz, J. and A. Weiss (1981) 'Credit rationing in markets with imperfect information', *American Economic Review*, 71, 393–430.

Stiglitz, J. and A. Weiss (1983) 'Incentive effects of terminations: applications to the credit and labour markets', *American Economic Review*, 73, 912–27.

Stolper, W. and P.A. Samuelson (1941) 'Protection and real wages', *Review of Economic* Studies, 9, 58–73.

Swann, D. (1988) *The Economics of the Common Market*, 6th edn, London: Penguin.

Taylor, M.P. (1989) 'Expectations, risk, and uncertainty in the forex market: some results based on survey data', *Manchester School*, 57, 142–53.

Tobin, J. (1982) 'A proposal for international monetary reform'. In J. Tobin, *Essays in Economics: Theory and Policy*, Cambridge, MA: MIT Press.

Tobin, J. (1987) 'Agenda for international coordination of macroeconomic policies'. In *International Monetary Cooperation: Essays in Honour of Henry C. Wallich*, Princeton Essays in International Finance 169, December, 61–9.

Venables, A.J. (1987) 'Customs unions and tariff reform under imperfect competition, *European Economic Review*, 31, 103–10.

Vickers, J. (1985) 'Delegation and the theory of the firm', *Economic Journal, Supplement (Conference Papers)*, 95, 138–41.

Viner, J. (1950) *The Customs Union Issue*, New York: Carnegie Endowment for International Peace.

Walters, A. (1986) *Britain's Economic Renaissance*, Oxford: Oxford University Press.

Weitzman, M.L. (1974) 'Prices vs. Quantities', *Review of Economic Studies*, 41, 477–91.

Werner, P. (1970) 'Interim report on the establishment by stages of economic and monetary union', *Bulletin of the European Communities*, Supplement, No. 7.

Whalley, J. (1984) ' "Trade, industrial policy, and Canadian manufacturing, by R.G. Harris (with the assistance of David Cox)": a review article', *Canadian Journal of Economics*, 17, 386–98.

Wigle, R. (1988) 'General equilibrium evaluation of Canada–US trade liberalization in a global context', *Canadian Journal of Economics*, 21, 539–64.

Williamson, J. (1983) *The Exchange Rate System Revised*, Washington, DC: Institute for international Economics.

Winters, L.A. (1987) 'The economic consequences of agricultural support: a survey', *OECD Economic Studies*, 9, Antumn, 7–54.

World Bank (1985, 1986, 1987) *World Development Report*, Washington, DC: World Bank.

World Bank (1988) *World Debt Tables, 1987–88*, Washington, DC: World Bank.

Index